Fundamentals of Franchising

Rupert M. Barkoff – Andrew C. Selden

Editors

 American Bar Association    Forum on Franchising

Cover design by Susan Lydon.

The materials contained herein represent the opinions of the authors and editors and should not be construed to be the action of either the American Bar Association or the Forum on Franchising unless adopted pursuant to the bylaws of the Association.

Nothing contained in this book is to be considered as the rendering of legal advice for specific cases, and readers are responsible for obtaining such advice from their own legal counsel. This book and any forms and agreements herein are intended for educational and informational purposes only.

The fundamentals of franchising/Rupert M. Barkoff, co-editor, Andrew
    C. Selden, co-editor.
        p.   cm.
    "Sponsored by: American Bar Association, Forum on Franchising"—T.p.
    Includes bibliographical references.
    ISBN 1-57073-384-8 (pbk.)
    1. Franchises (Retail trade)—Law and legislation—United States.
I. Barkoff, Rupert M.   II. Selden, Andrew C.   III. American Bar
Association. Forum on Franchising.
KF2023.F86 1997
346.7304′8—DC21   96-50881
                                                                          CIP

Discounts are available for books ordered in bulk. Special consideration is given to state bars, CLE programs, and other bar-related organizations. Inquire at Book Publishing, American Bar Association, 750 North Lake Shore Drive, Chicago, Illinois 60611.

01 00 99 98 97   5 4 3 2 1

Contents

This will make more sense when I send you the videotape. cll

Foreword

Fundamentals of Franchising, sponsored by the American Bar Association's Forum on Franchising, exemplifies our organization's commitment to educate practictioners about franchise law through the publication of comprehensive, unbiased works.

Fundamentals of Franchising presents in a single volume all the essentials of franchise law for practitioners new to the field and even for nonlawyers. We are particularly proud that this is a collaborative work prepared by over three dozen authors, who have enhanced its value as an important authority by explaining franchise law from a wide range of experiences and viewpoints. No other primer on franchise law existing today addresses franchising with equal diversity.

Co-editors Rupert M. Barkoff and Andrew C. Selden, each a past chair of the Forum on Franchising, fully comprehend the Forum's mission to study and advance franchise law responsibly, and have done so ably with this work. As members of the Forum's leadership when the *Fundamentals of Franchising* project was first concieved in the mid–1980s, both gentlemen were instrumental in publishing the original *Fundamentals of Franchising* book in 1987 in connection with the 10th Annual Forum in Tucson, Arizona. Since then, they have assumed responsibility for seeing it updated almost annually and for expanding, reformatting, and editing the work anew for this publication's general circulation. They have contributed countless hours to creating an important sustaining franchise legal publication and a vital authority on franchise law.

On behalf of the Forum on Franchising, I am enormously grateful to Rupert, Andy, and to each one of the distinguished contributing authors over the years, all of whom are recognized in the acknowledgments. Without the collective participation of so many Forum members, this book could not claim its special place on the franchise bookshelf. My thanks are also extended to the law firms of Kilpatrick Stockton, L.L.P. and Briggs and Morgan, P.C. for generously contributing editorial assistance to enable us to complete this special project in a timely fashion.

Rochelle B. Spandorf, Chair
Forum on Franchising

Preface

Fundamentals of Franchising represents the culmination of nine years of work by thirty-one contributors. The *Fundamentals* project was conceived in January 1987 to fill a void in franchise law publications. At that time many books covered certain aspects of franchise law at both beginning and advanced levels. However, there was no publication designed to give a broad overview of the law of franchising. Consistent with the mission of the American Bar Association's Forum on Franchising—to educate its members in the field of franchise law—*Fundamentals* is intended to introduce its readers to the legal areas in which franchise practitioners must be conversant to represent their clients properly, effectively, and professionally.

In October 1987, the first "Fundamentals of Franchising" program was presented as a half-day seminar to some seventy attendees in Tucson, Arizona, in conjunction with the ABA's Tenth Annual Forum on Franchising Annual Program. Altogether, "Fundamentals" has now been presented nineteen times. The total attendance to date exceeds eight hundred.

The materials presented in this book are direct descendants of the papers developed for the Tucson program. The materials have been updated almost annually and, for purposes of this book, have been re-edited and reformatted. Many of the authors in this book were original participants at the Tucson program. We have, however, added at least one additional author to each chapter to broaden the perspective of each paper and to ensure that the papers, which in some instances express opinions not shared by all, are within the mainstream views of franchise law practitioners. The authors and editors of this edition have, in the aggregate, more than three hundred years of legal experience. The papers necessarily reflect the experience, perspectives, and views of their respective authors and do not purport to represent the position or opinion of the American Bar Association or the Forum on Franchising.

This edition of *Fundamentals* and its updated successors will supplant the program materials that have historically been used as part of the program. For those readers who have been unable to attend a "Fundamentals" seminar program, we strongly encourage you to do so. After all, there is no substitute for live entertainment.

Rupert M. Barkoff
Andrew C. Selden
Editors

Acknowledgments

We, as editors of *Fundamentals of Franchising,* constitute only the tip of the iceberg of contributors to this publication. We would like to extend our thanks and appreciation to the following:

To the authors who prepared the manuscripts included in this book, and to the other contributors who have assisted in updating the *Fundamentals* materials since they first appeared in 1987:

Chapter 1
Authors: Laurence R. Hefter and William A. Finkelstein
Contributors: Mark H. Miller and Louis T. Pirkey

Chapter 2
Authors: Andrew A. Caffey, Stuart Hershman, and Lewis G. Rudnick
Contributors: John R. F. Baer and Charles S. Modell

Chapter 3
Authors: Judith Bailey and Dennis Wieczorek
Contributors: Gayle Cannon, Ann Hurwitz, Carol McErlean, and Ronald P. Roman

Chapter 4
Authors: Rochelle B. Spandorf and Mark B. Forseth
Contributors: Kenneth R. Darrow and Ann Hurwitz

Chapter 5
Authors: Thomas M. Pitegoff and M. Christine Carty
Contributor: W. Michael Garner

Chapter 6
Authors: Robert T. Joseph, Michael M. Eaton, and Alan M. Maclin
Contributors: Arthur I. Cantor and Michael J. Lockerby

Chapter 7
Authors: Rupert M. Barkoff and Andrew C. Selden
Contributors: Patrick J. Carter, Jan M. Davidson, and David Laufer

To our colleagues at Kilpatrick Stockton L.L.P. and Briggs and Morgan, P.A., who assisted in proofreading, cite checking, and otherwise preparing this edition for publication. These include Elaine W. Arnold, James Coblin, Jerome Connell, Jan M. Davidson, Cecil Davis, Neil Falis, Randolph Houchins, Lynne Henry, Wei Hu, Alan Maclin, Kris Melby, and Faye Taylor.

To Michael Garner, who, as Publications Officer of the Forum on Franchising, acted as coordinator for this project, and to Brett Lowell and Shelley Spandorf for their support as Chairs of the Forum on Franchising during the term of this project.

And, to the Forum on Franchising itself, for sponsoring this publication.

Rupert M. Barkoff

Andrew C. Selden

Editors

CHAPTER 1

Trademark Law and Related Franchising Issues

Laurence R. Hefter and William A. Finkelstein

Contents

This chapter focuses on trademark law as it relates to franchising. Among the major issues addressed are the types, selection, and clearance of marks; state and federal registration; enforcement of trademark rights; trademark licensing in the franchise agreement; and international protections.

Overview of Concepts

Trademarks and Service Marks

Trademarks and service marks are at the heart of the modern day marketing of consumer goods and services.[1] These marks can be symbols, words, pictures, slogans, colors, configurations, or virtually any other indicia that identify the goods

---

1. For simplicity, the word "trademark" will frequently be used to cover both trademarks and service marks. A trademark identifies products, while a service mark identifies services. Frequently the same mark is used as both a trademark (*e.g.,* "Taco Bell" for burritos) and a service mark (*e.g.,* "Taco Bell" for restaurant services).

or services of a particular party—be it a manufacturer, merchant, or offerer of services—and that distinguish these from the goods and services of others. Simply put, trademarks and service marks help consumers select goods or services by identifying those that have been satisfactory in the past while rejecting those that have not.

By identifying the source of goods or services, trademarks convey valuable data to consumers while reducing the costs (i.e., time, trial and error, and inconvenience) of acquiring information about the particular products or services, since consumers can come to rely on a trademark and the brand image it conveys. Moreover, trademarks fix responsibility, thereby inducing higher quality goods and services, and provide the framework for effective advertising.

Trade Names

A trade name is the name by which a legal entity does business or is known to the public, suppliers, or creditors. It is usually the same as a corporate name, although this is not always the case, especially in situations involving partnerships or sole proprietors. It often—but not necessarily—contains the key mark of the franchise system.

There is no federal registration of trade names as such. A trade name may only be registered as a trademark if it is used and presented to the consuming public in the form of a mark.[2] For example, "Pizza Hut, Inc." is a trade name, but "Pizza Hut" is the mark presented to, seen by, and used by customers of the restaurants.

Trademark Value

Trademarks are symbols used to convey to the minds of consumers the desirability of the goods or services the marks identify. As a result of successful performance, trademarks can develop commercial magnetism: a well recognized and respected trademark can become a business asset of incalculable value, usually referred to as business goodwill. Furthermore, the owner of a well recognized mark is more likely to attract business partners (i.e., franchisees) willing to make an investment and pay royalties because above-average opportunities exist for introducing goods or services with an already established trademark image and recognition.

Goodwill

Goodwill in a trademark develops as a result of favorable consumer recognition and association. Trademark law is designed to protect business goodwill by protecting consumers from confusing various producers of goods or providers of services. Confusingly similar marks not only deceive consumers but dilute the value of the goodwill of the legitimate mark.

---

2. *In re* Diamond Hill Farms, 32 U.S.P.Q.2d (BNA) 1383 (T.T.A.B. Bd. 1994).

Licensing and Franchising

The law allows the trademark owner to license the use of the mark to others provided that the owner maintains control over the quality of the goods and services provided by the licensee under the mark. Trademark licensing is, in almost all cases, the cornerstone of a franchise system.[3] It is a legally sanctioned business agreement between the owner of a trademark and another party that desires to use the trademark, including its associated goodwill, as the central element in its business to identify its product or service to the public while guaranteeing a uniform expectation of quality.

Franchising, in its simplest terms, is a complex program or system of trademark licensing. Franchising most often involves a system of marketing and distributing goods and services in accordance with standards and practices established by the trademark owner, who furnishes a well-established trademark and brand image, expertise, training, stability, and marketing know-how. In return, the trademark owner, or franchisor, obtains new sources of expansion capital, new distribution markets, and self-motivated vendors of its products or services.

The key to success for any franchise relationship is to implement properly the franchisor's marketing plan and business format, keeping in mind that protection of the trademark is essential. The best way to reach this objective is by achieving uniformity and consistency of the products, services, or business formats used in the franchise, coupled with a corresponding uniformity and consistency in presenting the trademark, brand identity, and image, and then vigorously protecting these legally.

The legal exclusivity that trademark rights afford to the franchisor and its franchisees offers the competitive advantage that is essential to a successful franchising business.

Overview of Trademark Law

Common Law

Trademark rights in the United States, unlike in most other countries, are obtained through use of the mark on or in connection with particular goods or services. Trademark rights accrue automatically—that is, without any formality or paperwork—to the first business using a particular mark to identify its goods or services. The first or "senior" user has the right to prevent competitors, including subsequent federal registrants, from using that or a confusingly similar mark in its geographic area of use as well as in any areas of reputation and natural expansion. Trademark rights that are brought into existence in this manner are called

---

3. Susser v. Carvel Corp., 206 F. Supp. 636 (S.D.N.Y. 1962), *aff'd*, 332 F.2d 505, 141 U.S.P.Q. (BNA) 609 (2d Cir. 1964).

"common-law rights." Common-law rights are subject, however, to limitation and even elimination by other parties that previously filed applications for federal registration or have already obtained federal registrations.

Registration

Although not mandatory for the protection of trademark rights, federal trademark registration provides many substantive and procedural benefits and is, therefore, highly recommended. For example, a federal registration provides a presumption of validity and ownership of the mark, allows the possibility of acquiring incontestability status five years after the registration has issued, and provides constructive notice of use nationally, thereby giving the trademark owner nationwide superior rights even if the owner does not use the mark throughout the entire territory of the United States. State trademark registrations are also available but offer few benefits and are recommended only in particular situations.

An application for federal registration of a mark may be based either on actual use of the mark or on "bona fide intent-to-use" the mark.[4] The intent-to-use application will not issue as a registration until the mark has actually been used. However, if the application matures to registration, the mark is deemed to have been "constructively used" throughout the United States as of the application's filing date.[5] Therefore, the first applicant obtains a key priority date over intervening users. This is of considerable importance because often long periods of time are necessary before a product or service is ready for market, and years may lapse between the adoption and the actual commercial use of a mark. Also, the mark is protected while test marketing is conducted or franchises are being offered and sold.

Use of the Mark

While an intent-to-use application effectively reserves the mark for a limited time period (up to approximately four years), the federal registration will not issue until actual use of the mark has commenced and specimens and dates of use have been submitted to the U.S. Patent and Trademark Office (PTO).[6] Therefore, it is important to note that actual commercial use is still the key requirement for acquisition, registration, and maintenance of trademark rights in the United States. The "use" required to satisfy the Lanham Act requirements is bona fide commercial use: token use is inadequate.[7] Acceptable commercial use varies depending

---

4. Lanham Act § 1(a),(b), 15 U.S.C. § 1051 (a),(b); the Lanham Act, 15 U.S.C. §§ 1051–1127, is the statute that governs the federal registration of trademarks and the rights of registrants.

5. 15 U.S.C. § 1057(c).

6. 15 U.S.C. § 1051(d).

7. 15 U.S.C. § 1127; Zazu Designs v. L'Oreal, S.A., 979 F.2d 499, 24 U.S.P.Q.2d (BNA) 1828 (7th Cir. 1992).

andard for a particular industry. For example, one restaurant site is al-
ʹays acceptable and a single shipment may be acceptable in an industry
ı single-unit sales are common, such as in heavy machinery, whereas for
er products, such as toys, larger and more continuous shipments may be
required.

Protectability

Courts will protect a trademark only if it truly identifies and distinguishes the
source of the goods or services. Not every word or symbol used in connection
with a product or service can be a trademark. Words that are the common name of
that particular good or service (generic terms) can never be marks because they
cannot identify the source. (For example, "Pocket Survival Tool" was found
generic for a compact folding tool.)[8]

A generic term is the understood term to identify a type of product (such
as "car" for a motorized vehicle). Generic terms legally can never obtain trademark status and, therefore, can never become the proprietary property of a
company.

To be protected under trademark law, a mark must be distinctive, that is, capable of identifying and distinguishing the product of one party from those of
competitors. Therefore, proper and thoughtful selection, thorough and diligent
clearance, appropriate and consistent usage, proper contractual arrangements,
and diligent policing are essential elements in the development and maintenance
of a protectable property interest in a mark.

Summary of Trademark Functions

Trademarks perform several key functions that are recognized and protected by
the courts:

1. They identify an owner's goods or services and distinguish them from
    those of competitors.
2. They signify that all goods or services bearing the mark emanate from a
    single, albeit sometimes anonymous, source or connote common spon-
    sorship.
3. They signify that all goods or services bearing the mark are of the same
    or similar quality.
4. They act as a tool for advertising the goods or services with which the
    mark is used.
5. They bind a franchise system together by providing a common identity
    with synergistic benefits for the franchisor and franchisees.

8. *In re* Leatherman Tool Group, 32 U.S.P.Q.2d (BNA) 1443 (Trademark Trial & App.
Bd. 1994).

Types of Marks

The range of words, names, symbols, or devices capable of serving as trademarks is virtually unlimited. It includes logos, slogans, colors, product shapes, packaging, designs—even smells—provided that they are inherently distinctive or have attained secondary meaning. "Secondary meaning" is a term of art used to describe borderline marks that are not inherently distinctive of a particular source but have, through usage in commerce, come to be associated with a particular source.

Words, Letters, and Numbers

[handwritten: most common.]

Words are the most common form of marks. They can be recognizable existing words or new, arbitrary combinations of letters or letters and numbers. Even an individual letter[9] (e.g., "S" for Singer sewing machines) or an arrangement of letters (e.g., "NBC") can function as a mark.

Likewise, numbers alone (e.g., "4711" for cologne) or in combination with letters (e.g., "A.1" for steak sauce)[10] can be marks, provided, however, that the numbers are in fact used in a trademark sense and not only descriptively to indicate the model, grade, or size of a product.

Even telephone number and letter combinations (e.g., "INJURY-1" for legal services) have been found to be descriptive and thus protectable upon proof of secondary meaning.[11]

Designs, Shapes, and Symbols

Designs, drawings, and symbols may serve as trademarks if they are perceived by customers as indicators of source and not only as ornamentation.[12] Realistic drawings illustrating the product or service or commonplace geometrical figures or product configurations (such as the "Coke" bottle) are protectable if they are inherently distinctive or upon a showing of secondary meaning.

Single Colors

For several years the courts were split on the question of whether a single color alone—that is, without a design—could be registered and protected as a mark.

---

9. Quality Semiconductors v. QLogic Corp., 31 U.S.P.Q.2d (BNA) 1627 (N.D. Cal. 1994).

10. Nabisco Brands, Inc. v. Kaye, 760 F. Supp. 25, 19 U.S.P.Q.2d (BNA) 1465 (D. Conn. 1991).

11. Dranoff-Perlstein Assoc. v. Sklar, 967 F.2d 852, 23 U.S.P.Q.2d (BNA) 1174 (3d Cir. 1992). However, since January 1994 the PTO examining attorneys are advised to refuse registration of generic or descriptive telephone number combinations. PTO Examination Guide No. 1–94, at 3 (January 28, 1994).

12. *In re* Swift & Co., 223 F.2d 950, 166 U.S.P.Q. (BNA) 286 (C.C.P.A. 1955).

The U.S. Supreme Court recently decided that a single color alone could indeed be a valid trademark under the Lanham Act if it (1) serves no utilitarian function and (2) has attained secondary meaning.[13]

The Supreme Court treated color as a descriptive term that can function as a mark only when the color has attained secondary meaning and therefore the public has come to identify a particular color on a product as signifying a brand. Moreover, a color must not be functional. The Supreme Court opinion quotes earlier cases holding, on the one hand, that competitors must be free to use the color green for farm machinery and black for outboard motors but, on the other hand, that the color pink could function as a trademark for fiberglass insulation, since other colors are equally available.[14] Under this opinion, the fact that there is a limited supply of colors that would soon be depleted by competitors is an "occasional problem [that should not] justify a blanket prohibition."

Composites or Combinations

A product or service can be identified by more than one mark, and labels and packages often contain a combination of several trademarks. Each designation that creates a separate commercial impression distinct from other material appearing on the label and that serves as a source indicator is considered a separate trademark.

House Marks versus Secondary Marks

Often a business uses its corporate name as its "house mark" (e.g., "Dupont" in the oval logo) in combination with many different "secondary marks" (e.g., "Teflon") for its various products. Most franchise systems use a house mark combined with a logo (e.g., "Burger King") to identify the franchise as a whole and several secondary marks (e.g., "Whopper") that identify individual products.

Slogans

Slogans may serve as trademarks if they are capable of identifying goods and services. Common promotional phrases like "Brand Names For Less" for clothing stores are not protectable because they are trite and highly descriptive.[15] However, even though the slogan "Extra Strength Pain Reliever" as used on Excedrin brand pain relievers is highly descriptive, it was given trademark protection upon showing of secondary meaning.[16]

---

13. Qualitex Co. v. Jacobson Prods. Co., 115 S. Ct. 1300, 34 U.S.P.Q.2d (BNA) 1161 (1995).

14. Deere & Co. v. Farmhand, Inc., 721 F.2d 253 (8th Cir. 1983); Brunswick Corp. v. British Seagull, 35 F.3d 1527, 1532, 32 U.S.P.Q.2d (BNA) 1120 (Fed. Cir. 1994); In re Owens-Corning Fiberglass Corp., 774 F.2d 1116, 227 U.S.P.Q. (BNA) 417 (Fed. Cir. 1985).

15. In re Melville Corp., 228 U.S.P.Q. 970 (Trademark Trial & App. Bd. 1986).

16. Bristol-Myers Co. v. Approved Pharmaceutical Corp., 149 U.S.P.Q. (BNA) 896 (N.Y. Sup. Ct. 1966).

Trade Dress

"Trade dress" refers to the combination of elements that make up the look, feel, or environment of a product or business. The term can refer to individual elements of a product or business image as well as to the image the combination of those elements creates as a whole.

There is neither a fixed list of features that constitute a business image nor a statutory definition of the term. A product's trade dress may include its size, shape, label, packaging, color, color combinations, texture, or graphics. The trade dress of a service may include exterior and interior architectural designs and decor, vehicle decoration, clothing, signs, menus, cuisine, or entertainment features—anything and everything that individually or in combination identifies and distinguishes a business.

Prominent examples of legally protectable trade dress include the exterior design of White Castle,[17] Howard Johnson,[18] and Kentucky Fried Chicken restaurants;[19] the interior decor of Fuddruckers' restaurants;[20] the overall appearance of a Ferrari automobile;[21] the Rubik's Cube puzzle;[22] and even the inverted "Y" design on Jockey shorts.[23]

Trade dress protection does not, however, extend to vague or abstract images or themes. For instance, courts have refused to extend trade dress protection to the concept of a "full-service restaurant serving down home country cooking in a relaxed and informal atmosphere"[24] or a Scandinavian marketing theme for ice cream.[25] Trade dress protection does attach to an arbitrary, extensive, and distinctive "signature" collection of interior design characteristics of a restaurant.[26]

Trade dress protection attempts to balance three public policy objectives:

1. The protection of consumers from confusion
2. The protection and reward of investment in unique and original features identifying a product or service

---

17. White Tower Sys., Inc. v. White Castle Sys., 90 F.2d 67 (6th Cir. 1937).

18. Clayton v. Howard Johnson Franchise Sys., Inc., 730 F. Supp., 1553 (M.D. Fl. 1988).

19. Kentucky Fried Chicken Corp. v. Diversified Packaging Corp., 549 F.2d 368, 193 U.S.P.Q. (BNA) 649 (5th Cir. 1977).

20. Fuddruckers, Inc. v. Doc's B.R. Others, Inc., 826 F.2d 837, 4 U.S.P.Q.2d (BNA) 1026, Bus. Franchise Guide (CCH) ¶ 8977 (9th Cir. 1987).

21. Ferrari S.p.A. v. McBurnie, 11 U.S.P.Q.2d (BNA) 1843 (S.D. Cal. 1989).

22. Ideal Toy Corp. v. Plawner Toy Mfg. Corp., 685 F.2d 78, 216 U.S.P.Q. (BNA) 102 (3rd Cir. 1982).

23. *In re* Jockey Int'l., Inc., 192 U.S.P.Q. (BNA) 579 (Trademark Trial & App. Bd. 1976).

24. Prufrock, Ltd. v. Lasater, 781 F.2d 129, 131–32, 228 U.S.P.Q. (BNA) 435, Bus. Franchise Guide (CCH) ¶ 8563 (8th Cir. 1986).

25. Haagen-Dazs, Inc. v. Frusen Gladje, Ltd., 493 F. Supp. 73, 210 U.S.P.Q. (BNA) 204 (S.D.N.Y. 1980).

26. Fuddruckers, Inc. v. Doc's B.R. Others, Inc., 826 F.2d 837, 4 U.S.P.Q.2d (BNA) 1026, Bus. Franchise Guide (CCH) ¶ 8977 (9th Cir. 1987).

3. The protection of the rights of others to compete freely by having unrestricted access to the ordinary public domain features of products or attributes of providing services, or design elements that are functional in nature or necessary to allow competition.

Although some trade dresses are unregistrable because of definition and specificity issues (like the interior design of a restaurant), the courts may protect such rights in infringement litigation brought under state law and under Section 43(a) of the Lanham Act.[27] To succeed in a claim for trade dress infringement, a trade dress owner must establish all of the following elements:

1. The specific nature and scope of its trade dress.
2. That the trade dress is nonfunctional, in that it has no function other than being an embellishment added for purpose of identification. However, the combination of otherwise unprotectable functional features can create trade dress that is protectable as a whole.[28]
3. That the trade dress either is inherently distinctive[29] or has acquired secondary meaning.[30]
4. That there is a likelihood of confusion between the parties' trade dress.[31]
5. That the trade dress owner has been or is likely to be damaged.

Trade dress in a product configuration is inherently distinctive if it is (1) unusual and memorable, (2) conceptually separable from the product, and (3) likely to serve primarily as a designator of origin of the product.[32]

Often the trade dress is used in conjunction with a word mark. For example, the producer of Excedrin PM sued the producer of Tylenol PM for infringement of the trade dress of the packaging. The court held that the similarity in trade dress was not likely to confuse the public because the famous word marks visually dominated the trade dresses and were the most prominent feature.[33]

---

27. 15 U.S.C. § 1125(a). *See* Fotomat Corp. v. Photo Drive-Thru, Inc., 425 F. Supp. 693, 193 U.S.P.Q. (BNA) 342 (D.N.J. 1977); Warehouse Restaurant, Inc. v. Customs House Restaurant, Inc., 217 U.S.P.Q. (BNA) 411 (N.D. Cal. 1982).

28. Aromatique, Inc. v. Gold Seal, 28 F.3d 863, 31 U.S.P.Q.2d (BNA) 1481 (8th Cir. 1994); Fuddruckers, Inc. v. Doc's B.R. Others, Inc., 826 F.2d 837, 4 U.S.P.Q.2d (BNA) 1026 (9th Cir. 1987).

29. Two Pesos, Inc. v. Taco Cabana, Inc., 112 S. Ct. 2753 (1992). "Inherently distinctive" is discussed in a later section of this chapter.

30. Aromatique, Inc. v. Goldseal, 28 F.3d 863, 31 U.S.P.Q.2d (BNA) 1481 (8th Cir. 1994); Duraco Prods. v. Joy Plastic Enters., 40 F.3d 1431, 32 U.S.P.Q.2d (BNA) 1724 (3rd Cir. 1994); George Basch Co. v. Blue Coral, Inc., 968 F.2d 1532, 23 U.S.P.Q.2d (BNA) 1724 (2nd Cir. 1992), *cert. denied,* 113 S. Ct. 510 (1992).

31. Prufrock Ltd. v. Lasater, 781 F.2d 129, 228 U.S.P.Q. (BNA) 435, Bus. Franchise Guide (CCH) ¶ 8563 (8th Cir. 1986).

32. Duraco Prods. v. Joy Plastic Enters., 40 F.3d 1431, 32 U.S.P.Q.2d (BNA) 1428 (3rd Cir. 1994).

33. Bristol-Myers Squibb Co. v. McNeil-P.P.C., Inc., 973 F.2d 1033, 24 U.S.P.Q.2d (BNA) 1161 (2nd Cir. 1992).

Selection of Marks

Choosing a Proper Mark

The selection of a proper mark can be crucial to the success of a franchise business. The mark is central to the franchise "personality." It can become the franchisor's most valuable asset. Yet the selection process is often given insufficient attention by franchisors.

Legally Protectable

First of all, the mark must be legally protectable and registrable. The consequences of choosing a mark with legal defects may cause expensive litigation, increase advertisement costs, or preclude the expansion of the use of the mark to new products or to additional countries. Counsel can be instrumental in focusing attention on this issue and channeling the selection process in a legally protectable direction.[34]

Marketable and Attractive

In addition to being legally protectable, a mark should be suitable for use in all advertising and other materials, easy to remember and pronounce, and free of hidden connotations in English and in foreign languages that may be familiar to the American public or where the mark will likely be used.

Appropriate for Expansion

The mark should be chosen bearing in mind possible future growth both geographically and into new types of products or services. A mark describing the nature of the product to be marketed today might be inappropriate if applied to a different product in the future, thus forcing the owner to create and introduce new marks for future products and losing the goodwill transfer benefit of trademarks. Consideration should be given to whether the selected mark is probably appropriate and legally acceptable in most target international markets. Every country has its own trademark laws containing different requirements regarding the protectability of marks. Surnames, geographic names, and terms with "official" or religious connotations are likely to cause problems in most foreign countries. Even if the mark is legally protectable and registrable in the foreign country, it might nevertheless be unacceptable for cultural reasons or because it sounds offensive (e.g., "Banana Republic" in a tropical nation). The mark may have an unacceptable meaning or connotation in the language of the foreign country. For example, the mark "Nova" for automobiles unfortunately means "does not go" in a Spanish-speaking country, and the fanciful mark "Mist" translates into "manure" in the German language. When used in a foreign language, a suggestive mark will probably lose its hidden message or even have an unwelcome one (e.g., "Coppertone," although used in Italy, does not suggest suntan in Italian, but rather "car tire"). Some marks, like "Whirlpool," are puzzling to pronounce for non-English speakers and are likely to be misspelled.

---

34. *See generally* Hefter, *Selection of Marks,* 2 FRANCHISE L.J. 3 (1982).

The Mark Must Be Legally Protectable and Registrable

To be protected under trademark law, a mark must be distinctive, that is, capable of identifying and distinguishing the goods or services of the proprietor from those of its competitors. To analyze their distinctiveness, marks can be placed on a continuum called "spectrum of distinctiveness."

Inherently Distinctive Marks

Inherently distinctive marks are legally protectable and registrable from the moment they are adopted in commerce. The following types of marks are inherently distinctive:

1. *Fanciful marks.* These are coined new words that have been invented to serve as marks and have no other meaning besides their identifying function (e.g., "Kodak," "Exxon").[35]
2. *Arbitrary marks.* These are dictionary words or common designs having a meaning that bears no relationship to the product they are meant to identify (e.g., "Domino's" for pizza, "Apple" for computers).
3. *Suggestive marks.* These require thought, imagination, and perception to associate the mark with the product or service it identifies (e.g., "Coppertone" for suntan oil, "Cork 'N Cleaver" for restaurant services).[36] These marks indirectly suggest characteristics or features of the goods or services without describing them.

Suggestive marks are popular because they are considered to be inherently distinctive and thus immediately protectable and registrable without requiring proof of secondary meaning while also being satisfactory marketing tools because they convey some information about the product or service.

Descriptive Marks

In contrast, descriptive marks are initially not considered distinctive and are thus not immediately protected as trademarks. Descriptive marks include (1) marks that merely describe in words or pictures the intended purpose, function, quality, size, ingredients, characteristics, class of users, or intended effect on the user of the goods or services they identify; (2) marks that primarily describe the geographical origin of the goods or services; and (3) marks that primarily constitute a person's surname.[37] If the description is inaccurate, the mark is "deceptively misdescriptive." All these marks are initially not considered distinctive and thus are not protected or registrable immediately upon use. Marks found by courts or the PTO to be merely descriptive will be denied protection and will also be found

---

35. Exxon Corp. v. Xoil Energy Resources, 552 F. Supp. 1008, 216 U.S.P.Q. (BNA) 634 (S.D.N.Y. 1981).

36. Cork 'N Cleaver of Colorado, Inc. v. Keg 'N Cleaver of Utica, Inc., 192 U.S.P.Q. (BNA) 148 (N.D.N.Y. 1975).

37. 15 U.S.C. § 1052(e).

unregistrable, unless secondary meaning can be shown (e.g., "Giant Hamburgers" for hamburgers and restaurant services,[38] "Pestaway" for pest control services,[39] "Beef & Brew" for restaurant services,[40] "Vision Center" for optical clinic services,[41] "First Southern Bank" for a bank in Florida).[42]

However, descriptive (and deceptively misdescriptive) marks may become distinctive and thus protectable if they attain "secondary meaning," that is, when owing to extensive use and advertisement the relevant consuming public has come mentally to associate the mark, not in its descriptive or surname sense, but as indicating a single source of the product or service.[43] Section 2(f) of the Lanham Act provides that proof of substantially exclusive and continuous use of a descriptive mark on goods or services for five years can be *prima facie* evidence of secondary meaning.

When choosing a mark, descriptive marks should be avoided because they are initially not protected by trademark law and are not immediately registrable. In addition, it can be difficult and expensive to establish secondary meaning.

Terms Not Protectable

The following matter is prohibited from serving as a mark:

1. Generic terms (words that are the common name of a product or service) can never be marks because they cannot distinguish those goods originating from a particular business from other goods of the same kind (e.g., "Discount Mufflers" is generic for repair and replacement muffler services).[44]
2. Deceptively misdescriptive terms (i.e., terms that falsely indicate certain material characteristics of the products if the prospective purchasers are likely to believe the misdescription) and marks that falsely suggest a connection with any person, living or dead, or with any institution or business organization.[45]
3. Immoral or scandalous matter and marks consisting of the flag or coat of arms of any state.[46]

38. Giant Food, Inc. v. Nation's Foodservice, Inc., 710 F.2d 1565, 218 U.S.P.Q. (BNA) 390 (Fed. Cir. 1983).

39. Couhig's Pestaway Co. v. Pestaway, Inc., 278 So.2d 519, 179 U.S.P.Q. (BNA) 112 (La. Ct. App. 1973).

40. beef & brew, inc., v. Beef & Brew, Inc., 389 F. Supp. 179, 185 U.S.P.Q. (BNA) 531 (D. Or. 1974).

41. Vision Center v. Opticks, Inc., 596 F.2d 111, 202 U.S.P.Q. (BNA) 333 (5th Cir. 1979).

42. Great S. Bank v. First S. Bank, 625 So.2d 463, 30 U.S.P.Q.2d (BNA) 1522 (Fla. 1993).

43. "Supercuts" for haircutting shops was found to be descriptive but to have achieved secondary meaning. Emra Corp. v. Superclips, Ltd., 559 F. Supp. 705, 218 U.S.P.Q. (BNA) 124, Bus. Franchise Guide (CCH) ¶ 8016 (E.D. Mich. 1983).

44. Discount Muffler Shop, Inc. v. Meineke Realty Corp., 535 F. Supp. 439, 217 U.S.P.Q. (BNA) 1154 (N.D. Ohio 1982).

45. 15 U.S.C. § 1052(a).

46. 15 U.S.C. § 1052(a), (b), (c).

The Mark Must Be Nonfunctional

Features that are essential to the use or purpose of the product or that affect the cost or quality of the product cannot be appropriated as trademarks or trade dress. Otherwise, a producer would obtain a perpetual monopoly over a useful feature even if it does not qualify for patent protection, thus inhibiting legitimate competition.[47]

Is the Mark Legally Available?

The selected mark must be clear from potential claims from prior users, applicants for federal registration, or federal registrants. A mark that is confusingly similar to a previously registered mark, a mark that is the subject of a prior pending application, or a mark or trade name previously used in connection with the same or related goods or services may not be able to achieve registration.[48] Also, if the proposed mark is confusingly similar to a mark that is the subject of an intent-to-use application, and if the applicant uses the mark while the application is pending, a registration will issue and the mark will be considered to have been in use as of the application's filing date. As a consequence, since one must not copy or imitate an existing mark, one must conduct an extensive trademark search to make sure that a mark is available (a process discussed later in this chapter).

Strength of the Mark

The more distinctive, unique, and well-known the mark is, the "stronger" it is considered to be. The strength of a mark defines the scope of protection it is accorded: the stronger the mark, the more extensive is the scope of legal protection against infringing marks over a wide range of product and service categories or geographic markets and a wider range of appearance, sound, and meaning variations.

Strength is a relative notion, and marks can be placed on a continuum ranging from very strong to weak. Strength is determined by three primary factors.

How Common the Mark Is in the Field of Use

Consumers are aware that marks such as "Star," "Gold Medal," and "Universal"[49] are used by many unrelated businesses. Therefore, they are weak source identifiers. When many similar marks exist on the market, each of these "crowd of marks" is not very distinctive and, therefore, is weak and has a relatively narrow

---

47. Qualitex Co. v. Jacobson Prods. Co., 115 S. Ct. 1300, 34 U.S.P.Q.2d (BNA) 1161 (1995); *In re* Bio Medicus, Inc., 31 U.S.P.Q.2d (BNA) 1254 (Trademark Trial & App. Bd. 1994) (configuration of a centrifugal veinless blood pump). Functional configurations may be protectable under the patent law.

48. 15 U.S.C. § 1052(d).

49. Universal Money Ctrs. v. American Tel. & Tel. Co., 22 F.3d 1527, 30 U.S.P.Q.2d (BNA) 1930 (10th Cir. 1994), *cert. denied,* 115 S. Ct. 655 (1994).

scope of protection.[50] Generally, marks consisting of one or two letters or numbers also are considered weak.[51]

How Descriptive the Mark Is in Relation to the Particular Goods or Services

The more descriptive the mark, the less distinctive and thus weaker it is initially. Fanciful and arbitrary marks are generally considered to be inherently strong and are, therefore, given a wider range of protection. Suggestive marks are in the middle ground and descriptive marks are, at least initially, at the weak end of the spectrum.

The Degree of Fame and Marketplace Recognition of the Mark

Even if a mark is fanciful or arbitrary, it might be relatively unknown to the public because of minimal sales and is thus commercially weak. Conversely, after significant use and advertising, a descriptive mark initially classified in the weaker part of the spectrum may become a strong mark. For example, "Kentucky Fried Chicken" (consisting of a geographic and generic term) and "McDonald's" (a surname and thus descriptive) have accumulated an amount of secondary meaning that far exceeds the minimum required for protectability and qualifies these marks as strong. For example, the use of "McDental" for dental services was enjoined based on McDonald's strong family of "Mc" marks, even though fast food and dentistry are not related.[52]

Marks Should Be Distinctive, Not Descriptive

When selecting marks, marketing people are often attracted to descriptive terms because they believe that the more descriptive the term is, the more it communicates about the product to the consumer. Legally, however, such terms tend to be less distinctive and thus less protectable. Therefore, the owner of a weak mark needs to invest significantly in marketing and advertising to educate the public that the mark is proprietary and, thereby, acquire secondary meaning. On the other hand, fanciful and arbitrary marks are inherently distinctive and strong, but they convey little or no message about the product to the consumer and might require expensive advertising to teach the consumer to remember the marks. The way out of this dilemma is to avoid both extremes and select a mark that is marketable and attractive and yet suggests features of the product.

Avoid Descriptive Terms

A simple misspelling is not enough, especially if the misspelling follows the pronunciation of the descriptive word (e.g., "Nite" for "night"). However, the mark

---

50. Pfizer, Inc. v. Astra Pharmaceutical Prods., 858 F. Supp. 1305, 33 U.S.P.Q.2d (BNA) 1545 (S.D.N.Y. 1994).

51. American Optical Corp. v. American Olean Tile Co., 185 U.S.P.Q. (BNA) 405 (S.D.N.Y. 1974).

52. McDonald's Corp. v. Druck and Gerner, D.D.S., P.C., 814 F. Supp. 1127 (N.D.N.Y. 1993).

"Muff-Funs" for mini-muffins was found registrable because it plays on the words "muffin" and "fun."[53] The simple translation of a descriptive term into a foreign language is insufficient (e.g., "Saporito" as the equivalent of "tasty" in Italian).[54] However, a combination of foreign and English words may result in a suggestive mark (e.g., "Le Crystal Naturel").[55]

The selection of a mark is a creative process seeking to send an attractive message to the consumer while avoiding mere description of the goods or services. The investment required to confer secondary meaning on a weak descriptive expression might be better invested in educating the public through advertising to associate a coined or arbitrary mark with a product. Coined marks may be used to create a family of related marks (e.g., "Kodak," "Kodacolor," "Kodachrome"). Moreover, once a strong mark is recognized in the market, it can be used as a magnet to introduce new products with less advertising costs and with a smaller risk that a third party may have already appropriated the mark in that category of goods. Descriptive and other weak types of marks present increased risks of third parties having superior common-law rights in local trading areas.

Success stories like the McDonald's and Kentucky Fried Chicken marks are the exception rather than the rule. On the other hand, one need not totally adopt invented names like Mr. Eastman did with "Kodak."

Avoid Geographic Names

Geographic names are particularly weak if the product is generally expected to, and in fact does, originate from that area. If, however, an area is not known for that type of product, the geographic name is protectable. For example, "Philadelphia" for cream cheese was found to be an arbitrary mark because this cheese is made in the small city of Philadelphia, New York (and not in the more obviously recognized city of Philadelphia, Pennsylvania), and neither of these two cities has a particular reputation for the production of cheese.[56]

Avoid Surnames

Surnames are likely to be already used as common-law marks somewhere in the United States. Moreover, these terms can present additional registrability prob-

---

53. *In re* Grand Metro. Foodservice, 30 U.S.P.Q.2d (BNA) 1974 (Trademark Trial & App. Bd. 1994).

54. *In re* Geo A. Hormel & Co., 227 U.S.P.Q. (BNA) 813 (Trademark Trial & App. Bd. 1985).

55. French Transit v. Modern Coupon Sys., 818 F. Supp. 635, 29 U.S.P.Q.2d (BNA) 1626 (S.D.N.Y. 1993).

56. Kraft Foods v. BC-USA, 840 F. Supp. 344, 29 U.S.P.Q.2d (BNA) 1919 (E.D. Pa. 1993). *See also In re* Harvey & Sons, 32 U.S.P.Q.2d (BNA) 1451 (Trademark Trial & App. Bd. 1994). According to Section 2(a) of the Lanham Act as amended to implement GATT and TRIPS, trademarks for wine or spirits that consist of a geographical designation that do not in fact originate in that geographic area will be refused registration if first used after January 1, 1996.

lems on an international level, since many foreign countries are more restrictive than the United States with regard to the registration of surnames.

Suggestive Marks Are Often the Answer

Suggestive marks do not describe but instead simply suggest a link to the goods or services. Drawing the line between suggestive and descriptive marks is often difficult. The amount of "imagination, thought, and perception" a term must require to be recognized by the PTO and the courts as "suggestive" rather than "descriptive" is hard to define. As a rule, if the term in question has been frequently used by competitors, it is likely that it will be found descriptive.[57]

Coin Both a Product Name and a Trademark

If, over time, the public uses and understands the trademark as the generic name of the product, the term will cease to be protected as a trademark and will be available for all to use as a generic name. This adoption by the public and consequent loss of rights has occurred in many instances. For example, "Cellophane,"[58] "Aspirin,"[59] and "Escalator" were once proprietary trademarks. For a new type of product for which a generic name is not commonly known, it is a good idea to coin and advertise both a trademark and a generic term for the product to preserve ownership of the trademark and provide a generic term for the public and competitors to use.[60]

When Bayer Company first introduced its "Aspirin" product, the only generic name available was the commercially unacceptable name "acetyl salicylic acid." Thus, "aspirin" became a generic name because the public could remember and pronounce it and "Bayer" became the trademark for aspirin.

Clearance of Marks

The Search Process

Before incurring the expense of adopting a mark, preparing packaging and promotional material, and filing a trademark application, a comprehensive search should be conducted to determine the availability of the mark. The comprehensive search encompasses marks registered and pending in the PTO, state trademark registrations, and marks and names that are in use but not registered (common-law marks). Similar searches can be conducted outside of the United States. The determination of the legal availability of marks, especially for services, is a process fraught with uncertainties and imperfections. Accordingly, the advice of counsel with specific expertise in trademark matters is recommended.

---

57. Shoe Corp. of America v. Juvenile Shoe Corp., 266 F.2d 793, 121 U.S.P.Q. (BNA) 510 (C.C.P.A. 1959).

58. DuPont Cellophane Co. v. Waxed Prods. Co., 85 F.2d 75, 81 (2nd Cir. 1936).

59. Bayer Co. v. United Drug Co., 272 F. 505 (D.N.Y. 1921).

60. *Id.*

Preliminary Considerations

Time Frame: "Haste Makes Waste"

An extensive trademark search takes time, but this time is well spent, considering the potential costs and delay caused by litigation over the use of the mark. The advent of computerized trademark searches has greatly reduced the search time. It is, however, a good idea to start searching the mark with sufficient lead time before the launch. Typically, at least one month should be allowed to conduct and evaluate a full search in the United States and two months should be allowed for an international search.

Costs: "Penny Wise and Pound Foolish"

The costs of a trademark search are negligible compared to the costs of litigation or the investment in package design and in an advertising campaign. It would be absurd to try to save a few thousand dollars when searching a mark, only to risk million-dollar liabilities. Obviously, it is cheaper to avoid or remove all third-party obstacles before launching the mark than to be caught by surprise and face litigation after launch.

Selection: "Don't Be Obvious"

The stronger the mark, the lesser the clearance risks. The more obvious and trite the mark, the higher the risk that someone somewhere is using it as an unregistered common-law mark that might escape detection during the search. There are probably dozens of eateries named "Tony's Pizza" in the United States.

Fallibility: "No System Is Perfect"

There is no single registry or comprehensive source of trademark usage information, and all databases from which searches are made are flawed to some degree. Therefore, searching common-law marks is by its nature incomplete. The client should be informed of the risks.

Why Conduct a Search?

Duty to Search

Although not mentioned in the Lanham Act, and not required by most courts, some cases imply a duty to conduct a trademark search, for instance, before launching a new mark in a national advertising campaign.[61]

Constructive Notice

Section 22 of the Lanham Act[62] provides that a federal registration constitutes nationwide constructive notice of the registrant's claim of ownership of the mark.

---

61. Sands, Taylor & Wood v. Quaker Oats Co., 18 U.S.P.Q.2d (BNA) 1457 (N.D. Ill. 1990), *aff'd on merits, remanded on damages,* 978 F.2d 947, 24 U.S.P.Q.2d (BNA) 1001 (7th Cir. 1992); Money Store v. Harriscorp Finance, Inc., 689 F.2d 666, 216 U.S.P.Q. (BNA) 11 (7th Cir. 1982).
62. 15 U.S.C. § 1072.

This means that a latecomer cannot defend its adoption and continued use of a mark on the grounds of innocence, good faith, or lack of knowledge of an earlier registration by another.[63]

Constructive Use

The filing of an application for federal registration constitutes constructive use of the mark, conferring to the first applicant a right of priority, contingent on eventual registration.[64] Thus, the existence of pending applications for federal registration (since November 16, 1989) indicates the existence of priority rights of others, provided that use commences and registration eventually issues.

Actual Knowledge and Duty to Avoid

The latecomer has a duty to differentiate its mark from all existing marks.[65] In the federal registration process, any doubt about confusing similarity is resolved against the newcomer.[66] If the existing mark is sufficiently strong and well-known, a latecomer may not be allowed to adopt it even on noncompeting goods or services because the consumer might infer a common sponsorship or because the value and awareness of the famous mark might become diluted. For instance, a court held that there was a likelihood of confusion between the defendant's use of "Hallmark" for an automobile dealership and the trademark of the famous greeting cards producer.[67]

Good Business Judgment

The failure to search, a faulty or incomplete search, or a failure to resolve problematic references properly can result in severe consequences: court injunctions against use and advertising, damages, loss of profit, loss of goodwill and investment, and suits against the franchisor by franchisees for damages and breach of contract.

Contents of the "Full" Search

PTO Search

The first step is to search the database of the PTO to identify federal registrations and pending applications that would clearly preclude use or registration of the mark searched, thus saving the further costs of a comprehensive search. However,

---

63. Dolfin Corp. v. Jem Sportswear, Inc., 218 U.S.P.Q. (BNA) 201 (C.D. Cal. 1982).

64. 15 U.S.C. § 1057(c).

65. Visa Int'l. Service Assoc. v. Visa Hotel Group, Inc., 561 F. Supp. 984, 218 U.S.P.Q. (BNA) 261 (D. Nev. 1983).

66. *In re* Shell Oil Co., 992 F.2d 1204, 26 U.S.P.Q.2d (BNA) 1687 (Fed. Cir. 1993) (RIGHT-A-WAY & Design for service station oil and lubrication change services blocked by RIGHT-A-WAY & Design for distributorship services in the field of automobile parts).

67. Hallmark Cards, Inc., v. Hallmark Dodge, Inc., 634 F. Supp. 990, 229 U.S.P.Q. (BNA) 882 (W.D. Mo. 1986).

this search alone does not reveal the most recent applications because, owing to backlogs at the PTO, there can be a gap of several months between the filing of an application and the time it appears in the PTO records. Furthermore, because of an international convention to which the United States is bound, an application filed in the United States within six months of its initial filing date in a foreign country is entitled in the United States to that initial filing date. Therefore, one cannot be sure there is no application of concern until a second search is conducted approximately nine months after the initial search.

State Registrations

A database is available to search the state registrations of all fifty states and it could indicate the existence of local common-law rights. (A separate search is required for Puerto Rico.)

Common-Law Marks

In the United States, trademark rights accrue both from common-law use and from registrations. Neither federal nor state registration is mandatory, and consequently common-law users with potential common-law rights may not be listed in a searchable database. At common law, the first to use a mark acquires exclusive protectable rights in the actual geographic area of use plus a zone of reputation, as well as possibly in areas of natural or probable expansion.[68]

There are, of course, thousands of companies doing business on a limited local level, and common-law trademark rights accrue automatically—without any formality or paperwork—to the first user in a given geographic area. Even a federal registration cannot defeat the common-law rights accrued to a user of an unregistered mark before the date of the registration's application filing date.

A prior local user of a common-law mark can prevent a subsequent user—even one who subsequently obtains a federal registration (unless the application leading to the registration was filed before the first user began use)—from entering its territory, thus effectively inhibiting a national sales program. For example, Whopper Burger restaurants in San Antonio, Texas, prevented Burger King from using "Whopper" for hamburger sandwiches there for many years.[69] Even if the local user was not the first user nationwide but just the first to use the mark in good faith in its geographic area, it will be permanently protected in its area of trade as long as it uses the mark, even if a later user subsequently obtains a registration.[70]

Therefore, even if the proposed mark passes the federal and state registration search, it is still possible that an identical or similar mark is in use as an unregis-

---

68. Weiner King, Inc. v. Wiener King Corp., 615 F.2d 512, 204 U.S.P.Q. (BNA) 820 (C.C.P.A. 1980); Parrot Jungle, Inc., Corp. of Florida v. Parrot Jungle, Inc., Corp. of New York, 512 F. Supp. 266, 213 U.S.P.Q. (BNA) 49 (S.D.N.Y. 1981).

69. *See also* Mesa Springs Enter., Inc. v. Cutco Industries, Inc., 736 P.2d 1251, 2 U.S.P.Q.2d (BNA) 1950 (Colo. App. 1986).

70. Burger King of Florida, Inc. v. Hoots, 403 F.2d 904, 159 U.S.P.Q. (BNA) 706 (7th Cir. 1968).

tered common-law mark. Such marks may be identified through a "full" search by checking sources like trade directories and trade publications, telephone and trade name listings, litigation citations, and internal sources of the owner.

However, even a full search is no guarantee that all pertinent common-law users will be revealed because some users do not show up in the databases normally searched. For example, Chi-Chi's national restaurant chain was unable to franchise or otherwise open restaurants in Pittsburgh, Pennsylvania, as a result of not uncovering a prior local user.[71]

Avoiding Adverse Consequences

It is obviously more cost-effective and less disruptive to remove all obstacles before launching a new mark than afterward. To ignore references to possible prior trademark rights by adopting a mark that may be considered an infringement of such rights without seeking a coexistence or consent agreement, the cancellation of a federal registration, a license, or an outright purchase can have disastrous consequences. For example, in such situations injunctions and million-dollar judgments have been awarded to owners of prior rights that subsequent users ignored.[72]

Registration

State Registration

State registrations are available in all states, and are easy, quick, and inexpensive to obtain but are of little value in most situations. They are sometimes useful for a local business that cannot satisfy the interstate commerce requirements for federal registration, although, in view of the broad interpretation of the term "in commerce," such situations are rare. In most states, no real substantive rights are acquired by these registrations because all one gets is whatever common-law rights one can prove.[73] Some states, however, do have constructive notice provisions in their statutes (notably, Texas and Massachusetts). Obtaining a state registration is a way to be entered quickly, right at the start of a business, into a searchable database to stake a claim, thereby warning off other potential users of that mark.

However, applications for federal registration are clearly the better choice, thus making state registrations unnecessary.

---

71. ChiChi's, Inc. v. Chi-Mex, Inc., 568 F. Supp. 731, 221 U.S.P.Q. (BNA) 906 (W.D. Pa. 1983).

72. More than $25 million was awarded in Sands, Taylor & Wood Co. v. Quaker Oats Co., 978 F.2d 947, 24 U.S.P.Q.2d (BNA) 1001 (7th Cir. 1992), *cert. denied,* 113 S. Ct. 1879 (1993), *on remand,* 1993 U.S. Dist. LEXIS 7893 (N.D. Ill. 1993), *aff'd in part and vacated and remanded in part,* 34 F.3d 1340, 1994 U.S. App. LEXIS 25238 (7th Cir. 1994), *corrected, substituted op., in part,* 44 F.3d 579 (7th Cir. 1995), *on remand,* LEXIS 4797 (N.D. Ill. April 11, 1995).

73. Spartan Food Sys., Inc. v. HFS Corp., 813 F.2d 1279, 2 U.S.P.Q.2d (BNA) 1063, Bus. Franchise Guide (CCH) ¶ 8797 (4th Cir. 1987).

Benefits of a Federal Registration

Federal registration affords significant benefits by strengthening the rights provided at common law and by affording additional rights as well. The following substantive and procedural advantages make obtaining a federal registration desirable, especially for an expanding business, such as a franchise.

Constructive Notice

Federal registration provides constructive notice to everyone of the registrant's claim of ownership, effective from the date of registration.[74] A registrant can assert superior rights even in those parts of the country where it does not actually use the mark if the registrant is expanding into that disputed territory.[75]

Presumption of Validity and Ownership

The registration is *prima facie* evidence of the validity of the registered mark and of the registrant's exclusive right to use the mark in nationwide commerce.[76]

Constructive Use

Once the registration has issued, the registrant is entitled to the application filing date as its nationwide "constructive use" date.[77]

Federal Court Jurisdiction

Registration provides jurisdiction in federal courts for infringement claims regardless of diversity of citizenship or the amount of damages.[78]

Incontestability

After the mark has been in continuous use for five years after registration, the registrant may apply to have the mark declared incontestable.[79] At this point, the *prima facie* evidence of validity and exclusive right to use the mark ripens into conclusive evidence.[80] The principal affirmative defenses that are no longer available five years after registration are (1) that the mark is merely descriptive and lacks secondary meaning and (2) that the registrant is not the senior user of the mark. Certain other defenses, such as that the registration was fraudulently procured, the mark has become generic, or the mark was abandoned, are always available.

---

74. 15 U.S.C. § 1072.

75. Dawn Donut Co. v. Hart's Food Stores, Inc., 267 F.2d 358, 121 U.S.P.Q. (BNA) 430 (2nd Cir. 1959); Lone Star Steakhouse & Saloon v. Alpha of Virginia, 43 F.3d 922, 33 U.S.P.Q.2d (BNA) 1481 (4th Cir. 1995).

76. 15 U.S.C. § 1115.

77. 15 U.S.C. § 1057(c).

78. 15 U.S.C. § 1121.

79. 15 U.S.C. § 1065.

80. 15 U.S.C. § 1115.

Remedies

The Lanham Act provides various remedies for infringement, including injunctions, damages, defendant's profits, treble damages, destruction of infringing articles, costs, and attorneys' fees.[81]

Prohibition against Importation of Infringing Articles

Federal registration is a basis for having the U.S. Customs Service exclude the unauthorized importation of articles that bear the registered mark.[82]

Special Remedies against Counterfeit Marks

Registration is a basis for *ex parte* seizure orders and special criminal sanctions for the use of counterfeit marks, that is, marks identical or substantially indistinguishable from a registered mark.[83]

Registration Symbol

Only federally registered marks may bear the ® symbol to put others on actual notice of the registration. If a registrant fails to give such notice, it will be precluded from recovering profits and damages in an infringement action under the Lanham Act, unless it can prove that the defendant had actual knowledge of the registration.[84]

Obtaining Federal Registration

As the basis for federally registering a mark, there are two options available:

1. If the mark has been used on goods shipped or services rendered in interstate commerce, an application may be filed on the basis of actual use of the mark in commerce.
2. If the mark has not been used in interstate commerce, an application may be based on an intent to use the mark. Such intent must qualify as "bona fide" intent to use the mark in the ordinary course of business, and not merely to reserve a right in a mark.[85] Furthermore, a registration will not issue until the mark has actually been used. If the intent-to-use application is not successfully opposed, the PTO will issue a "Notice of Allowance" giving the applicant a time limit of six months to submit a verified statement of use showing the mark in actual use. The time limit for filing the statement of use may be extended for additional six-month periods up to a maximum of three years.[86]

---

81. 15 U.S.C. §§ 1116–1118.
82. 15 U.S.C. § 1124.
83. 15 U.S.C. §§ 1116, 1117(b); 18 U.S.C. § 2320.
84. 15 U.S.C. § 1111.
85. 15 U.S.C. § 1051(b).
86. 15 U.S.C. §§ 1051(d), 1063(b)(2).

To satisfy the jurisdictional requirement of the "commerce clause," the use upon which the registration is based must be use directly affecting interstate commerce or other commerce regulated by Congress. As a consequence, even a local restaurant may be in interstate commerce. For instance, the service mark "Bozo's" for a single-location restaurant was found to satisfy the "use in commerce" requirement because it was located near Memphis, whose metropolitan area comprises portions of three states, and was often patronized by customers from other states.[87]

Examination

The application must comply with precise statutory requirements. An application based on actual use requires specimens showing the mark used in connection with the goods or services.

After the application is filed with the PTO, an examining attorney considers whether there are any grounds for rejecting the registration (e.g., if the mark is primarily geographic or a surname or too descriptive to function as a mark) and conducts a search to determine whether there is any likelihood of confusion with any prior registrations or pending applications. Thus, another party's mark can block registration without any action by that party.

Opposition

Once approved by the examining attorney, the mark is published in the PTO's *Official Gazette* to give any party that believes that it would be damaged by the registration the opportunity to file an "opposition." If an opposition is filed, an *inter partes* administrative proceeding, including discovery, is conducted before the Trademark Trial and Appeal Board. In principle, an opposition can be based on any statutory ground, but most often it is predicated on confusing similarity with a prior registered (or sometimes prior used, common-law) mark.[88] Not infrequently, opposition proceedings take several years to resolve.

Registration

If the application is based on actual use and the application has not been challenged successfully, the mark will be registered on the Principal Register. If the application is based on intent to use the mark in the future, the PTO will issue a "Notice of Allowance" and will register the mark after the applicant has used the mark and filed its statement of use. Registrations are issued for a period of ten years, provided that the registrant files an affidavit during the fifth year showing that the mark is still in use. Registrations may be renewed for additional ten-year terms indefinitely, for as long as the mark remains in use.[89]

---

87. Larry Harmon Pictures Corp. v. Williams Restaurant Corp., 929 F.2d 662, 18 U.S.P.Q.2d (BNA) 1292 (Fed. Cir. 1991), *cert. denied,* 112 S. Ct. 85 (1991).

88. Burger Chef Sys., Inc. v. Burger Man, Inc., 492 F.2d 1398, 181 U.S.P.Q. (BNA) 168 (C.C.P.A. 1974); Burger Chef Sys., Inc. v. Sandwich Chef, Inc., 608 F.2d 875, 203 U.S.P.Q. (BNA) 733 (C.C.P.A. 1979).

89. 15 U.S.C. §§ 1058–1059.

Marks that are descriptive but not yet registrable because they have not yet acquired secondary meaning may be registered in the Supplemental Register.[90] However, such registration provides no substantive rights beyond those available at common law and provides little advantage besides the fact that the mark will appear in databases, thus giving notice of the claim in the mark to those clearing new marks and being available for citation by the examining attorney against later filed applications.

Cancellations

Even if no oppositions are filed and the mark proceeds to registration, interested parties have five years after registration to file a petition to cancel the mark on the same grounds upon which they could have opposed.[91] Cancellation proceedings are much less frequent than opposition proceedings but, nonetheless, add a note of caution to the registration process. After five years, only a few grounds for cancellation are available, primarily that the mark has been obtained fraudulently, has been abandoned, or has become generic.[92]

Concurrent Use

The issuance of concurrent use registrations limited to geographic areas not yet occupied by an earlier user is an infrequently invoked procedure, most typically used to allocate the rights to the same or similar mark, usually service marks, used by two different parties in geographically disparate areas of the country.

Enforcement of Trademark Rights

Causes of Action

Different causes of action are available depending on whether the trademark to be enforced is registered and whether state or federal law is at issue.

Infringement of a Federally Registered Mark

The holder of a federally registered mark may sue in federal court or state court for infringement by any person using a mark in a way that is likely to cause a significant number of consumers to be confused as to the source of the defendant's goods or services by thinking that they originate from or are endorsed by the plaintiff.[93]

Federal Unfair Competition

Subsection 43(a) of the Lanham Act gives a common-law owner of an unregistered mark the option to sue in federal courts for claims of infringement. The benefits

---

90. 15 U.S.C. §§ 1091–1096.
91. 15 U.S.C. § 1064(1).
92. 15 U.S.C. § 1064(3).
93. 15 U.S.C. §§ 1114–1121.

of registration afforded by the Lanham Act (presumption of validity, incontestability, etc.) will not apply, but the remedies available under Subsection 43(a) are the same as for infringement of registered marks. Of course, the owner of a common-law mark may also sue in state court.[94]

Federal Trademark Counterfeiting Act of 1984

The 1984 amendments to the Lanham Act provide a cause of action to seek *ex parte* seizure orders and certain mandatory monetary remedies, as well as criminal penalties, for counterfeiting.[95]

State Common Law

States have developed their own common law giving a cause of action for the infringement of trademarks. State common law has developed several unfair competition theories providing causes of action against infringement of trade name, misappropriation, false advertising, disparagement, dilution, and the like. These actions typically are joined with an action under the Lanham Act and may be brought in federal court.

Various State Statutes

The majority of states have enacted state trademark registration statutes, but they generally confer few substantive benefits (as discussed earlier).

Dilution Statutes

What if a company begins selling "Baskin Robbins" oven cleaner? What about "Kodak" doughnut stores? Although such uses would probably not satisfy the traditional trademark infringement standard of likelihood of confusion, such uses on noncompeting services or goods could "dilute" a famous mark by eroding its distinctiveness and uniqueness.[96] To prevent such pirating of another's goodwill, a majority of the states have adopted specific dilution statutes.  Although typically not explicitly required by these statutes, most courts have held that protection against dilution under such state statutes is only available to strong, relatively famous marks.[97] To remedy the inconsistent judicial interpretations of the vague language in many of these statutes, as well as the fact that many states do not offer such protection, the Federal Trademark Dilution Action of 1995 was added as Subsection 43(c) to Section 1125(c) of the Lanham Act, effective January 16, 1996. This act creates a federal cause of action for the unauthorized use of a famous mark that dilutes the distinctive quality of a mark, irrespective of

---

94. 15 U.S.C. § 1125(a).

95. 18 U.S.C. § 2320; 15 U.S.C. § 1116.

96. Ameritech, Inc. v. American Information Technologies Corp., 811 F.2d 960, 1 U.S.P.Q.2d (BNA) 1861 (6th Cir. 1987); Exxon Corp. v. Exxene Corp., 696 F.2d 544, 217 U.S.P.Q. (BNA) 215 (7th Cir. 1982).

97. Accuride Int'l, Inc. v. Accuride Corp., 871 F.2d 1531, 10 U.S.P.Q.2d (BNA) 1589 (9th Cir. 1989); Hyatt Corp. v. Hyatt Legal Serv., 736 F.2d 1153, 222 U.S.P.Q. (BNA) 669 (7th Cir. 1984); *but see* Amstar Corp. v. Domino's Pizza Inc., 615 F.2d 252 (5th Cir. 1980).

whether the mark's owner has a federal registration and regardless of the presence or absence of competition or a likelihood of confusion. Thus, a mark that is judged to be "famous" (the act lists numerous factors bearing on this determination) in connection with one type of services or goods could be protected against another's use of the mark on unrelated services or goods. While this can be a powerful tool for trademark protection, it should be noted that many marks used in franchising that indeed may be quite well-known nonetheless might not qualify for dilution protection since they contain surnames, geographic names, or descriptive or generic terminology that others are entitled to use in unrelated fields. It is presumed that the courts will demand a high burden of proof to be met by a trademark owner seeking to use this form of relief.

State deceptive trade practice acts codify certain unfair competition theories developed under state common law.

State anticounterfeiting statutes have lost much of their significance since the enactment of the Federal Trademark Counterfeiting Act of 1984 amending the Lanham Act. However, a number of states have recently enacted tough anticounterfeiting laws.

Proof of Infringement

The five elements required to bring an action for federal trademark infringement are as follows: (1) use of a reproduction, copy, or colorable imitation of a (2) registered mark (3) in commerce (4) in connection with the sale, offer for sale, distribution, or advertising of any goods or services (5) that is likely to cause confusion, mistake, or deception as to the source of the products or services.

In practice, elements (2), (3), and (4) are rarely in dispute. The other elements are combined into the question of whether an "appreciable number of reasonable buyers" are likely to be confused by the similarity of the marks.

"Likelihood of confusion" is the test of both common law and federal statutory trademark infringement and is determined by a number of factors, including the similarity of appearance, phonetics, and meaning of the marks; the proximity of the products or services; the similarity of the relevant segment of the purchasing public; the sophistication of the customers and the cost of the goods or services; the strength of the plaintiff's mark; and the similarity of the channels of trade and advertising.[98]

It is sufficient to prove likelihood of confusion. However, evidence of *actual* confusion is often the best way to prove its likelihood.[99] Properly conducted consumer surveys showing that consumers would probably confuse two nonidentical but similar marks may also be used to prove likelihood of confusion.

---

98. *See* Polaroid Corp. v. Polarad Electronics Corp., 287 F.2d 492, 128 U.S.P.Q. (BNA) 411 (2nd Cir. 1961), *cert. denied,* 368 U.S. 820 (1961); AMF, Inc. v. Sleekcraft Boats, 599 F.2d 341, 204 U.S.P.Q. (BNA) 808 (9th Cir. 1979).

99. Union Carbide Corp. v. Ever-Ready, Inc., 531 F.2d 366, 188 U.S.P.Q. (BNA) 623 (7th Cir. 1976), *cert. denied,* 429 U.S. 830 (1976).

This determination is highly factual and can be a question for the jury.[100] As a practical matter, however, a large number of trademark disputes are decided at a preliminary injunction level where the question of confusing similarity is decided by a judge. Although the defendant's intent is not a necessary element of a trademark infringement suit, it may constitute very effective evidence of likelihood of confusion: the very act of intentionally imitating another's mark can raise a presumption that the defendant sought to create consumer confusion.[101]

When the owner of the well-known "Jim Beam" mark for Kentucky bourbon sued for infringement arising out of use of "Beamish" for Irish stout, no likelihood of confusion was found because the packaging was different, the labels indicated dissimilar geographic origins, bar patrons are unlikely to confuse beer with bourbon, there was no evidence that the bourbon producer intended to enter the beer market, both products coexisted in Ireland without evidence of actual confusion, and there was no intent by the defendant to capitalize on the plaintiff's reputation.[102]

The focus of a determination of unfair competition or infringement of an unregistered mark or trade dress under Section 43(a) of the Lanham Act is usually whether the defendant's use is a false or misleading representation likely to cause confusion as to affiliation, connection, association, origin, or sponsorship of the products or services.

Remedies

Courts may order several types of remedies against trademark infringement.

Injunctions

The most common relief for trademark infringement is an injunction preventing the infringer from continuing its unauthorized use of the mark. The court may also issue injunctions ordering the infringer to publish corrective advertising, to withdraw from the market, or to destroy the infringing products.[103] The court may grant preliminary injunctions and temporary restraining orders to protect the trademark owners at the outset of and during the litigation.

Monetary Recovery

One or more of the following monetary awards may be sought under the Lanham Act for infringement of federally registered marks, and for unregistered marks based on Section 43(a).

Plaintiff's actual damages resulting from loss of sales and goodwill may be recovered but are difficult to quantify. In a case involving a motel franchisee

---

100. Soweco, Inc. v. Shell Oil Co., 617 F.2d 1178, 207 U.S.P.Q. (BNA) 278 (5th Cir. 1980), *cert. denied,* 450 U.S. 981 (1981).

101. Osem Food Indus., Ltd. v. Sherwood Foods, Inc., 917 F.2d 161, 16 U.S.P.Q.2d (BNA) 1646 (4th Cir. 1990); Fleischmann Distilling Corp. v. Maier Brewing Co., 314 F.2d 149, 158, 137 U.S.P.Q. (BNA) 913 (9th Cir. 1963), *cert. denied,* 374 U.S. 830 (1963).

102. Jim Beam Brands Co. v. Beamish & Crawford Ltd., 852 F. Supp. 196, 31 U.S.P.Q.2d (BNA) 1518 (S.D.N.Y. 1994).

103. 15 U.S.C. §§ 1116, 1118.

holding over and failing to change the mark after termination of the contract, a court found that the lost royalties are the basis for compensation.[104]

Defendant's profits are awarded if the plaintiff can show that the infringement was intentional and resulted in an unjust enrichment of the defendant.

The court is given the discretion to increase or reduce the amount of recovery based on the actual damages (up to three times such amount) or the defendant's profits if the court finds it necessary to compensate the plaintiff adequately, particularly if the defendant acted willfully.[105]

The prevailing plaintiff is, as a rule, entitled to recover the costs of the action.[106]

Attorneys' fees may be awarded to the prevailing party only in "exceptional cases."[107]

In a recent case, a Dunkin' Donuts franchisee in Texas had opened four "Donkin' Donas" donut shops in Mexico. The court found intentional violation of Dunkin' Donuts' trade dress and granted award of treble damages, attorneys' fees, and costs.[108]

Confiscation and destruction of infringing articles or instruments for making them may be ordered by the court.[109]

The court may impose the use of a notice disclaiming the affiliation with the other party.

In any action involving a registered trademark, the court may order the cancellation or a modification of the registration. However, cancellation cannot be the sole basis for a plaintiff's suit.[110] If it is, a cancellation proceeding should be initiated in the PTO rather than in court.

Finally, criminal penalties may be imposed. Trafficking in counterfeit goods is punishable by up to five years imprisonment and $250,000 in fines.[111]

Policing Marks

A franchisor should constantly monitor the market and intervene against unauthorized uses of identical or confusingly similar marks to avoid serious weakening of the mark. Valuable marks should be policed promptly, diligently, and vigorously. Failure to do so can result in a diminished scope of legal protection, potential inability to protect the mark, or even a technical abandonment of the mark.[112] The

---

104. Howard Johnson Co. v. Khimani, 892 F.2d 1512, 13 U.S.P.Q.2d (BNA) 1808 (11th Cir. 1990).

105. 15 U.S.C. § 1117(a).

106. *Id.*

107. *Id.*

108. Dunkin' Donuts v. Mercantile Ventures, 32 U.S.P.Q.2d (BNA) 1460, Bus. Franchise Guide (CCH) ¶ 10,521 (W.D. Tex. 1994).

109. 15 U.S.C. § 1118.

110. 15 U.S.C. § 1119.

111. 18 U.S.C. § 2320.

112. 1 J. Thomas McCarthy, McCarthy on Trademarks and Unfair Competition, § 11.28 (1995).

more the public is exposed to numerous sources using similar marks, the less it will rely on the franchisor's mark as a symbol of uniform quality. From a practical standpoint, disgruntled franchisees may have a breach of contract cause of action against a franchisor that fails to police the mark properly owing to the reduced value of the mark.

A franchisor should also ensure that its franchisees do not infringe another's trademark rights, since a franchisor may be found liable for contributory trademark infringement if one of its franchisees infringes the trademark of a third party.[113]

Trademarks and The Franchise Relationship

A trademark license is usually the core of a franchise relationship. The license to use the trademark is the vehicle for the franchisee to become part of a business system with uniform format and quality standards. The necessity and the role of the trademark license depend on the type of franchise system at issue.

When a Trademark License Is Necessary

A trademark license is necessary if the franchisee manufactures and sells a product bearing the trademark to someone other than the trademark owner or those operating under license from the trademark owner.

It is also necessary if the franchisee uses the trademark in performing a service under license from the trademark owner, for example, as part of a franchising system.

When a Trademark License Is Not Necessary

A trademark license is not necessary if one party merely distributes or sells the product for the trademark owner without conducting business under the owner's mark or name. For example, a gas station franchisee does not need to obtain a trademark license from soda producers to sell sodas.

The license is also unnecessary if one party manufactures the product for the trademark owner (or its licensees) and the trademark owner itself (or licensee) sells or distributes the product. For example, manufacturing T-shirts for the trademark owner's promotional use does not require a trademark license.

The Role of Trademarks in Different Types of Franchise Systems

A product distribution franchise relationship is used for the marketing of products that are made by or for the account of the franchisor. Its purpose is to provide the

---

113. Mini Maid Servs. Co. v. Maid Brigade Sys., Inc., 967 F.2d 1516, 23 U.S.P.Q.2d (BNA) 1871, Bus. Franchise Guide (CCH) ¶ 10,072 (11th Cir. 1992).

franchisor with a distribution system to market its products. It is similar to an ordinary supplier-dealer relationship, but the franchisee has a greater identification with the franchisor's trademark and might be precluded from selling competitors' products. Examples include gas stations and automobile dealerships.

Under a business format franchise relationship, the franchisor provides a license under a mark and also provides a business format for the retail sale of goods or services under the mark. The franchisor typically does not manufacture any products but may offer to supply equipment, ingredients, raw materials, packaging materials, advertising, and so forth. The franchisee typically performs services but may sell products in conjunction with those services. The franchisee usually deals exclusively in the franchisor's sponsored services and is required to adopt the franchisor's mark and overall presentation format as its exclusive trade identity. Examples include restaurants, hotels and motels, and auto repair, car rental, and temporary employment services.

Under an affiliation franchise relationship, the franchisor recruits into its system as licensees persons who are already established in the particular line of business. Each of the businesses is required to adopt and use the franchisor's mark, but they may be permitted to continue using their own marks as secondary marks. These businesses rarely use the same overall presentation or identity format except for the mark itself. Examples are insurance, financial, and real estate brokerage services.

Trademark Licensing in the Franchise Agreement

Important Considerations

Detailed Documentation

While in theory there is no legal requirement that a trademark license be in writing,[114] it is clearly sound business practice to set out the franchise relationship in a comprehensive document. Moreover, it is essential that a written franchise agreement contain the appropriate detailed trademark licensing provisions, both to protect the franchisor vis-à-vis the franchisee as well as to protect the mark itself, that is, to preserve its legal validity for both of them vis-à-vis third parties.

Quality Control

The indispensable element of a trademark license is quality control.[115] The nexus of the franchisor-franchisee relationship is the control of the consistency and quality of the goods and services bearing the trademark. The crucial importance of this aspect is twofold:

---

114. Nestle Co. v. Nash-Finch Co., 4 U.S.P.Q.2d (BNA) 1085 (Trademark Trial & App. Bd. 1987).

115. Kentucky Fried Chicken Corp. v. Diversified Packaging Corp., 549 F.2d 368, 193 U.S.P.Q. (BNA) 649 (5th Cir. 1977).

1. From a practical perspective, it is clear that the success of the business usually depends on a consistent and uniform level of quality throughout the franchise system.
2. Legally, the franchisor may lose its right in the mark if it fails to control the nature and quality of the goods or services sold by its franchisees. Quality control is mandatory so that franchisor and franchisees can qualify as "related companies" in order to
   • establish trademark rights,[116]
   • enforce trademark rights against others,[117] and
   • avoid a legal determination of abandonment of the mark.[118]

Legal Basis

The Lanham Act allows the use of a mark by someone other than the owner only when the owner exercises sufficient control over the nature and quality of the goods or services sold under the mark by the other.

Under the Lanham Act, the use of a registered mark by another inures to the benefit of the registrant if the parties are "related companies."[119] A related company is one that is controlled by the owner with respect to the quality of the goods or services.[120] It can be an entity controlled through stock ownership or by agreement between two arms-length parties.

Actual Exercise of Control

It is not sufficient merely to recite a right to control in the franchise agreement to qualify for "related company" status. The franchisor should actually exercise this right in practice, or else the license might be held invalid as having been abandoned.[121] Because the Lanham Act does not define quality control, it is a factual question as to whether the means of control or the degree of control is sufficiently exercised under the particular circumstances.[122]

Policing Licensees

The courts have generally placed an affirmative duty upon franchisors to take reasonable measures to detect and prevent misleading uses of the mark by li-

---

116. 15 U.S.C. § 1055, codifying Turner v. HMH Pub. Co., 380 F.2d 224, 154 U.S.P.Q. (BNA) 330 (5th Cir. 1967), *cert. denied,* 389 U.S. 1006 (1967).

117. Yocum v. Covington, 216 U.S.P.Q. (BNA) 210 (Trademark Trial & App. Bd. 1982).

118. Heaton Enter. of Nevada, Inc. v. Lang, 7 U.S.P.Q.2d (BNA) 1842 (Trademark Trial & App. Bd. 1988).

119. 15 U.S.C. § 1055.

120. 15 U.S.C. § 1127.

121. Alligator Co. v. Robert Bruce, Inc., 176 F. Supp. 377, 122 U.S.P.Q. (BNA) 276 (D. Pa. 1959).

122. Dawn Donut Co. v. Hart's Food Stores, Inc., 267 F.2d 358, 121 U.S.P.Q. (BNA) 430 (2nd Cir. 1959); Weight Watchers of Quebec, Ltd. v. Weight Watchers Int., Inc., 398 F. Supp 1047, 188 U.S.P.Q. (BNA) 16, Bus. Franchise Guide (CCH) ¶ 7709 (E.D.N.Y. 1975).

censees (franchisees) who use the franchisor's mark on products of inferior quality or on unauthorized products.[123]

Typical Licensing Provisions in Franchise Contracts

There can be no standard licensing provisions that fit all franchising agreements. Rather, the licensing provisions in franchise agreements should be carefully tailored to the type of business involved to reflect the particular circumstances. The following are typical trademark-specific provisions contained in franchising agreements.

Preamble

In addition to describing the parties and the subject matter of the agreement, the preamble offers the opportunity to emphasize the uniqueness, value, distinctiveness, and importance of the trademark(s) to the entire franchise relationship and agreement, thus justifying such items as franchise fees, royalties, strict quality control standards, and stringent termination provisions.

Granting Clause

The granting clause is the key provision in which the franchisor actually grants the franchisee the right to use the marks of the system. It should specify whether the right to use the marks on particular goods or services in a particular geographic area is exclusive or nonexclusive.

There are two types of exclusive licenses:

1. Exclusive in the sense that the franchisor cannot itself use the licensed marks
2. Exclusive except for the franchisor's own
   - equivalent use (e.g., on another restaurant in other territories);
   - overlapping use (e.g., packaged food goods to be sold in grocery stores under the same mark in the same territory as the restaurant); and
   - different use (e.g., merchandise items such as toys or clothing displaying the mark).

If the agreement is silent with regard to exclusivity, it will usually be construed as nonexclusive. However, the intent of the parties will be controlling.

If the agreement gives an "exclusive" grant but is otherwise silent as to the rights of the franchisor, it may preclude uses such as those listed in the second clause above unless the circumstances and intent of the parties clearly prove otherwise (e.g., the restaurant franchisor already sold grocery store items). Carefully defining the geographic area of exclusivity and what constitutes encroachment is essential.

Even if the agreement uses the word "license," care must be taken to ensure that an exclusive license cannot be interpreted as an assignment of the mark.

---

123. Jordan K. Rand, Ltd. v. Lazoff Brothers, Inc., 537 F. Supp. 587, 217 U.S.P.Q. (BNA) 795 (D.P.R. 1982).

The agreement should state whether the franchisee has the right to sublicense or subfranchise. If the agreement is silent, generally no such right will be presumed, but it is best specifically to recite either the prohibition or the permission under certain detailed conditions.

The agreement should enumerate the circumstances in which the franchisee may transfer an existing license to a new location. In a recent case, a licensee of Arby's fast-food chain was found to have infringed the "Arby's" trademark when, following the expiration of its lease, the franchisee opened a new restaurant at a new location, because the contract enumerated four circumstances in which a licensee could transfer a license to a new location and the expiration of the lease was not among them.[124]

Goods and Services

The particular goods and services on which the franchisee shall use each mark should be set forth in specific, clear, and unambiguous language to prevent future misunderstandings. The franchisee should be allowed to use the mark only on licensed products or services and, depending on the nature of the business, should be prohibited from selling products or services with other marks in conjunction with the franchised business.

Trademark Relationship

The following provisions are essential:

1. The franchisee's acknowledgment that the mark is valid, that the franchisor is the owner of the mark and of the goodwill associated therewith, and that the franchisee will not contest the validity of the mark or any relevant registrations during the term of the agreement or thereafter ("licensee estoppel")
2. The franchisee's acknowledgment that all use of the mark by the franchisee inures to the benefit of the franchisor ("related companies")
3. The franchisee's acknowledgment that it acquires no right, title, or interest in the mark or any associated goodwill, save for the limited license under the agreement (not an assignment).

Display of the Mark

It should be stated that the franchisee shall only display the mark in such manner and form as are prescribed by the franchisor's guidelines and standards or as instructed by the franchisor. The franchisor should reserve the right to approve all materials, advertising, and the like that display the mark.

Quality Control

While it is acceptable to list all the types of control procedures contemplated, this could be risky if in practice not all are exercised. It is preferable to delineate

124. Licensee Trust v. Arby's, 1995 U.S. App. LEXIS 1395 (4th Cir. Jan. 24, 1995).

the goals (i.e., uniform and consistent compliance with franchise standards) and the rights of the franchisor to achieve those goals, including, for example, inspection, supervision, receiving samples, training manuals and schools, and adherence to specifications set forth from time to time by the franchisor, such as in an operating manual.

Trademark Policing

While not "guaranteeing" the mark, franchisors should always reserve the right to protect and defend it, with all decisions involving such matters being in the franchisor's sole discretion and specifically prohibiting franchisees from litigating without permission. Absent such a bar, a court could find an exclusive franchisee qualified to bring suit, thus potentially placing the validity of the mark in the hands of the franchisee without any input or control by the franchisor. While protection and defense costs usually are borne by the franchisor, the franchisee should agree to cooperate fully in any litigation and to report promptly any infringements it discovers.

Effects of Expiration or Termination

The right to use the mark ceases at expiration or termination of the agreement, even without an express provision.[125] However, it is recommended to include a provision mandating immediate discontinuance of all uses of the mark and any trade dress, including steps to be taken such as notification to phone companies, cancellation of assumed name registrations, and de-identification of principal physical attributes, if appropriate. For instance, the franchisee may be required to change distinctive building design elements or colors and to remove signs. Use of the mark after expiration is usually considered trademark infringement and can be the best cause of action to pursue in a "holdover" or "breakaway" situation.[126] For example, failure to de-identify the premises where services are conducted can be the basis for effective action by a mark's owner, but it usually entails a difficult burden of proof. Thus, it is essential that the agreement contain detailed de-identification provisions so that the fact pattern can support both infringement and breach of contract actions.[127]

Miscellaneous Trademark Provisions

There are several miscellaneous trademark provisions to note:

1. A franchisee should be expressly prohibited from assigning the licensed rights or the agreement without the franchisor's permission.
2. In view of decisions expanding tort liability, the franchisee should indemnify the franchisor for all claims arising out of the franchisee's use of the mark and operations. The franchisee should seek to limit the

---

125. United States Jaycees v. Philadelphia Jaycees, 639 F.2d 134, 1209 U.S.P.Q. (BNA) 457 (3d Cir. 1981).

126. *Id.*

127. Long John Silver's, Inc. v. Washington Franchise, Inc., 209 U.S.P.Q. (BNA) 146, Bus. Franchise Guide (CCH) ¶ 7738 (E.D. Va. 1980).

indemnification to exclude liabilities that result from the act or omission of the franchisor (e.g., defectively designed equipment specified by the franchisor as "required" for the franchise that subsequently injures an employee or customer, or contaminated food procured from an "approved vendor" that causes illness to a customer). In addition, the franchisee should be required to carry sufficient insurance and to name the franchisor as an additional insured.

3. The franchisee should not be allowed to use the mark, or the franchisor's name, as part of its trade name.

4. The franchisor should reserve the right to change or modify the mark at its discretion at any time upon reasonable notice, with reasonable time for the franchisee to dispose of inventory and accomplish the transition.

International Trademark Protection

Trademark Rights as Territorial

Trademark rights are geographically limited. Trademark rights obtained in the United States convey no rights in other countries. There is no automatic protection of a U.S. trademark outside of the territory of the United States. Further, there is no worldwide centralized registration system.[128]

Trademark rights must be sought on a country-by-country basis and this process is fairly unpredictable and expensive. Each of the approximately two hundred jurisdictions around the world has its own trademark laws, and the requirements for obtaining trademark registration and protection vary from country to country. As a consequence, a U.S. franchisor must clear the mark and file separate registration applications in every country where it contemplates future expansion.

Because the registrability standards differ from country to country, a valid and successful mark in the United States may not be registrable or protectable in other countries. One should never assume that a successful U.S. trademark will be commercially or linguistically or culturally suitable for use in other countries. The meaning of a mark may change if used in or translated into a foreign language. For example, "Pizza Hut" literally means "Pizza Hat" in German. It is therefore essential to choose, from the beginning, a mark that will be suitable for use in all target countries.

Common Law versus Civil Law

In most countries, the first to file an application for trademark registration will obtain superior rights in the trademark. Only in a minority of countries (mainly those with a common-law system) is use required or sufficient to acquire trademark

---

128. The "Madrid Arrangement" is an important international treaty with approximately thirty member states, which provides a centralized filing system for trademark registrations, but the United States is not a member.

rights. The mixed common law and registration approach in the United States does not exist in many countries. In most civil law countries, there is no trademark protection without registration. Unregistered "marks" may be protected in some countries under a theory of unfair competition but with far less predictable results.

Because in most civil law countries it is sufficient to be the first to file an application for registration to obtain priority, a franchisor is exposed to the risk of trademark piracy: someone else may register the franchisor's mark first, thus blocking the franchisor's registration. Conversely, civil law jurisdictions allow the franchisor to register the mark legitimately well before the launching of the products or services in that country. In such countries it is essential that filing to register be made promptly to prevent trademark piracy. In 1996, companies with a business location in the European Union became able to file a single registration application effective in all EU countries.

Registration

International Classification of Goods

Most countries have adopted a system of classification of goods and services and they generally tend to apply it in a rigid way such that the registration for an entire class of goods or services gives protection within that class regardless of actual use. Conversely, the protection is construed very narrowly with regard to goods or services that do not strictly fall under the registered class. Therefore, it is best to register the mark in all classes that may directly or indirectly come within the scope of the business.

Service Marks

Owing to recent changes in the law of several countries, today most industrial countries and a significant number of developing countries provide for the registrability of service marks. However, service mark protection is still not available in several jurisdictions. Therefore, registration in such countries should include those classes of goods corresponding to the services so that the services rendered are properly protected. For instance, to protect a mark used for restaurant services, registration should be obtained for the food classes and the classes covering containers, paper goods, and printed matter.

Translation of the Mark

In addition to the mark actually used, the registrant should also consider registering the mark's translations and transliterations as well as the trade dress (since the latter will rarely be protected without registration).

Recordation of Franchisees

Unlike U.S. law, the laws of many jurisdictions require recordation of a trademark license with a government entity to validate the license and to legitimize the franchisee's use as inuring to the franchisor's benefit. Failure to record could result in the loss of a mark or preclude enforcement of trademark rights.

The Paris Convention

The Paris Convention has been joined by virtually all commercially significant countries and is based on the principle that each member state shall grant the same protection to nationals of other member states as it would to its own citizens. Moreover, this convention provides that once an applicant files a registration application in one country, it has a six-month period to file corresponding applications in other member states to obtain as a priority date the date of the initial filing. An application filed in member states after six months will receive the actual filing date as its priority date. This can be significant in the event a third party files an application for the same or a confusingly similar mark after the applicant's initial filing date but before the subsequent filing in member countries.

The Impact of GATT on Trademark Law

The Uruguay Round of the General Agreement on Tariffs and Trade (GATT) led to the adoption of the Agreement on Trade-Related Aspects of Intellectual Property Rights (TRIPS), which establishes comprehensive standards for the protection of intellectual property rights within the member states of the World Trade Organization (WTO). The member countries of the WTO are obliged to bring their trademark legislation in line with TRIPS within the next few years.[129] In the long run, TRIPS will have the effect of introducing minimal standards and harmonizing the intellectual property protection within the WTO. In particular, the new WTO dispute settlement system will apply to international intellectual property disputes and is expected to offer an effective enforcement mechanism.

TRIPS incorporates the Paris Convention by reference and requires its member states, among other things, to grant most-favored-nation treatment to nationals of other member states.[130] With regard to trademarks, TRIPS requires member states to refuse the registration of misleading geographical indications of origin if that area has a reputation regarding the goods at issue and provides for additional protection for geographical indications for wine and spirits.[131] TRIPS states that actual use shall not be a condition for filing an application for registration,[132] and it prohibits the compulsory licensing of trademarks.[133]

Summary of International Trademark Protection

International trademark practice confronts the owner of a U.S. mark with different legal systems, languages, and cultural values. To minimize the risks and expenses, the following recommendations should be followed:

129. TRIPS, art. 65. TRIPS constitutes Annex 1C to the Agreement Establishing the Multilateral Trade Organization of the Final Act Embodying the Results of the Uruguay Round of the Multilateral Trade Negotiations (version of 15 December 1993) of the General Agreement on Tarriffs and Trade.
130. TRIPS, arts. 3, 4.
131. TRIPS, arts. 22–24; The Lanham Act, Section 2(a), has been amended accordingly.
132. TRIPS, art. 15, sec. 3.
133. TRIPS, art. 21.

1. The franchisor should be farsighted in selecting a mark that is acceptable and protectable in possible future international target markets.
2. Consideration should be given to registering the mark promptly and in all relevant classes of goods and services in all countries of possible future international expansion. However, since an international registration program can be very expensive, a careful practical evaluation should be undertaken.
3. Legal counsel with experience in international trademark practice should be consulted.

Conclusion

Trademarks are the cornerstone of the franchise method of doing business. Through use of a trademark readily recognizable to consumers, a franchise business is able to communicate the message that each of its units belongs to a franchise system with uniform format and quality standards.

The selection of a proper mark is crucial to the success of a franchise system. The mark must be legally protectable and registrable. Moreover, the mark should send an attractive message to the consumer while avoiding mere description of the goods or services and should be appropriate for expansion. Geographic terms, surnames, and trite laudatory terms are to be avoided. The more distinctive and unique the mark is, the more extensive the scope of legal protection is.

To be legally available, the chosen mark must be sufficiently distinct from marks previously adopted by others for the same or similar goods or services. A comprehensive trademark search should be conducted before beginning use of a mark and seeking its registration. The failure to search a mark properly before its adoption and to protect an important mark by the early filing of an application for registration may result in expensive litigation and a disruptive requirement to change the mark.

The trademark license is the core of the relationship between a franchisor and franchisee. The franchisor must control the quality and consistency of the goods and services bearing the trademark, or else the license might be held invalid and the mark abandoned. In many countries, the license or licensee should be registered or recorded.

Legal counsel with experience in trademark practice should be consulted for the clearing and protecting of a proposed mark and for the drafting of a franchise agreement.

CHAPTER 2

Structuring the Franchise Relationship

Andrew A. Caffey, Stuart Hershman, and Lewis G. Rudnick

Contents

This chapter discusses the considerations to be taken into account in structuring a franchise system. It focuses on the legal aspects of structuring, leaving the issues of the desirability of the different structures to others.

The first part of this chapter gives an overview of the typical types of franchise structures. This discussion is followed by an in-depth analysis of the unit franchise structure, which is the most typical type of franchise structure. Then, the other types of franchise structures are briefly analyzed.

Types of Franchise Structures

There are several different ways the franchise relationship can be structured. Two types of franchise relationships are the individual or unit franchises and area franchises.

Unit Franchises

Individual or unit franchises are those in which a franchisee is granted the right to develop and operate one outlet at a specific location or within a defined territory. Rights to acquire additional franchises may be granted within a defined area, subject to performance criteria and structured as either options or rights of first refusal. Rights of first refusal, however, will make it more difficult to attract qualified buyers for locations that are subject to such rights.

Unit franchises may also be offered as an incentive for growth for existing franchise owners, with additional franchises granted to successful franchisees. Franchisors should exercise caution in granting any sort of contractual obligation to grant additional unit franchises. Most companies simply adopt companywide policies regarding the incentive program.

The typical uses of an individual or unit franchise are as follows:

1. For a service business, in which the expertise of the franchisee is critical to the success of the operation. Some examples of service businesses are real estate, home inspection, and dental businesses.
2. For businesses requiring an owner-operator.
3. For active investors who are willing to "get their hands dirty." This type of franchise would not be appropriate for a passive investor.

Area Franchises

Area franchises are those with multiple outlet franchises or area development agreements and may include subfranchisors and master franchisors. Under these arrangements, a franchisee may be granted the right to develop and operate two or more outlets within a defined territory or, in some instances, the right to subfranchise some of these development responsibilities. Following are the significant elements of an area franchise agreement:

1. Territory and exclusivity
2. The number of outlets to be developed
3. The time frames for development
4. Franchisor assistance in development
5. Fee obligations
6. Site selection and approval responsibilities of the parties
7. Termination and its consequences (i.e., the effect of termination of the development agreement on existing individual outlet franchises and the effect of termination of outlet franchises on the development agreement and other outlet franchises must be addressed).

In area franchises, a single development agreement is used to grant development rights for all outlets to be developed by the franchisee. Separate franchise agreements are then used to grant specific rights related to each outlet. Minority ownership of individual outlets (such as by outlet managers or passive investors) may be permitted.

Typically, area franchises are used for businesses that require a single franchise owner in a market to avoid encroachment and advertising problems that might otherwise arise if multiple owners develop a single market. Area franchises may also be attractive for businesses able to sustain a salary of an on-site manager, supervised by a franchisee owning multiple units. Given the management aspects of area franchise development, area franchisees should expect to have management experience and people skills.

Subfranchising

Subfranchising is another structural approach to large market area development. A subfranchise allows the franchisor to grant others (subfranchisors) the right to operate outlets by directly entering into franchise agreements with each subfranchisee.

The franchisor reserves final subfranchisee approval and site approval rights and may dictate the economic relationship between subfranchisor and subfranchisee (e.g., fees charged to subfranchisees for the purchase of subfranchise rights). There are significant antitrust considerations in these arrangements with respect to price-fixing and non-price restraints.

This type of relationship requires substantial investment on behalf of the franchisor and subfranchisor. Both parties perform services to the subfranchisee. The sharing of revenue between franchisor and subfranchisor will depend on their relative investment, services, and contribution to the system.

Unique problems may arise as to the status of the subfranchisee upon termination or expiration of the subfranchisor relationship. The subfranchisor agreement generally provides for the automatic assignment of subfranchises to the franchisor. A more conservative approach would allow the franchisor the option to buy the subfranchise agreements using either the fixed price or formula price method to establish a selling price.

Typical applications for the subfranchise system include businesses in which the ultimate owner-operator need be trained not in the operation of the business, but rather in the systems of the franchise. For instance, in a real estate brokerage affiliation franchise, a properly trained franchisee can survive even with a weak subfranchisor.

The principal attraction of subfranchising to entrepreneurs is the potential for exponential expansion and rapid development. The sale of ten subfranchises to persons each then selling ten subfranchises results in one hundred operating units. As attractive as this prospect is, it may lead to problems such as one subfranchisor's permeating the entire market, perhaps expanding too quickly.

Master Franchising

Master franchising is used successfully in many franchise systems as an alternative to subfranchising. This alternative features a master franchise agreement between the franchisor and the master franchisee granting limited rights to recruit new franchisees and imposing on the master franchisee responsibility for providing certain field support services. The franchisor and the master franchisee may both be parties to the unit agreement, which often is structured as a three-party contract.

A master franchisee may be responsible for one or more of the following:

- Soliciting, screening, and qualifying prospects
- Site selection and lease or purchase negotiations
- Outlet development
- Training and opening assistance
- Inspection, supervision, and assistance
- Enforcement of system standards and compliance.

As with subfranchising, the franchisor generally retains the right of final approval of franchisee selection and site location. Franchise fees, royalties, and other payments are divided between the franchisor and master franchisee in an appropriate formula. Master franchise relationships avoid some of the problems of subfranchising, such as the franchisor's control over the unit franchise relationship and effective trademark protection. A master franchise program also eliminates the assignment problems associated with termination or nonrenewal of a subfranchisor.

Typical uses for master franchising are similar to those for subfranchising.

Development Quotas

Development quotas for area franchisees are essential to avoid the problem of a franchisor's being unable to develop fully the exclusive area granted to an area franchisee. The consequences of failure to meet development quotas might include loss of exclusive rights, termination of the area franchise, or reduction of the size of the exclusive area.

Advantages and Disadvantages

Area franchising has both advantages and disadvantages. Area franchisees are generally stronger economically and more sophisticated and independent than single-outlet franchisees. It maximizes the capacity for rapid and self-sustaining development. Having fewer franchisees simplifies contract administration, changes in the system are easier to implement, and reacquisition of any franchised units may be simpler. However, area franchising can also result in tougher bargaining on the part of the area franchisee and more difficulty in maintaining uniformity among franchisees. Termination of an area franchise relationship can be far more complex and difficult than terminating a unit franchise, and the difficulties that a franchisor may have in a unit franchise relationship are magnified by an area development program.

Legal Documentation of the Franchise Relationship

Franchising relationships are complex legal arrangements. The franchise agreement is just the beginning of the subjects treated by written contract between the parties. The following is a list of contracts that often appear in franchise relationships:

1. Franchise or license agreement
2. Area development agreement
3. Subfranchise or sublicense agreement
4. Master franchise agreement
5. Three-party agreement (franchisor/subfranchisor or master franchisee/franchisee)
6. Franchise commitment agreement (used at the time the application is approved)

7. Site selection agreement (where no site has been selected at the time the franchise agreement is signed)
8. Preliminary agreement
9. Lease or sublease
10. Collateral lease assignment
11. Facility development agreement
12. Management agreement
13. Promissory note and security agreement
14. Outlet repurchase agreement
15. Outlet sale agreement for sale of corporate-owned outlets to franchisees.
16. Assignment agreement
17. Guarantees (when the franchisee is a corporation).

Other agreements or relationships between a franchisor and franchisees include: (1) landlord-tenant; (2) supplier-dealer; and (3) lender-borrower.

Structuring a Unit Franchise Relationship

This section focuses on the details of structuring the relationship between the franchisor and franchisee.

Term and Renewal of the Franchise

A threshold consideration in structuring a franchise relationship is the term for which the franchisor will grant the franchise and whether the franchisee will have any renewal rights. The initial term may be expressed in a fixed number of years or be coextensive with the underlying lease or sublease for the premises of the franchisee's business. Before franchising's growth spread to many industries during the past three or four decades, many franchisors granted perpetual franchises, but this practice has largely been abandoned. Product franchisors traditionally have granted short-term franchises that are renewed automatically unless either party terminates the franchise by specified prior notice.

In selecting the term's duration, several considerations are relevant. The term must be long enough for the franchisee to amortize its investment in fixed assets and realize a reasonable profit. It is not realistic to require a franchisee to invest $50,000 to $100,000 in equipment and fixtures yet grant a franchise for only a five-year term. In capital-intensive franchises (e.g., fast food and lodging), terms of ten to twenty-five years are typical. A longer term may be in the franchisor's best interests if franchisees would be inclined to operate independently of the franchise after they have acquired sufficient knowledge of the business. The franchisor will have a breach of contract claim against a franchisee who repudiates its contract during its term, and a covenant not to compete is more likely to be enforceable against a franchisee who has breached its contract than against one who has merely declined an offer to renew the relationship.

Franchise renewal has become a much debated topic in recent years. This is attributable primarily to the large number of expiring franchises and franchisee uncertainty over prospects for terms of renewal. Nonrenewal is an especially sensitive issue when the franchisor also is the lessor of the franchisee's business premises. Expiration of the franchise results in the franchisee's losing the right to occupy the premises, and the franchisee does not have the option to continue its business at the same location independent of the franchise.

If statistics are believed, franchisor refusals to renew expiring franchises are rare occurrences. Nonrenewal typically is the franchisee's decision, or the franchisor's and franchisee's mutual decision, and frequently involves the franchisee's selling its business to the franchisor or a successor franchisee. The high percentage of renewals suggests that the renewal terms franchisors offer have not been impediments to renewal.

Despite the fact that nonrenewal does not appear to be a real issue in franchising, much state and federal legislation enacted during the past twenty years to regulate franchise and dealership terminations also regulates renewal and imposes prior notice or other conditions for refusal to renew a franchise. These laws should be consulted in planning this aspect of a franchise relationship.

Many franchisors, particularly established companies whose franchises are in demand, offer no renewal rights. Some franchisors adopting this approach do agree to give substantial prior notice (up to two years) of a decision not to renew and to allow the franchisee to sell its business to a successor franchisee (unless the franchisor discontinues operations at the franchisee's location or in its market). The opportunity to sell the business enables the franchisee to realize any goodwill that it has established independent of the franchise's goodwill. (The franchisee can also realize some goodwill attributable to the franchise if the price at which it can sell the business is not affected by higher fees that the franchisor will charge in the franchise issued to the buyer.)

Other franchisors who do not grant renewal rights permit the franchisee, when the initial term expires, to continue the same business at the same location (or in the same market), requiring only that the franchisee remove signs and all other indicia of the franchise.

If renewal rights are granted, they typically require the franchisee to satisfy certain conditions. A fundamental condition is that the franchisee must have complied with the franchise agreement during the initial term. Equally significant is renewing the lease for the premises and upgrading the business facility to current standards or, if this is not economical or advisable (e.g., the neighborhood has changed considerably), relocating the business to a new acceptable site or premises and developing those premises according to current standards.

Renewing a franchise is more accurately characterized as extending the franchise relationship or granting a successor franchise under modified terms, generally the terms on which the franchisor is granting new franchises at renewal time (though an initial fee typically is waived and training obligations are either waived entirely or reduced). Modern practice dictates continuing the relationship on the franchisor's then current form of franchise agreement.

Another consideration is whether the initial franchise agreement should provide for a single renewal for a specific term (or a term coextensive with the extended or new lease) or for a series of future renewals (a fixed number or in perpetuity). The former method preserves maximum flexibility for the franchisor because any subsequent rights to extend the relationship beyond the first extension period will be governed by the terms of the franchise agreement signed for that period.

Functional Exclusivity

A franchisor must consider the territorial exclusivity it will grant to franchisees and whether it must or should reserve for itself certain types of customers (e.g., national accounts) for the goods or services that franchisees sell. The franchisor should also consider whether it should reserve the right to operate comparable business outlets and to sell the same product or service in another distribution channel under the same trademark or service mark (or only under a different mark). A fast-food franchisor might have an opportunity to market a food product bearing its trademark in supermarkets (e.g., A&W Root Beer). An employment agency franchisor might initially specialize in temporary help and subsequently expand into permanent employee placements or stratify its market by occupational specialty. The franchisor might develop a new business concept that it will want to market, and perhaps franchise, under its already well-known trademark. That concept might or might not be competitive with the existing franchise system.

Though the franchisor frequently will elect to expand the business conducted under the original franchise system (marketing economics or franchisee goodwill considerations frequently will compel this decision), if it has thought through these issues in advance and structured its franchise relationship to anticipate future opportunities, it will preserve the flexibility to evaluate all possible methods for exploiting a future opportunity.

Territorial and Customer Rights and Restrictions

The threshold issue in formulating a franchisor's territorial and customer policy is whether to grant any form of territorial exclusivity to franchisees. The form of territorial protection typically granted to franchisees is the franchisor's commitment not to operate, or allow other franchisees to operate, additional outlets conducting the same business within a defined geographic market. The franchisor might retain some flexibility by qualifying this commitment. The qualification might be a limitation on the number of outlets that it will franchise or operate within a defined territory, perhaps related to the territory's population. In a variation of this policy, the franchisor initially will grant exclusivity but reserve the right to add outlets if the market changes in a prescribed manner (e.g., population increase, commercial development) or the franchisee fails to achieve prescribed market penetration (e.g., sales quotas). The reserved right to introduce additional outlets might take the form of shrinking the territory originally granted or establishing additional outlets within the initially defined territory and allowing the new outlets to compete with the original franchisee.

The converse of the exclusive territory is a policy of territorial confinement. If the franchisee is mobile and can market goods or services outside of a defined exclusive territory, territorial confinement prohibits the franchisee from soliciting or making sales outside of its exclusive territory. Where the franchisee operates from a fixed location, a territorial confinement policy takes the form of a location restriction, that is, a grant of a franchise only for a specific location, which the franchisee may not unilaterally change. The franchisee might also be prohibited from soliciting customers or making sales outside of its exclusive territory through other means (e.g., by mail order or through retailers located in other markets).

Other approaches that franchisors have taken to discourage extraterritorial sales include areas of primary responsibility, profit passovers, and other financial penalties imposed on sales made outside of a defined territory. The area of primary responsibility concept requires the franchisee to concentrate its sales efforts within a defined territory (typically coextensive with its exclusive territory) and might impose a sales quota to be fulfilled within the territory (or an obligation to make a specified percentage of its sales within its territory).

A profit passover obligates the franchisee to surrender a percentage of the gross sale price on an extraterritorial sale to the franchisee in whose territory the sale is made. The theory of this obligation and similar economic penalties is to compensate the franchisee who will have ongoing warranty, service, or other obligations to the customers who purchase goods from outside suppliers. This concept is limited to product franchise systems and has declined in significance in recent years.

Territorial restrictions complete the concept of an exclusive territory: the franchisee receives an exclusive right to market the franchisor's goods or services within a defined territory, is insulated from some or all intrabrand competition from the franchisor and other franchisee outlets (which may not be established within that territory), and is partially or totally prohibited from soliciting or making sales outside of that territory (or is penalized for doing so). From the late 1960s until the late 1970s, complete territorial confinement restrictions generally were considered to be *per se* (i.e., automatic) violations of federal antitrust law.[1] Lesser territorial restrictions (e.g., location restrictions, areas of primary responsibility, and profit passovers), on the other hand, generally qualified for Rule of Reason analysis under federal antitrust law unless they operated in practice as a closed territory system. Lower federal courts were uncomfortable with the *per se* concept, and the U.S. Supreme Court in 1977 reversed its earlier decision and applied the Rule of Reason to all vertically imposed territorial restrictions.[2] In a multitude of decisions since then, both federal and state courts have upheld ver-

---

1. For a discussion of antitrust issues, see Chapter 6.

2. *Compare* Continental T.V., Inc. v. GTE Sylvania, Inc., 433 U.S. 36 (1977) *with* United States v. Arnold, Schwinn & Co., 388 U.S. 365 (1967).

tical territorial restraints in Rule of Reason analyses. These decisions place the burden of proof of an unreasonable restraint of trade on the plaintiff franchisee and reject claims that territorial restraints are horizontal merely because the franchisor engages in dual distribution by owning some of its retail outlets. Federal courts sanction territorial restrictions even where the franchisor and its franchisees face little or no interbrand competition from other sellers of the same product or service.

The evolving law of territorial restrictions has expanded the choices that a franchisor faces in structuring its franchise relationship.

When a franchisor prefers to preserve maximum flexibility regarding the location and ownership of future franchised outlets, it will grant no territorial protection to its franchisees (or perhaps very limited protection within the franchisee's immediate market) and probably no options or rights of first refusal to acquire franchises for outlets to be established at locations proximate to their markets. The franchisor might want to retain complete flexibility concerning future outlet placement and ownership and to be in a position either to reward cooperative and productive franchisees with additional franchises or to deny to uncooperative or less effective operators the right to expand within the system. This policy is known as franchising by address or "location franchising." The franchise is granted for a specific address or location (e.g., shopping mall), and the franchisor reserves the right to grant additional franchises and establish franchisor-owned or operated outlets at any other location. This practice might become increasingly common among large, mature franchisors who grant a large percentage of new franchises to existing franchisees and whose franchise is in such demand that it is unnecessary to enhance its appeal with territorial protection.

The decline in territorial protection has caused concern among franchisees that their franchisors, faced with declining markets for expansion, will introduce additional outlets into their markets, reducing sales growth potential or even causing actual sales declines. This concern, generally termed "encroachment," already has generated significant litigation in mature systems and provided the impetus for state regulation of franchisor expansion rights. As its franchise system develops, a franchisor should continually review its policy on outlet spacing and franchisee expansion and communicate that policy to its franchisees. A misunderstood franchisor policy can adversely affect franchisee performance and interest in the system.

Customer restrictions are relatively rare in franchising and have generated little litigation. A franchisor sometimes reserves certain customers for itself for bidding or other sales efforts, though actual sales of goods or services frequently are made by its franchisees. Government and national (or regional) accounts are examples of customers that franchisors reserve. Customer restrictions do raise antitrust issues. The restriction itself is subject to a Rule of Reason analysis and generally will be upheld if the franchisee could not deal effectively with a restricted customer (particularly if the franchisee is offered an opportunity to service the customer in the franchisee's market). Another issue is the status of a service contract that the franchisor negotiates with a national account. If the franchisee must service the national account customer at a prenegotiated price, an unlawful vertical price-fixing issue is raised. However, if the franchisee simply is given an option to perform part of the national contract and can still independently solicit the customer, no price-fixing issue is likely to exist. Of course, the franchisor must develop a contingency plan for those franchisees who decline to participate under the national contract.

Developing the Franchisee's Business Facility

The threshold determination in developing the franchisee's business facility is the franchisor's and franchisee's relative responsibilities for the development. Franchisor practice runs the gamut from total franchisor to total franchisee responsibility. Furnishing a complete turnkey facility is not a common franchisor practice. It normally is feasible and appropriate only for an established and well-financed franchisor. However, the expansion of franchise outlets in regional malls, high interest rates, scarcity of financing, and the large cash flow generated by mature franchisors or franchisors that have been acquired by larger companies have generated more turnkey outlets subleased to franchisees. Regional malls prefer to deal with franchisors and to have a commitment that their franchisor tenant will develop the leased space. Franchisee inability to finance outlet development has confronted franchisors with the choice of providing financing (e.g., by leasing developed real estate) or accepting slow system expansion. A strong stimulus to expanding the turnkey approach has been the combined benefits to the franchisor of outlet control (leading to enhanced quality and uniformity control) and real estate investment that can generate an income stream that will increase with inflation and higher outlet sales volume. Nonetheless, the turnkey franchise is found among only a small number of franchises.

When the franchisor is also the franchisee's landlord, it must determine whether it will sublease to the franchisee at the same rent it pays or increase the rent charged to compensate for the additional risk it assumes and to generate profits. When the franchisor owns the real estate leased to the franchisee, it must decide whether to lease at a fixed return on its cost (usually with inflation escalation) or at the greater of a fixed rental or a percentage of the outlet's revenue.

At the other end of the spectrum, some franchise programs impose on the franchisee exclusive responsibility for outlet development and financing. This approach is common among newer and smaller franchisors whose financial resources limit their involvement in developing or financing the franchisee's outlet. These franchisors usually will reserve the right to approve the site the franchisee selects and furnish at least general plans and specifications for construction or remodeling. When the site is leased, many franchisors reserve the right to approve the lease's terms or to prescribe certain required lease clauses. Examples are clauses providing for notice to the franchisor of the franchisee's default under the lease and granting the franchisor the right to cure the default and substitute as tenant for the franchisee; embodying the landlord's agreement that the lease may be assigned to the franchisor; allowing the franchisor to enter the premises to take down signs; allowing the landlord to report sales to the franchisor; and tying the lease to the franchise by making termination of the franchise a default of the lease, resulting in either an automatic transfer of the lease to the franchisor (which can be dangerous if the lease is on unfavorable terms for a poor location) or the franchisor's option to acquire the lease.

Another technique that franchisors widely use to avoid responsibility for franchisee outlets is to obtain a lease assignment as security for the franchisee's performance. If the franchisor terminates the franchise agreement for cause or the franchisee terminates the franchise agreement without cause, the franchisor may enforce the lease assignment and take control of the former franchisee's outlet. This allows the franchisor to decide on a case-by-case basis whether to incur liability for lease obligations. Controls of this kind are important only when the franchisee's business facility is significant to its business. If the franchisee can readily relocate without a significant loss of goodwill, outlet control is relatively unimportant. This technique also provides no protection when the franchisee has fully performed its obligations.

There are various degrees of franchisor involvement between the extremes of the turnkey outlet and total franchisee responsibility for developing and financing the outlet. Beginning with site selection, responsibility for proposing sites may be placed on the franchisee, assumed by the franchisor, or shared by both. The method selected will depend on the franchisor's size, experience, and perception of the franchisee's ability to expedite site selection. The next phase of outlet development is leasing or purchasing the site or premises. Substantially the same variations in assigning responsibility apply to site acquisition, although it is less common for franchisors to assume total responsibility for lease or purchase negotiations when they will not have a leasehold or ownership interest in the outlet. However, even relatively small and inexperienced franchisors typically commit to "assist" with lease negotiations.

Undertaking responsibility for site selection and acquisition can be a trap for the neophyte franchisor. The drain on manpower and travel and other expenses can escalate quickly, exceeding the franchisor's capacity to fulfill its commitments. This can lead to hasty and ill-advised site selection, excessive acquisition costs, or the franchisor's failure to fulfill its obligations to franchisees. Site selection and acquisition are critical elements of a franchise system's expansion. In structuring a franchise program, a franchisor's personnel and financial resources must be carefully considered to determine its responsibility.

The franchisor should recognize that failing franchisees frequently claim that the franchisor supplied them with a bad location. Location is critical to the success of a retail business and, in any expanding franchise system, the risk of selecting a poor location is unavoidable. Consequently, whatever the franchisor's and franchisee's relative responsibilities for site selection, their agreements should reflect the franchisee's acceptance of the location, its recognition that site selection is an exercise of business judgment and not foolproof, and its acknowledgment that the franchisor does not guarantee the success of the franchisee's business at that location.

The franchisee's business facility might consist of a motel, a freestanding restaurant, a large retail store with extensive fixtures, a simple office, a small retail storefront, or even a vehicle. If real estate is involved, the next phases in developing the franchise outlet will be constructing a new structure or a finished store or remodeling an existing structure; acquiring and installing fixtures, furnishings, equipment, and signs; decorating the facility; and purchasing an opening inventory of merchandise or supplies. Where a freestanding building must be constructed, development may include determining and complying with zoning variations; obtaining utility, environmental, and building permits and local government approvals; preparing architectural plans and specifications; participating in construction bidding and contracts; and drafting various contracts for fixtures, furnishings, equipment, signs, decorating, merchandise, and supplies.

With the exception of the relatively few franchisors that customarily furnish a turnkey facility to their franchisees, franchisees assume responsibility for constructing, fixturing, furnishing, and equipping their facilities. Recognizing that franchisees (particularly new franchisees) generally cannot undertake complex outlet development, franchisors customarily furnish varying degrees of support in several elements of development. For example, if complex construction is required, franchisors typically give plans and specifications for one or more prototype buildings. These plans and specifications frequently require modifications to meet local building codes and other restrictions and approval by a locally licensed architect but save the franchisee money and time and simplify this phase of its outlet's development.

Franchisors often furnish ongoing assistance to the franchisee during the outlet's development. This assistance often includes recommending contractors with whom the franchisor or its other franchisees have worked successfully; furnishing a list of approved suppliers for the fixtures, furnishings, equipment, and signs the franchisee requires for its outlet; periodically inspecting development to ensure that the outlet meets the franchisor's requirements; and assisting in purchasing an opening merchandise inventory.

This assistance can become so extensive as to be virtually indistinguishable from providing a turnkey facility. Some franchisors therefore offer to supplement their franchise agreements with an outlet development agreement. A franchisee has the option to assume responsibility for development or, in effect, to hire the franchisor to develop its outlet. Outlet development agreements discuss the franchisor's obligation to develop the facility, set forth the procedure for financing development (e.g., depositing funds with the franchisor or a financing arrangement with a lender permitting the franchisor to draw funds as needed during development), and state the franchisor's fee for its services. To encourage franchisees to use the franchisor's development services, some franchisors charge a higher initial franchise fee (payable without regard to whether the franchisor develops the franchisee's outlet) and a relatively low development fee.

A number of subsidiary questions concerning outlet development must be answered in structuring a franchise relationship. For example, the facility's location, local zoning or building restrictions, or neighborhood resistance to the facility may require modifications to standard formats and designs. The franchisor must decide who will be responsible for dealing with these issues and implementing any agreed-on modifications.

If the franchisee has development responsibility, the franchise agreement should identify a time period within which development must be completed and the outlet opened for business. The franchise agreement should also specify what happens if the franchisee fails to complete development within the prescribed period. Unless owing to conditions or events beyond the franchisee's control, failure to complete development properly and timely is typically a ground for termination. However, the problems potentially arising from an incomplete business facility are not resolved simply by terminating the franchise. The franchisor generally should reserve an option to acquire the lease to the premises or ownership of the property on an equitable basis. Alternatively, the franchisor could reserve the right to require sale or lease to a successor franchisee. Lenders will be involved and may insist on some form of franchisor guarantee of complete development. Even if the guarantee is not demanded, a lender cannot be expected to permit either franchisor takeover or sale or lease to a successor franchisee without a right of approval and adequate security.

In addition to construction or remodeling, the franchisee's facility may require fixtures, furnishings, equipment, signs, or merchandise inventory at substantial cost. The franchisor must determine the extent to which it must control the sources of these assets and will assist the franchisee in acquiring them. Control methods include furnishing specifications as to type, brand, or model of each item required; identifying approved suppliers; and designating one or perhaps a few suppliers with whom the franchisee must deal. If approved or designated suppliers are used, the franchisor must determine if, and under what conditions, it will approve additional sources for any item. If a designated or approved supplier (which may include the franchisor) offers a complete package or one or more of the required assets, the franchisor must determine whether to permit the franchisee to buy less than the complete package.

In some cases, the franchisor may go as far as to require that franchisees purchase these items from the franchisor or its designated sources and refrain from purchasing goods of other companies. The avowed purpose of restrictive purchasing requirements may be to protect and enhance the franchise system's image, trademark, and goodwill by assuring product or service quality and standardization and consistently prompt production and delivery schedules or to lower costs by concentrating purchases with one or a few suppliers. On the other hand, they may be imposed to create a "revenue center" for the franchisor, arising from the franchisor's (or an affiliate's) direct sales and leases to franchisees or the franchisor's receipt of payments from third-party suppliers with whom the franchisees are directed to deal. Whatever the motive, a franchisor risks liability under antitrust laws if its franchisees are obligated to deal with the franchisor or its designees (including affiliates) as a supplier, lessor, or lender.[3]

In the early years of business format franchising, franchisors frequently required their franchisees to purchase equipment, merchandise, and supplies di-

---

3. *See* Siegal v. Chicken Delight, Inc., 448 F.2d 43 (9th Cir. 1971), *cert. denied,* 405 U.S. 955 (1972); Ungar v. Dunkin' Donuts of Am., Inc., 531 F.2d 1211 (3d. Cir. 1970), *cert. denied,* 429 U.S. 823 (1976).

rectly from them or their designated suppliers (from whom the franchisors received commissions). The profits and commissions from these sales frequently represented the franchisor's sole or principal income, the imposition of royalties and related fees being relatively insignificant. These purchasing restrictions were first challenged during the 1960s as unlawful "tying arrangements" under the antitrust laws. Indeed, alleged "tie-ins" have been the predominant subject of franchisor-franchisee antitrust litigation, hundreds of lawsuits having been filed between the late 1960s and early 1980s by franchisees claiming that their franchisors forced them to buy equipment, supplies, or other goods or services, or to lease real property, as a condition of acquiring or retaining their franchises. The plaintiff franchisee sought in many cases to bring its lawsuit as a class action on behalf of all similarly situated franchisees.[4] The history of this litigation is voluminous and replete with issues with which federal courts wrestled for some time.

The concern with tying arrangements is that they foreclose the access of competing sellers to the tied product market (e.g., the product the franchisee also must buy from the franchisor to acquire or retain the franchise), not because of competitive merit but as a result of the seller's power in the tying product market (i.e., the market for the franchise itself). Buyers are compelled to forego free choice between competing sellers in the tied product market. A series of judicial decisions since the late 1970s and early 1980s, however, has eviscerated most tying claims.[5] In the current antitrust climate, a plaintiff generally must establish the following to convince a court to find a supply source restriction to be a *per se* illegal tying arrangement: (1) that the seller offered two separate and distinct products or services; (2) that sale of the tying product was conditioned on purchase of the tied product; (3) that the seller possessed sufficient power in the tying product market to restrain competition appreciably in the tied product market; and (4) that a not insubstantial amount of interstate commerce was affected. As in all antitrust cases, a plaintiff also must overcome available defenses and prove damages.[6]

Several references have been made to financing the development of the franchisee's business facility. This is an obviously significant element in structuring a franchise relationship. Many industries in which franchise systems prevail are characterized by capital-intensive retail outlets. Franchisors have always assisted their franchisees in raising needed capital. Some franchisors lease turnkey facilities to their franchisees. Others have arranged sales and leasebacks of real estate, sometimes packaging several facilities for sale to an investor who leases to the franchisee, or to the franchisor for sublease to the franchisee (thereby incorporating a credit guaranty by the franchisor), in exchange for which the franchisor acquires outlet control and additional revenue. Still others have given partial or full guarantees for lease and conventional financing

---

4. *See, e.g.,* Ungar v. Dunkin' Donuts of Am., Inc., 531 F.2d 1211 (3d Cir. 1970), *cert. denied,* 429 U.S. 823 (1976).

5. *See, e.g.,* Jefferson Parish Hosp. Dist. No. 2 v. Hyde, 466 U.S. 2 (1984).

6. *See* Chapter 6.

granted to their franchisees. Franchisors have even extended financing guarantees in the form of inventory repurchase agreements, which are assignable by the franchisee to its lender, thereby assuring the lender that, if the franchisee defaults, the franchisor's repurchase of qualified merchandise will generate funds for repayment, a more effective type of security than traditional Uniform Commercial Code security interests.

Many franchisors have encouraged franchisees to use Small Business Administration (SBA) guaranteed loans and assisted their franchisees in securing them. SBA guaranteed loans have played a major role in financing franchisee expansion. Recent changes in the procedures for seeking SBA loans, and the SBA's increasing acceptance of the franchising method of distribution, will further augment SBA financing of franchisee expansion.

Increasing capital requirements over the years have stimulated a search for new capital sources. One source is the large and well-financed area developer who commits to develop multiple outlets in a defined territory. Some area developers are medium-size or even large companies that successfully operate another business and are seeking diversification. Others are wealthy individuals attracted to the opportunity to establish a chain of outlets in a protected territory. An area developer satisfies the traditional capital contribution function of the franchisee more effectively than an individual franchisee. Area developer arrangements continue to expand. In fact, a sizable number of franchisors will grant only multiple outlet franchises.

A second source (adopted by a few franchisors) is the formation of a small business investment company (SBIC) or a minority enterprise small business investment company (MESBIC). SBICs are subject to fewer restrictions and are more common than MESBICs. SBICs and MESBICs that meet certain capital and other requirements and are certified by the SBA may borrow significantly beyond their capital from the SBA at interest rates substantially below prevailing market rates for comparable loans. SBICs and MESBICs may make loans to, and equity investments in, eligible small businesses.

A third capital-raising technique is the publicly offered limited partnership in a pool of outlets to be developed for lease to franchisees. The traditional sale and leaseback investor makes a large investment in one or a few outlets. The publicly offered limited partnership is an effort to tap the vast pool of small investors, a variation of the real estate investment trust. Franchisors have not promoted these public offerings but have approved them and, in fact, may be the lessee for some of the outlets developed with the offering's proceeds.

Financing the development of franchisee outlets can be difficult when capital is in short supply, subject to fierce competition, and expensive. Franchisors may be required to develop other approaches to and sources of financing. For example, as a franchisor expands in foreign countries, it may develop a foreign capital source that is sufficiently impressed by the franchisor's success in the foreign country that it becomes a source of capital for further United States expansion. It is clear that, in many franchise systems, financing the franchisee's business outlet cannot be taken for granted and must be considered and reflected in structuring the franchise relationship.

Training Program

The franchise documents should address the training program's content, duration, and location. This is where the franchisee will learn the business. The content typically consists of a training school (e.g., classroom instruction on operating the business), field experience (e.g., training and working in a franchisor or franchisee outlet), and training manuals and materials. The duration typically will be fixed but may be flexible depending on the franchisee's aptitude and facility in learning the business. Training usually is conducted at the franchisor's principal office, regional training facilities, or operating outlets. The people to whom training is furnished vary from system to system but typically include the franchisee (or a principal or managing owner), outlet managers and assistant managers, subsequently hired managers, and other employees.

The franchisee (or its principal or managing owner) or its managers usually must complete the training program satisfactorily. The franchisor should develop objective criteria for determining satisfactory participation in the form of examinations and on-the-job evaluations. A franchisor often will reserve the right to terminate the franchise agreement if the franchisee (or its principal or managing owner) fails to complete the training program satisfactorily. In many cases, it will refund the initial fees to the franchisee and assist in disposing of the franchisee's business facility and operating assets. The franchisor usually will not terminate the franchisee if a non-owner manager fails to complete the training program satisfactorily. Instead, the franchisee must replace the manager with somebody else who can satisfactorily complete training.

Franchisors frequently offer refresher training programs for the franchisee and its personnel. These may be optional or mandatory, depending on their content and location. Franchisors usually will not charge separately for the training they offer to new franchisees and a minimum number of personnel. These fees normally are encompassed within the initial franchise fee, although franchisors often reserve the right to charge separately for additional employees who attend the training program. In virtually all cases, however, the franchisee is responsible for the travel and living expenses that its personnel incur while attending the training program.

Operating Assistance or Guidance

The operating assistance or guidance that the franchisor provides to the franchisee during their relationship usually is contained within an operating manual. The operating manual may take many forms, including written materials, audiotapes, videotapes, software, and related media. Whatever its form, it contains standards and specifications that will assist the franchisee in opening and operating its business. There often will be additional assistance, beyond that contained in the "four corners" of the operating manual, that the franchisor will provide to the franchisee.

The franchisor customarily will assist the franchisee in advertising and promoting the opening of its outlet. The franchisor might direct the advertising and promotion on the franchisee's behalf and at the franchisee's expense or simply supervise the franchisee's administration of its advertising and promotion program. The franchisee may be required to spend a minimum amount for a grand opening advertising and promotion program. While the franchisee may have some discretion in the amount it spends and how it spends that amount, the franchisor typically will control the content and media of the advertising and promotion.

Besides advertising and promotion, the franchisor typically will send one or more employees to the franchisee's outlet or territory, depending on the business, to assist the franchisee in opening its business. This assistance may be for a specified time period before and after the opening or may be at the franchisor's discretion.

General operating assistance that the franchisor provides after the business opens customarily includes inspecting and evaluating the franchisee's performance; assisting with specific operating problems, such as training employees and evaluating employees' performance; consulting on the business facility's appearance and service, product quality, adherence to specifications and standards, efficiency, and costs of operation; advertising and promotion programs; purchase of goods, supplies, and services; inventory control advice; bookkeeping and accounting programs; administrative procedures; insurance; and other services. This guidance is furnished via the operating manuals, other written communications, field assistance, periodic refresher training courses, and telephone consultations. The franchisor will provide much of this assistance at no additional cost but will reserve the right to charge the franchisee separate fees for assistance or guidance beyond a "reasonable" amount (to protect against unreasonable franchisee demands) or for special or additional training that the franchisor requires or the franchisee requests.

Supplying Franchisees

As discussed earlier, the franchisor may become involved in supplying goods or services to franchisees. The franchisor may be the designated or sole supplier of a particular product or service or merely one of several approved suppliers. The franchisor will also participate in negotiating supply and distribution contracts, in which case it often will require franchisees to commit to a certain level of purchases. Franchisor-owned and operated commissaries or distribution facilities are increasingly in vogue, as franchisors seek to regulate their system's operation and the quality of the products and services sold through the system. While it is not unreasonable for the franchisor to seek a profit from its supply programs, the prices ultimately charged to franchisees must be competitive. Franchisees are increasingly playing roles in the supply side of a franchise program, whether by forming purchasing or distribution cooperatives or establishing franchisee advisory councils, which, as the term suggests, advise the franchisor on how it should proceed in the area.

While the antitrust considerations prevalent in the 1970s and early 1980s have ebbed significantly, the franchisor should always be aware of tying issues,

Robinson-Patman Act issues (concerning price discrimination), and related antitrust matters.

Franchisors must manage franchisee credit risk to the extent that they are involved directly as suppliers to franchisees. A franchisor must consider the terms and conditions of the sale of products and services, the late charges or interest that will be added to past due accounts, whether it will require personal guarantees (as is traditional) covering all of the franchisee's monetary obligations or seek purchase money or blanket security interests in the items it sells to the franchisee, and the effects of these various methods on the franchisee's ability to seek other financing. The key for the franchisor is to remember its primary business. It should not let the supply relationship put a strain on the franchise relationship. After all, franchisees expect franchisors to provide competitive, if not "better," prices than those available elsewhere. Deficiencies on the supplier side of the relationship could severely jeopardize the franchise relationship.

The franchisor might organize and administer the supply program by developing and modifying specifications and standards and maintaining quality control. It might also negotiate purchase and distribution agreements with manufacturers and distributors. Typically, the franchisor does not take title to the goods or guarantee payment (except for its own outlets). On the other hand, there may be a buying entity in the supply program, for example, a corporation that acts as the franchisee's and franchisor's purchasing agent. Depending on its role in the distribution process, the franchisor may be able to receive a functional discount for its activities.

Franchisee participation in the supply side of the franchise system has led to increasing numbers of franchisee buying cooperatives. These cooperatives typically operate on a national or regional basis and likewise will negotiate supply programs with manufacturers and distributors. These cooperatives may take title to the goods purchased or simply function as an intermediary, with title passed directly to the ordering franchisees. When franchisees become directly involved in the supply process, there tends to be less suspicion regarding the franchisor's benefit from the supply program, which, in turn, reduces the chances of litigation. Nonetheless, the franchisor can play a role by providing technical advice and guidance on supply sources and, to the extent it operates company-owned outlets, as a member of the buying cooperative.

Whether the franchisor or franchisees administer the supply process, there will be restrictions on the franchisees' sources of products, ingredients, materials, and supplies. Franchisees often will have to buy approved brands, buy from approved suppliers, or buy according to certain specifications. The suppliers may, depending on the system and the products involved, be limited to the franchisor, its affiliates, or certain designated sources or may encompass a number of approved suppliers. Whether the franchisor or its designees will be the sole source of particular products often depends on whether the products are made with proprietary information.

While there may be sourcing restrictions, there will also be procedures for requesting approval of new brands or suppliers and investigating those new brands and suppliers. Usually, a franchisor will have criteria for approving additional suppliers and will communicate those criteria to the suppliers directly or to the franchisees who request them. The franchisor often will limit the number of approved suppliers to concentrate purchases for better prices and service or to achieve administrative and monitoring effectiveness. In the supplier approval process, the franchisor may charge a fee for reviewing and evaluating a proposed brand or supplier. This fee often will simply cover the franchisor's out-of-pocket costs of making the decision. However, there are systems in which the franchisor requires suppliers to pay a royalty for using the franchisor's trademark and selling to franchisees in the system.

Advertising and Marketing Programs

In many, if not most, franchise systems, the franchisor administers, or reserves the right to administer at a later date, an advertising or marketing program. Any marketing program typically will be supported by advertising fees or contributions from franchisees and franchisor outlets. The contributions will be either a percentage of the franchisee's revenue or a fixed dollar amount. The formula depends on the nature of the business and the method by which the franchisor calculates the money that the franchisee must pay. While the franchisor customarily administers the advertising program directly, it may set up a separate corporation or trust to do so.

A fund's potential uses are limited to advertising or promotion, public relations, market research, and payment of expenses and salaries of the franchisor's advertising department. The franchisor will reserve the right to overspend and borrow the difference or underspend and invest excess funds for future use. There may be income tax considerations, depending on how monies flow into and out of any advertising fund.

The franchisor must decide whether formulating advertising, selecting advertising and public relations agencies and media, and implementing advertising campaigns will be accomplished unilaterally or determined after input from the franchisee's advisory council (which may operate on a national, regional, or local basis). Advertising and promotional materials will be furnished to the franchisee at the franchisor's direct cost or on another basis.

While the franchisor may administer an advertising or marketing program on a national or regional basis, often the franchisee must advertise and promote its business locally. This means that the franchisee must spend a minimum amount on approved advertising media in its immediate trading area, including classified telephone directory listings and advertisements. Franchisees are frequently required by their franchisors to advertise jointly with other franchisees located or operating within a particular area. While franchisees may cooperate in administering regional or local advertising programs, there are antitrust restrictions on coercing franchisees to follow the prices identified in the advertising materials.

Maintenance of Standards

The franchise agreement will describe the specifications, standards, and operating procedures that the franchisee must follow in operating its business. While it may be desirable to articulate in detail the most significant specifications, standards, and operating procedures, it is too cumbersome and inflexible to enunciate all of them. For that reason, many franchisors reserve the right to establish and periodically modify and augment the governing specifications, standards, and operating procedures. The franchisor will categorize these areas for reference purposes and articulate the general parameters of its discretion rather than detail the specific specifications, standards, and operating procedures. The covered areas generally include the business facility's condition and appearance and periodic maintenance and repair; authorized and required products and services and product and service categories; designated or approved suppliers from which the franchisee may procure operating assets and supplies; standards of service; appearance of employees; use and display of trademarks and service marks; terms and conditions of the sale and delivery of, and terms and methods of payment for, goods and services that the franchisee obtains from the franchisor or affiliated suppliers; insurance requirements; production, presentation, packaging, and delivery of products and services; sales, marketing, advertising, and promotional programs and materials and media used in these programs; authorized warranties and obligations to honor warranties issued by other franchisees; the franchisee's operational control and management; business hours; forms and reports; signs, posters, and displays; staffing levels, management issues, and employee performance; credit practices and acceptance of credit and debit cards; and compliance with specific laws and regulations. Standards, specifications, and operating procedures are communicated in the operating manual and other written communications, at national and regional meetings of franchisees, and during field inspections and refresher training programs.

Another type of standard with which the franchisee must comply concerns accounting, record-keeping, and reporting requirements. The franchisee might be required to maintain a standard accounting system (chart of accounts) and to routinize records establishment and maintenance. The franchisee must submit periodic reports of its sales and revenue, typically weekly or monthly; various financial statements, typically monthly, quarterly, or annually, the latter of which might have to be audited or reviewed by a certified public accountant; and sales and income tax returns, either automatically or at the franchisor's request. If the franchisee must maintain a computer system to gather and organize certain information, the franchisor should retain the right to access that information directly.

Some franchisors provide accounting services to their franchisees, including monthly and year-to-date profit and loss statements, current balance sheets, other financial reports, and comparative statistical analyses. This might also include payment of the franchisee's bills from a jointly controlled bank account. Some franchisors will mandate this service to control the franchisee's operation indirectly (by maintaining a close watch on its operations). Franchisors typically will charge a separate fee for these services, whether mandatory or voluntary.

To ensure that the franchisee is complying with the franchise agreement and the franchisor's standards, specifications, and operating procedures, franchisors reserve the right to inspect the franchisee's outlet, and sometimes to photograph and videotape the outlet's operation, interview employees and customers, take or observe an inventory of the franchisee's outlet, and examine, copy, and audit all of the franchisee's books and records (to the extent they pertain to the particular franchise). For most types of inspections (e.g., a physical inspection or sampling), the franchisor need not provide notice before its arrival. For other types of inspections (e.g., examination of books and records), the franchisor might agree to give the franchisee minimum notice, typically ranging from twenty-four to seventy-two hours. While most inspections occur at the franchisor's expense, the franchisee typically must reimburse the franchisor for the costs of the examination or audit if it occurs because of the franchisee's failure to furnish required information in a timely manner, or at all, or reveals that the franchisee understated its revenue.

Protection of Trade Secrets and Noncompetition Provisions

Virtually all franchise agreements have in-term covenants prohibiting the franchisee's or its owners' association with or interest in a competitive business. The definition of a competitive business will vary from system to system. Ideally, it is broad enough to protect the franchisor and its proprietary information from possible leakage into related businesses yet sufficiently narrow to be enforceable in most states. In-term covenants (i.e., those that apply only during the term of the franchise agreement) are enforced more universally than are postterm covenants. In-term covenants proscribe direct or indirect, controlling or noncontrolling, legal, or beneficial ownership interests in competitive businesses; performing services as an officer, director, employee, manager, consultant, representative, agent, or in any other capacity for a competitive business; soliciting the franchisor's or other franchisees' employees; and other conduct that might divert business from the franchise system. Postterm covenants are more limited. Courts will enforce these provisions, if at all, only if they are reasonably limited in geography, duration, and scope of prohibited activities. The franchise agreement should apply these covenants after termination, expiration, or transfer of the franchised business (whether the transfer is to another franchisee or the franchisor or its affiliates). These covenants typically apply within the market where the franchisee operated.

The nondisclosure provisions should define or identify the nature of the trade secrets or other proprietary information, prohibit their disclosure and unauthorized use during and after the franchise agreement's term, and require franchisees to obtain nondisclosure agreements from managerial employees or others who may have access to the proprietary information. While most franchisors believe that it is impractical to require a franchisee's managerial employees to sign these nondisclosure agreements as a condition of employment, failure to do so may eviscerate a franchisor's later attempts to protect its proprietary information from improper use.

License to Use Trademarks and Service Marks

The trademark sections of a franchise agreement are fairly elaborate and prescribe how the franchisee may or may not use the franchisor's commercial symbols, identify the symbols' ownership, regulate the modification or discontinuation of a particular trademark's or service mark's usage, and indemnify (at least when the trademark is strong) the franchisee if it ultimately is held liable in or incurs expenses in defending a trademark infringement lawsuit. Franchisors always require franchisees to use appropriate registration symbols and dictate the products and materials on which the marks must be placed. Franchisees may not use the marks with unauthorized products or services, in their corporate or legal business names, or in another unauthorized form. The franchise agreement routinely reserves to the franchisor all goodwill arising from the franchisee's use of the trademarks. The franchisor also retains control of all litigation and administrative proceedings concerning the licensed marks. The franchisee must notify the franchisor promptly of any challenge to its use of the franchisor's commercial symbols or any claim by any third party of any rights in a confusingly similar commercial symbol. The franchisee usually must cooperate with the franchisor and its counsel in any litigation or administrative proceedings arising from the use of the commercial symbols. The franchisor, as noted, customarily indemnifies the franchisee against damages and expenses arising in trademark infringement proceedings.

If the franchisor believes that it is appropriate or necessary for the franchisee to modify or discontinue using a mark, the franchisee must comply with the franchisor's directions within a reasonable period of time after receiving notice. The franchisor might agree to reimburse the franchisee for its direct, out-of-pocket costs of changing signs; however, the franchisor typically will not reimburse the franchisee for any loss of revenue attributable to using a modified or new trademark or for any expenses it incurs to promote that new mark.

Above all, the franchisee is expressly estopped from challenging the franchisor's rights in the licensed trademarks.

Sources of Revenue

Franchisors have numerous sources of revenue from a franchise relationship. First and foremost are the initial fees that the franchisee pays for the franchise. Initial fees include the initial franchise fee, fees for developing the franchisee's business facility, training fees, fees for development rights, and option fees (to the extent the franchisee may acquire additional franchises). Franchisors sometimes lump all of these fees into one large fee. Most would agree that the initial franchise fee is not designed to generate significant profit. It should compensate the franchisor for its costs and expenses in establishing each franchise and training the franchisee in operating the business. While there may be a small profit, it should not be too excessive.

Franchisors generally agree that their key revenue source is the continuing fees that the franchisee pays during the term of the franchise agreement. Continuing fees include royalty fees, service or assistance fees, advertising fees, and transfer and renewal fees. The royalty and service fees are based on the franchisee's revenue or sales. They might be measured by a fixed percentage of revenue or sales or by escalating or declining percentages (depending on revenue levels), or even be a specific dollar amount (in which case there may be a cost of living adjustment). Revenue is defined in most cases to include all of the franchisee's receipts from operating its business, including sales to employees and credit sales that remain uncollected. Customarily excluded from "gross" revenue are monies collected for payment to taxing authorities and refunds, adjustments, credits, and allowances that the franchisee actually provides to its customers. Franchisors may distinguish between the cash and accrual bases for collecting fees. Fees may be payable weekly or monthly and by check or, as is increasingly in vogue, by account "sweeping" and automatic funds transfers. The latter method avoids the "check is in the mail" excuse and reduces paperwork. This method does not, however, avoid the insufficient funds check problem if the franchisee fails to deposit into its business checking account the amounts that the franchisor will withdraw electronically.

Advertising and marketing payments might be made to a separate advertising and marketing fund that is administered as a trust. Contributions are not taxable income to the franchisor, and there may be fiduciary obligations to those who have contributed to the trust. If advertising and marketing fees are paid directly to the franchisor, however, they may be taxable income to the franchisor, and the franchisor may have contractual (and maybe fiduciary) obligations to spend the fees as the franchise agreement prescribes.

There are numerous other revenue sources for the franchisor. The franchisor might profit from an override on the business facility's lease. It might derive revenue from selling various items to franchisees, including equipment, fixtures, furniture, and signs; finished products, ingredients, materials, and supplies; commissary or distribution services; advertising services and materials; accounting and data processing services; training and consulting; and other services or assistance.

Franchisors frequently derive revenue from sales to franchisees made by independent third-party suppliers. These take the form of commissions on sales to franchisees, inspection and technical assistance fees, royalties for using the franchisor's trademark, and advertising allowances. The franchisor should be wary of the antitrust considerations arising from its financial interest in sales by third-party suppliers.

Some franchisors also derive revenue from interest and loan fees. These result from the franchisor's direct loans to franchisees or placing loans with third-party lenders. Security deposits also comprise a form of revenue. Security deposits may be in cash or may be a letter of credit or a collateral assignment of the business facility's lease. These payments are security for all the amounts that the franchisee might ultimately owe to the franchisor under the franchise agreement for performing nondisclosure and noncompetition obligations and performing other franchisee obligations.

Modification of the System

All franchisors reserve the right to modify the franchise system's image, market position, format, product mix, and services. Some modifications require the franchisee's significant capital investment in the business. Franchisors often limit the amount that the franchisee must spend on capital investment during the term of the franchise agreement. This may be a fixed amount or a flexible limitation based on the franchisee's revenue. There also might be limits on the time period during which the franchisor may require the franchisee to spend these amounts. There at least should be a sufficient remaining term for the franchisee to amortize its capital investment. If not, the franchisor should be willing to extend the term so that the franchisee's investment can be amortized. Exceptions to these limitations are capital modifications required by law.

As a safety measure for the franchisee, the franchisor might agree that it will not impose modifications unless the franchisor likewise modifies it own outlets, everybody in the system modifies their outlets, the franchisee association or another advisory committee approves the proposed modifications, or a majority or supermajority of franchisees approves the capital modifications. The franchisor must consider the practical enforceability of capital modifications during the term of the franchise agreement. Nonetheless, the franchisor should reserve the right to impose a capital modification requirement as a condition of the franchisee's renewal of the franchise or acquisition of a successor franchise.

Transfer of the Franchise

Before addressing the conditions that franchisors typically impose on prospective transfers, one should understand the franchisee's nature and composition. Some franchisors will grant franchises only to individuals or partnerships, although they then will permit transfer to a corporation for convenience. The purpose is to ensure that all individuals signing the franchise agreement are personally liable for all of the contractual obligations. Most franchisors, however, will grant franchises directly to a corporation or limited liability company as long as that entity's shareholders or members guarantee all of its obligations as franchisee and agree to be personally bound by, and personally liable for the breach of, each and every obligation that the franchise agreement contains. These include monetary, nondisclosure, noncompetition, and standard maintenance obligations. For added protection, some franchisors will require the members of the owner's family to agree to certain obligations. As a practical matter, though, many franchisors make a business decision to limit the personal guarantee requirement to significant rather than all shareholders. In those circumstances, however, the "minority" owners still should agree to the nondisclosure, noncompetition, and related obligations.

Most franchisors reserve for themselves an unlimited right to transfer the franchise agreement. This is essential to maintain flexibility, especially if the franchisor's acquisition by another company is foreseeable. Franchisees, however, may not effect transfers without the franchisor's approval. These restrictions apply to transfers of the franchise and the franchise agreement, an ownership interest in the franchisee, the business facility and its assets, and subleases. These restrictions apply to voluntary and involuntary transfers, lifetime (*inter vivos*) transfers, and transfers on death and disability. There typically are exceptions for transfers to an entity that the franchisee controls or transfers of a specific percentage of the entity when the entity will be limited to operating the franchised business and all, or perhaps all significant, shareholders or members agree to be bound by the franchise agreement. Other exceptions may include transfers among owners or family members that do not shift control of the franchise.

There are numerous criteria for approval that the franchisor might impose. Some relate specifically to the transferee, including character, financial and operational capability, experience, aptitude and attitude, involvement in prohibited competitive businesses, and satisfactory completion of the franchisor's training program. Other conditions will mandate the cure of all outstanding defaults, including payment of all amounts due and submission of all outstanding reports. The terms of the sale also will be an issue. The transferee might be required to assume the selling franchisee's franchise agreement or to sign the franchisor's then current form of franchise agreement. The franchisor should require that the purchase price not be excessive in terms of the buyer's ability (or the transferred business's ability) to meet both purchase obligations and the franchisee's financial obligations. The selling parties typically subordinate the buyer's purchase obligations to the buyer's royalty and other obligations to the franchisor. Either the franchisee or the transferee must pay a transfer fee, and the assigning franchisee and its owners must agree to comply with the franchisor's noncompete and de-identification provisions. Lastly, the franchisee and its owners will be expected to sign a general release of the franchisor and its affiliates and their respective shareholders, officers, directors, and employees.

Even if these criteria are satisfied, the franchisor might exercise a right of first refusal to purchase the ownership interest or assets proposed for transfer. The right of first refusal might apply to transfers among owners and family members as well as to transfers to unaffiliated third parties. The franchisee usually must obtain a bona fide written offer, which includes all material terms of purchase, and identify the buyer. The franchisor might require the payment of earnest money so that it knows that the offer should be taken seriously. The franchise agreement will identify the time periods within which the franchisor must exercise its option and, if exercised, within which the sale must be consummated. Franchisors retain the right to substitute cash for non-cash consideration that the offeror presents or to take advantage of the same credit terms. (Not to be overlooked are several state relationship laws that affect the restrictions that a franchisor can impose on transfers.)

Termination by the Franchisor

The franchise agreement will identify numerous grounds upon which the franchisor may terminate the franchise agreement either immediately or after a cure period has expired. The franchisor may reserve the right to terminate the franchise relationship at its inception owing to the franchisee's failure to lease or purchase an acceptable business facility, develop the business facility in a timely fashion, satisfactorily complete training, or open the franchised business on a timely basis. There also will be numerous grounds for terminating the franchise agreement after the business opens. The franchisor often will reserve the right to terminate the franchise agreement immediately, without giving the franchisee an opportunity to cure the alleged default (unless otherwise required by state law), upon bankruptcy, insolvency, and similar events (although these may not be enforceable under the U.S. Bankruptcy Code); discovery of material misrepresentations; abandonment of the franchised business; loss of the right to possess the premises; understating revenue (either by a specified percentage for a minimum period or on two or more occasions); repeated breaches, whether or not cured after notice (sometimes limited to repeated breaches of the same obligation); operation of the business in an unsafe manner; assignment or transfer without the franchisor's approval; conviction by a trial court of or pleading no contest to a felony or other crime; interference with inspection rights; dishonest or unethical conduct adversely affecting the trademarks; failure to pay taxes; termination of other franchises that the franchisee has with the franchisor; unauthorized use of the licensed trademarks or disclosure of confidential information; failure to transfer the business facility and franchise agreement, or an ownership interest in the franchisee, upon the franchisee's or its managing or principal owner's death or disability; or the franchisor's withdrawal from the franchisee's market. Nonpayment of royalties, rent, amounts for purchases, and other items, as well as operational defaults not identified above, typically are curable within a ten- to thirty-day period. Nonetheless, there are almost twenty generally applicable state relationship and termination statutes that will override the franchise agreement's termination provisions and prohibit termination for one of the specified grounds or grant the franchisee a cure period (or longer cure period).

While not all franchise agreements give the franchisee a contractual right to terminate, the better practice is to include this type of provision. This provision allows the franchisee to terminate the franchise agreement if the franchisor fails to cure a material default after receiving notice of that default from the franchisee. The provision prevents the franchisee from simply declaring a breach of the franchise agreement and walking away from the relationship (which generally is the franchisee's common-law right upon a material default). It gives the franchisor an opportunity to identify and then cure or combat the alleged default. Depending on the system, the franchisee may have the right to terminate the franchise agreement at any time and with or without cause. In a few franchise systems, the franchisee may terminate the franchise agreement by paying an agreed-on amount or an amount determined by formula.

The Franchisee's Obligations upon Termination or Expiration

The franchisee normally has numerous obligations after the franchise agreement's termination or expiration. It must pay all amounts due to the franchisor, return operating manuals and other proprietary materials, surrender signs or sign faces, surrender or destroy all materials bearing the franchisor's commercial symbols, cancel all assumed or fictitious name registrations, consent to a transfer of the telephone numbers to the franchisor, and modify the business facility's appearance (which includes construction and equipment, fixture, sign, and color scheme changes).

To protect the franchisor from unwelcome and unwarranted competition, the franchisee and its owners must agree to certain noncompetition obligations. These may apply in one or more of the following circumstances: the franchisor's termination of the franchise agreement for cause, the franchisee's unilateral termination of the franchise agreement without cause, or expiration of the franchise agreement without renewal. The franchise agreement must identify the prohibited activities and relationships and their geographic and temporal scope. The franchise agreement should include a "savings" clause, wherein the parties agree in advance that a court or arbitrator may reduce the scope of the noncompetition provisions to the extent necessary to comply with applicable law, although some courts refuse to "blue pencil" (i.e., rewrite) noncompetition provisions.

Some franchisors will allow the franchisee to sell its business to a successor franchisee upon the franchisor's termination or refusal to renew the franchise agreement or upon the franchisee's death or disability. The franchise agreement will specify the time during which the franchisee will be allowed to find a buyer (with or without the franchisor's assistance). The franchise agreement may also regulate management of the business during the franchisee's attempt to sell it, or the franchisee may be allowed to manage the business as long as it complies with the franchise agreement during the interim period. The franchisor might agree to postpone payment of royalties and other amounts until closing. Allowing the franchisee to sell the business reduces the chances of litigation or arbitration and allows the franchisee to preserve the goodwill or going business value of its business. The franchisor might retain a right of first refusal on these sales as well and typically will grant a franchise to the successor franchisee on its then current terms. While the franchise agreement might regulate franchisee sales in these circumstances, the franchisor may prefer to have a flexible policy on this matter.

The Franchisor's Option to Purchase the Business

The franchisor may reserve the right to purchase the franchised business under limited circumstances, for example, upon the franchisor's termination of the franchise agreement for cause or the franchisee's unilateral termination of the franchise agreement without cause. The franchise agreement will identify the procedures that the parties must follow if the franchisor chooses to exercise this right. Foremost is determining the applicable purchase price. The franchise agreement may contain various formulas, such as a percentage or multiple of sales, profits, book value, or a combination of these factors, or it may dictate appraisals or other independent valuations.

The Franchisor's Obligations upon Termination or Expiration

The franchise agreement will not contain many provisions concerning the franchisor's obligations upon the franchise agreement's termination or expiration. The franchisor might commit to repurchase certain assets, such as "logoed" items or other materials that originally were purchased from the franchisor. State relationship and termination laws may impose certain statutory requirements on the franchisor.

Boilerplate Provisions

A substantial part of the franchise agreement contains so-called boilerplate provisions, which regulate enforcing and interpreting the franchise agreement, dispute resolution, governing law, and related matters.

The gist of the "severability" provision is to delete invalid provisions of the franchise agreement while maintaining "legal" provisions. The "waiver" provision permits the franchisor to waive unilaterally any of the franchisee's obligations. At the same time, the provision prohibits the franchisee from relying continuously on any expressly granted waiver. The waiver is limited to the particular situation and is irrelevant for future activities. The franchise agreement should declare that the franchisor's failure to enforce a particular provision against the franchisee or other franchisees—its course of conduct or dealing—is not a waiver of the franchisor's contractual rights.

The governing law section should recite that the franchise agreement will be governed by the federal arbitration (if the franchisor so decides) and trademark laws. With respect to contract interpretation and the parties' relationship, the franchise agreement might apply the law of the franchisor's domicile, the law of the franchisee's domicile, the law of the state in which the business facility is located, or another state's law. There may be state public policy limitations that restrict the enforceability of a governing law provision.

Judicial Enforcement

The franchise agreement may contain provisions concerning the state or states with jurisdiction over disputes and the venue where disputes will be resolved. The franchise agreement generally may divest courts of the franchisee's home state of jurisdiction or venue, although some states' laws prohibit such provisions. It sometimes will just confer jurisdiction and venue on courts of the franchisor's home state. The parties will reserve the right to seek or obtain temporary and permanent injunctive relief. The prevailing party typically will have the right to recover attorneys' fees and costs. There also may be waivers of jury trial and punitive damages and limitations on the time frame within which legal proceedings must commence.

Arbitration

The franchise agreement might require the parties to resolve their disputes through arbitration or mediation. Arbitration's asserted advantages are lower costs, earlier determinations, less formal and less confrontational proceedings, final and binding decisions, and no precedential effect of decisions. Asserted disadvantages include limited ability to discover the opponent's case and other important information; arbitrators tend to seek a compromise; awards are not appealable (except for gross abuse of the arbitrator's discretion); and problems in enforcing arbitration awards. While the franchise agreement may cite arbitration as the preferred dispute resolution vehicle, the franchisor might wish to except certain disputes from arbitration, including trademark and trade dress law disputes, real estate disputes, the franchisee's liquidated indebtedness, antitrust issues, and enforcement of noncompetition provisions. The franchisor might except these so that it may go into court immediately to enforce these rights and avoid having to go through the arbitration procedures. The franchisor might also wish to have a court, rather than an arbitrator, determine important contract or other rights. Whether or not the franchisor excepts certain matters from arbitration, the arbitration provision should be used concurrently with preliminary injunction rights. In other words, the franchisor and the franchisee should be able to seek temporary and preliminary injunctive relief in appropriate circumstances to preserve rights immediately threatened as long as they submit their dispute for arbitration on the merits.

The location of the arbitration proceedings often will be the location of the franchisor's principal place of business or state of operation, although state franchise registration statutes may limit these provisions as a condition of the franchisor's registration in the state. The agreement typically will specify one to three arbitrators, preferably those with franchise experience, and call for the commercial arbitration rules of the American Arbitration Association to govern. To protect its interests, the franchisor may prohibit the arbitrator from awarding exemplary damages and prohibit class arbitration or joinder of two or more arbitrations. (The latter provisions prevent franchisees from teaming up against the franchisor.)

Integration Clause

The franchise agreement should include an integration clause, which establishes that the only terms and agreements that govern the parties' relationship are contained within the four corners of the franchise agreement (and any other agreements signed simultaneously with the franchise agreement) and that there are no other franchisor promises or representations upon which the franchisee has relied. It is hoped that this will prevent the franchisee at a later date from raising promises and other statements that the franchisor allegedly made before, and as an inducement to, the franchise sale.

Relationship of the Franchisor and Franchisee

The franchise agreement will recite that the franchisor and franchisee are independent contractors, that neither party may bind the other except as expressly provided in writing, and that the franchisor will not be responsible for claims arising from the franchisee's operation of its business, including any taxes levied on the franchisee's business facility or operations. The franchise agreement will require the franchisee to indemnify the franchisor for all claims and liabilities that arise from the franchisee's operation. These claims and liabilities include actual and consequential damages, costs, attorneys' fees, and similar expenses that the franchisor incurs in defending against third-party claims that are brought against the franchisor because of its assumed "deeper pockets."

Structuring a Multiple Outlet Relationship

The relationship between the franchisor and area franchisee may be structured in a variety of ways. Both the development schedule and the territorial rights granted will vary, depending on the options granted in the franchisor-area franchisee agreement. This section describes how these provisions may be structured.

Term, Territory, and Termination

The territory may consist of either fixed or fluid boundaries subject to modifications, with rights to modify being reserved by the franchisor.

The term of the agreement may be perpetual or fixed.

Renewal rights may be conditioned on compliance with the development schedule. The parties have the flexibility to extend the development schedule, negotiate a new schedule, or revise the development rights into a lower level of commitment, such as a right of first refusal to purchase new franchises in the development area.

Development rights may include an option to develop additional territories and may include a cap on the maximum number of outlets allowed.

Fee Structure

Fees charged may include development and option fees. A fee may be charged for renewal of the agreement, and the area franchisee may receive a portion of unit franchise fees.

Development Obligations

Unit franchises may be granted through a separate franchise agreement for each franchise granted, and the terms may be fixed or variable. The area contract may provide for cross default provisions with the unit agreements. An alternate structure would combine the unit agreement with the development agreement, with each unit outlet identified in an addendum.

The area developer would typically be required to fulfill development obligations based on the number of outlets in operation or under development at the end of each agreement year. The area developer's failure to comply may result in termination of the development agreement or development rights, partial surrender of territory, or payment of unit development fees as if the development schedule had been met.

The area developer assumes certain financial and management obligations to comply with financial criteria and to develop and maintain operations management. Noncompliance with these obligations usually results in termination of the development agreement or the franchisor's refusal to grant additional franchises.

The contract should specify whether the franchisor or the developer undertakes the obligations relating to site selection and unit development.

To protect confidential system information owned by the franchisor, the developer is typically restricted from becoming involved in competing activity.

The Effects of Transfer and Termination

Transfer provisions must specify whether the developer has authority to transfer the entire development agreement or sell off partial interests through a public offering and, if so, how the transfer will affect the status of the unit franchises in the area. In many systems, the franchisor reserves a right of first refusal.

An area franchise may be terminated for a variety of reasons, including failure to comply with development obligations, termination of a unit agreement for cause, noncompliance with other obligations under the agreement, failure to cure a default (if applicable), and the death or disability of the developer.

The effect of a termination should be detailed. Unlike unit franchise agreements (where all aspects of the relationship may be severed), a developer may remain very much involved in the system through ownership of various unit operations in the area.

Dispute resolution clauses often call for arbitration or mediation.

Structuring a Subfranchise Relationship

Financial Arrangements

The franchisor controls the economics of the franchise by dictating whether a two- or three-party franchise agreement is signed. For example, a three-party franchise agreement would include all three players. Alternatively, the company may prefer that the subfranchisor not be a party and that just the franchisor and unit franchisee sign the franchise agreement. The amount of fees payable by the subfranchisor may vary. For example, there may be an increase in the percentage of the fee due the franchisor as fees payable by the subfranchisee are increased over a specified percentage or amount.

To guarantee the performance of the subfranchisor, the franchisor generally requires some type of security arrangements to be made by the subfranchisor. This may include collateral assignment of franchises, leases, or subleases; pledging stock of a leasing corporation; or personal guaranties.

The Role of the Subfranchisor

The agreements may require that a subfranchisor own and operate one or more units before it may grant unit franchises or that it operate one or more units throughout the term of the subfranchise relationship.

The subfranchisor may be required to operate its unit franchises under separate franchise agreements as a separate legal entity, making the subfranchisor a franchisee as well.

Other obligations of the subfranchisor may include the use of a prescribed form of franchise agreement, site selection and acquisition guidelines, unit development specifications, franchisee selection standards, franchisee training obligations, unit operating assistance requirements, franchisee assistance and guidance requirements, inspection and franchise agreement enforcement, and regional and local advertising and marketing.

Most subfranchise agreements include an indemnification of the franchisor by the subfranchisor. The contract should specify the areas subject to indemnification, who pays for damages and the costs of the legal defense of a covered claim, the right to select counsel for the defense, and whether the subfranchisor must provide some form of security for the indemnification.

The franchisor may have in place an advertising fund requiring monthly contributions from the subfranchisor or its franchisees based on a percentage of their revenues.

The franchisor typically reserves site approval, final franchisee approval, the right to inspect and audit operations, and the ultimate right to enforce system standards.

Registration and Disclosure

Compliance with disclosure regulations is generally the primary responsibility of the subfranchisor. Depending on the amount of involvement exhibited by the franchisor, a registration may be filed jointly or the franchisor might furnish a "form" of offering circular to the subfranchisor reserving the right to approve the subfranchisor's offering circular before use.

The allocation of fees between the franchisor and subfranchisor is detailed and may include liquidated damages for defined operational failures and the sharing of initial franchise fees and royalty fees.

Termination and Transfer of Subfranchise Rights

Transfer provisions must specify whether the subfranchisor has authority to transfer the entire subfranchise agreement or, perhaps, sell off partial interests through a public offering. If permitted, how will the transfer affect the status of the unit franchises in the area? In many systems, the franchisor reserves a right of first refusal.

A subfranchise may be terminated on a number of grounds, including failure to comply with a development schedule; failure of the subfranchisor to supervise and assist subfranchisees; failure of the subfranchisor to enforce specifications, standards, or operating procedures; termination of the franchise owned by the subfranchisor; and noncompliance with other terms or conditions of the subfranchise agreement. The agreement may call for a period in which the subfranchisor may have a minimum amount of time in which to cure certain defaults. The death or disability of the subfranchisor or its principal owner may also result in termination unless the franchise is transferred pursuant to the agreement.

If a subfranchisor is terminated or fails to renew the subfranchise agreement, the situation will require a determination of the status of the unit subfranchises. Among the options are: the unit agreements are automatically transferred to the franchisor; the franchisor retains an option to purchase the unit agreements; or the franchisor retains an option to terminate them.

CHAPTER 3

Franchise Disclosure Issues

Judith Bailey and Dennis Wieczorek

Contents

Disclosure laws have been enacted to ensure that a prospective franchisee is provided essential information about the franchise business and contract, the relationship of the parties, and the prior business experience of the franchisor. This information reduces the opportunities for fraud, helps to counterbalance any greater bargaining power of the franchisor, and allows the franchisee to make an informed investment decision based on more complete and reliable information.[1]

    1. *See, e.g.,* Chapter III of the Statement of Basis and Purpose Relating to Disclosure Requirements and Prohibitions Concerning Franchising and Business Opportunity Ventures, 43 Fed. Reg. 59,614 (1978), Bus. Franchise Guide (CCH) ¶¶ 6300 *et. seq.,* at ¶ 6305; and CAL. CORP. CODE § 31001, Bus. Franchise Guide (CCH) ¶ 3050.02 (the California legislature's statement of need in connection with the 1970 enactment of the first state franchise disclosure law).

Reasons for Disclosure and Disclosure Requirements

Business Benefits

From the franchisor's perspective, the required disclosure document can also be a sales tool that includes positive information about the franchisor and its franchise program. Furthermore, full disclosure helps prevent misunderstandings and false assumptions by a franchisee. It is to the advantage of both the franchisor and the franchisee that each makes a fully informed decision that the franchisee is qualified and capable to operate within the franchise system. Sales to uninformed or unprepared franchisees (who are "qualified" only by virtue of being able to pay the initial fee) carry tremendous risks of failure for all concerned, especially for the start-up franchisor, since the failure of a system's first franchisees may doom the franchisor as well.

Legal Requirements

The so-called FTC Rule,[2] which was adopted by the Federal Trade Commission (FTC) in 1978 and became effective in 1979, requires disclosure by franchisors and sellers of certain business opportunities before any offer or sale is made unless an exemption applies. No federal filing or registration is required.[3] The FTC Rule only preempts state disclosure laws that are inconsistent with the FTC Rule or provide less protection to prospective franchisees.[4]

More than half of the states have either general franchise[5] or business opportunity[6] laws or both. If applicable, and if no exemption exists, these laws also require disclosure before any offer or sale (either with or without prior registration, depending on the state, the parties involved, and the nature of the offering). A few states also have laws or regulations requiring disclosure before the sale of franchises in specific industries.[7]

---

2. Disclosure Requirements and Prohibitions Concerning Franchising and Business Opportunity Ventures, 16 C.F.R. pt. 436 (1979), Bus. Franchise Guide (CCH) ¶¶ 6080 *et. seq.* (hereinafter the FTC Rule).

3. FTC Rule Interpretive Guides to Franchising and Business Opportunity Ventures Trade Regulation Rule, 44 Fed. Reg. 49,966 (1979). Introduction, Bus. Franchise Guide (CCH) ¶¶ 6201 *et. seq.* (hereinafter FTC Rule Interpretive Guides).

4. FTC Rule Interpretive Guides § I.D.2, Bus. Franchise Guide (CCH) ¶ 6228.

5. Fifteen states have laws governing the offer and sale of franchises: California, Hawaii, Illinois, Indiana, Maryland, Michigan, Minnesota, New York, North Dakota, Oregon, Rhode Island, South Dakota, Virginia, Washington, and Wisconsin.

6. Laws governing the sale of business opportunities (also called seller-assisted marketing plans) exist in twenty-three states: California, Connecticut, Florida, Georgia, Indiana, Iowa, Kentucky, Louisiana, Maine, Maryland, Michigan, Minnesota, Nebraska, New Hampshire, North Carolina, Ohio, Oklahoma, South Carolina, South Dakota, Texas, Utah, Virginia, and Washington.

7. *See, e.g.,* ALASKA STAT. §§ 45.50.800 *et. seq.* (gasoline dealers); MINN. ADMIN. RULES §§ 2860.7100 *et. seq.*, Bus. Franchise Guide (CCH) ¶¶ 5230.44 *et. seq.* (hardware franchises).

Misleading disclosure, or a failure to disclose when there is a duty to do so, may also give rise to common-law actions for fraudulent misrepresentation or concealment.[8]

Exemptions

Certain transactions do not require disclosure. The FTC Rule expressly exempts from its coverage some transactions, such as employment and general partnerships,[9] based on the relationship between the parties. Others, such as fractional franchises,[10] are exempted because of the nature of the franchisee's business. Certain industries have been exempted based on an FTC determination that the application of the FTC Rule is not necessary to prevent unfair and deceptive practices.[11]

Under the FTC Rule and most state franchise laws, the sale of a franchise by a franchisee does not require disclosure by the franchisor unless the buyer has significant contacts with the franchisor or the terms of the franchise are changed materially.[12] Likewise, renewals of existing franchise agreements,[13] contract

---

8. *See, e.g.,* Williams v. Dresser Indus., Inc., 795 F. Supp. 1144 (N.D. Ga. 1992) (concealment of material fact from prospective franchisee constituted fraudulent misrepresentation where franchisor had common-law duty of disclosure based on negotiating circumstances).

9. FTC Rule at 436.2(a)(4)(i), Bus. Franchise Guide (CCH) ¶ 6165.

10. *Id.* at 436.2(a)(3)(i), Bus. Franchise Guide (CCH) ¶ 6164. A "fractional franchise" exemption is available if the franchisee or any of its directors or executive officers have been in the type of business being franchised for more than two years, and the parties reasonably anticipate that sales from the franchise will not exceed 20 percent of the franchisee's total dollar sales. *Id.* at 436.2(h), Bus. Franchise Guide (CCH) ¶ 6173. *See also* FTC Rule Interpretive Guides § I.A.3.a, Bus. Franchise Guide (CCH) ¶ 6210; ILL. REV. STAT. § 705/3(1)(ii), Bus. Franchise Guide (CCH) ¶ 3130.03; MICH. COMP. LAWS § 445.1506(1)(h), Bus. Franchise Guide (CCH) ¶ 3220.06; MINN. STAT. §§ 80C.03(f), .06(5), Bus. Franchise Guide (CCH) ¶¶ 3230.03, .06.

11. *See, e.g.,* Porsche Cars of North Am., Inc., Bus. Franchise Guide (CCH) ¶ 10,153 (FTC Order 1993).

12. FTC Rule Interpretive Guides §§ I.B.1, .2., Bus. Franchise Guide (CCH) ¶¶ 6219, 6220; CAL. CORP. CODE §§ 31102, 31119, Bus. Franchise Guide (CCH) ¶¶ 3050.26, .38; HAW. REV. STAT. § 482E-4(a)(7), Bus. Franchise Guide (CCH) ¶ 3110.04; ILL. REV. STAT. § 705/7, Bus. Franchise Guide (CCH) ¶ 3130.07; IND. CODE § 4, Bus. Franchise Guide (CCH) ¶ 3140.04; MICH. COMP. LAWS § 445.1506(1)(f), Bus. Franchise Guide (CCH) ¶ 3220.06; MINN. STAT. §§ 80C.03(a), .06(5), Bus. Franchise Guide (CCH) ¶¶ 3230.03, .06; R.I. GEN. LAWS §§ 19-28.1-6(b), -8(b), Bus. Franchise Guide (CCH) ¶¶ 3390.06, .08; and WASH. REV. CODE §§ 19.100.030(1) .080, Bus. Franchise Guide (CCH) ¶¶ 3470.03, .08.

13. FTC Rule Interpretive Guides § I.B.2, Bus. Franchise Guide (CCH) ¶ 6220. With respect to state laws, *see, e.g.,* HAW. REV. STAT. § 482E-4(a)(5), Bus. Franchise Guide (CCH) ¶ 3110.04; ILL. REV. STAT. § 705/7, Bus. Franchise Guide (CCH) ¶ 3130.07; MICH. COMP. LAWS § 445.1506(1)(e), Bus. Franchise Guide (CCH) ¶ 3220.06; OR. ADMIN. RULES § 441-325-030(2), Bus. Franchise Guide (CCH) ¶ 5370.03; and R.I. GEN. LAWS §§ 19-28.1-6(f), -8(b), Bus. Franchise Guide (CCH) ¶¶ 3390.06, .08.

amendments,[14] and the opening of additional outlets[15] generally do not require disclosure.

Liability for Failure to Disclose

Laws Imposing Liability

The FTC can impose civil penalties of up to $10,000 per violation of the FTC Rule.[16] The FTC can also require rescission, reformation, payment of refunds or damages, or combinations of these remedies,[17] and it can issue cease-and-desist orders.[18]

Currently, there is no private right of action for violations of the FTC Rule.[19] Remedies do, however, exist under state law. State franchise[20] and business opportunity[21] laws, and state consumer fraud or "little FTC acts," which typically cover the sale of franchises[22] and frequently make any violation of the FTC Rule a state law violation,[23] generally provide a private right of action for rescission, damages, costs and attorneys' fees, and sometimes multiple[24] or punitive dam-

---

14. *See, e.g.,* HAW. REV. STAT. § 482E-4(a)(5), Bus. Franchise Guide (CCH) ¶ 3110.04; ILL. REV. STAT. § 705/7, Bus. Franchise Guide (CCH) ¶ 3130.07; MICH. COMP. LAWS § 445.1506(1)(e), Bus. Franchise Guide (CCH) ¶ 3220.06; OR. ADMIN. RULES § 441-325-030(2), Bus. Franchise Guide (CCH) ¶ 5370.03; and R.I. GEN. LAWS §§ 19-28.1-6(f), -8(b), Bus. Franchise Guide (CCH) ¶¶ 3390.06, .08; *but see* CAL. CORP. CODE § 31125(b), Bus. Franchise Guide (CCH) ¶ 3050.44, requiring registration and disclosure for modifications solicited by a franchisor.

15. FTC Rule Interpretive Guides § I.B.2, Bus. Franchise Guide (CCH) ¶ 6220. With respect to state laws, *see, e.g.,* HAW. REV. STAT. § 482E-4(a)(6), Bus. Franchise Guide (CCH) ¶ 3110.04; MICH. COMP. LAWS § 445.1506(1)(g), Bus. Franchise Guide (CCH) ¶ 3220.06; N.Y. GEN. BUS. LAW § 33-684(3)(d), Bus. Franchise Guide (CCH) ¶ 3320.05; R.I. GEN. LAWS §§ 19-28.1-6(e), -8(b), Bus. Franchise Guide (CCH) ¶¶ 3390.06, .08; and WASH. REV. CODE § 19.100.030(6), Bus. Franchise Guide (CCH) ¶3470.03.

16. 15 U.S.C. § 45(m)(1).

17. 15 U.S.C. § 57(b).

18. 15 U.S.C. § 45(b).

19. Mon-Shore Management, Inc. v. Family Media, Inc., 584 F. Supp. 186, Bus. Franchise Guide (CCH) ¶ 8494 (S.D.N.Y. 1985). Over the years a number of bills have been introduced in Congress to provide for a private right of action for injunctive relief and damages for violations of the FTC Rule, and in some cases to add mandatory disclosure requirements for additional categories of information such as earnings and operating data, but none of this legislation has been enacted.

20. *See, e.g.,* CAL. CORP. CODE § 31300, Bus. Franchise Guide (CCH) ¶ 3050.60.

21. *See, e.g.,* FLA. STAT. §§ 559.813(1), (3), Bus. Franchise Guide (CCH) ¶ 3098.08.

22. *See, e.g.,* Arizona Consumer Fraud Act, ARIZ. REV. STAT. §§ 44-1521 *et. seq.*; Flower World of America, Inc. v. Wenzel, 122 Ariz. 319, 594 P.2d 1015 (Ct. App. 1979).

23. *See, e.g.,* Morgan v. Air Brook Limousine, Inc., Bus. Franchise Guide (CCH) ¶ 8560 (N.J. Super, Ct. Law Div. 1986) (violation of disclosure requirements of FTC Rule is an automatic violation of New Jersey's "little FTC act"); *but see* Symes v. Bahama Joe's, Inc., Bus. Franchise Guide (CCH) ¶ 9192 (D. Mass. August 12, 1988); LeBlanc v. Belt Center, Inc., 509 So.2d 134, Bus. Franchise Guide (CCH) ¶ 8971 (La. Ct. App. 1987).

24. *See, e.g.,* Olivetti Corp. v. Ames Business Sys., Inc., Bus. Franchise Guide (CCH) ¶ 8691 (N.C. Ct. App. 1986) (treble damages).

ages.[25] Willful violations of state laws may also result in crimir cluding fines and imprisonment.[26]

Liable Individuals

In addition to the franchisor company itself, most state laws exp joint and several liability for disclosure violations on all partners, d cipal officers, controlling persons, and employees who aid a violati sponsible for compliance.[27] The FTC has imposed liability for FTC Rule violations on the officers and directors of corporate franchisors—and has even extended restraining orders to their spouses.[28]

If a franchisor has sales brokers, subfranchisors, or area developers who sell franchises, all of them are jointly responsible for compliance with all franchise disclosure laws and all are jointly liable for any violations.[29] This can create a particularly risky situation for franchisors who do not participate in the sales activities of their subfranchisors or area developers and lack any opportunity to police such activities.

Finally, lawyers and accountants also have some risk of liability for violations of these disclosure laws. Although the general rule is that professionals are liable only to their clients, an exception is made when a lawyer or accountant prepares material upon which it is foreseeable that third parties will rely.[30]

The Disclosure Document

Document Contents

The previous section discussed the reasons for disclosure before the sale of a franchise. This section reviews the disclosure document, including the choice of format for the disclosure document, the Uniform Franchising Offering Circular Guidelines, and the use of a multistate document for such disclosures.

Regardless of its format, the disclosure document must provide a prospective franchisee with basic information about the following:

The Franchisor
    1. Its business activities and corporate family

25. Sellinger v. Freeway Mobile Home Sales, Inc., 110 Ariz. 573,521 P.2d 1119 (1974).

26. *See, e.g.*, WIS. STAT. § 553.52, Bus. Franchise Guide (CCH) ¶ 3490.16 (fines of up to $5,000 or imprisonment of up to five years or both).

27. *See, e.g.*, CAL. CORP. CODE § 31302, Bus. Franchise Guide (CCH) ¶ 3050.62.

28. *See, e.g.*, Bus. Franchise Guide (CCH) ¶ 9999 (report on court order approving amended FTC complaint naming wives as defendants and extending asset freeze to them).

29. FTC Rule Interpretive Guides § I.B.1, Bus. Franchise Guide (CCH) ¶ 6219.

30. *See, e.g.*, Courtney v. Waring, 237 Cal. Rptr. 233 (Cal. Ct. App. 1987) (attorney liable to franchisees for legal malpractice for negligent preparation of offering circular; the defendant was an officer and director of the franchisor, but that fact was not relied upon in the decision).

2. Background of its officers and directors
3. Litigation history of the company, directors, and officers
4. Bankruptcy history of the franchisor and certain individuals
5. Financial statements.

The Franchised Business
1. The franchisee's initial investment
2. Source-restricted purchases or leases
3. Financing and other services provided by the franchisor
4. Advertising programs
5. Trademarks, patents, and copyrights
6. Restrictions on the franchisee's sales of products or services
7. Information about existing and former franchisees
8. Site selection
9. Training programs
10. Optional earnings claims.

The Franchise Agreement
1. Initial and ongoing fees
2. Territorial rights
3. Requirements that the franchisee be personally involved in the business
4. Term of the franchise and renewal rights
5. Termination of the franchise
6. Repurchase of the franchise by the franchisor
7. Transfer
8. Death or disability of the franchisee
9. Covenants not to compete.

Electing the FTC Rule or UFOC Format

Disclosure documents must be prepared in conformity with either the FTC Rule[31] or the Uniform Franchise Offering Circular (UFOC) Guidelines developed by the North American Securities Administrator's Association (NASAA).[32] The FTC Rule and UFOC format circulars cover similar categories of information, but there are material differences in the degree of detail and types of information required. Although each of these formats has certain advantages and disadvantages from a disclosure perspective, the decision about which format to use often is influenced by the geographic areas in which the franchisor wishes to sell its franchises. Also, a UFOC format circular that is registered[33] with a state agency regulating franchising carries a rebuttable presumption of "sufficiency, adequacy, and

---

31. 16 C.F.R. pt. 436 (1979), Bus. Franchise Guide (CCH) ¶¶ 6080 *et. seq.*
32. On April 25, 1993, NASAA, after public comment periods, hearings, and much debate, unanimously approved revised UFOC Guidelines. Bus. Franchise Guide (CCH) ¶¶ 5900-5932.

accuracy,"[34] while an FTC Rule format circular, unless registered in a particular state, does not carry such a presumption.

Where the FTC Rule and the UFOC Format Can Be Used

The FTC Rule format circular can be used in all states that do not have franchise registration or disclosure statutes. An FTC Rule format circular will not be accepted for registration by state agencies in states that have adopted their own disclosure and registration requirements (except in Hawaii, Illinois, Indiana, Michigan, New York, North Dakota, and Wisconsin). Even in the seven "registration" states that accept disclosure documents prepared under the FTC Rule, state administrators may require substantial revisions to the offering circular, thereby nullifying many of the disclosure advantages of the FTC Rule format. Practically speaking, a franchisor must use the UFOC format to sell franchises in the states with registration or disclosure statutes and, having done so, would incur substantial cost to prepare a second format disclosure document for use elsewhere.

A UFOC format circular with minor modifications can be used to offer and sell franchises in all states. Although all of the registration states accept the basic disclosure UFOC format, some states also may require the franchisor to make extra or special disclosures, either in the offering circular itself or in an addendum to the offering circular.

The FTC Rule acknowledges that disclosures required under the UFOC format provide equal or greater protection to a prospective franchisee than do the disclosures required under the FTC Rule. Therefore, the FTC Rule allows the UFOC format to be used in lieu of the FTC Rule format, even if the UFOC format circular has not yet been registered in any state requiring registration.[35]

Considerations in Electing a Format

The main advantage of initially selecting the UFOC format is that there is no subsequent need to deal with two separate formats or to change to another format when the decision is made to offer and sell franchises in certain registration or disclosure states. Because use of the UFOC format satisfies the requirements of the FTC Rule, all other factors being equal, it would be the format of choice. There may be good reasons to select either an FTC Rule or UFOC format depending on the type of disclosures each requires, the nature of the franchisor's business concept and history, and the franchisor's expansion plans. Generally speaking, the UFOC format requires more detail on a greater range of subjects than does the FTC Rule format. The FTC Rule format requires lists of all designated and approved suppliers. This alone may render the format unacceptable to some franchisors, but it is the principal area where more information is required than under the UFOC format. Other factors, such as the phase-in of audited financial statements and somewhat less onerous disclosure requirements relating to advertising and training programs, bankruptcy and litigation history, computer sys-

33. *See* Chapter 4 for a discussion of registration of a franchise.
34. *See* FTC Rule Interpretive Guides, Bus. Franchise Guide (CCH) ¶ 6227.
35. *Id.*

tems, and franchise terminations, may influence a start-up franchisor to consider using an FTC Rule format offering circular.

The franchisor cannot pick and choose between sections of the formats in a single offering circular. A disclosure document must follow one format or the other in its entirety. Since the overwhelming majority of franchisors choose to prepare disclosure documents pursuant to the UFOC Guidelines, these guidelines will be reviewed in the next section.

UFOC Guidelines

The UFOC Guidelines consist of the disclosure requirements, specific instructions, and sample answers for twenty-three separate items. In addition to the UFOC Guidelines, the NASAA Franchise and Business Opportunities Committee promulgated a commentary on the UFOC, dated June 21, 1994,[36] to clarify and provide interpretations of specific provisions of the UFOC Guidelines. This article is not a substitute for careful review of the UFOC Guidelines and the UFOC Commentary, but merely a summary of each item.

General Instructions and Cover Page

The general instructions to the UFOC Guidelines require that all offering circulars be written in plain English, avoiding legal antiques and repetitive phrases, with a stated preference for the active voice over the passive voice. The general instructions contain numerous examples of the types of phrases and words that should be avoided. Franchise examiners in various states strictly enforce the plain English mandate and have summarily rejected UFOCs for failure to comply with this requirement even if the franchisor makes the required substantive disclosures.

Ancillary documents, such as operations manuals, which are not included in the UFOC, must not make any representations or impose conditions that contradict or are materially different from the information disclosed in the UFOC. Franchisors must carefully review all these documents and materials to ensure that no such contradictions or differences exist, or they must make the appropriate revisions to these other documents.

The general instructions provide that a single offering circular may be used for the registration of both single-unit and multiunit franchises if the UFOC is not confusing. However, the UFOC Guidelines do not specify the disclosures required with respect to a franchisor and a subfranchisor in the various items. State policies (which sometimes are not published) generally determine the scope of such disclosure.

The cover page to the UFOC must contain certain identifying information, a brief description of the franchised business, the franchisee's initial franchise fee, and the franchisee's initial investment. The cover page must also disclose certain risk factors, using specified language in boldface type, with respect to choice-of-

---

36. Bus. Franchise Guide (CCH) ¶ 5950 (hereinafter the UFOC Commentary).

law and forum selection clauses in the franchise agreement. State regulators can require disclosure of additional risk factors at their sole discretion. The cover page must contain additional required language, but many of the warning legends and disclaimers (mandated in prior UFOC formats) have been moved to Item 23, the offering circular receipt.

Item 1: The Franchisor, Its Predecessors, and Affiliates

Continuing the plain English requirement in the general instructions, the word "we," initials, or one or two words must define the franchisor, while the word "you" must define the franchisee throughout the UFOC.

The UFOC Guidelines require disclosure of basic identifying information regarding the franchisor and its predecessors[37] and affiliates,[38] the prior business experience (including franchising activities) of the franchisor and its predecessors and affiliates, and its agent for service of process. The franchisor must also describe its business and the franchises it offers, along with information regarding the general market for the product or service the franchisee will offer. In addition, it must disclose, in general terms, any regulations specific to the industry in which the franchise business operates. It is not necessary, however, to include laws or regulations that apply to businesses generally, such as child labor laws, even if these laws disproportionately affect the franchised business.[39]

Item 2: Business Experience

The franchisor must disclose a list of the names and positions of the directors, the trustees and general partners, the principal officers, and other executives or subfranchisors who have management responsibility relating to the franchises offered, along with each person's principal occupations and employers during the preceding five years. Item 2 also requires disclosure regarding a corporation serving as a franchise broker and its directors, principal officers, and executives with management responsibility to market and service franchises sold.

---

37. Defined as "a person from whom the franchisor acquired directly or indirectly a major portion of the franchisor's assets."

38. The term "affiliate" has different definitions throughout the UFOC. In all cases, as a beginning point, an affiliate is a "person (other than a natural person) controlled by, controlling, or under common control with the franchisor." For purposes of Item 1, disclosure covers only an affiliate that is "offering franchises in any line of business or is providing products or services to the franchisees of the franchisor." For purposes of Item 3, the term "affiliate" covers only those affiliates that offer franchises under the franchisor's principal mark. For all other purposes throughout the UFOC, franchisors must employ the basic definition (i.e., a person (other than a natural person) controlled by, controlling, or under common control with the franchisor), but disclosure is required only if the affiliate has a bankruptcy history (Item 4); provides products, services, or financing to franchisees or receives rebates for their purchases (Items 5, 6, 8, and 10); or competes or may compete with franchisees by operating similar outlets or offering similar products or services (Items 12 and 20). *See* UFOC Commentary Issue #7.

39. UFOC Commentary Issue #8.

Item 3: Litigation

The litigation history of the franchisor and persons listed in Item 2 must be disclosed, as must litigation involving the franchisor's predecessors and any affiliates offering franchises under the franchisor's principal trademark. In addition to pending actions, the disclosure must cover actions concluded in the past ten years. The enumerated list of disclosable claims includes administrative, criminal, and material civil actions alleging violation of a franchise; antitrust, or securities law; fraud; unfair or deceptive practices; or comparable allegations. The franchisor need not disclose ordinary routine litigation incidental to the business (e.g., slip and fall, employment, or similar cases). However, any pending material actions[40] (with materiality determined by reference to the number of franchisees or the size, nature, or financial condition of the system or its operations), regardless of whether such actions involve any of the enumerated types of claims, must be disclosed. A franchisor must carefully evaluate the nature and potential impact of such claims and, when in doubt, provide such disclosure. In addition, a settlement of any of these actions in which the franchisor agrees to pay material consideration or agrees to be bound by obligations materially adverse to its interests must be disclosed, whether or not the settlement is confidential.[41]

Item 4: Bankruptcy

The bankruptcy histories of the franchisor and its affiliates, predecessors, officers, and general partners during the ten-year period immediately preceding the date of the offering circular must be disclosed. This requirement also covers situations in which the franchisor's officer was a principal officer of another company during the period that it filed for bankruptcy protection. The triggering event for this disclosure is the filing of a petition, either on a voluntary or involuntary basis, under the U.S. Bankruptcy Code, or obtaining a discharge of debts under the U.S. Bankruptcy Code. Actions under the laws of foreign nations in the nature of bankruptcy proceedings must also be included.

Item 5: Initial Franchise Fee

The franchisor is required to disclose its initial fee, which includes all fees and payments for services or goods received from the franchisor before the franchisee's business opens, and the conditions, if any, under which this fee is refundable. Thus, in addition to the standard initial franchise fee charged by the franchisor, it must disclose information on a variety of initial payments to the franchisor and its affiliates, including payments for inventory, software license fees, grand opening payments, and similar amounts paid or incurred before the

---

40. "Actions" include complaints, cross-claims, counterclaims, third-party complaints, and the like along with any claim made in arbitration. The definition also includes foreign litigation. *See* UFOC Commentary Issue #12.

41. UFOC Commentary Issue #9. However, the UFOC Commentary also states that disclosure of confidential settlements is not required for those entered into before April 25, 1993, the date of NASAA's approval of the revised UFOC Guidelines.

franchisee's opening. If the initial fee is not uniform, the formula or the range of the initial fee paid in the previous fiscal year and the factors that determined the amount must be disclosed.

Item 6: Other Fees

Other recurring or isolated fees or payments that the franchisee must pay to the franchisor or its affiliates, or that the franchisor or its affiliates impose or collect on behalf of a third party, must be disclosed in tabular form. The headings for the table's columns include the name or type of the fee, the amount, the due date, and remarks to elaborate on information or to disclose caveats. The formula used to compute these other fees and payments and the conditions, if any, under which each fee or payment is refundable also must be disclosed.

With regard to advertising cooperatives, the franchisor must disclose the voting power of franchisor-owned outlets over any fees imposed by such cooperatives and a range for the fees if franchisor-owned outlets have controlling voting power.

Item 7: Initial Investment

Item 7 requires the franchisor to disclose, in chart form, five specific categories of initial expenditures and any other payments that the franchisee must make to begin operations. The five categories are: (1) real property (if the expenditure for real property is neither estimable nor describable by a low-high range, the franchisor may describe its requirements, such as the property type, location, and building size); (2) equipment, fixtures, other fixed assets, construction, remodeling, leasehold improvements, and decorating costs; (3) inventory required to begin operations; (4) security deposits, utility deposits, business licenses, and other prepaid expenses; and (5) additional funds required by the franchisee before operations begin and during the initial phase of the franchise business. This additional funds entry is intended to disclose all costs necessary to begin and maintain operation of the franchise for at least three months or during a different start-up period that is reasonable for the particular industry involved. Because the duration of the initial phase may vary from industry to industry, the franchisor must disclose the length of the initial phase.[42] Item 7 also requires the franchisor to describe, in general terms, the factors, basis, and experience that the franchisor relied on in arriving at the amount required for the additional funds. The disclosures in Item 7 must be in chart form and include information regarding to whom the payments are made, when the payments are due, the refundability of each payment, and whether a portion of the initial investment may be financed.

---

42. *See* UFOC Commentary Issue #15. The Commentary indicates that, in most cases, only the additional funds line item need cover the initial phase period. It may be appropriate to include real estate costs during the initial phase, and possibly royalties and other fees (if earnings claims problems can be avoided). All other line items in Item 7 are intended to include expenses only through the opening date.

Item 8: Restrictions on Sources of Products and Services

Item 8 must provide the prospective franchisee with information regarding its obligations to purchase or lease from the franchisor, the franchisor's designee, or suppliers the franchisor approves or whose goods or services meet the franchisor's specifications. In addition, the categories of goods and services for which the franchisor (or its affiliates) are approved or the only approved suppliers must be disclosed. The UFOC Guidelines also require disclosure of the estimated proportion of all source-restricted purchases and leases to all purchases and leases by the franchisee of goods and services in establishing and operating the franchise.

The franchisor must disclose significant information concerning its financial interest in the purchases or leases made by franchisees and reveal the extent to which it relies on the franchisees' purchases as a source of revenue. The franchisor must report its total revenues and the portion of those revenues represented by sales or leases to franchisees. Sales or leases to franchisees by the franchisor's affiliates also must be disclosed.

The franchisor must disclose the existence of purchasing or distribution cooperatives and describe how it issues specifications and approves suppliers. Item 8 must indicate whether the franchisor negotiates purchase arrangements with suppliers for its franchisees and whether franchisees are rewarded with material benefits for patronizing certain suppliers. The franchisor must also disclose rebates and other considerations (expressed as a dollar amount or as a percentage of purchases) that it receives from all third-party, unaffiliated suppliers as a result of transactions with franchisees.

Item 9: Franchisee's Obligations

The disclosure required under Item 9 consists of a tabular listing of the franchisee's principal obligations under the franchise agreement and other agreements with cross-references to such agreements and to the items in the UFOC that disclose such obligations. The twenty-four obligations that require disclosure are specified and the franchisor may not change the heading for any obligation. The franchisor may add additional obligations it deems important to the franchise.

Item 10: Financing

The franchisor must disclose the terms and conditions of each financing arrangement (including franchisor guaranties of franchisee notes or leases) that the franchisor, its agents, or affiliates offer directly or indirectly to the franchisee. An indirect offer of financing includes a written arrangement between a franchisor or its affiliate and a lender for the lender to offer financing to the franchisee or an arrangement in which the franchisor or its affiliate receives benefits from the lender from franchisee financing. Item 10 must include information about the franchisee's potential liabilities upon default, including any accelerated obligation to pay the entire amount due, payment of court costs and attorney's fees for collection, waivers of defenses, and potential termination of the franchise.

The franchisor may, but is not required to, summarize the terms of each financing arrangement in tabular form, using footnotes to provide additional required information not included in the chart. Specimen copies of each financing document must be attached to the UFOC as an exhibit and referenced by section in the narrative disclosure.

Item 11: Franchisor's Obligations

Item 11 is typically one of the more lengthy items in a franchisor's offering circular because it requires disclosure of a wide range of information. Generally, the franchisor must disclose all obligations that it is bound to perform before and during the operation of the franchise business.

Disclosure regarding the franchisor's advertising programs is also required. Among other information, the franchisor must disclose the media that may be used for its advertising programs; the scope of its dissemination; the source of the advertising; the conditions under which franchisees may use their own advertising material; details regarding the operation and governance of any advertising advisory council, advertising cooperative, or advertising fund; and the amounts the franchisor is required to spend on advertising in the franchisee's area. With respect to advertising funds, the franchisor must indicate the percentages spent on media placement, production, administration, and other costs.

Recognizing that computers play an increasing role in franchised businesses, Item 11 requires the franchisor to provide detailed information about any required computer or electronic cash register systems in nontechnical language, including information on hardware components and software programs, the purpose and intended use of such hardware and software, maintenance and upgrades, the availability of substitutes, and the franchisor's access to the franchisee's data.

The franchisor must disclose the table of contents of the operations manual along with the corresponding number of pages per section of the manual or allow the prospective franchisee to view the manual before purchasing the franchise. If the franchisor chooses to allow the prospective franchisee to view the manual, it may require the prospective franchisee to execute a confidentiality agreement to prohibit the dissemination of confidential information contained in the manual. Franchisors should be aware, however, that such an agreement will be treated like a franchise agreement for purposes of disclosure delivery rules, and the franchisee must have had the UFOC for ten business days before executing the confidentiality agreement.[43]

The franchisor must also disclose information concerning the methods it uses to select or approve the location of the franchisee's business as well as the typical length of time between signing the franchise agreement or the first payment of consideration for the franchise and the opening of the franchisee's business.

In a tabular format, the franchisor must disclose detailed information regarding its training program, including the subjects taught during initial training, the time when training begins, what instructional materials are used, how many

---

43. *See* UFOC Commentary Issue #25.

hours of classroom and on-the-job training are required, and the experience of the instructors for each course.

Item 12: Territory

The franchisor must describe the franchisee's rights with respect to any territory granted pursuant to the franchise agreement, including any exclusive territory, and the franchisee's right to relocate or establish additional outlets. The franchisor must also disclose whether other franchised or franchisor-owned outlets may be opened in the franchisee's area. Disclosure of whether the franchisor or its affiliates may establish other channels of distribution, including sales in supermarkets, by mail order, or any other method, using the franchisor's trademarks is required.

The franchisor must provide extensive disclosure as to whether it or its affiliates operate or franchise, or have any plans to operate or franchise, a business under a different trademark where the business sells products or services similar to those offered in the franchisee's business. In particular, the franchisor must provide various information about the competitive program and describe how conflicts between franchisees of each system regarding the territory, customers, or franchisor support will be resolved.

Item 13: Trademarks

Item 13 requires a list of the principal trademarks to be licensed to the franchisee. If the franchisor does not have a federally registered trademark, a specific disclaimer, which warns the franchisee that without such a registration the franchisor does not have certain presumptive legal rights granted by such a registration, must be included in this item. Material agreements, litigation, and infringement, opposition, or cancellation proceedings with respect to the principal trademarks also must be disclosed.

Item 14: Patents, Copyrights, and Proprietary Information

The franchisor must describe any rights it owns in any patents or copyrights that are material to the franchise and the relationship of such rights to the franchise. If the franchisor claims proprietary rights in confidential information or trade secrets, their general subject matter and the terms for use by the franchisee must be disclosed. Material agreements, litigation, and infringement, opposition, or cancellation proceedings with respect to material patents or copyrights also must be disclosed.

Item 15: Obligations to Participate in the Actual Operation of the Franchise Business

Disclosure of the franchisee's obligations to participate personally in the business, whether they arise from a written agreement, the franchisor's practice, or other documents, is required. The restrictions that the franchisee must place on its manager, and any agreements or guaranties to be signed by the owners or managers, must be described.

Item 16: Restrictions on What the Franchisee May Sell

Restrictions or conditions the franchisor imposes regarding the goods or services that the franchisee may sell, and the customers to whom the franchisee may sell goods or services, must be disclosed. The franchisor must specifically indicate whether it has the right to change the types of approved goods or services and whether there are limits on its right to make such changes.

Item 17: Renewal, Termination, Transfer, and Dispute Resolution

A tabular format must be used to summarize and cross-reference certain important provisions of the franchise agreement. The table must have three headings: "Provision," "Section in Franchise Agreement," and "Summary" and must cover twenty-three categories of information. These categories include subjects relating to term, termination, transfer, rights of first refusal, purchase options, death or disability, noncompetition covenants, integration or merger clauses, dispute resolution by arbitration or mediation, choice of forum, and choice of law, along with a concise summary of such provisions.

A separate table should describe the provisions of any other significant franchise-related documents. Since the UFOC Guidelines do not provide direction as to the scope of this requirement, the franchisor may be required to create separate tables describing provisions of area agreements, preliminary agreements, leases, and other agreements entered into with the franchisor.

Item 18: Public Figures

This item requires disclosure about public figures used in the franchise name or symbol, public figures used in selling franchises to franchisees, such public figures' compensation or other benefits, and such public figures' total investment in the franchisor.

Item 19: Earnings Claims

A franchisor may choose whether or not to make an "earnings claim," which encompasses any information regarding sales, costs, income, or profits of a franchise. Any earnings claim made in connection with an offer of a franchise must be included in full and must have a reasonable basis at the time it is made. An earnings claim must include a description of its factual basis and the material assumptions underlying its preparation and presentation. If no earnings claim is made, the franchisor must recite a required negative disclosure in this item. In 1994 NASAA began discussing the possibility of mandating some form of earnings claim presentation.

Item 20: List of Outlets

The franchisor must disclose information regarding the size of its system. In tabular format, the franchisor must disclose, on a state-by-state basis, as of the close of each of the past three fiscal years, the number of franchised and franchisor-owned outlets in operation. The table must list the number of franchised outlets that have transferred controlling ownership, have been canceled or terminated by the franchisor, have not been renewed by the franchisor, have been reacquired by the franchisor, or have been reasonably known by the franchisor to have otherwise ceased to do business in the system. A projection of the number of franchises to be sold (and franchisor-owned outlets to be opened) during the one-year period following the close of the franchisor's most recent fiscal year also must be provided on a state-by-state basis.

The franchisor must list the names of all franchisees and the addresses and telephone numbers of all their outlets. (Alternatively, the franchisor may limit the information to the state where the franchise is being offered, but if there are less than one hundred outlets in the state, the franchisor must list outlets from all contiguous states, and then the next closest state(s) until at least 100 are listed.) The franchisor must also provide the name and last known home address and telephone number of every franchisee who has been or had an outlet terminated, canceled, not renewed, or otherwise voluntarily or involuntarily ceased to do business under the franchise agreement during the most recently completed fiscal year, or who has not communicated with the franchisor within the preceding ten weeks.

Item 21: Financial Statements

The franchisor must include audited balance sheets for its past two fiscal years and statements of operations, stockholders' equity, and cash flows for the past three fiscal years, in a format of columns that compares at least two fiscal years. If a franchisor files any registration application more than ninety days after its fiscal year ends, it must submit current unaudited financial statements. Audited financial statements of an affiliate of the franchisor are acceptable in lieu of an audit of the franchisor's statements if they are accompanied by the affiliate's guarantee of the performance of the franchisor.

Item 22: Contracts

All agreements proposed for use regarding the offering of the franchise, including the franchise agreement, leases, options, and purchase agreements, must be listed in Item 22 and attached as exhibits to the offering circular.

Item 23: Receipt

The last page of the UFOC is a detachable document acknowledging receipt of the offering circular by the prospective franchisee. It must be in boldface type and include a recitation of the FTC Rule requirements regarding document delivery. It must also contain a paragraph stating that if the franchisor fails to deliver the UFOC on time or if the UFOC contains false or misleading information, the franchisor may have violated state and federal law and should be reported to the FTC or state regulator. Two copies of the receipt must appear in the circular: one to be retained by the franchisee and one to be returned to the franchisor.

Multistate Document

Both the FTC Rule and state laws require disclosure of state-specific information. It is possible to have a separate document for each state, to combine the disclo-

sures for a number of states into a single document, or to combin
for all states into a single document. Franchisors may choos
documents for each registration state (because of required an
changes) and a single document for non-registration states. In any ca
sential to include all the information a particular state requires when ofte
sell franchises in that state.

The UFOC Guidelines now recognize and, in some instances, facilitate the
use of a single circular in all states. A multistate document will require the use of
state riders to the franchise agreement and state addenda to the offering circular
to incorporate state-specific comments. The disadvantages to preparing a single
UFOC are that franchisors must disclose all the information that any state requires to all prospective franchisees and it may be confusing to determine exactly
which rider(s) must be signed. The benefits to preparing a single UFOC are that
the franchisor need not send multiple UFOCs to a prospective franchisee, the
chance of the franchisor's staff mistakenly providing a prospective franchisee
with the wrong circular is reduced, and it is easier to work with one document
instead of many.

In December 1990 the NASAA Franchise and Business Opportunities Committee completed its State Specific Project.[44] The project provides a centralized source
for much of the information (e.g., filing fees, number and type of copies, agent for
service of process) that is required of franchisors for various types of filings. Parts 3
through 6 of the project contain standard language relating to certain specific disclosure items, such as renewal and termination rights, post-term covenants not to compete, termination upon bankruptcy, and liquidated damages provisions.

The Disclosure Process

Timing

The FTC Rule requires that the disclosure document, with copies of the forms of all
franchise agreements and financing documents and the franchisor's financial statements, be given to a prospective franchisee at the earlier of the first personal face-to-
face meeting held for the purpose of discussing the possible sale of a franchise or ten
business days before the execution of any binding documents or the franchisee's
payment of any consideration.[45] State laws have similar requirements.[46] In addition,
copies of all the agreements to be executed, completed except for signatures, must be
given to a prospect at least five business days before their execution.[47]

---

44. Appendix B-1 to the UFOC Guidelines, Bus. Franchise Guide (CCH) ¶ 5826.
45. FTC Rule §§ 436.1(a), 436.2(g), and 436.2(o), Bus. Franchise Guide (CCH) ¶¶
6100, 6172, and 6183.
46. *See, e.g.,* ILL. REV. STAT. § 705/5(2), Bus. Franchise Guide (CCH) ¶ 3130.05.
47. FTC Rule § 436.1(g), Bus. Franchise Guide (CCH) ¶ 6149.

Multiple State Disclosure

Depending on the particular laws of each state, disclosure laws can be triggered if any one or more of the following occur within a state:[48]

1. The prospect is a state resident
2. The offer originates from the state
3. The offer is received in the state
4. Meetings between the franchisor and prospective franchisee occur in the state
5. The offer is accepted in the state
6. The franchised business will be operated in the state
7. The franchise territory is entirely or partially in the state.

If the laws of more than one state apply, it may be necessary (unless exemptions exist)[49] to provide a prospect with disclosure documents for each state whose laws apply.[50] If one or more of the states is a registration state, it is possible that the offering circulars will differ.

Policing the Process

The franchisor should obtain receipts for the delivery of the disclosure document, any addenda, and the FTC Earnings Claim Document (if used) and should also obtain receipts for delivery of the completed execution copies of the agreements. Such receipts will be needed in the event of future disputes regarding delivery dates. In addition, one state, Illinois, requires that photocopies of the receipts for delivery of the offering circular for each franchise sold be filed with the franchisor's annual renewal application.[51]

It is also important to be sure that disclosure materials are delivered to the right people: each individual franchisee, a principal officer of a corporate franchisee, the managing general partner of a partnership, or the manager of a limited-liability company.[52]

In addition to obtaining receipts, a franchisor may want to verify sales procedures and the timing of disclosures and deliveries before closing a franchise sale. A few franchisors videotape interviews with prospective franchisees, while most rely on oral interviews, with or without some form of written certificate. Whatever the format, the following points should be covered:

---

48. *See, e.g.,* CAL. CORP. CODE § 31013, Bus. Franchise Guide (CCH) ¶ 3050.15.

49. *See, e.g.,* CAL. ADMIN. RULE § 310.100.1, Bus. Franchise Guide (CCH) ¶ 5050.07.

50. For a case in which the disclosure laws of California, Maryland, and Virginia and the FTC Rule all applied, see Dollar Systems, Inc. v. Avcar Leasing Systems, Inc., Bus. Franchise Guide (CCH) ¶ 8954 (C.D. Cal. 1987).

51. ILL. ADMIN. RULE § 200.603(a)(2), Bus. Franchise Guide (CCH) ¶ 5130.45.

52. *See, e.g.,* ILL. REV. STAT. § 705/5(2), Bus. Franchise Guide (CCH) ¶ 3130.05.

1. The date the disclosure document was received by the prospect
2. The date each addendum to the disclosure document was received
3. The date of the first face-to-face meeting with a representative of the franchisor, who should be identified
4. The date completed copies of all agreements to be executed were received by the prospect
5. The date that the first agreement was signed by the prospect
6. The earliest date a check, cash, or other consideration was delivered by the prospect to a representative of the franchisor, and the name of that individual.

In addition to confirming the disclosure schedule, it is important to confirm that no oral, written, or visual claim or representation was made to calculate, state, or suggest any sales, income, or profit levels if the disclosure document does not contain earnings claims. Alternatively, if the franchisor's disclosure document does contain earnings claims, the prospect should be asked to confirm that no oral, written, or visual claim or representation was made that contradicted the disclosure document.

Unfortunately, there are no quick or easy ways to correct disclosure violations. The FTC Rule has no "cure" provisions, and neither do most state laws. Except in states like California, where certain violations can be cured by providing franchisees with a written notice preapproved by the state,[53] franchisors must rely on common-law settlements and releases, obtained after adequate disclosure and for consideration, to "cure" violations.[54]

Changes to the Disclosure Document

Annual Updates

Disclosure documents must be updated completely on at least an annual basis. In registration states, renewals (or amendments or annual reports in states having indefinite registrations) are typically required within 90 to 120 days after the franchisor's fiscal year-end.[55] Under the FTC Rule, if the franchisor is using a disclosure document in non-registration states and that document is currently regis-

---

53. CAL. CORP. CODE § 31303, Bus. Franchise Guide (CCH) ¶ 3050.64.

54. *See* MICH. COMP. LAWS § 445.1527(b), Bus. Franchise Guide (CCH) ¶ 3220.27. Advance waivers are illegal and void under most franchise laws. *See, e.g., id.,* and N.Y. GEN. BUS. LAW §§ 687.3, .4, Bus. Franchise Guide (CCH) ¶ 3320.08.

55. *See, e.g.,* CAL. CORP. CODE § 31121, Bus. Franchise Guide (CCH) ¶ 3050.40, and CAL. ADMIN. RULE § 310.120, Bus. Franchise Guide (CCH) ¶ 5050.25 (registration expires 110 days after franchisor's fiscal year-end, and renewal application must be filed 15 business days before expiration, or approximately 100 days after fiscal year-end); MINN. STAT. § 80C.08(1), Bus. Franchise Guide (CCH) ¶ 3230.08 (annual report due within 120 days of franchisor's fiscal year-end).

tered in at least one of the registration states, then the document can be updated as required by the registration state. If, however, a disclosure document is used in non-registration states and is not registered in at least one registration state, the document must be updated within 90 days of the franchisor's fiscal year-end. In that case, if the updated disclosure document is not available for use at the end of the 90-day period, the franchisor's sales activities must stop.[56]

Wise franchisors begin preparing to obtain audited financial statements early. Failure to get audited financial statements on time is one of the most frequent causes for late updating and renewal. As part of the overall process for annual updating, franchisors should consider problems that arose and program and contract changes that were suggested in the prior year. Franchisors, and those in charge of key franchisor operations, should reread the entire disclosure document for updates, inaccuracies, and inconsistencies. In particular, initial investment estimates should be verified against the recent experiences of franchisees and the costs for opening company outlets; earnings claims should be updated to reflect current data; and all contract amendments and letters of clarification should be reviewed to determine if the contract or disclosure document should be revised or a form amendment should be included. Finally, the franchisor should consider whether there are other possible issues beyond the required categories of disclosures that could be material to the prospective franchisee's investment decision and need to be included in the disclosure document.[57] Examples of such issues may include a contemplated sale of the franchisor or a major marketing shift.

Interim Amendments for Material Changes

The FTC Rule definition of a material change is analogous to the traditional securities law definition: anything with a substantial likelihood of influencing a reasonable prospective franchisee in making a significant decision relating to the franchise or having a significant financial impact.[58] State law definitions generally contain the same broad concept,[59] but many also specify nonexclusive lists of defined occurrences that constitute material changes.[60] In the case of a small or start-up franchisor, small changes may well be material. Common examples of involuntary changes include personnel resignations, new litigation or developments in existing litigation, a financial decline, and the loss of franchisees. Typi-

---

56. FTC Rule Interpretive Guides, § I.D.1.c, Bus. Franchise Guide (CCH) ¶ 6227.

57. *See, e.g.,* Noble v. C.E.D.O., Inc., Bus. Franchise Guide (CCH) ¶ 8429 (Minn. Ct. App. 1985).

58. FTC Rule Interpretive Guides § I.F.1, Bus. Franchise Guide (CCH) ¶ 6231.

59. *See, e.g.,* N.D. CENT. CODE § 51-19-11.2(b), Bus. Franchise Guide (CCH) ¶ 3340.11.

60. *See, e.g.,* MD. REGS. CODE tit. 02, § 01.01.10.01B(1), Bus. Franchise Guide (CCH) ¶ 5200.01 (the termination or failure within three months of the greater of 1 percent or five franchisees regardless of location or the lesser of 15 percent or two franchisees in Maryland); N.Y. ADMIN. RULE § 200.5(b)(4)(v), Bus. Franchise Guide (CCH) ¶ 5320.05 (a 5 percent or greater change in net profits or losses in any six-month period).

cal voluntary changes include contract, fee, or program changes and the addition of new personnel.

Negotiated Changes

Item 5 of the offering circular specifically requires disclosure of any variation in initial fees that the franchisor is willing to negotiate or has negotiated in the previous fiscal year. A franchisor's general willingness to negotiate any other provision of its agreements also must be disclosed in the offering circular. This requirement is founded on the fundamental premise of all franchise disclosure laws that all prospective franchisees be fully informed, treated equally, and have the same opportunities without regard to their individual bargaining power if they are similarly situated.[61]

State law on the subject of negotiated changes has varied to extremes. Under Virginia law, a franchisee has the option for a brief period of voiding the franchise if not given the opportunity to negotiate all provisions other than uniform image and quality standards.[62] Conversely, some state regulators historically have taken the position that a franchisor can sell only the agreement that is registered. For example, before 1989, California did not permit negotiated changes, although California regulations now permit negotiated changes in certain limited situations.[63] New York also prohibited negotiated changes until a court ruled in 1990 that New York's franchise registration law does not prohibit negotiated changes to the registered form of agreements.[64]

Finally, six states have franchise laws that prohibit discrimination among franchisees, with certain exceptions and qualifications.[65] In these states, when a concession is made to one franchisee, it may need to be offered to others, both existing and prospective, unless there is a material time lapse or some justifiable reason for treating them differently.

Franchisors can avoid (or at least minimize) both the legal and practical problems of negotiated agreements by attempting to accommodate the reasonable and foreseeable needs of franchisees. A small or start-up franchisor does not have the marketing leverage to sell unconscionable contracts in any event, and such contracts are more likely to generate ill will and litigation without necessarily being ultimately enforceable.

---

61. *See, e.g.,* WASH. REV. CODE § 19.100.180(2)(c), Bus. Franchise Guide (CCH) ¶ 4470.01.

62. VA. CODE § 13.1-565(b), Bus. Franchise Guide (CCH) ¶ 3460.09.

63. CAL. ADMIN. RULE § 310.100.2, Bus. Franchise Guide (CCH) ¶ 5050.071.

64. The Southland Corp. v. Attorney General, Bus. Franchise Guide (CCH) ¶ 9661 (August 3, 1990).

65. HAW. REV. STAT. § 482E-6(2)(C), Bus. Franchise Guide (CCH) ¶ 4110.01; ILL. REV. STAT. § 705/18, Bus. Franchise Guide (CCH) ¶ 3130.18; IND. CODE § 2(5), Bus. Franchise Guide (CCH) ¶ 4140.02; MICH. COMP. LAWS § 445.1527(e), Bus. Franchise Guide (CCH) ¶ 3220.27; MINN. ADMIN. RULE § 2860.4400(B), Bus. Franchise Guide (CCH) ¶ 5230.31; WASH. REV. CODE § 19.100.180(2)(c), Bus. Franchise Guide (CCH) ¶ 4470.01.

Sometimes a formula or other basis can be used to disclose how a term will be determined. In other cases, it may be appropriate to use standard addenda for recurring special cases such as an individual franchisee's incorporation or the sale of multiple unit franchises.

When a change not contemplated by the disclosure document is negotiated, the franchisor may need to amend its disclosure document unless the negotiated change was made under such unique circumstances or for such unique reasons that it is highly unlikely to be made again.[66]

Procedures for Amending the Disclosure Document

In registration states, the franchisor must "promptly" file a post-effective amendment with the addendum or revised pages and stop marketing activities until the amendment is approved, unless the state approves interim sales.[67]

In states where registration is not required, and only the disclosure obligations of the FTC Rule apply, the offering circular must be updated for material changes on a quarterly basis, but prospects have to be informed of material changes before entering into the franchise relationship. If a separate FTC Earnings Claim Document is used, it must be current at all times.[68]

For a disclosure document that is not registered anywhere, a material change may be reflected in an addendum or by changing the affected pages. In the latter case, the word "revised" and the revision date should be placed on each affected page, on the cover (under the effective date), in the index following the caption of each affected item, and on the receipt. It is not necessary to update the entire disclosure document when updating is done for a material change, but all material changes should be made.

When a material change occurs after a prospective franchisee has received a disclosure document but before the transaction is completed, the prospect must be given an addendum or the revised disclosure document and ten more business days must elapse before the franchisor receives any payment or the prospective franchisee signs any contract.

---

66. *See, e.g.,* ILL. ADMIN. RULE § 200.114, Bus. Franchise Guide (CCH) ¶ 5130.141.

67. *See, e.g.,* CAL. CORP. CODE §§ 31123, 31124, Bus. Franchise Guide (CCH) ¶¶ 3050.42, .43.

68. FTC Rule Interpretive Guides § I.C.4, Bus. Franchise Guide (CCH) ¶ 6225.

CHAPTER 4

Franchise Registration

Rochelle B. Spandorf and Mark B. Forseth

Contents

Until 1970, when California enacted its Franchise Investment Law,[1] franchise selling practices were virtually unchecked, both practically and legally speaking. Franchising had been a sleeping industry until the 1950s, despite historical beginnings traceable to the previous century,[2] but expanded rapidly through the 1950s and 1960s in a laissez-faire legal environment.[3] The explosive growth of franchising forced a change in legal climate, triggering a chain reaction of state regulatory activity starting in 1970 and a judicial awakening to franchising as a distinct legal relationship.[4]

With the dramatic growth of franchising came a corresponding growth in complaints about the franchise selling practices being employed.[5] The magic of "rags to riches" stories, often sensationalized by the press, induced an easily influenced and relatively unsophisticated audience to make investments in franchise opportunities based on a paucity of information.[6]

Following California's legislative response in 1970, the Federal Trade Commission (FTC) devoted the next nine years to investigating the franchising industry. It finally concluded in October 1979 that the abuses in franchise selling practices were both attributable to and compounded by a serious informational imbalance between franchisor and franchisee, usually accompanied by economic disparity between the parties.[7] The legal response to these abuses has been government regulation, directed mainly at franchise selling practices,[8] but in more recent years broadened to reach certain substantive aspects of the franchise relationship.

1. CAL. CORP. CODE §§ 31000–31516, Bus. Franchise Guide (CCH) ¶¶ 3050.01–3050.90, became effective on January 1, 1971.

2. FTC Statement of Basis and Purpose, Bus. Franchise Guide (CCH) ¶ 6302. Singer Sewing Machine's use of a network of independent sales agents in 1851 to distribute its sewing machines is often cited as the first modern-day example of a franchise system. LUXENBERG, ROADSIDE EMPIRES: HOW THE CHAINS FRANCHISED AMERICA (1985). Some claim that the concept of franchising is traceable as far back as the Middle Ages to the network of tax collectors established by the Catholic Church. KINCH, FRANCHISING: THE INSIDE STORY (1986).

3. Rudnick, *The Franchise Relationship: Problem Areas for the 1980s*, 2 FRANCHISE L. J. 1 (1982). Franchising's expansion has continued through the 1970s, 1980s, and 1990s despite a proliferation of legislative activity during this period. Sales of goods and services through franchising reached $757.8 billion in 1991. Retail sales by franchised establishments represented an estimated 35 percent of all U.S. retail sales in 1991. Horwath International, *Franchising in the Economy 1991*, at 1.

4. Franchising operated in a "regulatory vacuum" until the 1970s mainly because franchising, as a business concept and legal relationship, failed to fit neatly into any recognized traditional legal mold. Zeidman, Ausbrook, & Lowell, CPS (BNA) *Franchising: Regulation of Buying and Selling a Franchise*, at A-1 (1983).

5. FTC Statement of Basis and Purpose, Bus. Franchise Guide (CCH) § 6304.

6. *Id.*

7. *Id.*

8. The record that impelled franchise legislation related predominately to franchise selling activities and attendant abuses during the 1960s and early 1970s. The evidence today suggests that selling abuses are not prevalent. The regulatory reaction appears to have served its reformatory function, which raises the political issue of the continuing need for expansive franchise legislation, such as franchise registration requirements, today.

Franchise sales regulation has reacted to the information imbalance by taking on the basic attributes of the federal securities laws,[9] requiring detailed disclosure of all material terms and conditions of the franchise agreement and any ancillary agreements between the parties, including detailed information about the franchisor, its litigation and bankruptcy history, financial condition, and identification of existing franchisees, before the franchisor may either accept any consideration for the franchise or execute any contract with the franchisee. Several states have also reacted by imposing a registration requirement, conditioning the right to offer or sell franchises in the state on approval by state regulators of the franchise disclosure documents and overall financial condition of the franchisor, and, further, requiring that franchisors submit to annual review to maintain their franchise licenses.

The focus of this chapter is on the legal response of registration, at the present time a legislative solution in fourteen states. An overview of the mechanics of registration—what, where, when, and how—is presented.[10] Connected to the legal response of registration, indeed an integral component of every franchise registration statute, is compliance with presale disclosure duties. (An analysis of franchise disclosure requirements is presented in Chapter 3.)

The Regulatory Scheme

State Regulation

Since California's enactment of franchise sales legislation in 1970, thirteen other states have followed suit, passing legislation imposing some form of franchise registration obligation on franchisors before the offer or sale of a franchise: Hawaii, Illinois, Indiana, Maryland, Michigan, Minnesota, New York, North Dakota, Rhode Island, South Dakota, Virginia, Washington, and Wisconsin.[11] While most of these statutes were initially patterned on California's law,[12] each statute is sufficiently different from the next, thereby leaving franchisors that offer franchises on a multistate basis to contend with an uneven patchwork of sales rules.

---

9. *See* Southland Corp. v. Keating, 465 U.S. 1 (1984).

10. To facilitate the reader's reference to statutory materials, statutory citations include a cross-reference to the Business Franchise Guide, published by Commerce Clearing House (herein cited as Bus. Franchise Guide (CCH)), the most comprehensive source of current franchise statutory and case law.

11. These states, together with Oregon, are sometimes collectively referred to in this chapter as "registration states." While Oregon does not require registration, its statute does mandate disclosure and certain record-keeping requirements. ORE. REV. STAT. §§ 650.005 *et seq.*, Bus. Franchise Guide (CCH) ¶ 3370.

12. *Compare* the Wisconsin registration statute, WIS. STAT. 553.01 *et seq.*, Bus. Franchise Guide (CCH) ¶ 3490, *with* the Illinois and California statutes, respectively ILL. REV. STAT. Ch. 85-551, §§ 1–44, Bus. Franchise Guide (CCH) ¶¶ 3130–3130.44; CAL. CORP. CODE § 31000–31516, Bus. Franchise Guide (CCH) ¶ 3050.01–3050.90.

Michigan's registration law requires that the franchisor file only a one-page notice before offering or selling franchises in the state identifying the franchisor and its agent for service of process. Registration is complete upon the notice's filing and is effective for one year, subject to annual renewal accomplished by completing the same filing process. Similarly, Wisconsin, effective July 1, 1996, amended its law to eliminate the review of the offering circular by state administrators so that registration will be completed by an annual filing (that includes a copy of the offering circular).[13]

Hawaii requires the disclosure document and requisite application forms to be filed with the appropriate state agency. Statutorily, the state registration requirement is satisfied upon filing.[14] In practice, however, franchise applications are subjected by Hawaii state securities examiners to a review process similar to that described later. The filing must be annually updated.[15]

In the remaining twelve states, the general mechanics of registration are identical, although differences exist not only in legal requirements but also in the scrutiny and standards of review applied. By way of summary, each state requires the franchisor to submit a franchise registration application, a consent for service of process, a disclosure document with exhibits (among them, audited financial statements for the franchisor entity), and a filing fee, which ranges between $50 and $750. Each state statutorily defines the form and content of the disclosure to be provided to the prospective franchisee and included in the application. Use of a disclosure document prepared in accordance with the Uniform Franchise Offering Circular (UFOC) Guidelines disclosure format eliminates the need to have more than one format of disclosure document (UFOC format, FTC Rule format, state law format) in circulation.[16] The registration must be accepted by the regulatory agency before the franchisor may offer or sell franchises in the state. Furthermore, the franchisor must comply with updating and renewal requirements to

---

13. MICH. COMP. LAWS ANN. § 445.1507a, Bus. Franchise Guide (CCH) ¶ 3220.07a; WIS. STAT. 553.26.

14. HAW. REV. STAT. Ch. 482 E. § 482 E-1 through E-12, Bus. Franchise Guide (CCH) ¶ 3110.

15. Haw. Dept. of Commerce and Consumer Affairs, tit. III, Business Registration, tit. 16, ch. 37, § 16-37-1, Bus. Franchise Guide (CCH) ¶ 5110.03.

16. The differences among formats and the considerations in selecting one format over another are discussed in Chapter 3. The North American Securities Administrators' Association (NASAA), on April 25, 1993, adopted a substantially revised UFOC format (the New UFOC). In accordance with Section 265 of the New UFOC, the New UFOC was to take effect six months after the FTC and each NASAA member whose jurisdiction requires presale registration of a franchise adopts the New UFOC. The FTC approved the New UFOC for use in the non-registration states for FTC Rule compliance effective January 1, 1994, and indicated that it would revoke the right to use the old UFOC format six months after the last registration state adopts the New UFOC. Bus. Franchise Guide (CCH) ¶ 6451, 58 Fed. Reg. 69,224 (1993). New York was the last registration state to adopt the New UFOC on July 28, 1995. While all of the registration states have accepted applications prepared under the New UFOC since January 1, 1994, after January 1, 1996, all initial franchise applications, renewals, and reregistrations must comply with the revised guidelines. Bus. Franchise Guide (CCH) ¶ 5900.

keep its franchise registration valid in these states. These registration mechanics are discussed in a later section of this chapter.

Federal regulation did not emerge until October 1979, when the FTC adopted its trade regulation rule, "Disclosure Requirements and Prohibitions Concerning Franchising and Business Opportunity Ventures."[17] The so-called FTC Rule is a disclosure rule only and does not require any registration, filing, or approval by the FTC or any other federal agency as a condition to offering or selling a franchise. The jurisdictional scope of the FTC Rule is coextensive with the most liberal construction of the relevant "in or affecting commerce" threshold established by the Federal Trade Commission Act.[18] Accordingly, the FTC Rule applies in all fifty states to nearly all franchise offerings, including intrastate sales where all relevant events involving the transaction are confined to a single state.[19]

The FTC Rule currently does not preempt state laws establishing a registration duty on franchisors, since registration is viewed as providing more protection to prospective franchisees than the protection provided by the FTC Rule.[20] The FTC Rule establishes minimum standards of disclosure, and states are free to require more expansive disclosures.[21] The FTC Rule preempts state registration laws only in limited areas.[22] In February 1989, the FTC issued an advance notice

---

17. 16 C.F.R. § 436 (1979) (the FTC Rule), reprinted at Bus. Franchise Guide (CCH) ¶¶ 6090–6193.

18. 15 U.S.C.A. § 45(a) (1973 Supp. 1995).

19. *See* FTC Statement of Basis and Purpose, Bus. Franchise Guide (CCH) ¶ 6316.

20. 16 C.F.R. § 436.3 n.2, Bus. Franchise Guide (CCH) ¶ 6192. It is perhaps more accurate to state that there is no federal preemption issue with respect to concurrent state laws establishing a registration duty on franchisors. Because there is no federal registration requirement under the FTC Rule, there is no conflict between federal and state law on this point and, therefore, no preemption question. Likewise, state relationship laws are not preempted since there is no corresponding federal legislation in conflict. *See* Mackey & Kurylak, *Interfaces of the FTC Trade Regulation Rule and State Franchise Laws,* 2 Ariz. St. L.J. 527 (1980).

21. 16 C.F.R. § 436.3 n.2, Bus. Franchise Guide (CCH) ¶ 6192.

22. The most significant areas of federal preemption are in the following:

1. The scope of transactions covered by the FTC Rule. Certain relationships may not be regulated by state law because they fall outside of the state definition of "franchise," or qualify for a state law exemption or exclusion, but will be subject to the federal disclosure rule, which contains its own "franchise" definition. Bus. Franchise Guide (CCH) ¶ 6203–6217.

2. The designation of persons responsible for compliance—e.g., the definition of "franchisor." Bus. Franchise Guide (CCH) ¶ 6219.

3. Instances where FTC Rule disclosure requirements are more expansive or demanding than state legislative requirements. Bus. Franchise Guide (CCH) ¶ 6228.

4. The timing requirements for delivery of the disclosure document mandated by the FTC Rule and contracts with all material terms completed. Bus. Franchise Guide (CCH) ¶ 6222.

5. Earnings claims made for "general dissemination" or "media claims." Bus. Franchise Guide (CCH) ¶ 6262.

Thus, businesses considering licensing and related methods for expanding must examine not only the state franchise definitions but counterpart FTC Rule definitions as well.

of proposed rule making (ANPR) seeking information on the impact of certain revisions to the earnings claim disclosure requirements and evidence of inconsistencies in state registration and disclosure requirements that would necessitate federal preemption.[23] The FTC announced in December 1993 that it would take no action to further preempt state franchise laws because it had received little evidence of inconsistencies in response to the ANPR.[24] More recently, in April 1995, the FTC announced that it was seeking public comment in connection with its systematic evaluation of the FTC Rule, a process routinely conducted by the FTC with respect to all of its trade regulation rules.[25] The FTC requested comment with regard to the overall costs and benefits of the FTC Rule and its overall regulatory and economic impact. More specifically, the FTC was seeking comment on: (1) whether the FTC disclosure document format should be replaced with the New UFOC format; (2) whether the scope of disclosure requirements for business opportunity ventures should be modified; (3) whether the FTC Rule should clarify its applicability to trade show promoters; and (4) whether the FTC Rule should be revised to mandate the provision of financial performance information related to the business being franchised (i.e., mandatory earnings claims). The relationship between federal and state disclosure laws, mandatory earnings claims, and federal preemption is addressed in the separate section on duties.

The Jurisdictional Scope of State Franchise Registration Laws

Generally, state registration laws follow a similar jurisdictional approach for determining whether an offer or sale of a franchise is subject to the state's regulation. The registration states apply their statutes when an "offer" or "sale" of a franchise is made "in this state." An "offer" of a franchise is broadly defined by all jurisdictions to include all methods of solicitation of an offer to buy a franchise. Thus, if jurisdiction applies, a franchisor may not advertise in that state before registration.[26] The phrase "in this state" is the key determinant of jurisdiction. Generally, an offer or sale is deemed to be made in the state when any of the following tests are met:

1. The meetings between the franchisor and prospective franchisee take place in the state
2. The offer to sell a franchise originates from the state
3. The offer to sell a franchise is directed to the state
4. The acceptance of a franchise is directed to the state

23. 54 Fed. Reg. 7,041 (1989).
24. 58 Fed. Reg. 69,223 (1993).
25. 60 Fed. Reg. 17,656 (1995).
26. *See,* e.g., CAL. CORP. CODE § 31018(b), Bus. Franchise Guide (CCH) ¶ 3050.21.

5. The prospective franchisee is domiciled in the state
6. The prospective franchisee resides in the state
7. The proposed franchise business will be located in the state
8. The sales territory granted to the franchisee is located in the state.

Under this approach, it is possible for the franchise laws of several states to apply to the sale of a single franchise. As an example, a California franchisor offers an Indiana resident a franchise to be located in New York, the prospective franchisee accepts the offer on vacation in Hawaii, and the parties sign the franchise agreement at a trade show in Illinois. In this example, five registration states—California, Indiana, New York, Hawaii, and Illinois—have jurisdiction, and the franchisor would deliver to the prospective franchisee all five registered disclosure documents, notwithstanding the substantial similarity of their contents.[27] Because of the broad jurisdictional scope of state franchise registration laws, sales activities can subject an unsuspecting franchisor to a registration law in a state where the franchisor is not registered.[28]

Several states, among them California, Maryland, Minnesota, and Wisconsin, provide an exemption from registration for "out-of-state" sales.[29] These are sales made by a resident franchisor to an out-of-state prospective franchisee who is not domiciled in the registration state or present in the registration state while negotiating or investigating the franchise, where the franchised business will not be operated in the registration state and the sale does not otherwise violate any federal or sister state law. This exemption facilitates a franchisor having a principal place of business in a registration state with such an out-of-state exemption to offer different programs to out-of-state prospects without having to register such

27. Typically, the only differences between the disclosure document prepared for one registration state and another are the inclusion of descriptions of particular substantive state laws regarding the franchise relationship, as described later in this chapter, and the idiosyncratic comments of the particular examiner assigned to the registration application. Under the New UFOC, many franchisors are attempting to register one form of disclosure document containing state-specific disclosure for all registration states within the one document to permit the franchisor to use one "uniform" disclosure document in all states.

28. *See* Mon-Shore Management, Inc. v. Family Media, Inc., 584 F. Supp. 186 (S.D.N.Y. 1984). Courts have shown reluctance, however, in ordering rescission or applying penalties in cases where the prospective franchisee, despite receiving an offering circular for the wrong state, or for fewer than all states having jurisdiction over the sale, received substantially the same information that he or she would have received from the correct offering circular. *See* Benson v. Sbarro Licensing, Inc., Bus. Franchise Guide (CCH) ¶ 7967 (D. Minn. Ct. 1983) (applying Minnesota Franchise Act); Golden West Insulation, Inc. v. Stardust Investment Corp., Bus. Franchise Guide (CCH) ¶ 7567 (Ore. Ct. App. 1980) (question of whether California document should have been given).

29. California: 10 CAL. ADMIN. CODE § 310.100.1, Bus. Franchise Guide (CCH) ¶ 5050.07; Maryland: MD. REGS. CODE § 02.02.08.10, Bus. Franchise Guide (CCH) ¶ 5200.10B; Minnesota: MINN. STAT. § 80C.03, Bus. Franchise Guide (CCH) ¶ 3230.03; Wisconsin: WIS. ADMIN. CODE, § 31.01, Bus. Franchise Guide (CCH) ¶ 5490.01(5).

programs in the franchisor's home state, if it is not offering that program within the state.[30]

New York, in contrast, claims extraterritorial jurisdiction, interpreting its registration statute to reach all sales activities taking place in New York (including circumstances in which the franchisee is domiciled in New York and the franchised business is or will be operated in New York) and from New York or directed to New York.[31]

Exemptions from Coverage

All registration states provide exemptions from registration duties to franchisors meeting specified conditions.[32] An exemption from registration, however, does not necessarily relieve the franchisor of its disclosure obligations. The FTC Rule requires all franchisors, even if exempt from state registration duties, to comply with federal presale disclosure, necessitating preparation and delivery of a disclosure document.

Furthermore, many states require disclosure to qualify for particular exemptions, such as the exemption for "large franchisors" discussed later. Compliance with disclosure duties makes up the lion's share of a franchisor's legal bill for franchise sales regulation compliance.

Nevertheless, a franchisor exempt from state registration, though subject to federal disclosure duties, has the advantage of being able to engage in franchise sales in the registration state without having to negotiate the bureaucratic hurdles of the registration process. Furthermore, a franchisor exempt from state registration, but subject to federal disclosure requirements, may be entitled to use the FTC disclosure format rather than the state-accepted format, which under certain circumstances may prove more desirable.[33]

---

30. The franchisor would have to comply with federal disclosure requirements with respect to such sales and any registration laws that might have jurisdiction, such as the laws of the prospect's resident state.

31. N.Y. Gen. Bus. Law § 681.12, Bus. Franchise Guide (CCH) ¶ 3320.02; Mon-Shore Management, Inc. v. Family Media, Inc., 584 F. Supp. 186 (S.D.N.Y. 1984).

32. Finding an exemption from registration duties becomes a concern once it is determined that the business relationship is a "franchise" as defined by the state registration law. A discussion of how the pivotal term "franchise" is defined by the various states and the FTC is beyond the scope of this chapter. Among the many difficulties associated with franchise regulation has been the inability of the states and the FTC to settle on a common, satisfactory definition of this term. Subtle, but in some cases significant and conflicting, differences exist in the definition of "franchise." It appears all jurisdictions endorse the same "over reach" philosophy, giving the term a broad application in an effort to reach any relationship that can conceivably be characterized as a franchise. See In the Matter of KIS Corporation, Bus. Franchise Guide (CCH) ¶ 8731 (Dec. 1986).

33. California, for example, does not accept use of the FTC Rule disclosure document. 10 Cal. Admin. Code § 310.114.1, Bus. Franchise Guide (CCH) ¶ 5050.23. However, a franchisor exempt from California registration and disclosure duties could use the FTC Rule disclosure format in California. The differences between disclosure formats are addressed in Chapter 3; however, see 60 Fed. Reg. 17,656 (1995).

The real value of an exemption from state registration is in those few instances when the FTC Rule may be inapplicable to a particular business arrangement (e.g., when an exemption from the FTC Rule applies or when the business relationship may be a franchise under state law, but not under the federal definition). In such a case, the franchisor might be able to avoid disclosure entirely for transactions in that state, assuming the state exemption also applied.

The registration exemption most frequently relied on is the "large franchisor" exemption, available to franchisors meeting minimum net worth or franchise experience standards.[34] The large franchisor remains subject to state disclosure requirements although exempt from registering itself or its offering materials.[35]

Another exemption of practical significance applies to sales made by existing franchisees for their own account that are not "effected by or through" the franchisor. The exemption removes any duty on the franchisee to register the sale or to make presale disclosures to the purchaser. The franchisor's right to approve the purchaser is generally recognized by the states as insufficient involvement to prevent application of the exemption.[36] The statutes do not, however, provide guidance on the type or extent of the franchisor's activities connected to the transaction that will prevent application of the exemption. By administrative interpretation, it appears that where the franchisor's approval of the sale by an existing franchisee is conditioned on the purchaser's execution of the franchisor's then current contract (forbidding the assumption of the franchisee-seller's contract), the franchisor is sufficiently involved in the franchisee's sale to require the franchisor (not the franchisee-seller) to register the new contract before offering it to the purchaser.[37]

---

34. The criteria and procedures for qualifying for the "large franchisor" exemption differ from state to state. Many states set the minimum net worth at $5,000,000 or $10,000,000 and require five years experience (or parent company experience) in the business to be franchised or experience with at least twenty-five franchisees conducting business at all times during the five years immediately preceding the offer or sale in that state.

35. *See* CAL. CORP. CODE § 31101, Bus. Franchise Guide (CCH) ¶ 3050.25; N.D. CENT. CODE ANN. § 51019-04, Bus. Franchise Guide (CCH) ¶ 3340.04; and S.D. COMP. LAWS § 37-5A-12, Bus. Franchise Guide (CCH) ¶ 3410.12; IND. CODE Ch. 2.5, § 3, Bus. Franchise Guide (CCH) ¶ 3140.3; MD. REGS. CODE tit. 2, subtit. 02, ch. 8, § 02.02.08.10, Bus. Franchise Guide (CCH) ¶ 5200.10; N.Y. GEN. BUS. LAW § 684.1; Bus. Franchise Guide (CCH) ¶ 3320.04; R. I. GEN. LAWS § 19-28.1-6, Bus. Franchise Guide (CCH) ¶ 3390.06; WASH. REV. CODE § 19.100.030, Bus. Franchise Guide (CCH) ¶ 3470.03.

36. *See,* e.g., CAL. CORP. CODE § 33102, Bus. Franchise Guide (CCH) ¶ 3050.26; N.Y. GEN. BUS. LAW § 684(5), Bus. Franchise Guide (CCH) ¶ 3320.07.

37. Other registration exemptions include sales to existing franchisees; sales by executors, administrators, sheriffs, receivers, bankruptcy trustees, or other judicial officers; offers or sales to financial institutions; sales of securities registered under state blue sky laws; industry-specific exemptions in favor of motor vehicle dealers, petroleum marketers, and bank credit card plans, among others; offers and sales to sophisticated franchisees; and limited offers directed by a franchisor to not more than a prescribed number of prospective franchisees. The specific state statutes, therefore, must be carefully checked to determine the availability of an exemption to a particular transaction. In addition, some

The Registration Process

There is no central "clearance" system for registration applications. In each registration state where the franchisor desires to sell franchises, the franchisor must apply for registration to the state agency designated by state law to review and respond to franchise application requests.[38]

The Application Filing Process

Registration commences with submission of a registration application to the state franchise administrator. All of the registration states accept use of the uniform franchise application forms prepared in accordance with the New UFOC, with minor deviations. These application forms consist of the following:

1. The Uniform Franchise Registration Application page or "facing page" eliciting identifying data on the franchisor (or subfranchisor, as applicable).
2. The Certification page or "signature page" to be notarized and acknowledged by an authorized representative of the applicant.
3. A Consent to Service of Process authorizing service of legal or other documents upon the state regulatory authority as agent for the franchisor.
4. A Sales Agent Disclosure Form containing information regarding the background and history of all persons authorized by the franchisor to offer or sell franchises in the state.
5. A Supplemental Information Form, which discloses other states that have registered or denied the franchisor's registration application. This document also asks for an estimate of the franchisor's total costs for performing its preopening obligations to provide goods or services in establishing each franchise (e.g., in providing training, equipment, site selection, inventory, operating manuals, and opening promotional assistance). The source of funds to be used in defraying these expenses must also be disclosed. The significance of this information is further explained later in this chapter.
6. Copies of all advertising or promotional literature proposed to be used in the state.
7. Two copies of the UFOC, with any state-specific changes from the uniform format required by the state's registration statute, including ex-

---

state administrators have discretionary authority to grant exemptions. Generally, discretionary exemptions are accomplished by formal opinion request process, a costly and time-consuming pursuit that, in the end and on balance, may not prove of significant advantage to the franchisor applicant, particularly if the exemption does not avoid the disclosure duties.

38. Several states designate the securities commissioner; in others, the reviewing authority may be the attorney general or the commissioner of corporations.

hibits. The exhibits consist of audited financial statements for the franchisor's three most recent fiscal years, the franchise agreement, and any other contracts that the franchisor regularly asks prospective franchisees to sign.

8. An auditors' consent (or photocopy of the consent), executed by the independent certified public accountant, to use the franchisor's latest audited financial statements in the offering circular.

9. The application fee.[39]

The Reply Process

Typically, state registration statutes grant the administrator a fixed period of time in which to approve or deny the registration application. These statutes generally provide that unless a stop order is in effect, registration automatically becomes effective on the day following the end of the fixed period from the date of filing.[40] When a franchise examiner is unable to complete his or her review of the registration application within the statutory period, rather than issue a stop order, an extreme measure, the examiner will ask the applicant to request that the automatic effectiveness rule be postponed indefinitely until the examiner has an opportunity to complete a review of the file. An applicant is hard-pressed to refuse such a request since refusal would only invite a stop order.[41]

Franchise registration applications are not subject to merit review. The standard of review applied by franchise examiners is not the "fair, just, and equitable" standard applied to securities offerings, but one of accuracy and completeness. The standard of review is to ascertain that each required disclosure category complies with the uniform guidelines and state-specific disclosure rules and that all material facts of the franchise sale are truthfully disclosed. Examiners rarely ask for independent verification of the disclosures made.

---

39. *See* Uniform Franchise Offering Circular Guidelines, Bus. Franchise Guide (CCH) ¶ 5901; *see also* Appendix A.

40. *See,* e.g., California—fifteen business days from date of filing, CAL. CORP. CODE § 31116(a), Bus. Franchise Guide (CCH) ¶ 3050.35; Illinois—twenty business days from date of filing, ILL. REV. STAT. Ch. 85-551, § 10, Bus. Franchise Guide (CCH) ¶ 3130.10; Maryland—thirty business days after an application or list amendment, MD. CODE ANN. § 14–48, Bus. Franchise Guide (CCH) § 3260.18; *but see* Minnesota—upon issuance of order of registration, MINN. STAT. Ch. 80C, § 80C.05, Bus. Franchise Guide (CCH) § 3230.05.

41. The registration statutes vest franchise administrators with discretionary authority to issue a stop order without prior notice, provided a hearing on the order is conducted within a stated number of days thereafter. *See,* e.g., CAL. CORP. CODE § 31402, Bus. Franchise Guide (CCH) ¶ 3050.70; *but see* The Kis Corp. v. Ulice Payne, Jr., Bus. Franchise Guide (CCH) ¶ 8617 (Cir. Ct. Wis., 1986), where the court held that the issuance of a summary stop order of the Wisconsin Commissioner of Securities violated basic due process and fundamental fairness guarantees provided by the U.S. Constitution. The stop order had been issued to a company believed to be engaging in the offer and sale of franchises without complying with the state's registration law. Notwithstanding infirmities in the order itself, which the court held did not adequately explain the reasons justifying the state's summary order, the court revoked the order on constitutional principles, but stopped short of declaring the summary action provision unconstitutional *per se.*

The registration process requires the applicant to include on the cover page of the registered prospectus, in boldface type, a statement that registration by the state does not constitute approval, recommendation, or endorsement by the state administrator of the franchise opportunity or a finding by the administrator that the information provided in the prospectus is true, complete, and not misleading. The registration states appear satisfied that this boldface disclaimer disassociates them from responsibility for the franchisor's compliance with state disclosure duties. There are no reported decisions in which a claimant has sought recovery against a state for negligently granting a franchise registration.

The state administrator's response is typically issued in a "deficiency" or "comment" letter to the applicant requesting additional information or revisions to the offering prospectus or application. It is not uncommon for more than one deficiency letter to be issued until all matters are resolved. The review period varies significantly from state to state and even within a particular state depending on a variety of factors, perhaps most significantly the workload of the examiner to whom review of the franchise registration application is assigned. The scrutiny applied in reviewing an application also varies significantly among states and among examiners. There is no procedure by which an applicant can request a particular examiner, and, once assigned, the examiner generally remains with the file from year to year.

Each registration state further grants its administrator authority to deny a registration application or summarily to suspend or revoke an effective registration based on broadly stated, but stringent, grounds when the administrator finds any of the following:

1. There has been a failure to comply with the provisions of state law
2. The offer or sale of the franchise would constitute a misrepresentation to purchasers or is or has been a fraud upon purchasers
3. An order imposing an escrow or impounding of franchise fees has not been complied with (discussed later in this chapter)
4. Any person identified in the franchisor's application or disclosure document has been convicted of a felony or held liable in a civil action involving certain specified causes relating to the sale of franchises and the state believes the continued involvement of such person in the sale or management of the franchise creates an unreasonable risk to prospective franchisees.[42]

The Registration Period: Renewal Obligations and Annual Reports

The statutes of all registration states, except Hawaii, Minnesota, New York, and South Dakota, provide that the franchise registration will expire at the end of a

---

42. *See,* e.g., CAL. CORP. CODE § 31115, Bus. Franchise Guide (CCH) ¶ 3050.34; WIS. STAT. § 553.28, Bus. Franchise Guide (CCH) ¶ 3490.10; N.Y. GEN. BUS. LAW § 683.7, Bus. Franchise Guide (CCH) ¶ 3320.04. However, the constitutionality of such summary stop orders has been questioned in The Kis Corp. v. Ulice Payne, Jr. *See supra* note 41.

fixed registration period, unless a renewal application is filed and approved. Generally, the registration period is one year,[43] placing upon franchisors an annual burden to renew their franchise registration.[44]

The renewal application is identical to the initial registration application, except that changes made to the existing filing must be highlighted. The renewal application filing fees are set forth in Appendix A. Even if the terms of the franchise offering are not modified at renewal time, the renewal offering circular must be updated to reflect all of the following:

1. Current information, specifically,
   - identification of existing franchisees (e.g., names, addresses, and telephone numbers of operating locations and franchisees who have not yet opened for business);
   - for the prior three years, the number of franchises that were transferred, terminated or canceled, not renewed, reacquired by the franchisor, or otherwise left the system or ceased doing business for any reason;
   - the name and last known home address and telephone number of every franchisee who, during the preceding twelve months, had an outlet terminated, canceled or not renewed, or otherwise voluntarily or involuntarily ceased to do business under their franchise agreement;
   - the name and last known home address and telephone number of every franchisee who has not communicated with the franchisor at any time during the ten weeks preceding the renewal filing;

---

43. The initial registration period may be less than one year. It is sometimes fixed to correlate with the franchisor's fiscal year, expiring a specified number of days thereafter (e.g., 110 days in California; 120 days in Rhode Island). Thereafter, each renewal term is for one year.

44. To provide administrators with sufficient time to review the renewal application, and to protect franchise companies against the possibility of a lapse in registration, the states with fixed registration periods each provide an "automatic effectiveness" rule. This rule automatically renews the registration if the renewal application is filed at least a specified number of days before the registration's expiration date, e.g., fifteen business days in California, twenty business days in Illinois. *See* Appendix A. These "automatic effectiveness" rules are of great benefit to franchisors whose selling activities need not be stalled because of an overburdened franchise examiner (although many examiners will request an applicant to waive automatic effectiveness). Franchisors who file for renewal after the automatic effectiveness date, but before the registration expires, are not guaranteed that the state administrator will approve the renewal application by the end of the then-current registration period, which could result in a lapse in the franchisor's ability to offer and sell franchises in that state until the renewal application is approved. As a rule, state administrators will not extend a registration period to allow franchisors additional time to file their renewal documents. In some cases, a lapse in registration is unavoidable where, for example, the audited financial statements for the franchisor's most recent fiscal year required with the renewal application cannot be completed by the automatic effectiveness filing deadline.

- statistics regarding company-owned and affiliate-owned stores during the preceding three years, specifically, openings, closures, and changes in ownership; and
  - a best estimate of the number of franchises to be sold during the franchisor's next fiscal year.
2. Changes in officers, directors, and key management personnel. These changes may affect the mandatory litigation and bankruptcy disclosures.
3. Audited financial statements for the most recent fiscal year. The offering circular must include audited financial statements for the franchisor's three most recent fiscal years presented in a comparative format. Thus, at renewal, the oldest statement is dropped and the most recent statement added.
4. During the most recent fiscal year, total revenue derived from franchisee purchases from required sources and the percentage such figure bears to total revenue from all sources. The same year-end information must be disclosed for each affiliate that sells or leases goods or services to franchisees.
5. Application of advertising funds during the most recent fiscal year.
6. Any changes in the initial investment figures or explanatory notes to reflect inflation or franchisee actual experience.

In Minnesota, New York, and South Dakota, franchise registration, in theory, is of indefinite duration, subject, however, to the overriding duty to keep the registration filing current. Since the availability of new financial statements is considered a material change, franchisors in these states must amend their registrations at least once annually to add the new financial statements to their registration and to update disclosures regarding advertising revenue and revenue from required purchases during the most recent fiscal year. It is at this time that franchisors selling in these states will also update outlet statistics in the manner described previously. Consequently, this annual amendment procedure in these states is, in substance, equivalent to an annual renewal filing. Additionally, these three states require franchisors to file an annual report disclosing new sales, which report must be filed within a specified number of days after the franchisor's year-end (currently 120 days in all three states). The amendment and annual report filings carry separate filing fees. A failure to file the annual report may constitute cause for cancellation of the registration.[45]

Amendment Requirements

Posteffective Changes

The statutes of all registration states require the filing of an amendment application in the event of a material change in the information contained in the registra-

---

45. Minn. Stat. § 80C.09, Bus. Franchise Guide (CCH) ¶ 3230.08.

tion application, which would include changes affecting information in the franchisor's offering circular. It is often difficult to determine what facts or circumstances in a given situation constitute a "material change." By regulation in Hawaii, Illinois, Maryland, Michigan, Minnesota, New York, Virginia, and Wisconsin, the term "material change" is defined. None of these definitions is all-inclusive; rather, "material change" is defined by way of example.

Instructive, if not controlling, on the issue of materiality is the definition of "material change," contained in the FTC Rule.[46] This definition, based on federal securities law, recognizes a "material change" as

> Any fact, circumstance, or set of conditions which has a substantial likelihood of influencing a reasonable franchisee or a reasonable prospective franchisee in the making of a decision relating to the named franchise business or which has any significant financial impact on a franchisee or prospective franchisee.

While the federal "substantial likelihood" standard is the ultimate test of materiality, the illustrations provided in state laws are instructive for purposes of practical application. Examples of "material change" include the following:

- The termination, closing, or purchase of or failure to renew a significant number of franchises
- A change in control or reorganization, or a significant change in the business condition, of the franchisor
- A change (other than a de minimis one) in any franchise fees or the introduction of new programs changing the franchisee's investment
- Any significant change in the obligations to be performed by the franchisor
- A change in franchisor personnel responsible for administering franchise services.

States that provide some definition of material change, and the FTC Rule, do not necessarily limit "materiality" to changes adverse to the franchisor's condition or to the franchisee's contractual position. Illinois, for example, cites a decrease in initial or continuing franchise fees as an example of a material change.[47] Even in states without rules defining "material" as such, franchise administrators have informally expressed the view that changes that improve the franchisee's position are nevertheless material to an investment decision—therefore, these changes must be added to the registration by an amendment before the "better deal" may be presented to a prospective franchisee.[48]

46. 16 C.F.R. § 436.2(n), Bus. Franchise Guide (CCH) ¶ 6182(a).

47. ILL. ADMIN. CODE, tit. 14, subtit. A, ch. II, § 200.110(a), Bus. Franchise Guide (CCH) ¶ 5130.11.

48. With respect to a negotiated change, the administrators who have offered their opinion point out that the materiality of the "better terms" is not for the benefit of the prospective franchisee who is offered the favorable deal but for prospective franchisees

An amendment application generally is limited to the filing of the modified pages of the application, disclosure document, or franchise agreement, properly highlighted to show the changes to the existing registration. The amendment application filing fees are set forth in Appendix A. The amendment is coined a "posteffective" amendment, since it is being made to an already effective registration.

The time within which registration states require that the amendment application be filed varies from state to state, generally measured not by days but by far less precise standards, for example "upon," "as soon as reasonably possible after," or "promptly" following the occurrence of the material change.[49] Material changes, however, can arise owing to events both within a franchisor's control, such as an increase in initial fees, and beyond a franchisor's immediate control, such as a change in key personnel, a significant adverse change in the franchisor's business condition, or the filing of significant litigation against the franchisor. Both types of material changes are subject to the posteffective amendment filing process.

The duty to file an amendment application "upon," "promptly," or "as soon as reasonably possible after" the material change or event occurs can have substantial implications for a franchisor's selling activities because, until the amendment application is approved and the approved and updated offering circular is furnished to a prospective franchisee in accordance with the state and federal delivery requirements, the franchisor's ability to engage in franchise selling activities is suspended.[50] It would be unlawful to furnish the revised offering circular to a prospective franchisee until the amendment application is approved, since to

---

who follow, who they claim are entitled to know in making their investment decision that the terms of the registered offering have been negotiated and that more favorable terms have been obtained. These administrators differ on how detailed the disclosure of the "better deal" must be. The UFOC disclosure guidelines specify for certain disclosure items (e.g., initial fees) that the franchisor state whether or not identical terms are offered to all prospective franchisees and, if not, the range or formula of the initial fees paid in the franchisor's last fiscal year. *Guidelines for Preparation of the Uniform Franchise Offering Circular and Related Documents,* prepared by the Midwest Securities Commissioners Assn., Bus. Franchise Guide (CCH) ¶ 5805, and those adopted by the NASAA, Bus. Franchise Guide (CCH) ¶ 5907.

49. Minnesota, South Dakota, and Wisconsin specifically require the filing to be made within a specified number of days (in each case, thirty days) after the material change or event occurs. MINN. STAT. § 80C.07, Bus. Franchise Guide (CCH) ¶ 3230.07; S.D. CODIFIED LAWS § 37-5A-40, Bus. Franchise Guide (CCH) ¶3410.40; WIS. STAT. § 553.31, Bus. Franchise Guide (CCH) ¶ 3490.13. *Compare,* e.g., ILL. REV. STAT. Ch. 85-551, § 11, Bus. Franchise Guide (CCH) ¶ 3130.11 ("upon the occurrence of any material change"); WASH. REV. CODE § 19.100.070(3), Bus. Franchise Guide (CCH) ¶ 3470.07 ("as soon as reasonably possible after"); CAL. CORP. CODE § 31123, Bus. Franchise Guide (CCH) ¶ 3050.42 and N.Y. GEN. BUS. LAW § 683.9, Bus. Franchise Guide (CCH) ¶ 3320.04 (which each require that the amendment be filed "promptly after" the material change).

50. Wisconsin appears to be the only state that, by rule, recognizes the problem of suspension; under Wisconsin law, the existing registration statement remains in effect while an application to amend is pending. WIS. ADMIN. CODE § 32.07(2), Bus. Franchise Guide (CCH) ¶5490.09. Suspension of franchise sales activities pending review and ap-

do so would constitute the offer of an unregistered franchise. Complicating this is the additional fact that only a few registration states—Indiana, Maryland, Virginia, and Wisconsin—provide an automatic effectiveness rule for amendment applications.[51] Elsewhere, state administrators are not required to approve a posteffective amendment application within a prescribed time period. The length of the resulting suspension is thus left to the uncertainties of the state examiner's workload.

Presale Negotiations

An amendment to the terms of a registration offering can also occur in the context of presale negotiations with a prospective franchisee. A handful of states—California, Illinois, Rhode Island, Washington, and Wisconsin—expressly speak to the issue of whether a franchisor must file an amendment for presale negotiated material changes.[52]

proval of a posteffective amendment is a critical issue when changes beyond a franchisor's control occur necessitating the amendment filing. It is generally not an issue, merely an inconvenience, with respect to the implementation of changes within the franchisor's control, since, for example, introduction of a new fee schedule can easily wait until an order approving the amendment is in hand. Technically, even in the latter case, once the amendment is approved, the old fee schedule is no longer the subject of a valid registration. Thus, consummation of a sale on the old terms, after the posteffective amendment is approved, would constitute the sale of an unregistered franchise. To avoid this technical trap, practitioners may consider requesting that the effective date of the amendment be a sufficient number of days ahead to permit any outstanding offers to be closed on the old terms.

51. IND. CODE § 20(b), Bus. Franchise Guide (CCH) ¶ 3140.20; MD. REGS. CODE § .02.02.08.06, Bus. Franchise Guide (CCH) ¶ 5200.06; VA. REGS. § 7.1, Bus. Franchise Guide (CCH) § 5490.071; WIS. ADMIN. CODE § 32.07, Bus. Franchise Guide (CCH) ¶ 5490.09. The Illinois statute does not contain an express automatic effectiveness rule, but does provide that the sale of a franchise that takes place after an amendment filing but before notice from the state administrator requesting additional changes will be treated as the sale of a registered franchise. ILL. REV. STAT. Ch. 85-551, § 11, Bus. Franchise Guide (CCH) ¶ 3130.11. The Virginia regulations provide that an application to amend or renew an effective registration if accompanied by an Affidavit of Compliance, prepared on the prescribed form, shall become effective immediately upon receipt by the Virginia Corporation Commission, provided certain conditions are met. VA. REGS. § 6, Bus. Franchise Guide (CCH) ¶ 5460.06.

52. Illinois, Rhode Island, and Wisconsin dispense with the posteffective amendment filing requirement for presale negotiations to allow franchisors and their prospects to negotiate changes in the standard contract. ILL. REV. STAT. ch. 85-551, § 11, Bus. Franchise Guide (CCH) ¶ 3130.11; R.I. GEN. LAWS § 19-28.1-10, Bus. Franchise Guide (CCH) ¶ 3390.10; WIS. STAT. § 553.31, Bus. Franchise Guide (CCH) ¶ 3490.13. Washington exempts franchisee-initiated negotiations from the amendment process. WASH. REV. CODE § 19.100.184, Bus. Franchise Guide (CCH) ¶ 3470.184. California exempts presale negotiated changes from the amendment process if certain conditions are met, which include filing a Notice of Negotiated Sale and identifying in the UFOC which disclosure items have been negotiated with other franchisees. 10 CAL. ADMIN. CODE § 310.100.2, Bus. Franchise Guide (CCH) ¶ 5050.071. New York's long-standing position against negotiated changes was rejected by a state trial court. The Southland Corp. v. Attorney General of New York, Bus. Franchise Guide (CCH) ¶ 9661 (N.Y. Sup. Ct. 1990).

The concern is that, arguably, new material terms negotiated with a prospect may constitute a new offer that must be registered as a posteffective amendment before a franchise on such negotiated terms may be sold.[53] Under this logic, a separate amendment filing must be made, and an amendment disclosure document redelivered, for each and every counteroffer in accordance with federal and state delivery rules—an extraordinarily burdensome requirement.

The FTC informally takes a more liberal position on the franchisor's duty to disclose presale negotiated changes. It requires that just the final negotiated contract, incorporating all of the material changes agreed on by the parties, be delivered to the prospective franchisee at least five business days before the franchisee signs the negotiated agreement or pays any consideration. The FTC interpretation dispenses with the need for repeated disclosures each time an offer and counteroffer is made.

Virginia takes a unique approach among registration states by requiring that the prospective franchisee be afforded the opportunity to negotiate the franchise agreement before signing it.[54] Otherwise, the franchisee has thirty days after signing to void the contract. The Virginia administrators, however, have never prosecuted an alleged violation of this provision and cannot comment on the degree of compliance.

Postsale Modifications

California and North Dakota are the only registration states to regulate material changes made to the terms of an executed franchise agreement. California requires registration of all "material modifications" to existing franchises before the franchisor may solicit a franchisee's agreement to such changes, despite the fact that the franchise contract may expressly recognize the right of the parties to amend the agreement and presale disclosure of such right is made. The California statute does not define "material change." The types of changes falling within the statutory ambit would be determined by reference to the guidelines for "materiality" applied in posteffective amendment situations. The material modification filing process requires registration of a "mini" offering circular that discloses the nature of the proposed contract revision, additional fees and expenses sought to be imposed on the franchisee, additional training requirements, and additional service obligations on the franchisee. The material modification filing obligations

---

53. Informally, some administrators claim that this result should follow regardless of whether the franchisor or franchisee initiates negotiation. For example, a prospective franchisee may seek a lower royalty fee than what is offered in the current circular. Some administrators are of the view that the franchisor may not accept and close the sale on the franchisee's terms without completing a posteffective amendment filing to register the change demanded by the franchisee and redelivering the amended circular to the franchisee. These administrators are not persuaded that the prospective franchisee who initiates the negotiation does not need the benefit of the modified disclosure. They argue that the franchisor's sale of such franchise at the lower royalty rate would constitute the sale of an unregistered franchise. Most administrators do not, however, hold this viewpoint.

54. VA. CODE ANN. § 13.1-454(b), Bus. Franchise Guide (CCH) ¶ 3460.09.

in California seriously impair a franchisor's ability to require unforeseeable, systemwide changes in the franchise program, often necessary for franchise systems to compete effectively in the marketplace. California has a separate material modification procedure for franchisors that are relying on the California net worth exemption. This procedure is identical to the procedure in North Dakota.[55]

With respect to a franchisor relying on North Dakota's net worth exemption, North Dakota law provides that, in the case of a material modification of an existing agreement, a franchisor must disclose in writing to each franchisee the specific provisions to be modified. A franchisee has the right to rescind its agreement to the material modification within ten days after the receipt of the writing describing the material modification. Unlike in California, there is no similar material modification requirement under North Dakota law applicable to a registered offering.[56]

The issue of postsale modifications raises another regulatory issue, which is the ability of a franchisor to reserve the right in the franchise agreement to modify the franchise program and franchise contract, from time to time, in the franchisor's discretion, and to enforce franchisee compliance with such changes, provided such unilateral right is adequately disclosed to the franchisee before the sale is made. For example, it is common for franchise agreements to require that franchisees sell all of the products dictated by the franchisor, as the list of products may be changed from time to time. The introduction, for example, of a new menu selection in a fast-food franchise may require a significant capital investment not disclosed in the offering circular delivered to the franchisee at the first personal (presigning) meeting (although the duty to conform to menu changes of all types is adequately disclosed). If the franchisee at the outset of the parties' relationship agreed to the franchisor's reservation of the right to impose menu changes from time to time, can the franchisee complain that the change was not adequately disclosed or that some registration violation has occurred? There is no reported case law on this issue.

Capitalization Requirements

All registration states vest in the state administrator the authority to condition approval of the franchise registration upon an adequate showing of the franchisor's financial ability to provide promised services and preopening support to franchisees. The state's interest in preventing thinly capitalized situations is in protecting against franchise sales being induced by grandiose promises of support that cannot be fulfilled unless paid for by the franchisee's own franchise fees.

A franchisor with inadequate development capital is typically heavily, and overly, dependent on initial franchise fees for cash flow, which can lead to an im-

---

55. CAL. CORP. CODE § 31125, Bus. Franchise Guide (CCH) ¶ 3050.44 and CAL. CORP. CODE § 31101(b)(2), Bus. Franchise Guide (CCH) ¶ 3050.25.
56. N.D. CENT. CODE ANN. § 51-19-04.1.d., Bus. Franchise Guide (CCH) ¶ 3340.04.

provident rate of franchise expansion beyond the franchisor's service capacity, eventually causing the whole house of cards to tumble.[57]

There is no practical explanation of the indicia used by state administrators in analyzing undercapitalization situations.[58] As a rule, however, no franchisor is likely to be granted registration by any state, at least not without an impound condition (as discussed later), if the franchisor is technically insolvent—that is, if current liabilities exceed current assets. A practical starting point in figuring minimum capital needs is to multiply the franchisor's estimated per-unit cost of providing promised preopening and opening services and support by the number of franchises the franchisor estimates it will sell in the state during the next year. Both the cost and sales estimates are mandatory disclosure items.[59] The product of per-unit cost and total projected sales for the state is then compared to the financial resources indicated by the franchisor's financial statements. In all cases, the minimum amount of available cash must be at least equal to this product, but it is not unusual for a state examiner, pursuant to its discretionary authority, to require that available cash be at least a multiple of this product (e.g., two times). Disappointingly, the registration statutes offer no guidance on the subject.

All registration states except Virginia authorize the franchise administrator to attach an impound, or escrow, condition to a registration if the franchisor cannot demonstrate sufficient sources of capital to meet these obligations.[60] Under an impound, the initial franchise fees must be held in an escrow account until the franchisor supplies written verification that all promised preopening obligations have been fulfilled and the franchisee has opened the franchise business.[61] In some states, the verification must also be signed by the franchisee.[62] An impound is an administrative and financial noose for franchisors, particularly when cash flow is an issue.

---

57. Franchise companies, as noted, are put to the annual burden of preparing audited financial statements by federal and state disclosure laws. It is for this reason that businesses with a previously unaudited history of operations may embark upon franchising through a newly formed subsidiary or affiliate company whose "clean slate" can readily be audited at relatively little expense.

58. Illinois regulations offer some direction, but no explanation of how the criteria mentioned in the regulations are applied in practice. *See* ILL. ADMIN. CODE tit. 14, subtit. A, ch. II, § 200.500, 200.513 *et seq.,* Bus. Franchise Guide (CCH) ¶¶ 5130.36, 5130.413.

59. The per-unit cost figures are included in the supplemental information page submitted with the franchise registration application and the sales estimate is disclosed in Item 20 of the offering circular.

60. State regulators view the sale of a franchise by an undercapitalized franchisor as an unreasonable risk contrary to the public interest and, in some states, a form of misrepresentation to prospective franchisees with respect to the franchisor's ability to fulfill contractual promises. State administrators have sufficient discretion to deny registration to undercapitalized companies; thus an impound, or escrow, condition may, for some applicants, be the only chance for getting started in the state.

61. *See,* e.g., ILL. ADMIN. CODE tit. 14, subtit. A, ch. II, § 200.502, § 200.503 and Appendix C thereto, Bus. Franchise Guide (CCH) ¶¶ 5130.38, 5130.39, 5130.74–5130.751.

62. *See,* e.g., 10 CAL. ADMIN. CODE § 310.113.4(f), Bus. Franchise Guide (CCH) ¶ 5050.20.

Franchise applicants determined to be undercapitalized by state administrators have alternatives to an impoundment of franchise fees, as discussed in the next sections.

Capital Infusion

One obvious method for correcting an undercapitalized situation is to obtain additional capital, that is, additional capital contributions to the franchisor corporation, not short-term borrowings that will equally increase both current assets and current liabilities and, therefore, not improve the net worth ratio. Long-term borrowings, even from officers or shareholders, may solve an undercapitalized situation, but only if expressly subordinated to the franchisor's obligations under the franchise agreement. In some cases, state administrators might require that such loans be paid from retained earnings and not from income.

Guarantee of Performance

Providing a corporate guarantee works to improve an undercapitalized situation only if the guarantor has audited financial statements that are filed with the registration application and made a part of the offering circular delivered to prospective franchisees. Most states require that the guarantor be a controlling company. Use of a controlling company guarantee arguably eliminates the obligation to file audited financial statements for the franchise company. A significant drawback in using a corporate guarantee is that it is not limited to the franchisor's performance of preopening obligations. The guarantee extends to the franchisor's performance throughout the term of the franchise agreement for each agreement signed during the period that the guarantee is in effect inasmuch as the franchisee has presumably relied on the guarantee in entering into the franchise agreement with the franchisor. Thus, recourse to the guarantor remains available to those franchisees who bought into the system when the guarantee was in place, notwithstanding that sometime later the franchisor may have corrected the undercapitalized situation and no longer is subject to an impound or alternative financial arrangement as a condition to its franchise registration.

Surety Bond

With the exception of Indiana, South Dakota, and Virginia,[63] the franchise statutes of all registration states permit an undercapitalized franchisor to post a surety bond in lieu of an impound arrangement. Typically, the amount of the bond required is the product of the initial franchise fees multiplied by the number of franchises the franchisor intends to sell in the state during the coming

63. Under Indiana and South Dakota law, the state administrators have discretionary authority to permit the posting of a surety bond. Virginia law does not recognize the surety bond alternative.

year.[64] As a practical matter, surety companies will be reluctant to write a bond for a franchisor who cannot otherwise meet the minimum capitalization standards asked for by the state administrator. Thus, the surety bond alternative is not necessarily available to all undercapitalized franchisors. Furthermore, many bonding companies require that the bond amount be personally guaranteed by an officer or shareholder, which diminishes the attraction of the bond alternative.

Nevertheless, unlike an impound or escrow, the bond does not tie up access to initial franchise fees, the principal source of cash flow for start-up franchise companies. Furthermore, unlike a corporate guarantee, the bond covers only the franchisor's performance of preopening services and recourse to the bond is canceled once the franchised unit opens.

Deferral of Initial Fees

Some states may waive the impound requirement if the franchise agreement provides that no monies are payable to the franchisor until after the franchise business opens. This stipulation ensures that the franchisor cannot use the money put up by the franchisee to discharge the franchisor's preopening duties owed to that franchisee (or for other purposes before the franchisee's opening for business).

Minimum Guidance

The lack of guidance provided by statutory authority, and the lack of uniformity among state administrators, makes it difficult to advise new franchisor clients of the minimum net worth required for registration in a particular state. The capital requirements on initial registration, however, appear to come under stricter scrutiny than on renewal. A track record of franchise sales, openings, and documented growth attaches credibility to the franchisor and seems to serve as a hidden persuader that financial conditions are not necessary. Existing units also generate cash flow through payment of continuing royalty fees. However, even on renewal, a company will not avoid an impound or escrow condition if its financial statements show a negative working capital. Compounding the difficulties in this area are franchisors who use puffed up plans for expansion. Projections for future franchise sales should be realistic, particularly since this is the key multiplier used by state administrators in determining the franchisor's minimum capital needs.[65]

---

64. Franchise administrators are generally unconcerned with projected franchise sales or existing franchise operations in other states notwithstanding that such activities represent a potential cash drain on the undercapitalized franchisor. The bond serves as a fund, or source of security, to resident franchisees, and only they would have access to the bond.

65. Franchisors should not inflate their projections for future franchise sales for other reasons as well. While franchisors generally hold the belief that the franchise program, particularly a new franchise program, will sell better if grandiose expansion plans are announced to convince the first several prospects that it is worth purchasing this yet unknown franchise name, when such goals fail to materialize, the franchisor's inflated claims may be the basis for an action for negligent misrepresentation, if not fraud, under common-law theories. Juries have shown sympathy with these claims. Although on appeal the franchisee plaintiffs have been unsuccessful in affirming their lower court victories, the potential exists for litigation in this area. *See,* e.g., Vaughn v. General Foods Corp.,

Other Registration Duties

Registration of Salespersons

All registration states except Virginia require identification or registration of franchise sales agents and other selling brokers. In most states, this is accomplished by filing the Uniform Sales Agent Disclosure Form—part of the North American Securities Administrators Association (NASAA) uniform application—with the state administrator.[66] Illinois, New York, and Washington distinguish salespersons from franchise brokers, requiring for the latter (defined as independent sales agents, not employees of the franchisor, engaged to represent the franchisor in soliciting prospective franchise sales) a more comprehensive application and registration process.[67] In California, if a franchisor files an application to add a salesperson separate and apart from any other application related to its registration (i.e., initial, renewal, or posteffective amendment), the filing of the sales agent application will be treated as a posteffective amendment and require the filing of an application form and payment of a filing fee.

The registration states have not developed a uniform form for notifying state administrators when a registered salesperson's authority to represent the franchisor has been terminated, but common-law agency principles dictate that notice promptly be given, which can be accomplished by letter.[68] The registration of salespersons is effective for the period of the franchisor's registration and therefore must be renewed annually in those states where renewal is required. The salesperson disclosure filing is part of a franchisor's registration application, but it is not included in the disclosure document delivered to prospective franchisees.

Advertising and Promotional Materials

All registration states, with the exception of Hawaii and Virginia, require that all advertising and promotional materials that offer franchises for sale be submitted to

---

797 F.2d 1403 (7th Cir., 1986), *cert. denied,* 479 U.S. 1087 (1987) (Seventh Circuit overturned the lower court's ratification of a $14 million jury verdict in favor of a group of franchisees on a claim of fraudulent misrepresentation based in part on the franchisor's lofty projections for future growth and expansion of the Burger Chef system while it was at the same time secretly exploring a suitable purchaser for the chain).

66. *See* Sales Agent Disclosure Form, Bus. Franchise Guide (CCH) ¶ 5931.

67. Franchise brokers must be separately identified in Item 2 of the franchisor's offering circular, which is the section describing officers, directors, and key management personnel. Salespeople, however, do not need to be identified in the offering circular unless they are an officer or director or have key management responsibilities for the franchisor. Officers, directors, and key management personnel are not generally exempt from the separate salesperson registration requirement because they are identified in the offering circular. Franchise brokers are subject to separate registration requirements in Illinois, New York, and Washington. ILL. REV. STAT. ch. 85–551 § 705/13, Bus. Franchise Guide (CCH) ¶ 3130.13; N.Y. GEN. BUS. LAW § 684.13, Bus. Franchise Guide (CCH) ¶ 3320.04; WASH. REV. CODE § 19.100.140, Bus. Franchise Guide (CCH) ¶ 3470.14.

68. Franchisors and their principals will be bound by the representations and admissions of their salespeople under common-law agency principles.

the state administrator for review several days before first publication or use in the state. All states requiring such filings provide that the advertising is deemed approved unless notice of disapproval is communicated to the applicant before the end of the waiting period.[69] The statutes define "advertising" expansively to include any communication used in connection with the offer or sale of a franchise, which would include recorded telephone messages, form letters, television and radio scripts, and audiovisual presentations.[70] Some states exclude from registration "tombstone" ads by a registered franchisor, which are limited to skeletal information concerning the franchisor, the franchise, and the total dollar investment.[71]

A franchise ad appearing in a publication in a registration state is not considered an offer to sell a franchise in that state if more than two-thirds of the publication's paid circulation resides outside of that state and the publication is not published in the state. Therefore, the advertising need not be registered with the state administrator.[72] This protection permits franchisors access to national and regional publications (e.g., *The Wall Street Journal,* which prints several regional editions, each covering a group of neighboring states) without having to be concerned that circulation in a registration state will inadvertently trigger application of the registration law. Of course, franchisors who rely on this limited protection are not free to engage in solicitation activities with residents of the registration state responding to the national or regional ad until registration in that state is completed.[73]

---

69. The waiting period starts upon the advertisement's filing. Filing may be delayed for two or three days after the state agency's actual receipt of the advertisement, in moving the article out of the central mail room to the examiner's desk. It is therefore advisable to submit the advertising with a postcard or duplicate copy of the transmittal letter and instruct the state to stamp the card or copy with the filing date and return it so that the applicant has a record of the filing date and when the waiting period ends.

70. *See,* e.g., CAL. CORP. CODE § 31003, Bus. Franchise Guide (CCH) ¶ 3050.04.

71. 10 CAL. ADMIN. CODE § 310.156.2, Bus. Franchise Guide (CCH) ¶ 5050.35.

72. *See,* e.g., MD. CODE ANN. § 14-203(a)(2), Bus. Franchise Guide (CCH) ¶ 3200.03; ILL. ADMIN. CODE, tit. 14, subtit. A, ch. II § 200.305(a), Bus. Franchise Guide (CCH) ¶ 5130.23. Note, however, that the Minnesota Franchise Law does not contain such an exclusion.

73. A franchisor's response to an inquiry from a registration state resident where the franchisor is not registered should be deliberately circumscribed. The franchisor's reason for using a national or regional publication for advertising should be to reach residents in the non-registration states covered in its circulation. Where the advertising also circulates in a registration state, the franchisor's response should be limited to taking down the name, address, and phone number of the inquirer and advising him or her that until registration in that state is completed the law prohibits any further discussion concerning franchise opportunities in that state. The franchisor should not send the registration state resident a copy of its offering circular used in another state, notwithstanding that its contents might ultimately prove to be identical, or nearly identical, to the disclosure that would be registered in that registration state. Nor should the franchisor invite the registration state resident to the franchisor's home state for further discussions or a tour of franchise operations. The registration state, in the interest of protecting its residents, has jurisdiction over the activities of the out-of-state franchisor. Before proceeding, the franchisor should review the jurisdictional application of the registration state's law, as such activities may constitute the offer of an unregistered franchise.

Subfranchisor Registration

Subfranchising is an arrangement whereby the franchisor grants to another (the subfranchisor) the right to sell and grant franchises to third parties, usually within a specified territory. Subfranchising involves two contractual layers: one between the franchisor and subfranchisor and the other between the subfranchisor and the third-party franchisee.[74] Subfranchising is one approach for multiunit or territorial expansion, distinguished from other expansion approaches by the fact that the subfranchisor, not the franchisor, executes the franchise contract with the third-party franchisee.

There are four common techniques for multiunit expansion: (1) area development, which grants the developer the right to open units within a specified territory all owned by the developer, subject to a minimum development commitment; (2) area representation, a hybrid of subfranchising, which grants to the area representative the right to offer franchises and service franchisees within a territory, but where the franchise contract is between the franchisor and franchisee; (3) franchise brokerage, involving a network of independent sales agents whose function is limited to franchise sales solicitation; and (4) subfranchising.[75] Because these relationships are for the most part conceptual, not statutory, regulation of these arrangements by the states is often inconsistent.[76]

---

74. Subfranchise rights are generally conditioned on the subfranchisor meeting agreed-on development commitments in the territory. Frequently, subfranchisors are permitted to meet development goals by developing some of the franchised units themselves, in which case they would be executing a franchise agreement with the franchisor for the units they open. A subfranchise is generally defined in most states as an agreement whereby the subfranchisor is granted the right, for consideration for that right, to sell or negotiate the sale of franchises in the name or on behalf of the franchisor. *See,* e.g., CAL. CORP. CODE § 31008.5, Bus. Franchise Guide (CCH) ¶ 3050.105.

75. A discussion and comparison of these four multiple-unit franchising approaches is beyond the scope of this chapter. See Chapter 2. An excellent review of these concepts is presented in a series of articles published in the IFA Franchise Legal Digest. *See* IFA LEGAL DIGEST (January 25–29, 1987) (area development approach); (March/April 1987) (subfranchising); and (July/August 1987) (area representation).

76. Area representation arrangements are often confused with subfranchising. The distinction between these two, however, is important, since subfranchising involves registration not only by the franchisor, but also by the subfranchisor. Area representation might not require separate registration of the area representative, although the area representative's role in providing services to franchisees and identity would have to be disclosed in the franchisor's offering circular. However, Illinois has amended its definition of "subfranchise" to include any agreement between a franchisor and franchisee whereby the subfranchisor is granted the right to *service franchises,* or to sell or negotiate the sale of franchises, in consideration of the payment of a franchise fee. ILL. REV. STAT. ch. 815, § 70513 (1992), Bus. Franchise Guide (CCH) ¶ 3130.03 (emphasis added). Thus, area representatives must be registered in Illinois. By administrative fiat, several examiners in California have taken the position that an area representative arrangement is a subfranchise and require that an area representative register separately as a subfranchisor. This can produce a rather absurd result requiring multiple registrations for the same franchise, each containing different minimal disclosure regarding the service representative.

Subfranchising imposes substantially greater registration requirements on franchisors than do the other multiple-unit arrangements. Registration states require separate registration by the franchisor of the offer of subfranchise rights. The franchisor's registration would include a separate description of the material terms of the subfranchise agreement (e.g., development duties in the territory, obligations to the franchisor, obligations to third-party franchisees). The subfranchisor is subject to its own registration duties in order to sell franchises in that state. Its offering circular will describe the material terms of the individual, or unit, franchise being offered.[77] Franchisors that engage both in subfranchising and in direct unit sales in a registration state are required to have two separate registrations in effect, one to offer and sell unit franchises and the second to offer and sell subfranchises. The subfranchisor, as noted, must also be registered in that state to sell franchises in its territory. The situation becomes even more complex if multiple subfranchises are sold within a single registration state.

Agent for Service of Process

All registration states require, as a condition of registration, that the franchisor irrevocably appoint an agent for service of process located in the state. Generally, such requirements dictate that the agency or its director responsible for the administration of the franchise law (or the secretary of state) be named, although private agents also are permitted. The service-of-process consent forms are part of the initial registration application (and the renewal application in some states, even though the consent filed with the initial application is irrevocable). These forms are not part of the disclosure materials delivered to prospective franchisees. However, the franchisor's agent for service of process must be listed on the cover page of the offering circular, or in an exhibit thereto.

77. Even where subfranchising is selected as the means for multiple-unit franchising, the terms of the subfranchisor's offer to third-party franchisees, with the exception of price (discussed below), are largely, if not completely, dictated by the franchisor. In many franchise systems, the offering documents registered by the subfranchisor are prepared by the franchisor, with the subfranchisor left to complete the application forms, the franchise fee schedule, and identifying information concerning the subfranchisor's personnel and to attach its audited financial statements. Since the subfranchisor's offering materials describe the franchisor and its franchise program, most franchise companies will want to control the disclosure contents.

U.S. antitrust laws prevent a franchisor from dictating the amount of the fees that a subfranchisor must charge the franchisees. Thus, even though a franchisor charges a $10,000 initial franchise fee to its franchisees on direct unit sales that it makes, the franchisor cannot require the subfranchisor to charge the same amount, or set minimum or maximum fees the subfranchisor is to charge. A partial solution is for the franchisor to specify a minimum dollar amount payable by the subfranchisor to the franchisor out of the initial franchise fees received from third-party franchisees.

Enforcement

All registration statutes create a comprehensive enforcement structure to deal with franchise sales abuses, vesting substantial investigatory and prosecuting power in the state administrator as well as providing for criminal enforcement and private litigation.[78]

Satisfying the uniform and state-specific disclosure categories may not prove an adequate defense to a state registration law violation in all cases. These statutes protect against fraudulent and unlawful practices in the sale of franchises and define such prohibited practices in the broadest terms. Thus, state law violations can be founded on events outside of the disclosure document delivered to franchisees, for example, upon (1) any intentional or willful making of an untrue statement of a material fact in the registration application; (2) any intentional or willful omission of a material fact that is necessary to render other statements in the application not misleading; (3) the breach of any order or condition imposed on the registration (e.g., the breach of an impound condition); or (4) the failure to notify the administrator in timely fashion of material changes in any application or report filed with the state. The failure to disclose a material fact, as materiality has been previously defined, notwithstanding that the particular disclosure is not specifically called for by the uniform or state-specific disclosure rules, is a fraudulent practice under state laws.[79]

---

78. There is no private right of action for FTC Rule violations. Mon-Shore Management, Inc. vs. Family Media, Inc., 584 F. Supp. 186 (S.D.N.Y. 1984); Holloway v. Bristol-Meyers Corp., 485 F.2d 986 (D.C. Cir. 1973). Generally, private litigants can obtain civil remedies for acts constituting FTC Rule violations by bringing actions under state "little FTC acts" which prohibit unfair and deceptive acts and practices in commerce. *See* Bailey Employment Sys. Inc. v. Hahn, 545 F. Supp. 62 (D. Conn. 1982), *aff'd per curiam* (unpublished opinion), 723 F.2d 895 (2d Cir. 1983). The FTC's enforcement powers include obtaining civil remedies on behalf of injured third parties and imposing penalties of up to $10,000 per day for each violation of the FTC Rule. 15 U.S.C. § 57(a)(1) and (b). The section on enforcement in this chapter is limited to the relief available for violation of franchise registration statutes. An excellent review of state remedies for franchise sales violations is presented in 5 IFA FRAN. L. DIG. 12 (1986).

79. Likewise, a material omission would violate the FTC Rule as a deceptive practice even if the missing information is not the subject of a specific disclosure category. Section 436.1(a)(21) of the FTC Rule (Bus. Franchise Guide (CCH) ¶ 6121) states that the information required to be disclosed by the FTC Rule "shall not contain any material or information other than that required by this part or by state law not preempted by this part." One could read this to mean that the FTC Rule prohibits any "extra" disclosures. On the other hand, one could read this language to compel disclosure of all material facts, regardless of whether they fit neatly within a prescribed disclosure category, if their omission would be actionable under state law as common-law fraud. The latter position—requiring franchisors to disclose all material information in the offering circular, whether specifically called for by disclosure rules or not—seems more persuasive since it results in greater protection to prospective franchisees.

Administrative Enforcement

The enforcement powers granted to state administrators are extremely broad. In practice they are limited mainly by budget constraints. Perhaps the most significant power reposed in the state administrator by statute is the ability to issue *ex parte* stop orders prohibiting franchise sales activities by individuals or entities whom the state administrator believes may be violating the franchise statute for up to a specified number of days until a hearing can be conducted.[80]

Furthermore, franchise administrators have authority to conduct both public and private investigations within, or outside of, the registration state; to seek injunctive orders; and, through the local district attorney's office, to prosecute criminal actions.

Some state statutes empower the franchise administrator to obtain restitution on behalf of victims of practices found to be fraudulent and illegal and, at any stage of litigation, to seek and obtain a court-ordered receivership of monies or property derived by a franchisor through fraudulent or unlawful means.[81]

Criminal Penalties

Criminal liability exists under all state registration statutes. Violation of state registration laws is punishable in all states as a felony. In addition, fines may be imposed for criminal violations and may be as high as $50,000 per violation. Criminal liability is predicated on "willful" or intentional violations.[82] California's law, which served as the model for other state registration statutes, permits criminal liability despite the absence of proof of any criminal intent or intent to violate the statute and does not excuse liability by proving ignorance of the law.[83]

Civil Actions

All registration states recognize private remedies (i.e., recovery of damages) for franchise registration law violations, including equitable relief and rescission.[84]

---

80. *But see supra* notes 41 and 42.

81. *See,* e.g., MD. CODE ANN. § 14-210, Bus. Franchise Guide (CCH) ¶ 3200.10.

82. ILL. REV. STAT. ch. 85–551 § 705/24, Bus. Franchise Guide (CCH) ¶ 3130.24.

83. People v. Gonda, 138 Cal. App. 3d 774, 188 Cal. Rptr. 295 (1982), Bus. Franchise Guide (CCH) ¶ 7968.

84. Some registration statutes limit rescission to "willful" statutory violations. *See,* e.g., CAL. CORP. CODE § 31300, Bus. Franchise Guide (CCH) ¶ 3050.60. The California appellate court decision in *Gonda* suggests that the California registration statute is a near-strict liability statute, thus permitting rescission for technical violations of the law if it can be shown that the franchisor knew what he or she was doing when he or she committed the statutory violation irrespective of whether or not he or she knew it was unlawful. *But see* HAW. REV. STAT. § 482E-9, Bus. Franchise Guide (CCH) ¶ 3110.09. This section provides that rescission is not available to the plaintiff if the defendant proves the plaintiff knew of the facts concerning the untruth or admission, or that the defendant exercised reasonable care and did not know, or if the defendant had exercised reasonable care and could not have known the untruth or admission.

Most of the state registration statutes do not provide for punitive damages. However, the Hawaii and Washington statutes permit the court, in its discretion, to award damages not to exceed three times actual damages sustained.[85]

Although there are not reported decisions in all of the registration states, the franchisor's ability to raise equitable defenses to rescission claims based on disclosure or registration law violations has received some judicial attention. The Hawaii, Maryland, Michigan, Minnesota, North Dakota, South Dakota, and Washington courts have recognized equitable defenses to rescission claims founded on technical violations of state registration statutes.[86] However, the Illinois courts have denied such equitable defenses.[87]

The registration states with a fair degree of uniformity extend joint and several liability to all controlling persons, partners, officers, directors, and persons falling under the catchall category of "occupying a similar status or performing similar functions" and to employees who "materially aid" in the violation committed. In-house counsel for franchisors found guilty of state law violations may, depending on the facts, come under the "aiding and abetting" category and have liability based on material inaccuracies or omissions in the registration filing or disclosure. Whether statutory liability should, or does, extend to outside counsel, assuming no actual knowledge of the material inaccuracy or omission, has been the subject of considerable debate and has yet to be addressed by any court.[88] However, outside lawyers who fail to perform due diligence and who prepare false and misleading offering materials may have liability for negligence to franchisees who rely on the inaccurate disclosures.[89]

85. HAW. REV. STAT. § 48 LE-9, Bus. Franchise Guide (CCH) ¶ 3110.09; WASH. REV. CODE § 19.100.190, Bus. Franchise Guide (CCH) ¶ 3470.19.

86. Fargo Biltmore Motor Hotel Corp. v. Best Western Int'l, 563 F. Supp. 1022 (D.N.D. 1983), *aff'd in part and remanded in part,* 742 F.2d 459 (8th Cir. 1984) (North Dakota Franchise Investment Law); Peck of Chehalis, Inc. v. C.K. of W. America, Inc., 304 N.W.2d 91 (N.D. Sup. Ct. 1981), Bus. Franchise Guide (CCH) ¶ 7627 (North Dakota Franchise Investment Law); Clapp v. Peterson, 327 N.W.2d 585 (Minn. 1982), Bus. Franchise Guide (CCH) ¶ 7907 (Minnesota Franchise Act); Benson v. Sbarro Licensing, Inc., Bus. Franchise Guide (CCH) ¶ 7967 (D. Minn. 1983) (Minnesota Franchise Act); Uncle John's of Hawaii v. Mid Pacific Restaurants, Bus. Franchise Guide (CCH) ¶ 9695 (Haw. Sup. Ct. 1990) (Hawaii Franchise Investment Law); Bagel Enters., Inc. v. Baskin & Sears, Bus. Franchise Guide (CCH) ¶ 8071 (Maryland Franchise Registration and Disclosure Act); Dynamic Enterprise, Inc. v. Fitness World of Jackson, Inc., Bus. Franchise Guide (CCH) ¶ 8054 (Bankr. M.D. Tenn. 1983) (Michigan Franchise Investment Law); Nielsen v. McCabe, Bus. Franchise Guide (CCH) ¶ 9432 (N.D. Sup. Ct. 1989) (South Dakota Franchise Act), and Harb v. Norrell Serv., Inc., Bus. Franchise Guide (CCH) ¶ 10,231 (W.D. Wash. 1993).

87. My Pie Int'l, Inc. v. Debould, Inc., 687 F.2d 919 (7th Cir. 1982), Bus. Franchise Guide (CCH) ¶ 7867 (interpreting Illinois Franchise Disclosure Act). The Illinois registration statute makes every franchise sold in violation of the statute voidable at the franchisee's election. ILL. REV. STAT. ch. 85-551, § 705/26, Bus. Franchise Guide (CCH) ¶ 3130.26.

88. *See* 4 ABA FRAN. L.J. 3 (Spring 1985) and 2 ABA FRAN. L.J. 1 (Spring 1982).

89. *See* Courtney v. Waring, 191 Cal. App. 3d 1434, 237 Cal. Rptr. 233 (1987), Bus. Franchise Guide (LLCH) ¶ 8887; Hanson v. Rudnick & Wolfe, Bus. Franchise Guide (CCH) ¶ 10,212, *decided on other grounds.*

Significantly, the franchisor's failure to register with a state does not void the franchise agreement or render it illegal. The statutory remedies for failure to register are the exclusive remedies for nonregistration. Unless state law makes the franchise contract voidable by the franchisee when there is a failure to register, the franchisee is not relieved of its contractual undertakings because of the franchisor's statutory violation. Certain states limit the franchisee's right to void the contract upon a showing that the franchisor's failure to register was "willful."[90] The measure of damages recoverable by a franchisee based on the sale of an unregistered franchise, when failure to register is the only violation of state law, has been addressed in only a handful of cases. The few considering the issue have not focused on calculating damages *per se* but on how to restore the injured party to its precontract position (in the context of rescission).[91]

In the states of Illinois, California, New York, and North Dakota, the private remedies extended to franchisees can be barred if the franchisor in question offers rescission before suit and offers to refund the difference between the consideration paid and the amount of income earned by the franchisee from operation of the franchise business.[92]

Franchise Relationship Laws

The franchise registration statutes discussed in this chapter focus on the procedural aspects of how franchises may be sold and marketed. They do not regulate the ongoing franchise relationship, that is, the relationship created by the fran-

---

90. *See* CAL. CORP. CODE § 31300, Bus. Franchise Guide (CCH) ¶ 3050.60; Pizza Time Theatre, Inc., v. Topeka Inn Management, Inc., Bus. Franchise Guide (CCH) ¶ 7790 (N.D. Cal. 1981) (court found that the failure to register was not "willful" and, therefore, franchisee was not entitled to rescission): *In Re* Dynamics Enters., Inc., Bus. Franchise Guide (CCH) ¶ 8054 (U.S. Bankruptcy Court, E.D. Tenn. 1983) (same result as *Pizza Time Theatre* under Michigan Franchise Investment Law).

91. *See* Kohr v. Gropp & Lehman Enterprises, 718 F.2d 1099 (6th Cir. 1983), Bus. Franchise Guide (CCH) ¶ 8124 (the court found that the franchisor had neither breached the franchise agreement nor made any untrue or misleading statements about the franchise; on the contrary, even though the franchisor had failed to register, the franchisor had provided more assistance than was required under the contract or promised in the offering circular; the franchisees' operating losses, according to the court, were due to their own mismanagement and would have been sustained even if the sale had been registered; thus, the court rejected plaintiffs' claim for operating losses, lost profits, and unpaid rent and limited the franchisee's recovery to a refund of the initial franchise fee); *cf.* Martin Investors, Inc. v. Vander Bie, 269 N.W.2d 868 (Minn. Sup. Ct. 1978) (rescission granted for failure to register franchises under Minnesota statute; rescission award included restitution of pretrial legal expenses, including cost of incorporating; court emphasized that such recovery did not constitute damages, but by-product of rescission).

92. Illinois: ILL. REV. STAT. ch. 85-551, § 26, Bus. Franchise Guide (CCH) ¶ 3130.26; New York: N.Y. GEN. BUS. LAW § 691.2, Bus. Franchise Guide (CCH) ¶ 3320.12; North Dakota: N.D. CENT. CODE ANN. § 51-19-12.4, Bus. Franchise Guide (CCH) ¶ 3340.12. *See also, supra* note 86, regarding waiver as a defense.

chise agreement. Franchise relationship laws of general application (not restricted to particular industries) exist in many states[93] and affect certain substantive aspects of the franchise relationship, most commonly termination and nonrenewal conditions.[94]

The regulatory reach of relationship statutes to termination and renewal provisions is aimed at preventing arbitrary and unfair forfeitures of franchise rights and franchise businesses without "good cause," in recognition of the substantial investment typically made by franchisees in their businesses. The relationship statutes vary both in their definition of "good cause" and in the procedural prerequisites for termination and nonrenewal. The majority of states define "good cause" nonexhaustively by way of examples.[95]

Many franchisors draft their franchise contracts to mirror the minimum requirements for termination and nonrenewal set forth in the state's relationship statute and, in this way, minimize the relationship laws' impact on the franchisor's disclosure document. While there is no reported decision or published administrative ruling on this point, it does not appear that a violation of the state registration statute would arise merely from the offer or sale of a franchise on terms permitting termination or nonrenewal in conflict with the state's relationship law. Generally, state administrators in registration states with a relationship law will not require, as a condition of registration, that franchisors rewrite their franchise contract to conform to the minimum protections required under the relationship statute but, instead, will require that franchisors include in their disclosure document notice of the existence of such laws, which may be done by state-specific addenda, and the inclusion of an amendment to the franchise agreement stating that to the extent the franchise agreement conflicts with the state's relationship law, the latter will control.[96]

Relationship laws in several states extend beyond issues of termination and nonrenewal and address such aspects of the franchise relationship as fair dealing, discrimination among franchisees, market protection for the franchisee (often referred to as encroachment on the part of the franchisor), the right to join franchisee associations, the alienability of franchise rights, choice of governing law for franchise contracts, and the situs for litigation and arbitration of contract disputes.[97] As franchising matures and competition in the marketplace increases,

---

93. A thorough discussion of this subject appears in Chapter 5.

94. The relationship statutes' limitation upon a franchisor's right to refuse renewal of a franchise purportedly applies only where a renewal right is given to the franchisee. See Chapter 5.

95. *See,* e.g., CAL. BUS. & PROF. CODE §§ 20021 and 20025, Bus. Franchise Guide (CCH) ¶¶ 4050.14 and 4050.15.

96. *See,* e.g., CAL. BUS. & PROF. CODE §§ 20021 and 20025, Bus. Franchise Guide (CCH) ¶¶ 4050.14 and 4050.15, and South Dakota Memorandum, Bus. Franchise Guide (CCH) ¶ 5410. Nevertheless, a violation of the relationship statute would arise if a franchisor sought to terminate a franchise on grounds not constituting "good cause" or in violation of the statute's procedural requirements, even though the grounds or procedures had been fully disclosed to the franchisee before the franchise sale was made.

97. *See,* e.g., IOWA CODE §§ 523H.1 to 523H.17 (1995).

this area continues to receive substantial legislative attention at the state and federal levels.[98]

Business Opportunity Laws

Business opportunity laws are an area of regulation frequently overlooked by franchise companies. These laws may, depending on the particular facts, reach franchise relationships. Compliance with business opportunity laws may involve fulfilling registration duties different from those addressed in this chapter.

Twenty-four states have enacted business opportunity laws.[99] In nearly all of these states, a franchise offering that complies with the state franchise sales law or FTC Rule will qualify for an exemption from the business opportunity registration duty, at least if the franchisor has a registered trademark. In a few states, a franchisor claiming an exemption must file a simple notice to qualify for the exemption.[100] In a few states, an exemption may not be available to franchisors notwithstanding compliance with the state's registration law or the FTC Rule. The issue then becomes one of statutory definition: whether the franchise relationship also constitutes a "business opportunity" as defined in the state's business opportunity law.[101]

The business opportunity laws were designed to reach distribution arrangements conceptually different from franchises, such as dealerships, vending machine and rack jobbing businesses, home manufacturing ventures, and electronic amusement machine routes, which typically require a low investment and historically have been marketed to unsophisticated purchasers. Mainly because of how franchises are sold, franchise relationships are touched by these laws.

---

98. *See* The Federal Fair Franchise Practices Act, H.R. 1717, Bus. Franchise Guide (CCH) extra ed. 187 (June 22, 1995). Various bills have been introduced in the U.S. House of Representatives since 1991 proposing federal franchise relationship legislation. H.R. 1717 is the latest of those bills and is discussed in greater detail later in this chapter.

99. Alabama, California, Connecticut, Florida, Georgia, Illinois, Indiana, Iowa, Kentucky, Louisiana, Maine, Maryland, Michigan, Nebraska, New Hampshire, North Carolina, Ohio, Oklahoma, South Carolina, South Dakota, Texas, Utah, Virginia, and Washington. *See* Appendix A. Each of these states has a specific statute that targets relationships termed "business opportunities" or something equivalent. (For example, the California statute regulates "seller assisted marketing plans.") The phrase "business opportunity" in one state's statute does not necessarily mean the same thing when used in another state's statute. In every case, the first inquiry should be with how the state statute defines the targeted relationship. Minnesota includes "business opportunities" in its franchise law. MSA 80C.01.

100. *See* Appendix A, Florida, Kentucky, Nebraska, Texas, and Utah.

101. As a separate issue, a relationship may fall within the state's definition of a "business opportunity" but not constitute a "franchise" under the state's franchise sales law (if any) or under the FTC Rule. In such case, the exemptions available to franchises may not apply. Again, the first inquiry must be with the state statute's definition of the targeted relationship (e.g., of the term "business opportunity," "seller assisted marketing plan," "franchise," and the like) and the particular facts at hand.

For the most part, business opportunity sales are defined as transactions involving the sale of products, equipment, or services to enable the purchaser to start a business that are accompanied by certain promises or representations regarding profitability, marketability, marketing assistance, or "buyback" of finished product. Franchise sales, by legal definition, typically include representations concerning marketing plans and assistance. Even in states that define business opportunities without reference to whether or not promises of marketing assistance are made, state administrators sometimes take an aggressive posture, claiming that franchise offers, by their nature, involve implied promises regarding profitability and income potential, and on that basis find reason to extend their business opportunity statutes to traditional franchise relationships.

Fortunately, as noted, nearly all states provide either an exception from the business opportunity definition or an exemption from the statute's application for franchisors. These exceptions and exemptions fall into four general categories:[102]

1. Coverage by a franchise registration law of the same state[103]
2. Exclusion from the definition of "business opportunity" where the offer of a marketing program is in conjunction with the licensing of a registered trademark[104]
3. Exclusion from the definition of "business opportunity" where the offer of a marketing program is in conjunction with a federally registered trademark[105]
4. Compliance with the FTC Rule disclosure duties.[106]

Business opportunity disclosure and registration duties are substantially similar to franchising rules. Indeed, in many business opportunity states, use of the UFOC disclosure format may satisfy state disclosure duties to business opportunity purchasers. As a practical matter, business opportunity filings do not come under the same degree of scrutiny as franchise registration filings. The application process, including amendment and renewal procedures, is similar to state franchise requirements.

Likewise, the statutory design for enforcement and penalties for business opportunity statute violations is very similar. Finally, some statutes provide busi-

---

102. Additional exemptions may be available to franchisors. These include, among others, business opportunity sales made by an "experienced seller" or to an "experienced buyer," as such terms are defined by state law, and sales involving an initial cash or total investment that is either above or below the jurisdictional range or industry-specific exemptions. The significant message here is for practitioners to recognize the possibility that business opportunity compliance may be required and to determine whether an exception or exemption to coverage is available.

103. California, Maryland, Virginia, and Washington.

104. Florida, Georgia, Louisiana, Maine, Maryland, South Carolina, Texas, and Utah.

105. Connecticut, Iowa, and North Carolina.

106. Nebraska, Ohio, and Texas.

ness opportunity purchasers with a postexecution "cooling off" period within which they may void the business opportunity sale.[107]

The Future of Franchise Regulation

What is the role of registration in the future of franchise regulation? Legislation affecting franchising was introduced in numerous states in the 1995–96 legislative sessions.[108] In several of these states, the bills that were introduced were franchise registration related. In the other states the bills were drafted to address issues relating to the franchise relationship. While the majority of these legislative proposals tended to focus on the franchise relationship area, in the 1993–94 legislative session, bills attempting to enact the NASAA Model Franchise Act were introduced in three states that do not currently have franchise registration and disclosure laws and in two states to supplant the existing franchise registration laws.[109] None of those bills proposing to enact the model act in the nonregistration states was successful. However, the model act was adopted in Rhode Island in 1993 to supplant the existing franchise law. Wisconsin and Hawaii revised their respective statutes in the 1996 session, with the changes in Wisconsin being from a full-blown registration and review process to a notification registration. No new states have adopted a registration law since New York did so in 1981.[110]

In addition to legislation at the state level, on May 25, 1995, Congressman John LaFalce introduced federal franchise legislation for the third time in four years. His proposal, H.R. 1717, is titled the Federal Fair Franchise Practices Act.[111] This proposal combines various aspects of three bills that had been introduced in the previous legislative session: the Federal Franchise Disclosure and Consumer Protection Act, the Federal Fair Franchise Practices Act, and the Federal Franchise Data and Public Information Act.[112]

H.R. 1717 seeks to codify and strengthen current federal law relating to disclosure and antifraud enforcement and to enhance the information available to the public concerning franchise opportunities. It seeks to accomplish these objectives through (1) expanding antifraud requirements; (2) creating a private right of

---

107. *See,* e.g., California—three business days; Iowa—three business days; Kentucky—thirty days; Maine—three business days; Ohio—five business days; Washington—seven days.

108. Bills were introduced in the states of Arkansas, Hawaii, Illinois, Indiana, Iowa, Louisiana, Maryland, Massachusetts, Michigan, Nevada, New Jersey, New York, South Carolina, South Dakota, Wisconsin, and Vermont.

109. Connecticut, Mississippi and South Carolina, and Indiana and Rhode Island, respectively.

110. Both Kentucky and Utah have enacted amendments to their respective business opportunity laws. *See* Appendix A.

111. H.R. 1717, Bus. Franchise Guide (CCH) extra ed. 187 (June 22, 1995).

112. H.R. 1315, H.R. 1316, and H.R. 1317, respectively, Bus. Franchise Guide (CCH) extra ed. 159 (March 24, 1993).

action that would permit persons injured by violations of its requirements to seek judicial redress; and (3) authorizing states attorneys general to bring action to enforce its requirements. While it has been suggested that the introduction of a federal private right of action would mitigate the need for state registration laws, it is unlikely that any measures will be taken federally to preempt state franchise registration and disclosure laws, and no such suggestions are contained in this bill.

H.R. 1717 prohibits certain practices that it deems deceptive and discriminatory. Among other things, the bill would make it unlawful for any franchisor to (1) prohibit a franchisee in many cases from obtaining equipment, fixtures, and supplies or services used in the franchised business from sources of the franchisee's choosing; (2) terminate or otherwise cancel a franchise before its expiration without "good cause"; and (3) prohibit any franchisee from engaging in any business at any location after expiration or termination of a franchise unless the franchisor offers in writing to purchase the assets of the franchise business for its fair market value as a going concern. The bill would also make it unlawful for a franchisor to hinder or prohibit, directly or indirectly, the free association of franchisees for any lawful purpose, and it provides an exemption from the Clayton Act[113] for the activities of franchisee associations. The bill also provides a federal restriction on "franchisor encroachment" by prohibiting a franchisor from establishing a new outlet or point of sale of goods or services similar to those offered by the franchisee and identified by the same trademark or advertising used by the franchisee within "unreasonable proximity" to the outlet or business licensed to the franchisee. The bill would also limit the effect of integration clauses, invalidate choice of venue provisions that would require a franchise to resolve disputes outside of its home state, and void any provisions purporting to waive liability under H.R. 1717. The bill also imposes standards of conduct in the franchise relationship by imposing a duty of good faith on the parties to a franchise agreement and a duty of due care on the part of the franchisor.

Another major issue facing franchising is the possible adoption by both federal and state regulators of a requirement that franchisors disclose the financial performance results of the business being franchised (or earnings claims, as noted earlier). This proposal, if enacted, would substantially alter the way earnings information is delivered to the prospective franchisee. The proposal is presently being studied by a committee of NASAA, together with representatives from the FTC.

On April 25, 1993, the NASAA membership voted unanimously to adopt the New UFOC Guidelines. The phase-in adopted by NASAA provides that the New UFOC Guidelines are effective six months after the FTC and each NASAA member whose jurisdiction requires presale registration of a franchise adopts the New UFOC. New York was the last state to adopt the New UFOC. As of January 1, 1996, all initial franchise applications and renewals must comply with the New UFOC.[114]

---

113. 15 U.S.C. § 12 *et seq.*
114. Bus. Franchise Guide (CCH) ¶ 5901.

One of the most significant roles the registration process will play in the next few years will be in the interpretation of the New UFOC Guidelines. On June 21, 1994, in response to concerns of its advisory committee, which consulted with NASAA during the drafting of the new UFOC, the NASAA Franchise and Business Opportunity Committee issued a "Commentary" to assist franchisors drafting offering circulars prepared under the New UFOC Guidelines and to assist state franchise examiners and enforcement agencies in their interpretation of franchisor compliance.[115] As state examiners review applications, and practitioners and examiners work together to resolve interpretational questions concerning the New UFOC Guidelines, it is hoped that the registration process will facilitate the development of a consistent (if not uniform) standard for interpreting the new disclosure requirements and will encourage the use of one offering circular for all the registration states.

115. Bus. Franchise Guide (CCH) ¶ 5950.

CHAPTER 5

Franchise Relationship Laws

Thomas M. Pitegoff and M. Christine Carty

Contents

This chapter provides an overview of the laws governing the franchise relationship after the franchise agreement has been signed.[1] (Franchise regulation relating to the sale of franchises is covered in Chapters 3 and 4.)

Appendices B through F provide more specific information regarding state franchise relationship laws, including statutory examples of good cause for termination, procedural requirements for termination and nonrenewal, and examples of unlawful practices not covered in the body of this chapter.

Brief History and Overview of Franchise Relationship Laws

Abuses

In the 1950s and 1960s, the early period of business format franchising, abuses were common. These abuses were exacerbated by the retrenchment and vertical integration in the motor vehicle fuel industry following the OPEC oil embargo in 1973. Franchisees argued that these abuses were not adequately addressed by common-law or antitrust remedies. The result was the successful passage of both franchise registration and relationship laws. The abuses to which relationship laws are aimed include the following:

- *Unjust terminations.* Either by contract or by economic or other pressures, the franchisor would attempt to terminate the franchise relationship, thereby depriving the franchisee of the fruits of his or her labor.

---

1. This chapter is based on Thomas M. Pitegoff's *Franchise Relationship Laws: A Minefield for Franchisors, in* BUILDING FRANCHISE RELATIONSHIPS: A GUIDE TO ANTICIPATING PROBLEMS, RESOLVING CONFLICTS, AND REPRESENTING CLIENTS 140 (Ann Hurwitz and Rochelle Buchsbaum Spandorf, eds., ABA 1996).

- *No renewal rights.* The franchise agreement typically was short-term, allowing the franchisor to capture the benefits of the business that the franchisee had developed once the stated term of the agreement had expired.
- *No right to assign.* The franchisor would prohibit the franchisee from transferring all or a portion of his or her interest in the franchise to a bona fide purchaser, or perhaps to a qualified member of the franchisee's family.
- *Other abuses.* The franchisor would place another unit (either company-owned or franchised) in close proximity to an existing franchised unit. This placement, known as encroachment, would result in the franchisee's business being "cannibalized." Franchisors also engaged in other practices objectionable to franchisees, such as restricting the right of free association among franchisees, discriminating among franchisees, and imposing unreasonable standards of performance on franchisees.

Federal Legislation

No franchise relationship law of general application exists at the federal level. While a federal franchise relationship law of general application was proposed as early as 1971, no such law has ever been adopted. Instead, the Federal Trade Commission (FTC) issued its "Disclosure Requirements and Prohibitions Concerning Franchising and Business Opportunity Ventures"[2] (the FTC Rule), which became effective in 1979. The FTC Rule requires presale disclosure, but it contains no requirements regarding termination, renewal, or assignment.

While broad legislative efforts failed at the federal level, certain industries were successful in obtaining legislation addressing specific needs. The first federal law specifically regulating franchising was the Automobile Dealer's Day in Court Act,[3] enacted in 1956. This statute basically requires automobile manufacturers to deal in good faith with dealers. More comprehensive laws governing the relationship between automobile manufacturers and dealers exist at the state level in most states.

In 1978, Congress adopted the Petroleum Marketing Practices Act (the PMPA),[4] which sets forth procedures that a gas station "franchisor" must follow before it may terminate or refuse to renew a dealer. The PMPA is of particular interest because it preempts state law in the areas of franchise termination and renewal. Therefore, the substantive protection provided by the states was abrogated by the federal act, an act that historically has not been viewed by many practitioners as being pro-dealer or franchisee and that is more procedural than substantive in content. The case law under the PMPA seems to support this view.[5]

---

2. 16 C.F.R. pt. 436. See Chapter 3 for a discussion of the FTC Rule.

3. 15 U.S.C. § 1221-1225.

4. 15 U.S.C. § 2801-2806.

5. *See generally* Lewis G. Rudnick, *The Franchise Relationship: A Look Back in Time,* I ABA ELEVENTH ANNUAL FORUM ON FRANCHISING (1988), tab 5 at 15.

The Sherman Act and other federal antitrust laws significantly influenced the early development of franchising arrangements, particularly with respect to vertical restrictions such as tying arrangements and exclusive territories. Since the late 1970s, however, antitrust laws have become less of an issue, as courts have allowed franchisors to impose reasonable vertical restrictions.

State Legislation

Franchisees have achieved greater success at the state level than at the federal level in creating protection against franchisor abuse. Statutes have been enacted to deal with specific problems in various industry sectors. The most common industry-specific statutes relate to the automotive, beer and wine, farm equipment, and construction equipment industries.[6]

In 1964, Puerto Rico became the first U.S. jurisdiction to pass a law protecting local dealers without regard to industry. The California Franchise Investment Law, enacted in 1970, was the first registration and disclosure law governing franchise sales. A number of other states also enacted franchise registration and disclosure laws during the 1970s. Most of the state franchise relationship laws also were enacted in the 1970s, either separately or as part of the registration and disclosure laws.

Seventeen states have laws of general applicability that govern the franchise relationship.[7] These laws were promulgated only after hard-fought battles in the legislative arenas. In seven of these states, the franchise relationship laws are part of a state franchise registration or disclosure law. Two other state have both disclosure and relationship laws. The remaining states have relationship laws but not disclosure laws. A state-by-state breakdown is set forth in Appendix C. The remainder of this chapter deals with state franchise relationship laws of general applicability.

The areas of primary concern under state relationship laws are the termination, renewal, and transfer of franchise rights. This chapter focuses on these issues. Franchise relationship laws prohibit a number of other practices of franchisors, such as the following:

---

6. The industry-specific statutes are collected in Bus. Franchise Guide (CCH) at ¶¶ 4000 *et seq.*

7. Arkansas, California, Connecticut, Delaware, Hawaii, Illinois, Indiana, Iowa, Michigan, Minnesota, Mississippi, Missouri, Nebraska, New Jersey, Virginia, Washington, and Wisconsin. The District of Columbia, Puerto Rico, and the U.S. Virgin Islands also have relationship laws. See Appendix B.

The South Dakota Division of Securities also has policies for registration that include a requirement that the franchise agreement afford the franchisee thirty days' notice of termination and an opportunity to cure. Bus. Franchise Guide (CCH) ¶ 5410.01. *See also* S.D. Codified Laws Ann. § 37-5A-51, referring to rules of the Division of Securities. No rules have yet been issued.

The Maryland Fair Distribution Act, which became effective October 1, 1995, applies to wholesale distributors of commercial goods who maintain an inventory of such goods for resale. This act specifically does not apply to franchises and business opportunities that fall under the state's registration and disclosure laws.

1. Restricting free association among franchisees
2. Discriminating between franchisees
3. Prohibiting changes in management without good cause
4. Encroaching on the franchisee's exclusive territory
5. Receiving payments from third parties based on the business dealings of such parties with franchisees
6. Requiring litigation or arbitration outside of the franchisee's state.

Examples of these prohibitions, with a breakdown by state, are listed in Appendix F.

The question of the effect of a contractual choice-of-law clause on the applicability of state relationship laws arises frequently. The effect of an attempt by a franchisor to avoid a franchise relationship statute by the contractual choice of law of another state is unpredictable.[8] In many states, a waiver of compliance with the relationship laws will be ineffective, and the selection of the law of another state will be held contrary to the fundamental policy of the franchisee's state.[9] In other cases, the selection of the laws of the franchisor's state will avoid the franchise relationship law of the franchisee's state.[10]

In a state in which the relationship requirements are part of the registration and disclosure law, the use of a franchise agreement that is contrary to the relationship requirements and is not qualified by reference to the local law may delay registration.

Definition of "Franchise" under State Relationship Laws

Breadth of Definition

The definition of a franchise varies widely among the relationship laws. The coverage of the franchise relationship laws, however, is often far broader than that of the registration and disclosure laws.

While each state relationship law has a different definition of the term "franchise," most definitions require that the following three elements be present:

---

8. *See* Thomas M. Pitegoff, *Choice of Law in Franchise Relationships: Staying within Bounds,* 14 Franchise L.J. 89 (1995); Thomas M. Pitegoff, *Choice of Law in Franchise Agreements,* 9 Franchise L.J. 1 (Summer 1989).

9. *See, e.g.,* Instructional Sys., Inc. v. Computer Curriculum Corp., 35 F.3d 813 (3d Cir. 1994), *cert. denied,* 115 S. Ct. 1176 (1995).

10. *See* Modern Computer Sys., Inc. v. Modern Banking Sys., Inc. 871 F.2d 734 (8th Cir. 1989) (holding that the franchise relationship law of Minnesota, the state in which the franchise was located, did not apply, citing the parties' choice of Nebraska law).

1. The relationship must involve the use of a trademark
2. There must be either a "community of interest" between the franchisor and the franchisee, or the franchisor must provide the franchisee with a "marketing plan"
3. The franchisor must charge the franchisee a fee.

The franchise laws of a few states cover not just franchises but many dealerships and distribution arrangements as well.[11] Manufacturers and suppliers who enter into agreements with distributors, wholesalers, or retailers in Arkansas, Connecticut, Missouri, New Jersey, or Wisconsin must be particularly careful. The relationship laws of these states define the term "franchise" without a fee element.

Some franchise laws cover only franchises that include a trademark license. A manufacturer or supplier can avoid the franchise relationship laws of Missouri and New Jersey, for example, by ensuring that agreements with its distributors in those states contain no implication of a grant of a license to use a trade name, trademark, or service mark, or anything that might be characterized as such.

The Arkansas Franchise Practices Act simply requires the grant of a license to use a trademark or service mark within an exclusive or nonexclusive territory to sell or distribute goods or services. There is no requirement of a franchise fee, a marketing plan, or a community of interest. This definition is extremely broad.

A Closer Look at the Elements of a Franchise

Marketing Plan

The term "marketing plan" refers to a grant of the right to engage in business under a marketing plan or system prescribed in substantial part by the franchisor.[12] Generally, a marketing plan exists whenever the franchisor presents the group of franchised outlets to the public as a unit, with the appearance of some central-

---

11. *See* K. H. Slade, *Applicability of Franchise and Business Opportunity Laws to Distribution and Licensing Agreements,* AIPLA Q.J. 1 (1987); H. B. Lowell & J. F. Dienelt, *Drafting Distribution Agreements: The Unwitting Sale of Franchises and Business Opportunities,* 11 DEL. J. CORP. L. 725 (1986).

12. Under the California Franchise Relations Act, for example, "franchise" means a contract or agreement, either expressed or implied, whether oral or written, between two or more persons by which:

1. A franchisee is granted the right to engage in the business of offering, selling, or distributing goods or services under a marketing plan or system prescribed in substantial part by a franchisor.
2. The operation of the franchisee's business pursuant to such plan or system is substantially associated with the franchisor's trademark, service mark, trade name, logotype, advertising, or other commercial symbol designating the franchisor or its affiliate.
3. The franchisee is required to pay, directly or indirectly, a franchise fee.

CAL. BUS. & PROF. CODE § 20001 (West 1981).

ized management and uniform standards.[13] This might be done, for example, through one of the following:

1. Advertising by the franchisor
2. Requirements regarding site selection, appearance of the premises, uniforms, or hours of operation
3. Limitations on products, services, or customers
4. Providing training
5. Requiring approval of advertising and signage
6. The use of a manual.

Community of Interest

Some of the franchise laws have a definitional requirement that the franchisor and franchisee have a community of interest in the marketing of the goods or services.[14] The community of interest element is usually far broader than the marketing plan element.

In Wisconsin, for example, a community of interest exists where the parties share a continuing financial interest and a degree of interdependence.[15] Some

---

13. The Illinois Franchise Disclosure Act of 1987, for example, provides as follows:
"Marketing plan or system" means a plan or system relating to some aspect of the conduct of a party to a contract in conducting business, including but not limited to (i) specification of price, or special pricing systems or discount plans, (ii) use of particular sales or display equipment or merchandising devices, (iii) use of specific sales techniques, and (iv) use of advertising or promotional materials or cooperation in advertising efforts. . . .
ILL. REV. STAT. ch. 121¹/₂, para. 1705 (1987). For a broad interpretation, *see* Petereit v. S.B. Thomas, Inc., 853 F. Supp. 55, Bus. Franchise Guide (CCH) ¶ 10,379 (D. Conn. 1993) (Connecticut law).

14. In Wisconsin, for example,
"Dealership" means a contract or agreement, either expressed or implied, whether oral or written, between 2 or more persons, by which a person is granted the right to sell or distribute goods or services, or use a trade name, trademark, service mark, logotype, advertising, or other commercial symbol, in which there is a community of interest in the business of offering, selling, or distributing goods or services at wholesale, retail, by lease, agreement, or otherwise.
WIS. STAT. § 135.02(3) (1985).

15. Cases discussing the community of interest requirement in Wisconsin include: Dodgeland Ag-Systems, Inc. v. Knight Mfg. Corp., Bus. Franchise Guide (CCH) ¶ 10,368 (1993), *rev. denied,* 515 N.W.2d 715 (Wis. 1994); Cajan of Wisconsin, Inc. v. Winston Furniture Co., Inc., 817 F. Supp. 778, Bus. Franchise Guide (CCH) ¶ 10,219 (E.D. Wis. 1993), *aff'd,* 21 F.3d 430, Bus. Franchise Guide (CCH) ¶ 10,458 (7th Cir. 1994); Ziegler Co., Inc. v. Rexnord, Inc., 139 Wis. 2d 593, 407 N.W.2d 873, Bus. Franchise Guide (CCH) ¶ 8882 (Wis. 1987), *remanded,* 147 Wis. 2d 308, 433 N.W.2d 8, Bus. Franchise Guide (CCH) ¶ 9317 (Wis. 1988); Lakefield Tel. Co. v. Northern Telecom, Inc., 696 F. Supp. 413, Bus. Franchise Guide (CCH) ¶ 9249 (E.D. Wis. 1988), *aff'd,* 970 F.2d 386, Bus. Franchise Guide (CCH) ¶ 10,064 (7th Cir. 1992).

Wisconsin courts have taken a simple view of this analysis in holding that a community of interest may exist in one of two circumstances: (1) when a large proportion of an alleged dealer's revenues are derived from the dealership; and (2) when the alleged dealer has made a sizable investment that is specialized in some way to the grantor's goods or services and thus is not fully recoverable upon termination.[16]

In New Jersey, the courts have construed "community of interest" more narrowly, looking to "the nature of the interdependence between the parties," and requiring a degree of control by the franchisor. In effect, there must be a sufficient inequality between the parties such that termination of the relationship by the stronger party would shock the court's sense of equity.[17] In one case, the court concluded that "the unequal bargaining power . . . in the franchise context arises when the relation between licensee and licensor has incidents that induce or require the licensee to invest in skills or assets that have no continuing value to the licensee if the license is terminated."[18] Another relevant factor under New Jersey law is whether the public perceives the putative franchisee and franchisor as "one and the same."[19]

In Minnesota, the payment of a volume-based royalty fee satisfies both the franchise fee element and the community of interest element of the definition of a franchise.[20]

Trademark

The trademark element of the state relationship laws will always be satisfied if the franchisee is licensed to do business under the franchisor's name or mark. Most of the marketing plan franchise laws, however, do not require a license. In some of these states, the operation of the franchisee's business must be "substantially associated" with the franchisor's trademark. In other states, the trademark element is satisfied where the franchisor's trademark or service mark identifies the goods or services sold, rather than the business itself. This would include

---

16. *See, e.g.,* Frieburg Farm Equip., Inc. v. Van Dale, Inc., 978 F.2d 395, Bus. Franchise Guide (CCH) ¶ 10,109 (7th Cir. 1992). *Cf.* Johnson v. Jingles Int'l, Ltd., 173 Wis.2d 304, 498 N.W.2d 912, Bus. Franchise Guide (CCH) ¶ 10,133 (Wis. Ct. App. 1992) (no community of interest where the distributor had less than $2,000 in inventory and purchased from the manufacturer on a COD or prepaid basis).

17. Pride Technologies, Inc. v. Sun Microsystems Computer Corp., Bus. Franchise Guide (CCH) ¶ 10,407 (N.D. Cal. 1994); Instructional Sys., Inc. v. Computer Curriculum Corp., 130 N.J. 324, 614 A.2d 124, Bus. Franchise Guide (CCH) ¶ 10,119 (1992); New Jersey Am., Inc. v. Allied Corp., 875 F.2d 58, Bus. Franchise Guide (CCH) ¶ 9395 (3d Cir. 1989); Colt Indus., Inc. v. Fidelco Pump & Compressor Corp., 844 F.2d 117, Bus. Franchise Guide (CCH) ¶ 9095 (3d Cir. 1988).

18. Cassidy Podell Lynch, Inc. v. Snyder General Corp., 944 F.2d 1131, 1142, Bus. Franchise Guide (CCH) ¶ 9885 (3d Cir. 1991).

19. Instructional Sys., Inc. v. Computer Curriculum Corp., 130 N.J. 324, 614 A.2d 124, Bus. Franchise Guide (CCH) ¶ 10,119 (1992); Freedman Truck Center, Inc. v. General Motors Corp., 784 F. Supp. 167, Bus. Franchise Guide (CCH) ¶ 9971 (D.N.J. 1992).

20. Martin Investors, Inc. v. Vander Bie, 269 N.W.2d 868 (Minn. 1978).

many ordinary distributorships.[21] If the relationship involves something less than a formal trademark license, the practitioner should examine the trademark element carefully.[22] For example, under Iowa law, this element is satisfied if the franchisor merely "allows" the business to be associated with its mark.[23] In one California case, the court held this element satisfied even though ultimate end users of the franchisees' services had no knowledge of the franchisor's name or mark.[24]

Fee

The fee element of the definition of a franchise generally means any fee or charge that the franchisee is required to pay for the right to do business under the franchise agreement. This payment does not have to be in the form of a franchise fee. It may also be royalties on sales. Most trademark license agreements contain provisions that would satisfy this requirement, as do most technology and "know-how" licenses. The fee may be a required payment for rent, advertising assistance, equipment and supplies, training, or other items. However, it generally does not include payment for a reasonable quantity of goods for resale at a bona fide wholesale price.[25]

In one case narrowly construing the meaning of a franchise fee for purposes of Minnesota's franchise law, the court held that minimum purchase requirements, required fees for advertising and training and to process warranty work, and a charge of 50 percent over the suggested sale price did not constitute franchise fees.[26] However, in two recent cases, Minnesota courts have broadly con-

---

21. For discussions of the trademark requirement, *see* Colt Indus., Inc. v. Fidelco Pump & Compressor Corp., 844 F.2d 117, Bus. Franchise Guide (CCH) ¶ 9095 (3d Cir. 1988) (New Jersey law); American Business Interiors, Inc. v. Haworth, Inc., 798 F.2d 1135, 1140, Bus. Franchise Guide (CCH) ¶ 8642 (8th Cir. 1986) (Missouri law).

22. A grant of limited use of a trademark can sometimes operate to avoid satisfaction of this element. *See, e.g.,* Smith v. Rainsoft Water Conditioning Co., 848 F. Supp. 1413, Bus. Franchise Guide (CCH) ¶ 10,447 (E.D. Wis. 1994); Pride Technologies, Inc. v. Sun Microsystems Computer Corp., Bus. Franchise Guide (CCH) ¶ 10,407 (N.D. Cal. 1994) (New Jersey law).

23. Iowa Code § 523 H.1.3.a (1)(c).

24. Kim v. Servosnax, Inc., 10 Cal. App. 4th 1346, 13 Cal. Rptr. 2d 422, Bus. Franchise Guide (CCH) ¶ 10,124 (Cal. Ct. App. 1992).

25. Cases discussing the fee requirement include: Continental Basketball Assoc., Inc. v. Ellenstein Enterprises, Inc., 640 N.E.2d 705, Bus. Franchise Guide (CCH) ¶ 10,541 (Ind. Ct. App. 1994) (Indiana law); Bryant Corp. v. Outboard Marine Corp., Bus. Franchise Guide (CCH) ¶ 10,604 (W.D. Wash. 1994); Boat & Motor Mart v. Sea Ray Boats, Inc., 825 F.2d 1285, Bus. Franchise Guide (CCH) ¶ 8846 (9th Cir. 1987) (California law); Cambee's Furniture, Inc. v. Doughboy Recreational, Inc., 825 F.2d 167, Bus. Franchise Guide (CCH) ¶ 8888 (8th Cir. 1987) (South Dakota law); Inland Printing Co. v. A.B. Dick Co., Bus. Franchise Guide (CCH) ¶ 8997 (W.D. Mo. 1987) (Illinois law); American Parts Sys., Inc. v. T & T Automotive, Inc., 358 N.W.2d 674, Bus. Franchise Guide (CCH) ¶ 8262 (Minn. Ct. App. 1984) (Minnesota law).

26. Brawley Distribution Co. v. Polaris Indus., Bus. Franchise Guide (CCH) ¶ 9388 (D. Minn. 1989).

strued the law to reach *any* payment (not specifically excluded in the statute) that is required as a condition of entering into the business relationship.[27]

"Good Cause" for Termination

Statutory "Good Cause" Requirements

Most franchise relationship laws require the franchisor to have good cause before terminating a franchise agreement. "Good cause" is defined in Minnesota, Nebraska, New Jersey, and Wisconsin as failure by the franchisee to comply substantially with the requirements imposed by the franchisor. Iowa defines good cause as "a legitimate business reason" and, uniquely, requires that the termination not be arbitrary or capricious when compared to the franchisor's acts in similar circumstances.

In the relationship laws of other states, the term "good cause" is not defined, except by way of examples. The failure of the franchisee to comply substantially with the requirements imposed by the franchisor is just one example of good cause in these states.

The Virginia Retail Franchising Act prohibits termination without "reasonable cause." The Delaware Franchise Security Law prohibits "unjust" termination, which means termination without good cause or in bad faith. Mississippi and Missouri do not have a good cause requirement for termination, but they do have notice requirements.[28]

Other specific statutory grounds for termination are listed in Appendix D.

Cases Interpreting Good Cause

Damage to the Franchisor's Reputation

In Minnesota, termination was found to have been lawful where the franchisee had engaged in consumer fraud, damaging the franchisor's reputation.[29] The New Jersey Franchise Practices Act has been held to permit termination where the franchisee violated the law.[30]

---

27. United Horizon Mktg., Inc. v. Precision Hub, Inc., 533 N.W.2d 63 (Minn. Ct. App. 1995); Current Technology Concepts, Inc. v. Irie Enterprises, Inc., 530 N.W.2d 539 (Minn. 1995).

28. *But see* ABA Distrib., Inc. v. Adolph Coors Co., 542 F. Supp. 1272, Bus. Franchise Guide (CCH) ¶ 7872 (W.D. Mo. 1982) (Missouri law).

29. AAMCO Indus., Inc. v. DeWolf, 250 N.W.2d 835 (Minn. 1977). In this case, the court also excused noncompliance with the law's procedural notice requirements, due to the severity of the breach with resulting consumer fraud and the "futility" of offering a cure period.

30. Amerada Hess Corp. v. Quinn, 143 N.J. Super. 237, 362 A.2d 1258 (1976); Anderson v. Amoco Oil, Bus. Franchise Guide (CCH) ¶ 8790 (D.N.J. 1987).

Unauthorized Use of a Trademark

In Minnesota, one court found good cause for termination where a franchisee sold competing products and palmed off unauthorized products under the franchisor's trademark.[31]

Sale of Competing Products

The sale by a franchisee of a competing line was held to be good cause for termination under Illinois law[32] and Wisconsin law.[33] Sale of a competing line was not good cause for termination under Connecticut law, however, when the distributorship agreement did not require exclusive dealing.[34]

Failure to Maintain Standards

An Illinois court found McDonald's to have had good cause to terminate when the franchisee failed to maintain the required standards of cleanliness, quality, and service.[35] In Delaware, a franchisor was found to have had good cause to terminate a franchise agreement when the franchisee failed to execute a renewal lease requiring additional rent for the possible installation of environmental control equipment.[36]

Failure to Meet Sales and Other Requirements

The Wisconsin Fair Dealership Law has been held to permit termination where the dealer failed to meet reasonable sales goals[37] or where the dealer became insolvent or unprofitable.[38] The New Jersey Franchise Practices Act has been held to permit termination in one case in which the franchisee failed to sell in the franchisee's entire territory, as required under the agreement,[39] and another in

---

31. Great Licks, Inc. v. Baskin-Robbins, U.S.A. Co., Bus. Franchise Guide (CCH) ¶ 9252 (D. Minn. 1988).

32. Inland Printing Co. v. A.B. Dick Co., Bus. Franchise Guide (CCH) ¶ 8997 (W.D. Mo. 1987).

33. Dade v. Day Food Co., Inc., 138 Wis. 2d 525, 406 N.W.2d 170, Bus. Franchise Guide (CCH) ¶ 8835 (Wis. Ct. App. 1987), *rev. denied,* 140 Wis. 2d 872, 416 N.W.2d 65 (1987). *But see* Reinders Bros., Inc. v. Rain Bird Eastern Sales Corp., 627 F.2d 44, Bus. Franchise Guide (CCH) ¶ 7544 (7th Cir. 1980).

34. Power Draulics-Nielsen, Inc. v. Libby Owens Ford Co., Bus. Franchise Guide (CCH) ¶ 9075 (S.D.N.Y. 1988).

35. Dayan v. McDonald's Corp., 125 Ill. App. 3d 972, 466 N.E.2d 958, Bus. Franchise Guide (CCH) ¶ 8223 (Ill. Ct. App. 1984).

36. Tulowitzki v. Atlantic Richfield Co., 396 A.2d 956 (Del. 1978).

37. Aring Equip. Co. v. Link-Belt Constr. Equip. Co., Bus. Franchise Guide (CCH) ¶ 8906 (Wis. Cir. Ct. 1987); L-O Distrib., Inc. v. Speed Queen Co., 611 F. Supp. 1569, Bus. Franchise Guide (CCH) ¶ 8430 (D. Minn. 1985); Al Bishop Agency, Inc. v. Lithonia Div. of Nat'l Serv. Indus. Inc., 474 F. Supp. 828 (E.D. Wis. 1979).

38. Lee Beverage Co., Inc. v. I.S.C. Wines of Calif., Inc., 623 F. Supp. 867, Bus. Franchise Guide (CCH) ¶ 8509 (E.D. Wis. 1985); Open Pantry Food Marts v. Garcia's Five, Inc., Bus. Franchise Guide (CCH) ¶ 8113 (Wis. Cir. Ct. 1984).

39. Carlo C. Gelardi Corp. v. Miller Brewing Co., 421 F. Supp. 237 (D.N.J. 1976).

which the franchisee intentionally underpaid royalties.[40] The latter termination was permitted even though the holdback occurred as a result of a legitimate commercial dispute between the franchisor and franchisee. A court interpreting the Puerto Rico Dealers' Act reached a contrary result and refused to permit termination for failure to meet sales goals and sale of competing goods, where the evidence showed that the deficiencies were caused, at least in part, by the franchisor's nearby competing outlet.[41]

Underreporting Sales

The New Jersey Franchise Practices Act and the Virginia Retail Franchising Act have been held to permit termination where the franchisee underreported sales.[42] The Wisconsin Fair Dealership Law has been held to permit termination where the dealer deliberately failed to report income.[43] Mississippi's franchise law has been interpreted to permit termination without notice in the event of submission of false credit information, incorrect purchase prices and down payments, and listing of fictitious trade-ins.[44]

Market Withdrawal by the Franchisor

When a franchisor discontinues business entirely, in a particular line of products, or in a particular geographic area, the question of whether ensuing terminations are for good cause requires careful and detailed analysis. Some states, such as Wisconsin, look to whether the supplier withdraws *completely* from selling its products or services on a nondiscriminatory basis; a change in distribution methods alone does not constitute good cause.[45] Other states look only to whether the franchisor or supplier has a sound business reason for the change, such as a failing market for a product line.[46]

---

40. Jiffy Lube Int'l, Inc. v. Weiss Bros., Inc., 834 F. Supp. 683, Bus. Franchise Guide (CCH) ¶ 10,388 (D.N.J. 1993).

41. Newell Puerto Rico, Ltd. v. Rubbermaid Inc., 20 F.3d 15, Bus. Franchise Guide (CCH) ¶ 10,413 (D.P.R. 1994).

42. Dunkin' Donuts of Am., Inc. v. Middletown Donut Corp., 100 N.J. Super. 166, 495 A.2d 66, Bus. Franchise Guide (CCH) ¶ 8408 (1985); Jackson Hewitt, Inc. v. Greene, 865 F. Supp. 1199, Bus. Franchise Guide (CCH) ¶ 10,591 (E.D. Va. 1994).

43. Open Pantry Food Marts v. Howell, Bus. Franchise Guide (CCH) ¶ 8072 (Wis. Cir. Ct. 1983).

44. Crosthwait Equip. Co. v. John Deere Co., 992 F.2d 525, Bus. Franchise Guide (CCH) ¶ 10,364 (5th Cir. 1993), *cert. denied,* 114 S. Ct. 549 (1993).

45. *See, e.g.,* Slowiak v. Hudson Foods, Inc., Bus. Franchise Guide (CCH) ¶ 10,006 (W.D. Wis. 1992), *aff'd,* 987 F.2d 1293, Bus. Franchise Guide (CCH) ¶ 10,180 (7th Cir. 1993); St. Joseph Equip. v. Massey-Ferguson, Inc., 546 F. Supp. 1245, Bus. Franchise Guide (CCH) ¶ 7895 (W.D. Wis. 1982); Kealey Pharmacy & Home Care Serv., Inc. v. Walgreen Co., 539 F. Supp. 1357, Bus. Franchise Guide (CCH) ¶ 7841 (W.D. Wis. 1982), *aff'd in relevant part,* 761 F.2d 345, Bus. Franchise Guide (CCH) ¶ 8351 (7th Cir. 1985).

46. Schott Motorcycle Supply, Inc. v. American Honda Motor Co., Inc., 976 F.2d 58, Bus. Franchise Guide (CCH) ¶ 10,091 (1st Cir. 1992) (Maine law); General Motors Corp. v. Gallo GMC Truck Sales, Inc., 711 F. Supp. 810, Bus. Franchise Guide (CCH) ¶ 9544 (D.N.J. 1989); Freedman Truck Center, Inc. v. General Motors Corp., 784 F. Supp. 167, Bus. Franchise Guide (CCH) ¶ 9971 (D.N.J. 1992) (New Jersey law); Medina & Medina v. Country

Unfair Actions by the Franchisor

A franchisor may not terminate in Wisconsin if the franchisor intends to replace a franchised outlet with its own store in the same marketing area as that of the franchisee after the franchisee has helped establish the franchisor's reputation[47] or, apparently, for failure to maintain standards determined to be minor or ancillary.[48] Similarly, courts have held, under the laws of both New Jersey and Connecticut, that a manufacturer may not transform an exclusive distributorship into a nonexclusive one, thereby putting itself in a position to compete directly with the distributor.[49] Such a transformation was held to constitute termination for purposes of these laws.

Cases dealing with termination upon transfer of a franchise are discussed later in the chapter.

Procedural Requirements for Termination

Statutory Procedural Requirements

Assuming that the franchisor has good cause to terminate the agreement, the franchisor must then comply with the procedural requirements for termination. This often means doing all of the following:

1. Giving written notice of termination the required number of days in advance
2. Including in the notice all of the reasons for termination
3. Including in the notice how much time, if any, the franchisee has to cure the default
4. Continuing to comply with the franchisor's obligations during the notice period.

The relationship laws of California, Illinois, Michigan, and Washington require that the franchisor give the franchisee notice of termination and a reasonable opportunity to cure, which in no event need be more than thirty days.

The Washington relationship law provides that if the default cannot be cured within thirty days, the franchisee can void the termination by initiating

---

Pride Foods, Ltd., 858 F.2d 817, Bus. Franchise Guide (CCH) ¶ 9245 (1st Cir. 1988) (Puerto Rico law).

47. Kealey Pharmacy & Home Care Serv., Inc. v. Walgreen Co., 761 F.2d 345, Bus. Franchise Guide (CCH) ¶ 8351 (7th Cir. 1985).

48. Tiesling v. White Hen Pantry Div., Jewel Co., Inc., Bus. Franchise Guide (CCH) ¶ 8175 (Wis. Cir. Ct.), *rev'd*, Bus. Franchise Guide (CCH) ¶ 8279 (Wis. Ct. App. 1984), *rev. denied*, 122 Wis. 2d 784, 367 N.W.2d 224 (Wis. 1985).

49. Carlos v. Philips Business Sys., Inc., 556 F. Supp. 769, Bus. Franchise Guide (CCH) ¶ 7949 (E.D.N.Y.), *aff'd*, 742 F.2d 1432 (2d Cir. 1983) (New Jersey and Connecticut law); Executive Business Sys. v. Philips Business Sys., Bus. Franchise Guide (CCH) ¶ 7703 (E.D.N.Y. 1981) (New Jersey law).

within thirty days "substantial and continuing action to cure such default." Washington also allows termination without prior notice and opportunity to cure in certain cases.

Other jurisdictions have specific minimum cure periods. Minnesota, the District of Columbia, and Wisconsin require that the franchisee be given sixty days to cure, except in certain specified cases. In Arkansas, the franchisor generally must allow the franchisee thirty days to cure. Arkansas permits a ten-day cure period for repeated breaches within a twelve-month period or failure by the franchisee to act in good faith and in a commercially reasonable manner. Iowa requires at least thirty days to cure, but the cure period need not be more than ninety days. Hawaii prohibits termination unless the franchisee is given notice and an opportunity to cure "within a reasonable period of time."

Some statutes provide that no cure period is required in the case of voluntary abandonment, criminal conviction, insolvency or bankruptcy, and certain other cases. The franchise relationship law of Virginia has no cure requirement and no minimum required notice period.

The specific state procedural requirements for termination are set forth in more detail in Appendix E.

Many franchise agreements purport to give the franchisor the right to terminate, often without notice or cure, upon a franchisee's bankruptcy. Some state laws also allow such termination. Section 365 of the Federal Bankruptcy Code, however, nullifies these provisions in most cases.

Cases Interpreting Procedural Requirements

Compliance with Notice Requirements

Failure to comply with the notice requirements in and of itself may constitute a violation of the law, regardless of whether the franchisor had good cause to terminate.[50] When the franchisor does not give the required statutory notice, the franchisor may be required to reinstate the relationship and, if appropriate, give the requisite statutory notice, even though the franchise agreement permits a shorter period.[51]

Franchisor Compliance during the Notice Period

After notice of termination has been given but before the effective date of termination, the franchisor must continue to do business with the franchisee and comply with its obligations under the franchise agreement. A refusal by a franchisor to provide pricing information during this period was held in one case to be a violation of the Missouri franchise relationship law.[52]

---

50. Designs in Medicine, Inc. v. Xomed, Inc., 522 F. Supp. 1054, Bus. Franchise Guide (CCH) ¶ 7733 (E.D. Wis. 1981) (Wisconsin law).

51. Maude v. General Motors Corp., 626 F. Supp. 1081, Bus. Franchise Guide (CCH) ¶ 8577 (W.D. Mo. 1986) (Missouri law).

52. American Business Interiors, Inc. v. Haworth, Inc., 798 F.2d 1135, Bus. Franchise Guide (CCH) ¶ 8642 (8th Cir. 1986).

Giving Reasons for Termination

In some states, the termination notice must contain all of the reasons for termination. This requirement can cause later difficulties for franchisors. It forces the franchisor to take a position at the time that the franchisor gives notice of termination and acts as an estoppel with respect to any reasons not contained in the notice. In a case interpreting Missouri law, for example, the franchisor was precluded from introducing evidence at trial concerning reasons for termination not contained in the notice.[53]

Insolvency

The Wisconsin Fair Dealership Law does not require prior notice and an opportunity to cure if the reason for termination is the dealer's insolvency. Even if the franchisee is insolvent, however, the franchisor is not excused from the notice and cure requirements if it did not know of the insolvency at the time of termination[54] or if insolvency was not the reason for termination as stated in the notice.[55]

Incurable Breaches

What must a franchisor do when the breach cannot be cured within the statutory cure period? Examples include failure to attain minimum sales, misuse of the franchisor's trademark, or damage to the franchisor's goodwill. Reported cases dealing with repeated breaches and cures by a franchisee do not appear to exist.

In Wisconsin, one court enjoined a franchisor from terminating the franchise agreement even though the requisite ninety-day notice was given and the franchisee was given sixty days to cure, as required by the statute, holding that the notice was "wholly inadequate in a practical sense."[56] Although the franchisee had failed to meet its minimum sales goals and was given the required notice and opportunity to cure, the court issued an injunction, holding that it would have been impossible for the franchisee to bring its whole year's sales up to the required level in only sixty days. In such a situation, complete cure by the franchisee may not be necessary. Reasonable steps by the franchisee to rectify the claimed deficiencies were held to be adequate to void the termination.

On the other hand, the Supreme Court of Minnesota has held that the statutory cure period was not required where the franchisee had already damaged the franchisor's goodwill and giving the franchisee an opportunity to cure would have been a "futile gesture."[57] In that case, the Minnesota Attorney General's office had brought an action against an AAMCO franchisee for consumer fraud. The

---

53. ABA Distrib., Inc. v. Adolph Coors Co., 542 F. Supp. 1272, Bus. Franchise Guide (CCH) ¶ 7872 (W.D. Mo. 1982).

54. Bruno Wine & Spirits, Inc. v. Guimarra Vineyards, 573 F. Supp. 337, Bus. Franchise Guide (CCH) ¶ 8081 (E.D. Wis. 1983).

55. Hammil v. Rickel Mfg. Corp., 719 F.2d 252, Bus. Franchise Guide (CCH) ¶ 8074 (7th Cir. 1983).

56. Al Bishop Agency, Inc. v. Lithonia Div. of Nat'l Serv. Indus., Inc., 474 F. Supp. 828, 834 (E.D. Wis. 1979).

57. AAMCO Indus., Inc. v. DeWolf, 250 N.W.2d 835, 840 (Minn. 1977). *See also* Smith v. Latham, Bus. Franchise Guide (CCH) ¶ 9259 (Minn. Dist. Ct. 1988).

franchisor terminated upon notice with immediate effect, notwithstanding the statutory requirement of a twenty-four-hour cure period.

Nonrenewal

Statutory Renewal Requirements

The provisions of the franchise relationship laws that restrict franchisors from refusing to renew franchise agreements are diverse.

The franchise relationship laws of Delaware, the District of Columbia, Hawaii, Iowa, New Jersey, and Wisconsin require good cause for nonrenewal by the franchisor. The Iowa statute requires six months' notice of the franchisor's intention not to renew. In addition, the franchisor must have good cause to refuse to renew, unless the parties agree to the nonrenewal, or the franchisor completely withdraws from the geographic market served by the franchisee and the franchisor agrees not to enforce a covenant not to compete. The Iowa statute also permits franchisors to condition renewal on a requirement that the franchisee meet the franchisor's then current requirements for franchises and that the franchisee execute a new agreement containing the then current terms and fees for new franchises.

California permits nonrenewal upon 180 days' notice for specified reasons, including failure by the franchisee to agree to the standard terms of the renewal franchise. Other states generally require good cause for nonrenewal but specifically allow nonrenewal in certain cases as well. In Arkansas, the franchisor may fail to renew, as long as the nonrenewal is in accordance with a policy that is not arbitrary or capricious. In Connecticut, the franchisor is permitted not to renew if the franchisor sells the premises on which the franchise is located or converts it to another use or the lease to the franchisee expires. In Indiana and Nebraska, the franchisor may refuse to renew if the agreement provides that it is not renewable upon expiration or that it is only renewable if the franchisee meets certain conditions specified in the agreement. In Minnesota, nonrenewal is permitted if the franchisee has been given an opportunity to operate the franchise over a period of time sufficient to enable the franchisee to recover the fair market value of the franchise as measured from the date of the failure to renew.

Illinois, Michigan, and Washington require renewal only in specified cases. Illinois requires renewal or repurchase of the franchise if there is a noncompete requirement. In Michigan, a franchisor may not refuse to renew without fairly compensating the franchisee by repurchase or other means if the agreement is for a term of less than five years and there is a noncompete requirement. In Washington, renewal or repurchase is required unless the franchisor agrees in writing not to enforce any covenant not to compete and gives the franchisee one year's notice of nonrenewal.[58] Iowa prohibits enforcement of the post-term restrictive covenant if the nonrenewal is occasioned by market withdrawal.

---

58. *See* Thompson v. Atlantic Richfield Co., 649 F. Supp. 969, Bus. Franchise Guide (CCH) ¶ 8805 (W.D. Wash. 1986).

Mississippi and Missouri have notice requirements regarding nonrenewal of the franchise agreement, but no substantive requirements. In California and Iowa, the franchisor must give the franchisee at least 180 days' notice of the franchisor's intention not to renew. In Washington, the franchisor must give the franchisee a full year's notice and must permit the franchisee to compete after the end of the term. Most other states require ninety days' notice or less. These requirements are set forth in Appendix E.

Cases Dealing with Nonrenewal

Although good cause is required for nonrenewal in Wisconsin, the Wisconsin Supreme Court has held that a franchisor may fail to renew a franchise agreement if the franchisee refuses to agree to changes in the franchisor's method of doing business, provided that such changes are "essential, reasonable, and nondiscriminatory."[59] The antidiscrimination provisions of the Michigan law have been interpreted to mean that franchisors must have legitimate, nondiscriminatory reasons for failing to renew a franchisee when compared to all similarly situated franchisees, not only to renewed franchisees.[60]

Several state courts have held that nondiscriminatory, necessary changes to the franchise agreement do not constitute either termination or a failure to renew.[61] However, the result may be the opposite if the franchisor uses threats of nonrenewal or termination to induce acceptance of the new agreement.[62]

Franchisees must also comply with the contractual renewal requirements. In one case under the Puerto Rico Dealers' Act, the franchisee failed to give notice of intent to renew as required under the agreement, and the court held that the franchisee was not entitled to renew the agreement.[63]

There is relatively little case law on the subject of nonrenewal. This is likely to change as many of the first-time franchises of the 1970s and 1980s come up for renewal. In particular, the question of the effect of the nonrenewal laws on the simple expiration of a fixed-term franchise that does not provide for a renewal option remains unsettled, as discussed in the next section.

59. Ziegler Co. v. Rexnord, Inc., 147 Wis. 2d 308, 433 N.W.2d 8, Bus. Franchise Guide (CCH) ¶ 9317 (1988).

60. General Aviation, Inc. v. The Cessna Aircraft Co., 13 F.3d 178, Bus. Franchise Guide (CCH) ¶ 10, 362 (6th Cir. 1993) (Michigan law).

61. Craig D. Corp v. Atlantic Richfield Co., 122 Wash. 2d 574, 860 P.2d 1015, Bus. Franchise Guide (CCH) ¶ 10,436 (Wash. 1993) (Washington law); Central GMC, Inc. v. General Motors Corp., 946 F.2d 327, Bus. Franchise Guide (CCH) ¶ 9896 (4th Cir. 1991), *cert. denied,* 503 U.S. 907 (1992) (Maryland law); Wisconsin Music Network, Inc. v. Muzak Ltd. Partnership, 5 F.3d 218, Bus. Franchise Guide (CCH) ¶ 10,283 (7th Cir. 1993); Remus v. Amoco Oil Co., 794 F.2d 1238, Bus. Franchise Guide (CCH) ¶ 8607 (7th Cir.), *cert. dismissed,* 479 U.S. 925 (1986) (Wisconsin law); Ziegler Co. v. Rexnord, Inc., 147 Wis. 2d 308, 433 N.W.2d 8, Bus. Franchise Guide (CCH) ¶ 9317 (1988) (Wisconsin law).

62. *See, e.g.,* Kansas City Trailer Sales v. Holiday Rambler Corp., Bus. Franchise Guide (CCH) ¶ 10,395 (W.D. Mo. 1994) (Missouri law).

63. Nike Int'l Ltd. v. Athletic Sales, Inc., 689 F. Supp. 1235, Bus. Franchise Guide (CCH) ¶ 9297 (D.P.R. 1988).

The Perpetual Agreement Problem

The Problem

State laws that require good cause for termination and nonrenewal, such as laws in New Jersey and Wisconsin, have the potential for turning contractual relationships of limited duration into perpetual relationships, giving franchisees something more akin to property rights than contract rights.

The franchisee may argue that he or she should not be deprived of the goodwill he or she has developed during the course of the relationship, which goodwill will either accrue to the franchisor if the franchisor takes over operation of the business or simply dissipate if the business is closed down.

The franchisee's position has appeal in some cases. However, the definition of a "franchise" is so broad that statutory protection is bound to extend to dealers who do not really need it. A franchise may be any arrangement from a simple dealership representing several suppliers to a tightly controlled business format franchise in which the franchisee must leave the premises and not compete with the franchisor upon termination of the franchise agreement. A dealership may be under an agreement of indefinite term, or no agreement at all, and the dealer may carry multiple lines and products, so that a termination of one line will not shut down the dealer's operations.

Types of Agreements

Franchise agreements usually have a fixed term, often ten or twenty years, and may or may not include a right of renewal. These agreements may require high initial fees.

Fixed-term agreements usually do not permit termination during the contract term except for reasons specified in the contract, such as breach. These reasons often will constitute good cause under the franchise laws.

Most franchise agreements contain renewal provisions. In some instances, successive renewals are permitted. In other cases, only one renewal may be permitted, but it may be for a lengthy period.

A fixed-term agreement that does not provide for renewal would expire in accordance with its terms under the common law. It is not clear whether the good cause requirement of some franchise laws mandates renewal of a fixed-term agreement, even one that clearly and explicitly provides that there will be no renewal.[64] Do these franchise laws cover agreements that the parties clearly intended to run for a limited period of time, with a well-defined expiration date? If so, the result could be an essentially perpetual agreement.

---

64. "In the rare but by no means unheard-of case where the parties actually have intended, from the beginning of their relationship, to have that relationship end with no possibility of continuation at the end of the specified term, it is neither desirable as a matter of policy nor necessary as a matter of fidelity to the legislature's intent to hold that the refusal to extend that relationship at the end of that term is a violation of section 135.03." Bowen & Butler, *The Wisconsin Fair Dealership Law* § 6.8 (State Bar of Wis. 1988).

Many dealership agreements have an indefinite term, particularly if they are not in writing. Such agreements generally are governed by the Uniform Commercial Code and are terminable by either party upon reasonable notice after the arrangement has been in existence for a reasonable period of time.[65]

These agreements generally require no initial franchise fee, and some are not in writing. Because many such agreements require a considerably smaller investment than a franchise, there is less need to protect a dealer than a franchisee.

A supplier of a dealer in New Jersey or Wisconsin, however, with an agreement of indefinite term, terminable by either party on sixty or ninety days' notice, may find that the agreement is essentially perpetual. One court has held that an unwritten twelve-month course of dealing, in contemplation of a franchise agreement, constituted a relationship governed by the Puerto Rico franchise act and subject to its notice provisions.[66]

At common law, an agreement that expressly provides that it may be terminated at any time without cause by giving the required notice generally can be terminated in accordance with its terms.[67] If, however, the supplier or franchisor attempts to terminate on grounds that are not enumerated in the agreement, it may be unable to do so.[68] Moreover, such a provision would not be enforceable in those states whose relationship laws require good cause for termination by the franchisor.

In contracts of indefinite duration, the good cause requirement is arguably analogous to the good cause requirement of some states in an employment context. This analogy may apply when the franchisee is an individual and the contract does not permit assignment by the franchisee. The analogy breaks down, however, when the franchisee is a corporation or when assignment is permitted by contract or required by law.

The Franchisor's Position

The concept of perpetual renewal, absent contractual language to the contrary, is troublesome to franchisors, in part because franchise agreements usually are

---

65. U.C.C. § 2-309(2). *See* Haagen-Dazs Co. v. Masterbrand Distrib., Inc., Bus. Franchise Guide (CCH) ¶ 9570 (S.D. Ga. 1989), *aff'd,* 918 F.2d 183 (11th Cir. 1990); Delta Serv. and Equip., Inc. v. Ryko Mfg. Co., 908 F.2d 7, Bus. Franchise Guide (CCH) ¶ 9668 (5th Cir. 1990). *See also* U.S. Surgical Corp. v. Oregon Medical & Surgical Specialties, Inc., 497 F. Supp. 68, Bus. Franchise Guide (CCH) ¶ 7580 (S.D.N.Y. 1980) (holding that a declaration by the licensor that a contract without an expressed duration had *expired* by reason of the passage of a "reasonable" period of time was not a "termination" requiring good cause under Minnesota law).

66. R.W. Int'l Corp. v. Welch Foods, Inc., Bus. Franchise Guide (CCH) ¶ 10,386 (1st Cir. 1994).

67. *See, e.g.,* Corenswet, Inc. v. Amana Refrigeration, Inc., 594 F.2d 129, 138–39 (5th Cir. 1979), *cert. denied,* 444 U.S. 938 (1979); S & R Corp. v. Jiffy Lube Int'l, Inc., 968 F.2d 371, Bus. Franchise Guide (CCH) ¶ 10,038 (3d Cir. 1992).

68. *See, e.g.,* Karl Wendt Farm Equip. Co. v. Int'l Harvester Co., 931 F.2d 1112, Bus. Franchise Guide (CCH) ¶ 9801 (6th Cir. 1991).

of lengthy duration, market circumstances can change over time, and franchisors feel that they need to be able to adjust their distribution methods over time.

Franchisors and suppliers object to good cause requirements as intrusions on their right to contract freely. Franchisors also need to exercise quality control. Franchise agreements are almost always trademark license agreements. Trademark licenses must allow for quality control if the licensor is to maintain the trademark rights. The threat of termination or nonrenewal is the primary method the franchisor has to police quality and protect the trademark. Continuation of substandard franchises reduces the value of the trademark to the franchisor and the other franchisees, while termination for reasons of quality control benefits other franchisees by preserving the goodwill of the system. Such termination also benefits consumers by ensuring that they receive products and services of the quality they expect. The relationship laws place the burden on the franchisor to prove that there was good cause. This makes termination more difficult and costly, even when good cause exists.

Judicial Relief

One Oregon court drew an analogy between franchise agreements and commercial leases.[69] Commercial leases typically run for fixed terms. Some have a right to renew and some do not. When there is no contractual right to renew, periodic renewals may give rise to expectations by the tenant that renewal is likely in the future. However, this does not create an obligation to renew. It makes no difference how much effort and money the tenant puts into the leased property. In addition, during the term of a fixed lease, the landlord cannot terminate except in accordance with the lease terms.

The Wisconsin Supreme Court declined to afford a dealer the protection of the Wisconsin Fair Dealership Law where the supplier failed to renew based on the dealer's rejection of the terms of the renewal agreement that were "essential, reasonable, and nondiscriminatory."[70] The court held that, although the Wisconsin Fair Dealership Law was intended to afford dealers substantial protection that had been unavailable at common law, "the Wisconsin legislature could not have intended to impose an eternal and unqualified duty of self-sacrifice upon every grantor that enters into a distributor-dealership agreement."[71] The court also held that the Wisconsin Fair Dealership Law was not intended to insulate dealers from economic reality by requiring dealerships to be continued, without change, in perpetuity.

Some courts have held that withdrawal from the market on a nondiscriminatory basis constitutes good cause for termination.[72] Courts sometimes follow

---

69. *See* William C. Cornitius, Inc. v. Wheeler, 276 Or. 747, 753, 556 P.2d 666, 671 (1976).
70. Ziegler Co. v. Rexnord, Inc., 407 N.W.2d 873, Bus. Franchise Guide (CCH) ¶ 8882 (Wis. 1987), *remanded,* 147 Wis. 2d 308, 433 N.W.2d 8, Bus. Franchise Guide (CCH) ¶ 9317 (Wis. 1988). *See also* cases cited *supra* at note 61.
71. *Id.* at 11.
72. *See supra* notes 45 and 46.

the rule that an agreement of indefinite duration may not be terminated until the dealer has had sufficient time to recoup any investment made in facilities, equipment, or other capital goods necessary to operate the dealership.[73] Courts have also found that the state franchise law did not apply because the arrangement in question did not constitute a "franchise."[74]

Remedies

Types of Remedies

The franchise relationship laws give franchisees a number of specific remedies in the event of termination or nonrenewal. Remedies available under the statutes or case law may include the following:

- Repurchase of inventory and other items
- Payment for goodwill
- Injunctive relief
- Damages, including lost profits, unrecouped expenses, and punitive damages
- Attorneys' fees.

Under some of these laws, state authorities also are empowered to seek civil remedies and criminal sanctions.

A court may require compensation of a terminated franchisee beyond that specifically referred to in the relevant statute. One franchisee, for example, was awarded lost profits under Wisconsin law.[75] Another franchisee was awarded damages in the amount of the reasonable value of the business under New Jersey law.[76] Damages available under Puerto Rico law have been held to include not only five times the average annual profit but possibly other "benefits," including goodwill.[77] Punitive damages were awarded in one case under Missouri law for tortious interference by a manufacturer with the business relationship between a franchisee and its prospective customers.[78]

---

73. Ag-Chem Equip. Co., Inc. v. Hahn, Inc., 480 F.2d 482 (8th Cir. 1973); U.S. Surgical Corp. v. Oregon Medical & Surgical Specialties, Inc., 497 F. Supp. 68, Bus. Franchise Guide (CCH) ¶ 7580 (S.D.N.Y. 1980). *But see* Mechanical Rubber & Supply Co. v. American Saw and Mfg. Co., 810 F. Supp. 986, Bus. Franchise Guide (CCH) ¶ 10,106 (C.D. Ill. 1990) (Illinois law recognizes recoupment doctrine only in agency relationships).

74. *See supra* note 26.

75. Kealey Pharmacy & Home Care Serv., Inc. v. Walgreen Co., 761 F.2d 345, Bus. Franchise Guide (CCH) ¶ 8351 (7th Cir. 1985).

76. Westfield Centre Serv., Inc. v. Cities Serv. Oil Co., 86 N.J. 453, 432 A.2d 48, Bus. Franchise Guide (CCH) ¶ 7668 (1981).

77. Ballester Hermanos, Inc. v. Campbell Soup Co., Bus. Franchise Guide (CCH) ¶ 10,346 (D.P.R. 1993).

78. American Business Interiors, Inc. v. Haworth, 798 F.2d 1135, Bus. Franchise Guide (CCH) ¶ 8642 (8th Cir. 1986).

On the other hand, in one case under California law, the court held that the only remedy available was repurchase of the franchisee's inventory.[79]

Repurchase

While the relationship laws of Arkansas, California, Connecticut, Hawaii, Michigan, Washington, and Wisconsin contain repurchase obligations, these laws differ from state to state on four issues:

1. Whether repurchase is required only when there is good cause for termination
2. Whether repurchase is required in the case of both termination and nonrenewal
3. What must be repurchased
4. The purchase price.

Must the franchisor repurchase if termination is with good cause? The franchise laws of Connecticut, Hawaii, and Wisconsin require the franchisor to repurchase inventory from the franchisee upon termination, regardless of whether the termination was with good cause. Arkansas and California require the franchisor to repurchase inventory only if termination was without good cause.

Must the franchisor repurchase upon termination and nonrenewal or only upon termination? Arkansas, Connecticut, and Wisconsin require repurchase of inventory only in the case of termination. Michigan requires repurchase only in the case of nonrenewal. California, Hawaii, and Washington require repurchase both in the case of termination and nonrenewal.

What must be repurchased? Arkansas, Connecticut, Hawaii, and Washington require repurchase of the franchisee's inventory, supplies, equipment, and furnishings purchased from the franchisor or a supplier designated by the franchisor. No compensation is required for personalized items that have no value to the franchisor. California and Wisconsin require repurchase of inventory only.

What price must the franchisor pay? Arkansas law provides that the franchisor must "repurchase at the franchisee's net cost, less a reasonable allowance for depreciation or obsolescence." In California, the amount is "the lower of the fair wholesale market value or the price paid by the franchisee." Connecticut requires "fair and reasonable compensation." In Hawaii and Washington, the amount is the fair market value at the time of the termination or expiration.

In Michigan, the franchisor must compensate the franchisee by repurchase or by other means for the fair market value at the time of expiration "of the franchisee's inventory, supplies, equipment, fixtures, and furnishings" if the term of the franchise is less than five years and either the franchisee is not permitted to

---

79. Boat & Motor Mart v. Sea Ray Boats, Inc., 825 F.2d 1285, Bus. Franchise Guide (CCH) ¶ 8846 (9th Cir. 1987).

continue substantially the same business under a different name or mark in the same area or notice of the nonrenewal is not given at least six months before expiration.

In Iowa, the franchisor may not enforce a post-term noncompete obligation unless the competing business "relies on a substantially similar marketing plan as the terminated or nonrenewed franchise" or unless the franchisor offers, before expiration of the franchise, to purchase the assets of the franchised business for its fair market value as a going concern. This requirement does not apply to the assets of a franchised business that the franchisee did not purchase from the franchisor or its agent.

As a practical matter, repurchase requirements are not onerous for franchisors, provided that the franchisee has acquired reasonable quantities of inventory and other items in reasonable reliance that the franchise would continue. Franchisors might repurchase such items in the absence of relationship laws because they might reasonably decide not to permit anyone other than franchisees or company-owned outlets to sell their goods or use their trademarks.

Goodwill

While Delaware, Indiana, Minnesota, Mississippi, Missouri, Nebraska, New Jersey, and Virginia do not require repurchase, the franchise laws of these states allow the franchisee to recover damages for a violation by the franchisor. Damages under the laws of these states may include goodwill. The Puerto Rico Dealers' Act also permits recovery for goodwill.[80]

In Illinois, a franchisor that refuses to renew a franchise must compensate the franchisee "by repurchase or by other means for the diminution in the value of the franchised business caused by the expiration of the franchise" if the franchisee is not permitted to continue substantially the same business under a different name or mark in the same area or if notice of the nonrenewal is not given at least six months before expiration.

A franchisee in Hawaii is entitled to the value of the goodwill of the business if the franchisor refuses to renew for the purpose of converting the franchise into a company-owned outlet. Goodwill must be paid to the franchisee in Washington upon the franchisor's refusal to renew, unless the franchisee has been given one year's notice of nonrenewal and the franchisor agrees in writing not to enforce any covenant not to compete with the franchisor.

The requirement to pay goodwill raises this question: Who owns the goodwill? In a trademark license agreement, the goodwill symbolized by the licensed trademarks is customarily owned by the licensor, not the licensee. The licensor typically invests enormous amounts of money to develop the goodwill associated with a national or international brand name, and it typically grants to the licensee a right to exploit the marks for a fixed period of time. To the extent that the franchisee is a licensee of the franchisor, the goodwill is owned by the fran-

---

80. Ballester Hermanos, Inc. v. Campbell Soup Co., Bus. Franchise Guide (CCH) ¶ 10,346 (D.P.R. 1993).

chisor, at least in the absence of the relationship laws. These laws may presume just the opposite. They may reflect the perception that a franchisee also develops a goodwill in the business, often called "sweat equity," that is separate and distinct from the goodwill inherent in the licensed trademarks.

One of the reasons many individuals buy franchises is to "be their own boss." While franchising allows the franchisee a large degree of autonomy, buying a franchise is very different from starting a new business. The franchisee obtains a license to use known trademarks and service marks and a proven system with a high chance of success. Such a system entails far less risk than starting a new business. This increased likelihood of success is owed in large part to the goodwill developed by the franchisor as well as to the special expertise of the franchisor and the training the franchisor provides. Ultimately, however, franchisors may want to be careful what they wish for. If it were widely understood by the public that a franchise is only a self-financed job, even for ten or twenty years, with no residual equity to the investor, franchises might become quite difficult to sell.

Injunctive Relief

Temporary injunctive relief is specifically available to franchisees in Delaware, Minnesota, and Wisconsin. In Wisconsin, any violation of the Fair Dealership Law is deemed to cause irreparable injury to the dealer for purposes of determining whether a temporary injunction should be issued. Much the same is true in Minnesota.[81] Injunctive relief is also specifically available to franchisees in Arkansas, the District of Columbia, Nebraska, and New Jersey, without any statutory indication of whether it is confined to temporary relief. "Equitable relief" also is available in Mississippi and Missouri.

Transfers

Grounds for Withholding Consent to Transfer

Iowa law contains the most extensive limitations on franchisors' rights to restrict transfers. Although the Iowa statute permits a franchisor to disapprove a transfer if the proposed transferee does not meet the franchisor's current financial requirements for franchisees, the refusal may not be "arbitrary or capricious when compared to the franchisor's actions in other similar circumstances." Certain transfers of ownership are deemed not to be transfers requiring consent of the franchisor, and the franchisor may not "interfere" with such dispositions. Exam-

---

81. For discussions of injunctive relief under Minnesota law, *see* Lano Equip., Inc. v. Clark Equip. Co., Inc., 399 N.W.2d 694, Bus. Franchise Guide (CCH) ¶ 8766 (Minn. Ct. App. 1987); OT Indus., Inc. v. OT-Tehdas Oy Santasalo-Sohlberg AB, 346 N.W.2d 162, Bus. Franchise Guide (CCH) ¶ 8128 (Minn. Ct. App. 1984).

ples are transfers by a sole proprietor franchisee to a wholly owned corporation, transfers of equity within an existing ownership group, and transfers to a spouse, child, or partner upon the franchisee's death or disability.

In Arkansas, Nebraska, and New Jersey, the franchisor can reject a proposed transfer of the franchise based on a material reason relating to the character, financial ability, or business experience of the proposed transferee, failing which the franchisor's approval is deemed granted. When these grounds do not exist, the franchisor is nevertheless not required to do business with a transferee that does not agree to comply with all the requirements of the franchise.

In Hawaii and Michigan, the franchisor may not refuse to permit a transfer of a franchise except for good cause. Good cause includes any of the following:

1. The failure of the proposed transferee to meet the franchisor's reasonable qualifications
2. The fact that the proposed transferee is a competitor of the franchisor
3. The unwillingness of the proposed transferee to agree to comply with all franchise obligations
4. The failure of the franchisee or proposed transferee to pay any sums owing to the franchisor and to cure any default.

In the District of Columbia, Minnesota, and Washington, the franchisor may not withhold consent to a proposed transfer when the proposed transferee meets the criteria for the purchase of a new franchise.

As a practical matter, transfers to qualified parties are not a problem for franchisors, and many franchisors permit such transfers in the absence of the relationship laws. Where it is of concern, some franchisors reserve a right of first refusal to purchase the franchise themselves when the franchisee desires to sell it. Such rights of first refusal may be limited by Section 365(f) of the Bankruptcy Code, which prevents antialienation clauses in agreements from defeating a trustee from realizing the full value of the debtor's assets.[82]

Procedural Requirements for Transfer

In Arkansas, the District of Columbia, Iowa, Nebraska, and New Jersey, the franchisee is specifically required to notify the franchisor of its intention to transfer or sell the franchise. The notice must include the prospective transferee's name, address, statement of financial qualification, and business experience during the previous five years. In these states, the franchisor has sixty days to reject the proposed transfer. In Iowa, only certain transfers are subject to franchisor notice and approval.

---

82. *See In re* Headquarters Dodge, Inc., 13 F.3d 674, Bus. Franchise Guide (CCH) ¶ 10,487 (3d Cir. 1993).

In Hawaii, the franchisor has thirty days after notice of a proposed transfer to approve or disapprove the proposed transfer, failing which the franchisor is deemed to have given its approval. In Iowa, the franchisor must have good cause to object to a public offering of securities as long as at least 50 percent of the voting power remains with the original franchisee.

Stock Transfers

In Hawaii, the prohibition against withholding consent except for good cause also covers the transfer of the ownership of the franchisee.

In Arkansas, Nebraska, and New Jersey, the franchisor may not restrict the sale, transfer, or issuance of any securities of the franchisee or prevent the sale, transfer, or issuance of shares of stock or debentures to employees of the franchisee, as long as basic financial requirements of the franchisor are complied with and any such sale, transfer, or issuance does not result in a sale of the franchise. The laws of these states and the District of Columbia also restrict the withholding of consent to a transfer of "an interest in a franchise." In Iowa, a transfer within an existing ownership group is deemed not to be a transfer requiring consent of the franchisor, provided that more than 50 percent of the franchise is held by persons who meet the franchisor's reasonable current qualifications.

In one New Jersey case, a franchisor was permitted to terminate the franchise where the shareholder of the franchisee sold stock to a new owner without the franchisor's consent.[83] The new owner also owned competing franchises. In a District of Columbia case, a preliminary injunction against termination based on the former president's sale of minority stock interest and withdrawal from management of the business was denied.[84]

Transfer upon the Death of a Franchisee

In California, the surviving spouse, heirs, and estate of the deceased franchisee or majority shareholder of the franchisee must be given the opportunity to participate in the ownership of the franchise for a reasonable time after the death of the franchisee or majority shareholder of the franchisee. If the heirs do not satisfy all of the then current qualifications for a purchaser of a franchise, they may transfer the franchise to a person who does satisfy the franchisor's then current standards for a new franchisee.

The franchisor's use of a right of first refusal in the case of the death of a franchisor is expressly permitted in California. In Indiana, the franchisor must also permit the surviving spouse, heirs, or estate of a deceased franchisee to participate in the ownership of the franchise for a reasonable time after the death of

---

83. Simmons v. General Motors Corp., 180 N.J. Super. 522, 435 A.2d 1167, Bus. Franchise Guide (CCH) ¶ 7725, *cert. denied,* 88 N.J. 498, 443 A.2d 712 (1981).
84. Beitzell & Co. v. Distillers Somerset Group, Inc., Bus. Franchise Guide (CCH) ¶ 8678 (D.D.C. 1986).

the franchisee. In Iowa, transfer to a spouse or child of the franchisee upon death or disability is not considered a transfer subject to the consent of the franchisor.

In Arkansas, Nebraska, and New Jersey, the franchisor may not restrict the sale, transfer, or issuance of any securities of the franchisee or prevent the sale, transfer, or issuance of shares of stock or debentures to heirs of the principal owner of the franchisee, as long as basic financial requirements of the franchisor are complied with and any such sale, transfer, or issuance does not result in a sale of the franchise.

In the District of Columbia, the franchisor may not refuse to consent or unreasonably delay consent to the bequest or intestate succession of a franchise to any person who meets the franchisor's reasonable qualifications.

In Washington, the death of a franchisee does not constitute good cause for termination where the franchisor does not rely on the unique talents of the franchisee. In such a case, transfer upon death should be permitted.[85]

In one case, the death of a franchisee was held to be valid grounds for termination under New Jersey law.[86] Termination for substantial change in ownership or control following the death of the principal of a distributor was upheld under Connecticut law where the franchise was run as a one-man operation.[87]

Common-Law Theories Affecting the Franchise Relationship

Breach of Contract

In the absence of franchise relationship laws, franchisees who suffer wrongful acts by franchisors can bring actions based on breach of contract.[88] There has been a strong tendency by the courts to uphold the sanctity of contracts. This tends to favor franchisors, however, since virtually all franchise agreements are drafted by the franchisor's counsel. For example, most agreements will devote pages to the obligations of the franchisee, while the franchisor's obligations will be set forth in, at most, a few paragraphs.

---

85. Bus. Franchise Guide (CCH) ¶ 4470.01. *See* Statement of Policy issued by the Dep't of Licensing, Securities Division (March 14, 1983).

86. Estate of Garo Mamourian v. Exxon Co., Bus. Franchise Guide (CCH) ¶ 8093 (D.N.J. 1983).

87. McKeown Dist., Inc. v. Gyp-Crete Corp., 618 F. Supp. 632, Bus. Franchise Guide (CCH) ¶ 8423 (D. Conn. 1985).

88. *See generally* Robert T. Joseph, *Do Franchisors Owe a Duty of Competence? in* BUILDING FRANCHISE RELATIONSHIPS: A GUIDE TO ANTICIPATING PROBLEMS, RESOLVING CONFLICTS, AND REPRESENTING CLIENTS 101 (Ann Hurwitz and Rochelle Buchsbaum Spandorf, eds., ABA 1996). Lee A. Rau, *Implied Obligations in Franchising: Beyond Terminations,* 47 BUS. LAW. 1053 (1992).

Promissory Estoppel and Recoupment

Franchisees who spend sums in reliance on the franchisor's promises outside of the contract can recover such sums on the basis of promissory estoppel[89] or recoupment.[90]

Injunctive Relief

Only in rare cases might a franchisee seek an injunction at common law for wrongful termination or nonrenewal. It is more likely that the franchisor would seek an injunction, for example, barring the franchisee from selling unauthorized goods under the franchisor's trademarks or continuing to use the franchisor's trademarks after termination of the franchise agreement. Franchisors can and do seek injunctions for trademark violations and breaches of post-term or in-term restrictive covenants.[91]

Noncompete Requirements

State common law limits the permissible scope of noncompete clauses.[92]

Consent to Transfer

Contractual clauses expressly prohibiting transfer without the consent of the franchisor or supplier, including clauses allowing the franchisor to withhold its consent "with or without cause," generally are upheld under the common law.[93] Such provisions would not be enforceable under some of the relationship laws.

When such a clause does not include the phrase "with or without cause," the court may imply an obligation of reasonableness. In one case under Colorado law, the court held that withholding of consent to transfer must not be arbitrary

---

89. *See, e.g.,* Triology Variety Stores, Ltd. v. City Prod. Corp., 523 F. Supp. 691 (S.D:N.Y. 1981).

90. *See, e.g.,* Sofa Gallery, Inc. v. Stratford Co., 872 F.2d 259, Bus. Franchise Guide (CCH) ¶ 9366 (8th Cir. 1989); Cambee's Furniture, Inc. v. Doughboy Recreational, Inc., 825 F.2d 167, Bus. Franchise Guide (CCH) ¶ 8888 (8th Cir. 1987); Schultz v. Onan Corp., 737 F.2d 339, Bus. Franchise Guide (CCH) ¶ 8189 (3d Cir. 1984); Allied Equip. Co. v. Weber Engineered Prod., Inc., 237 F.2d 879 (4th Cir. 1956).

91. *See, e.g.,* Haagen-Dazs Shoppe Co. v. Morton, Bus. Franchise Guide (CCH) ¶ 10,587 (D. Co. 1994).

92. For a state-by-state compendium of the law on noncompete covenants, see COVENANTS AGAINST COMPETITION IN FRANCHISE AGREEMENTS (Peter J. Klarfeld, ed., ABA 1992).

93. *See* C. Pappas, Inc. Co. v. E & J Gallo Winery, 610 F. Supp. 662, Bus. Franchise Guide (CCH) ¶ 8378 (E.D. Cal. 1985), *aff'd,* 801 F.2d 399, Bus. Franchise Guide (CCH) ¶ 8671 (9th Cir. 1986); San Francisco Newspaper Printing Co., Inc. v. Superior Court of Santa Clara County, 170 Cal. App. 3d 438, 216 Cal. Rptr. 462, Bus. Franchise Guide (CCH) ¶ 8422 (Cal. Ct. App. 1985); American Can Co. v. A.B. Dick Co., Bus. Franchise Guide (CCH) ¶ 8097 (S.D.N.Y. 1983).

or unreasonable unless the agreement expressly grants the franchisor an absolute right to refuse to consent.[94]

When the contract is entirely silent on the question of assignability, some courts allow the franchisor or supplier to prevent transfer on the basis that the contract is one for personal services.[95]

When the contract includes the grant of an exclusive territory, courts in states with no franchise relationship law have allowed the franchisor or supplier to refuse to consent to a proposed transfer to a competitor on the basis that the proposed franchisee would be unable to fulfill its implied best efforts obligation.[96]

A franchisor at common law may also withhold consent to a transfer on the basis that the price at which the franchisee is offering to sell the franchise is so high that it would jeopardize the financial stability of the business and hinder the transferee's ability to succeed.[97] The franchisor has an interest in ensuring that the purchaser will have a chance to realize a reasonable return on his or her investment and thereby be financially able to operate in accordance with system requirements.

Encroachment

In Indiana, a franchise agreement may not permit the franchisor to compete "unfairly" with the franchisee "within a reasonable area." The franchise relationship law of Iowa specifically grants franchisees territorial rights regardless of the contractual provisions between the parties to the contrary. In Iowa, the franchisor

---

94. Larese v. Creamland Dairies, Inc., 767 F.2d 716, Bus. Franchise Guide (CCH) ¶ 8398 (10th Cir. 1985).

95. *See* Berliner Foods Corp. v. Pillsbury Co., 633 F. Supp. 557, Bus. Franchise Guide (CCH) ¶ 8566 (D. Md. 1986); Jennings v. Foremost Dairies, Inc., 37 Misc. 2d 328, 235 N.Y.S.2d 566 (1962); Paige v. Faure, 229 N.Y. 114, 127 N.E. 898 (1920); Smith v. Craig, 211 N.Y. 456, 105 N.E. 798 (1914); Quinn v. Whitney, 204 N.Y. 363, 97 N.E. 724 (N.Y. 1912), *reh'g denied,* 204 N.Y. 688, 98 N.E. 1113 (1912). Where the franchisee or dealer is a corporation, there may be an issue of whether the parties contemplated such personal services. *See* Sally Beauty Co, Inc. v. Nexxus Prod. Co., Inc., 801 F.2d 1001, Bus. Franchise Guide (CCH) ¶ 8677 (7th Cir. 1986) (Posner, J., dissenting).

96. *See, e.g., Sally Beauty, supra* note 95, at 1007 (best efforts obligation under Texas U.C.C. § 2-306(b)).

97. *See, e.g., In re* Beverages International, Ltd., Bus. Franchise Guide (CCH) ¶ 8636 (Bankr. D. Mass. 1986); Walner v. Baskin-Robbins Ice Cream Co., 514 F. Supp. 1028, Bus. Franchise Guide (CCH) ¶ 7723 (N.D. Tex. 1981); Hawkins v. Holiday Inns, Inc., 634 F.2d 342, Bus. Franchise Guide (CCH) ¶ 7568 (6th Cir. 1980), *cert. denied,* 451 U.S. 987 (1981); Kestenbaum v. Falstaff Brewing Corp., 514 F.2d 690 (5th Cir. 1975), *cert. denied,* 424 U.S. 943 (1976); Hanigan v. Wheeler, 504 P.2d 972 (Ariz. Ct. App. 1972).

Courts generally have held that the proposed transferee does not have standing to sue where the franchisor has not consented to the transfer. *See, e.g.,* Superlease Rent-A-Car, Inc. v. Budget Rent-A-Car of Md., Inc., Bus. Franchise Guide (CCH) ¶ 9368 (D.D.C. 1989).

Franchisors also have the right to transfer franchise agreements. *See* Marc's Big Boy Corp. v. Marriott Corp., Bus. Franchise Guide (CCH) ¶ 9100 (E.D. Wis. 1988); O'Neal v. Burger Chef Sys., Inc., 860 F.2d 1341, Bus. Franchise Guide (CCH) ¶ 9251 (6th Cir. 1988).

must compensate the franchisee for lost profits if the franchisee's annual gross sales are adversely affected by 5 percent or more by a new outlet, unless the franchisor has first offered the new outlet or location to the existing franchisee, or unless the franchisee does not meet then current system standards for a new franchisee. The franchisor can avoid this requirement if the franchisor establishes a formal procedure for hearing and acting upon encroachment claims by an existing franchisee and a procedure for awarding compensation to a franchisee to offset lost profits caused by encroachment.

The franchise relationship laws of other states purport to protect franchisees against encroachment on their exclusive territories by the franchisor.[98] Generally, this protection is no broader than that available at common law, since it applies only where the agreement provides for an exclusive territory.[99]

In all states except Iowa and Indiana, the issue in encroachment cases is what the parties have agreed to, regardless of whether relationship laws apply. Where the contract gives the franchisee an exclusive territory, the courts will not permit encroachment. Where the contract provides for a nonexclusive territory, most courts will not stop a franchisor from establishing another franchise or company-owned outlet near the location of the first franchise.[100] Some courts, however, have held that contractual language stating that the franchise was for a specific location did not necessarily give the franchisor the right to place additional outlets nearby.[101]

On the other hand, if the franchisor saturates the market to drive franchisees out of business, a court may hold that the franchisor's acts are in bad faith and violate the antitrust laws.[102]

---

98. *See* Appendix F.

99. *See, e.g.,* CCR Data Sys., Inc. v. Panasonic Communications & Sys. Co., Bus. Franchise Guide (CCH) ¶ 10,624 (D.N.H. 1995).

100. *See* Eichman v. Fotomat Corp., 880 F.2d 149, Bus. Franchise Guide (CCH) ¶ 9352 (9th Cir. 1989); Super Valu Stores, Inc. v. D-Mart Food Stores, Inc., 431 N.W.2d 721, Bus. Franchise Guide (CCH) ¶ 9255 (Wis. Ct. App. 1988), *rev. denied,* 147 Wis.2d 888, 436 N.W.2d 29 (Wis. 1988); KFC v. Vangeloff, Bus. Franchise Guide (CCH) ¶ 9160 (W.D. Ky. 1988); Spahn Enterprises v. Badger Northland, Inc., Bus. Franchise Guide (CCH) ¶ 9009 (Wis. Cir. Ct. 1987) (Wisconsin law); McLane v. Pizza King Franchises, Inc., Bus. Franchise Guide (CCH) ¶ 8963 (Ind. Super. Ct. 1987); Patel v. Dunkin' Donuts, 496 N.E.2d 1159, Bus. Franchise Guide (CCH) ¶ 9258 (Ill. Ct. App. 1986) (Illinois law); Wellcraft Marine, Inc. v. Dauterive, 482 So.2d 1002, Bus. Franchise Guide (CCH) ¶ 8565 (La. Ct. App. 1986) (Louisiana law); Domed Stadium Hotel, Inc. v. Holiday Inns, Inc., 732 F.2d 480, Bus. Franchise Guide (CCH) ¶ 8176 (5th Cir. 1984). *But see* May v. Roundy's, Inc., Bus. Franchise Guide (CCH) ¶ 10,550 (Wis. Ct. App. 1994) (Wisconsin law).

101. Scheck v. Burger King Corp., 756 F. Supp. 543, Bus. Franchise Guide (CCH) ¶ 9760 (S.D. Fla. 1991), *on reconsideration,* 798 F. Supp. 692, Bus. Franchise Guide (CCH) ¶ 10,049 (S.D. Fla. 1992). *See also* Burger King Corp. v. C.R. Weaver and M-W-M, Inc., 798 F. Supp. 684, Bus. Franchise Guide (CCH) ¶ 10,019 (S.D. Fla. 1992); May B-Stores, Inc. v. Roundy's, Inc., 188 Wis. 2d 78, 524 N.W.2d 647, Bus. Franchise Guide (CCH) ¶ 10,550 (Wis. Ct. App. 1994). *But see* Richard Chang v. McDonald's Corp., Bus. Franchise Guide (CCH) ¶ 10,677 (N.D. Cal. 1995).

102. *See* Photovest Corp. v. Fotomat Corp., 606 F.2d 704 (7th Cir. 1979), *cert. denied,* 445 U.S. 917 (1980).

Fraud

In the context of the franchise relationship (as distinguished from the franchise sales setting), fraud has not provided a viable means to prevent franchisor abuse. For one thing, fraud is difficult to prove. Once the franchise relationship has been established, it is unlikely that the franchisee will be able to show that the franchisor made *any* representations to the franchisee, much less one that the franchisor knew to be false at the time it made it. Usually, the representations made to the franchisee will have been made in connection with the sales process (and are, therefore, outside the scope of this discussion).

In litigation involving the Burger Chef chain, however, certain franchisees asserted that the franchisor misrepresented its intentions by stating that it was committed to the franchisor's system, when in fact the franchisor was actively looking for a buyer. From that, the franchisees claimed that they had been damaged as a result of the franchisor's alleged fraud. There have been two reported cases litigated in this context. In both cases, the franchisees were victorious at the trial level, but the decisions were reversed on appeal.[103]

Fiduciary Relationship

During the late 1970s and early 1980s, several franchisees alleged in litigation that their franchises created fiduciary relationships because the franchisees were highly dependent on the franchisor and the franchisor had superior knowledge about its system and the marketplace.

One court accepted this reasoning, at least in terms of the language it used to express its decision.[104] However, a subsequent decision by the Eighth Circuit essentially limited the decision to its facts and may even have gone so far as to undercut the decision completely.[105]

Virtually all of the reported cases suggest that no fiduciary duty exists generally between franchisors and franchisees,[106] although there are suggestions in some of the decisions that the higher level of duty could exist in limited situations.

---

103. *See* Vaughn v. General Foods Corp., 797 F.2d 1403, Bus. Franchise Guide (CCH) ¶ 8630 (7th Cir. 1986), *cert. denied,* 479 U.S. 1087 (1987); O'Neal v. Burger Chef Sys., Inc., 860 F.2d 1341, Bus. Franchise Guide (CCH) ¶ 9251 (6th Cir. 1988).

104. Arnott v. American Oil Co., 609 F.2d 873 (8th Cir. 1979), *cert. denied,* 446 U.S. 918 (1980).

105. Bain v. Champlin Petroleum Co., 692 F.2d 43, Bus. Franchise Guide (CCH) ¶ 7861 (8th Cir. 1982).

106. *See, e.g.,* O'Neal v. Burger Chef Sys., Inc., 860 F.2d 1341, Bus. Franchise Guide (CCH) ¶ 9251 (6th Cir. 1988) (and cases cited at 1349 n. 4); Premier Wine & Spirits v. E&J Gallo Winery, 846 F.2d 537, Bus. Franchise Guide (CCH) ¶ 9106 (9th Cir. 1988); Coca-Cola Bottling Co. of Elizabethtown, Inc. v. Coca-Cola Co., 696 F. Supp. 57 (D. Del. 1988), *aff'd,* 988 F.2d 386 (3d Cir.), *cert. denied,* 114 S. Ct. 289 (1993); Seaward Yacht Sales, Ltd. v. Murray Chris-Craft Cruisers, Inc., 701 F. Supp. 766, Bus. Franchise Guide (CCH) ¶ 9287 (D. Or. 1988); Cambee's Furniture, Inc. v. Doughboy Recreational, Inc., 825 F.2d 167, Bus. Franchise Guide (CCH) ¶ 8888 (8th Cir. 1987); Boat & Motor Mart v. Sea Ray Boats, Inc., 825 F.2d 1285, Bus. Franchise Guide (CCH) ¶ 8846 (9th Cir. 1987); Wallach Marine Corp. v. Donzi Marine Corp., 675 F. Supp. 838, Bus. Franchise Guide (CCH) ¶ 9014 (S.D.N.Y. 1987).

Good Faith

Courts in most states consistently have held that an implied covenant of good faith and fair dealing exists in any franchise agreement.[107] Franchisees who feel that they have been aggrieved by their franchisors' post-sale conduct frequently cite this principle. The Iowa statute specifically provides that the covenant of good faith is part of every franchise relationship.

The covenant of good faith and fair dealing assists in interpreting the intention of the parties where the contract is silent. It will not override express contractual provisions.[108] To a large degree, it acts as a limitation on the reserved discretion of a party to a franchise agreement.

In essence, the covenant provides that the parties to a contract must act honestly and observe reasonable commercial standards of fair dealing in the trade. The covenant has also been interpreted to mean that neither party will act in such a manner as to deprive the other party of the benefit of the contract.[109] For example, if the franchisor opens a unit immediately adjacent to a franchisee who has been granted a franchise only for a specified site and who has expressly acknowledged that he or she has no rights to territorial protection, the franchisee will have a strong argument that the franchisor's action deprived the franchisee of the benefit of the contract.

In some instances, the covenant has been applied to prevent abusive conduct by a franchisor.[110] The covenant has also been applied in various situations to prevent unjust terminations.[111]

---

107. *Id. See also* U.C.C. §§ 1-203, 1-102(3); Restatement (Second) of Contracts § 205 (1979).

108. *See, e.g.,* Davis v. Sears, Roebuck and Co., 873 F.2d 888, Bus. Franchise Guide (CCH) ¶ 9384 (6th Cir. 1989); Tulsa Trailer & Body, Inc. v. Trailmobile, Inc., Bus. Franchise Guide (CCH) ¶ 8615 (N.D. Okla. 1986); Jack Walters & Sons Corp. v. Morton Building, Inc., 737 F.2d 698, Bus. Franchise Guide (CCH) ¶ 8192 (7th Cir. 1984), *cert. denied,* 469 U.S. 1018 (1984); Corenswet, Inc. v. Amana Refrigeration, Inc., 594 F.2d 129 (5th Cir.), *cert. denied,* 444 U.S. 938 (1979). *But see* Overhead Door Co. of Reno, Inc. v. Overhead Door Corp., 734 P.2d 1233, Bus. Franchise Guide (CCH) ¶ 8812 (Nev. 1987). *See also* Dayan v. McDonald's Corp., 126 Ill. App. 3d 11, 466 N.E.2d 945, Bus. Franchise Guide (CCH) ¶ 8185 (Ill. Ct. App. 1984). *See generally* T.M. McLaughlin & C. Jacobs, *Termination of Franchises: Application of the Implied Covenant of Good Faith and Fair Dealing,* 7 Franchise L.J. 1 (Summer 1987).

109. *See* Report to the House of Delegates of the ABA regarding the enactment by state legislatures of the "Franchise and Business Opportunities Act" of the National Conference of Commissioners on Uniform State Laws [presented in February 1988 and prepared by the Franchising Committee of the Section of Antitrust Law of the ABA], at 4-12 (hereinafter Task Force Report).

110. The most notable might be Photovest Corp. v. Fotomat Corp., 606 F.2d 704 (7th Cir. 1979), *cert. denied,* 445 U.S. 917 (1980), where there was abundant evidence suggesting that the franchisor was trying to drive the franchisee out of business.

111. *See* Task Force Report, *supra* note 109, nn. 11-13.

Although the covenant of good faith and fair dealing probably is law in most jurisdictions,[112] there are very few cases where that principle, by itself, has led to a ruling favorable to a franchisee.

Antitrust

In the early 1970s, the federal antitrust laws, as then interpreted and applied by the courts, provided a powerful basis for claims against franchisors. The antitrust laws provide in many circumstances for treble damages as well as attorneys' fee awards. At that time, the legality of vertical restrictions was in doubt. In practice, many franchisors were engaging in tying practices. Many franchisees were forced to buy equipment from the franchisor or its affiliates when there were perfectly acceptable alternative sources of supply.

As a result of changes in practices in the industry and changes in the attitudes of regulatory and judicial officials toward antitrust laws, claims of antitrust violations dropped off significantly in the 1980s. Antitrust laws today are used by franchisees only in the more egregious cases.[113]

Conclusion

Between 1979, when the FTC Rule went into effect, and 1992, very little franchise relationship legislation was enacted, although many bills were introduced. To a large extent, the disclosures required by the FTC Rule appeared to have lessened the abuses at which the relationship laws were aimed.

In 1992, Iowa enacted a new franchise relationship law. Initiatives followed in other states, although no other states have yet enacted new franchise relationship laws. Nevertheless, franchise relationship laws remain in effect in several states.

Counsel for franchisors, manufacturers, and suppliers will want to advise their clients of the risks under the franchise relationship laws of terminating franchise and dealership agreements and of withholding consent to their renewal or assignment. The advice should come before any agreement is signed, so that the client can make an informed decision whether to sign the agreement, restructure the arrangement, or not sign. When the client desires to terminate or withhold consent to a renewal or assignment, the client will need assistance in navigating through these laws to minimize the risk of litigation.

Counsel for dealers and franchisees should advise their clients of their rights under these laws. Wherever possible, counsel for dealers and franchisees will want to structure the arrangement in a way that brings it within the coverage of the relationship laws and to use contractual language that reinforces this coverage. When the franchisor, manufacturer, or supplier terminates or withholds consent to the renewal or assignment, the dealer or franchisee will need to know its rights and available remedies.

---

112. *See* Task Force Report, *supra* note 109, at 4.

113. *See* Photovest Corp. v. Fotomat Corp., 606 F.2d 704 (7th Cir. 1979), *cert. denied*, 445 U.S. 917 (1980).

CHAPTER 6

Antitrust Law

Robert T. Joseph, Michael M. Eaton, and Alan H. Maclin

Contents

This chapter focuses on antitrust law. It begins by discussing basic antitrust principles, and it then addresses vertical price and non-price restraints. Finally, it looks in detail at antitrust tie-in issues that are raised when the franchisor sells to franchisees.

Basic Antitrust Principles

The Governing Statutes

Section 1 of the Sherman Act:[1]

Every contract, combination in the form of trust or otherwise, or conspiracy, in restraint of trade or commerce among the several States, or with foreign nations, is declared to be illegal.

Section 2 of the Sherman Act:[2]

Every person who shall monopolize, or attempt to monopolize, or combine or conspire with any other person or persons, to monopolize any part of the trade or commerce among the several States, or with foreign nations, shall be deemed guilty of a felony, and, on conviction thereof, shall be punished by fine not exceeding $10,000,000 if a corporation, or, if any other person, $350,000, or by imprisonment not exceeding three years, or by both said punishments, in the discretion of the court.

Section 5 of the Federal Trade Commission Act:[3]

(a)(1) Unfair methods of competition in or affecting commerce, and unfair or deceptive acts or practices in or affecting commerce, are declared unlawful.

Section 3 of the Clayton Act:[4]

It shall be unlawful for any person engaged in commerce, in the course of such commerce, to lease or make a sale or contract for sale of goods, wares, merchandise, machinery, supplies, or other commodities . . . on the condition, agreement, or understanding that the lessee or purchaser thereof shall not use or deal in the goods, wares, merchandise, machinery, supplies, or other commodities of a competitor or competitors of the lessor or seller, where the effect . . . may be to substantially lessen competition or tend to create a monopoly in any line of commerce.

Private Actions

Although the Department of Justice and the Federal Trade Commission (FTC) are primarily responsible for federal antitrust enforcement, government suits are far outnumbered by private actions, particularly in the distribution area. Damages may be obtained under Section 4 of the Clayton Act[5] by "any person . . . injured in his business or property by reason of anything forbidden in the antitrust laws." Treble damages plus attorneys' fees and costs are awarded. In-

---

1. 15 U.S.C. § 1 (1988 & Supp. V 1993).
2. 15 U.S.C. § 2 (1988 & Supp. V 1993).
3. 15 U.S.C. § 45 (1988 & Supp. V 1993).
4. 15 U.S.C. § 14 (1988).
5. 15 U.S.C. § 15(a) (1988).

junctive relief may be obtained under Section 16 of the Clayton Act by "any person . . . threatened (with) loss or damage by a violation of the antitrust laws. . . . In any action under this section in which the plaintiff substantially prevails, the court shall award the cost of suit, including a reasonable attorney's fee, to such plaintiff."[6]

State Antitrust Enforcement

Most states have their own state antitrust statutes, often providing for both governmental and private enforcement.[7] Moreover, many states have "little FTC acts" that provide for private causes of action, including treble damages.[8] These laws can be of significant impact because of the unwillingness of the federal courts to find a private right of action under the Federal Trade Commission Act.[9]

Preliminary Principles

Rule of Reason versus *Per Se* Violation

Read literally, Section 1 of the Sherman Act would prohibit all concerted activity in restraint of trade. However, the Supreme Court has construed Section 1 to render unlawful only those restraints of trade that unreasonably restrict competition.[10] A presumption exists in favor of the Rule of Reason standard. Departure from the standard must be justified by demonstrable economic effect, such as facilitation of cartelizing, rather than formalistic distinctions.[11] In assessing whether a restraint violates Section 1, the fact finder is to evaluate the competitive effect by analyzing the facts peculiar to the business, the history of the restraint, and the reasons why it was imposed.[12]

There are, however, "certain agreements or practices which because of their pernicious effect on competition and lack of any redeeming virtue are conclusively presumed to be unreasonable and therefore illegal without elaborate inquiry as to the precise harm they have caused or the business excuse for their use."[13] The "nature and necessary effect" of such agreements "are so plainly anti-

---

6. 15 U.S.C. § 26 (1988).

7. *See generally* ABA Antitrust Section, State Antitrust Practice and Statutes (ABA 1991).

8. *See, e.g.,* N.C. Gen. Stat. §§ 75-1.1, 16.

9. *See, e.g.,* Brill v. Catfish Shaks of Am., Inc., 727 F. Supp. 1035, 1041 (E.D. La. 1989); Days Inn of Am. Franchising, Inc. v. Windham, 699 F. Supp. 1581, 1582–83, Bus. Franchise Guide (CCH) ¶ 9296 (N.D. Ga. 1988); Akers v. Bonifasi, 629 F. Supp. 1212, 1221, Bus. Franchise Guide (CCH) ¶ 8614 (M.D. Tenn. 1984); Freedman v. Meldy's, Inc., 587 F. Supp. 658, Bus. Franchise Guide (CCH) ¶ 8213 (E.D. Pa. 1984).

10. *See* Standard Oil Co. v. United States, 221 U.S. 1, 58 (1911); National Soc'y of Professional Eng'rs v. United States, 435 U.S. 679, 687–88 (1978).

11. Business Elecs. Corp. v. Sharp Elecs. Corp., 485 U.S. 717, Bus. Franchise Guide (CCH) ¶ 9103 (1988).

12. National Soc'y of Professional Eng'rs v. United States, 435 U.S. 679, 692 (1978).

13. Northern Pac. Ry. v. United States, 356 U.S. 1, 5 (1958) ("Northern Pac. Ry.").

competitive that no elaborate study of the industry is needed to establish their illegality—they are illegal 'per se.' "[14] The categories of restraints that are currently held to be *per se* unlawful include horizontal price-fixing, bid rigging and market division, vertical price-fixing, certain group boycotts, and some tying arrangements.[15] In recent years, lower courts have approached with caution efforts to apply and expand the *per se* rule.[16]

Vertical versus Horizontal

Horizontal restraints are agreements between competitors at the *same* level of market structure. Vertical restraints are combinations of persons at *different* levels of the market structure, such as manufacturers and distributors. Horizontal restraints have been scrutinized more strictly than vertical restraints.

Unilateral versus Concerted Action

To prevail under Section 1 of the Sherman Act, a plaintiff must establish a "contract, combination . . . or conspiracy" in unreasonable restraint of trade. Regardless of its purpose or effect, Section 1 does not prohibit independent action or business decisions. The conduct of a single firm is governed by Section 2 (monopolization and attempted monopolization) alone.[17]

Interbrand versus Intrabrand Competition

Interbrand competition (e.g., among different rental car franchisors) is competition among manufacturers of the same generic product. Intrabrand competition is competition between distributors—wholesale or retail—of the product of a particular manufacturer. Competition between or among franchisees of the same franchisor is intrabrand competition. When interbrand competition exists, "it provides a significant check on the exploitation of intrabrand market power because of the ability of consumers to substitute a different brand of the same product."[18]

---

14. National Soc'y of Professional Eng'rs, *supra* note 12, 435 U.S. at 692.

15. *See, e.g.,* Union Processing Corp. v. Atkin, 465 U.S. 1038, 1040 (1984) (market divisions) (White, J., dissenting in denial of cert.); United States v. Citizens & Southern Nat'l Bank, 422 U.S. 86, 118 (1975); Northern Pac. Ry., *supra* note 13, 356 U.S. at 5 (price fixing); Hahn v. Oregon Physicians' Serv., 868 F.2d 1022, 1026 (9th Cir. 1988) (on motion for rehearing), *cert. denied*, 493 U.S. 846 (1989) (horizontal price fixing, market divisions, group boycotts); Car Carriers, Inc. v. Ford Motor Co., 745 F.2d 1101, 1108 (7th Cir. 1984) ("Car Carriers, Inc."), *cert. denied*, 470 U.S. 1054 (1985).

16. *See, e.g.,* Hennessy Indus., Inc. v. FMC Corp., 779 F.2d 402, 403 (7th Cir. 1985); Car Carriers, Inc., *supra* note 15, 745 F.2d at 1108.

17. *See* Copperweld Corp. v. Independence Tube Corp., 467 U.S. 752 (1984); Monsanto Co. v. Spray-Rite Serv. Corp., 465 U.S. 752, Bus. Franchise Guide (CCH) ¶ 8141 (1984).

18. Continental T.V., Inc. v. GTE Sylvania, Inc., 433 U.S. 36, 52 n.19, Bus. Franchise Guide (CCH) ¶ 1635 (1977).

Vertical Price and Non-Price Restraints

Proof of Contract, Combination, or Conspiracy

Basic Standard for Finding Concerted Action

Section 1 of the Sherman Act requires that there be a "contract, combination . . . or conspiracy"[19] between two or more separate entities to establish a violation. Independent action by a single entity is not proscribed.

In *Monsanto v. Spray-Rite Service Corp.,*[20] the Supreme Court considered the circumstances under which a vertical price-fixing agreement may be inferred when a supplier terminates a discounting dealer following complaints from other, nondiscounting dealers. The Seventh Circuit had held in *Monsanto* that "proof of termination following competitor complaints is sufficient to support an inference of [conspiracy]."[21] The Supreme Court affirmed the holding of the Seventh Circuit but rejected its reasoning, finding that "something more than evidence of complaints is needed" to support an inference of concerted action.[22] According to the Court, "[t]he correct standard is that there must be evidence that tends to exclude the possibility of independent action by the manufacturer and distributor. That is, there must be direct or circumstantial evidence that reasonably tends to prove that the manufacturer and others had a conscious commitment to a common scheme designed to achieve an unlawful objective."[23] Circumstantial evidence may include actions by manufacturer and distributor after the refusal to deal occurs.[24]

A supplier generally has a right to deal, or refuse to deal, with whomever it likes, as long as it does so independently.[25] As the Court stated in Monsanto:[26] "Under [*United States v.*] *Colgate,* the manufacturer can announce its resale prices in advance and refuse to deal with those who fail to comply. And a distributor is free to acquiesce in the manufacturer's demand in order to avoid termination."[27]

---

19. 5 U.S.C. § 1 (1988 & Supp. V 1993).

20. 465 U.S. 752 (1984) ("Monsanto").

21. Spray-Rite Serv. Corp. v. Monsanto, 684 F.2d 1226, 1238 (7th Cir. 1982).

22. Monsanto, *supra* note 20, at 764.

23. *Id.* at 768.

24. Storer Cable Communications, Inc. v. City of Montgomery, 826 F. Supp. 1338 (M.D. Ala. 1993), *vacated*, 866 F. Supp. 1376 (M.D. Ala. 1993) (allegations of a contract, combination, or conspiracy are sufficient for Section 1 violation where, shortly after a complaining operator contacted supplier and the supplier refused to deal, an existing operator was awarded an exclusive contract with the supplier).

25. United States v. Colgate & Co., 250 U.S. 300, 307 (1919).

26. Monsanto, *supra* note 20, at 761.

27. *See also* Russell Stover Candies, Inc. v. FTC, 718 F.2d 256, 260 (8th Cir. 1983) ("simple refusal to sell to customers who will not sell at prices suggested by the seller is permissible under the Sherman Act"); H.L. Moore Drug Exchange v. Eli Lilly & Co., 662 F.2d 935, 946 (2d Cir. 1981), *cert. denied*, 459 U.S. 880 (1982) ("we need not consider whether Lilly's action was motivated by anticompetitive reasons, since a unilateral decision to terminate, no matter what the reason, does not constitute a violation of the antitrust laws").

The Court in *Monsanto* specifically noted that the concept of "a meeting of the minds" or "a common scheme" "includes *more than a showing that the distributor conformed to the suggested price.* It means as well that evidence must be presented both that the distributor communicated its acquiescence or agreement, and that this was sought by the manufacturer."[28] Whether a supplier's actions in attempting to influence the resale prices of its distributors went beyond the type of unilateral acts permitted by *Colgate* has been addressed in a number of other cases by the Supreme Court.[29] The line between unilateral action under *Colgate* and formation of an impermissible combination or conspiracy is not an easy one to draw.

Common Situations in Which the Concerted Action Issue Is Raised— Concerted Action Theories

Termination of Distributors or Imposition of Other Restraints Following Receipt of Complaints by Competing Distributors ("Distributor Noise"). A frequent theory of private treble damage litigants is that the supplier's refusal to deal resulted from a conspiracy between the supplier and one or more other distributors, pursuant to which the plaintiff was terminated because of its price-cutting activities. To what extent can a plaintiff's case be based on complaints from other distributors followed by termination? Before *Monsanto* a division existed among the courts of appeals over whether a plaintiff could survive a motion for a directed verdict if it established that a supplier terminated a price-cutting distributor in response to or following complaints by other distributors.

In *Monsanto* the Court stated that concerted action cannot be inferred merely from a refusal to deal following receipt of complaints from other distributors. There must be evidence that tends to exclude the possibility that the supplier and nonterminated distributors were acting independently. The Court recognized that complaints arise in the normal course of business; that distributors "are an important source of information for manufacturers"; and that manufacturers and distributors "constantly must coordinate their activities to assure that their product will reach the consumer persuasively and efficiently." The Court stated: "To bar a manufacturer from acting solely because the information upon which it acts originated as a price complaint would create an irrational dislocation in the market."[30] The Court, to be sure, recognized that evidence of complaints could have some probative value but concluded that the "burden remains on the antitrust plaintiff to introduce additional evidence sufficient to support a finding of an unlawful contract, combination, or conspiracy."[31]

---

28. Monsanto, *supra* note 20, at 764 n.9. (emphasis added).

29. *See* Business Elecs. Corp. v. Sharp Elecs. Corp., 485 U.S. 717 (1988); Matsushita Elec. Indus. Co. v. Zenith Radio Corp., 475 U.S. 574 (1986); Continental T.V., Inc. v. GTE Sylvania, Inc., 433 U.S. 36 (1977).

30. Monsanto, *supra* note 20, at 763–64. *See also* Oreck Corp. v. Whirlpool Corp., 639 F.2d 75, 80 (2d Cir. 1980), *cert. denied*, 454 U.S. 1083 (1981); Borger v. Yamaha Int'l Corp., 625 F.2d 390, 395 (2d Cir. 1980).

31. Monsanto, *supra* note 20, at 764 n.8.

Post-*Monsanto* cases have grappled with application of its standards to the "distributor noise" situation.[32]

32. *See, e.g.,* Ben Sheftall Distrib. Co. v. Mirta de Perales, Inc., 791 F. Supp. 1575 (S.D. Ga. 1992) (agreement to terminate price-cutting distributor cannot be implied from complaints from other distributors); Slowiak v. Hudson Foods, Inc., Bus. Franchise Guide (CCH) ¶ 10,006, 1992-1 Trade Cas. (CCH) ¶ 69,821 (W.D. Wis. 1992), *aff'd*, 987 F.2d 1293 (7th Cir. 1993) (meat manufacturer's announcement of retail prices on price lists did not constitute illegal conspiracy to fix maximum resale prices); Bailey's, Inc. v. Windsor America, Inc., 948 F.2d 1018, 1030 (6th Cir. 1991) (although evidence supported reasonable inference that manufacturer terminated direct sales to one dealer to retain and increase the volume of sales to others, there was no evidence of any agreement with dealers to control or fix prices); Bi-Rite Oil v. Indiana Farm Bureau Coop. Ass'n, 908 F.2d 200, 203 (7th Cir. 1990) (no evidence of agreement to set prices; thus vertical agreement between manufacturer and dealer to terminate a second dealer was not *per se* illegal); Parkway Gallery Furniture, Inc. v. Kittinger/Pennsylvania House Group, Inc., 878 F.2d 801, 805, 806 n.4, Bus. Franchise Guide (CCH) ¶ 9460 (4th Cir. 1989) (evidence that manufacturer implemented marketing policy in response to retailers' complaints and that retailers supported enforcement of the policy, insufficient to support conspiracy theory in non-price restriction claim); The Jeanery, Inc. v. James Jeans, Inc., 849 F.2d 1148, 1158, Bus. Franchise Guide (CCH) ¶ 9117 (9th Cir. 1988) (evidence of competitors' complaints about a retailer's price-cutting, the manufacturer's statement that it would "take care of things," alleged coercive tactics and lack of business justification for termination was not sufficient to permit case to reach a jury); Winn v. Edna Hibel Corp., 858 F.2d 1517, Bus. Franchise Guide (CCH) ¶ 9236 (11th Cir. 1988) (evidence of termination following complaints by other distributors insufficient to show "agreement" because supplier had independent reason to terminate discounter); McCabe's Furniture, Inc. v. La-Z-Boy Chair Co., 798 F.2d 323, Bus. Franchise Guide (CCH) ¶ 8638 (8th Cir. 1986), *cert. denied*, 486 U.S. 1005 (1988) (plaintiff presented adequate evidence that its termination as a dealer resulted from a conspiracy between the manufacturer and a competing dealer, but there was insufficient evidence that the purpose of the conspiracy was to maintain resale prices); National Marine Elec. Distribs., Inc. v. Raytheon Co., 778 F.2d 190, Bus. Franchise Guide (CCH) ¶ 8473 (4th Cir. 1985) (although Raytheon's decision to change its marketing strategy occurred in the context of dealer complaints, there was no evidence that reasonably tended to prove that Raytheon and one of the complaining dealers schemed to terminate plaintiff for the purpose of restraining price competition); World of Sleep, Inc. v. La-Z-Boy Chair Co., 756 F.2d 1467 (10th Cir.), *cert. denied*, 474 U.S. 823 (1985) (no conspiracy could be inferred where a retailer independently set its own prices and a manufacturer unilaterally terminated a competing retailer for failing to keep its prices up; although the retailer complained about the competitor's prices and the manufacturer responded by terminating, this was insufficient evidence of a conspiracy); Landmark Dev. Corp. v. Chambers Corp., 752 F.2d 369, Bus. Franchise Guide (CCH) ¶ 8295 (9th Cir. 1985); Magid Mfg. Co. v. U.S.D. Corp., 654 F. Supp. 325, Bus. Franchise Guide (CCH) ¶ 8783 (N.D. Ill. 1987) (insufficient proof of conspiracy based on distributor complaints about plaintiff's pricing, where manufacturer offered substantial evidence of independent intent to implement a new marketing plan); Garment Dist., Inc. v. Belk Stores Servs., Inc., 617 F. Supp. 944 (W.D.N.C. 1985), *aff'd*, 799 F.2d 905 (4th Cir.), *cert. denied*, 486 U.S. 1005 (1988); Pink Supply Corp. v. Hiebert, Inc., 612 F. Supp. 1334, Bus. Franchise Guide (CCH) ¶ 8362 (D. Minn. 1985), *aff'd*, 788 F.2d 1313 (8th Cir. 1986) (distributor's burden of proof could not be met under *Monsanto* solely by showing that the manufacturer terminated the distributor after receiving complaints from competing distributors regarding distributor's pricing or that the termination was in response to the other dealer's complaints; evidence of shared concerns about dealer profits between the manufacturer and its dealers, the manufacturer's furnishing of a suggested price list, dis-

Once concerted action has been established, it is necessary to consider the competitive impact of that concerted action.[33] Thus, there must be evidence that the complaining dealer agreed to set its prices at some level (although perhaps not a specific one). The complaining dealer cannot retain complete freedom to set whatever price it chooses. It will not be enough to prove that the supplier agreed to terminate the price-cutting dealer in the face of a demand by the remaining, complaining dealer. In *Sharp Electronics,* the Supreme Court reasoned that, absent an agreement on price, an agreement to terminate a distributor creates no greater risk of anticompetitive effects than a nonprice vertical restraint. It rejected the argument that vertical price agreements generally underlie agreements to terminate price cutters. Thus, an agreement between a manufacturer and a distributor to terminate another distributor because of the latter's pricing practices, without any agreement about the prices or price levels that will be charged by the remaining distributor or distributors, would constitute concerted action but not concerted action to fix resale prices. Consequently, the legality of such concerted action would be analyzed under the Rule of Reason, not the *per se* rule.

---

cussions of pricing with distributors, a manufacturer's sales agent's telling the distributor that a prospective customer belonged to another distributor, and a sales agent's suggesting termination because of the distributor's low bids was insufficient to show conspiracy); Gilchrist Mach. Co. v. Komatsu Am. Corp., 601 F. Supp. 1192, Bus. Franchise Guide (CCH) ¶ 8294 (S.D. Miss. 1984); Gillette Tire Jobbers, Inc. v. Appliance Indus., Inc., 596 F. Supp. 1277 (E.D. La. 1984) (summary judgment for defendant; since plaintiff's only admissible evidence consisted of complaints of other distributors followed by a reduction in the discount given to him, *Monsanto* governed, and there was insufficient evidence to establish a conspiracy); Burlington Coat Factory Warehouse Corp. v. Esprit de Corp, 769 F.2d 919, Bus. Franchise Guide (CCH) ¶ 8424 (2d Cir. 1985) (summary judgment for defendant; mere proximity of time between department store's announcement of plans to refuse to deal with wholesalers who supplied discount retailers and a clothing manufacturer's refusal to deal with such a retailer was not sufficient circumstantial evidence to constitute a Section 1 violation); Terry's Floor Fashions, Inc. v. Burlington Indus., Inc., 763 F.2d 604, Bus. Franchise Guide (CCH) ¶ 8390 (4th Cir. 1985) (actions taken by defendant were consistent with the marketing strategy of discouraging "bootlegging," and plaintiff was terminated when it stated its intention to continue violating this policy); Computer Place, Inc. v. Hewlett-Packard Co., 607 F. Supp. 822, Bus. Franchise Guide (CCH) ¶ 8250 (N.D. Cal. 1984), *aff'd without opinion,* 779 F.2d 56 (9th Cir. 1985) (summary judgment for defendant; plaintiff failed to satisfy standards; supplier showed its actions were unilateral and taken to further a market strategy de-emphasizing mail order distribution in favor of distributors who would provide full service); Glacier Optical, Inc. v. Optique Du Monde, Ltd., 816 F. Supp. 646, 652, Bus. Franchise Guide (CCH) ¶ 10,008 (D. Or. 1993), *aff'd,* 46 F.3d 1141 (9th Cir. 1995) (defendant's termination of distributor that refused to agree to customer restrictions held not to violate antitrust laws because defendant acted unilaterally; complaints by other distributors do not rise to the level of concerted activity); Matrix Essentials, Inc. v. Emporium Drug Mart, Inc., 988 F.2d 587, 594 (5th Cir. 1993) (distributor complaints regarding unauthorized sale of hair care products by retail drug store chain are not in themselves indicative of an illegal conspiracy).

33. In Business Elecs. Corp. v. Sharp Elecs. Corp., 485 U.S. 717 (1988), the Supreme Court held that a vertical restraint of trade is not *per se* illegal under Section 1 of the Sherman Act unless it includes some agreement on price or price levels.

Existence of a Horizontal Agreement. Franchisees also may be able to avoid the *Sharp* and *Monsanto* rules if they can prove the existence of a horizontal agreement (as opposed to a vertical agreement) among competing franchisees. This analysis flows from the Supreme Court's interpretation of a group boycott in *United States v. General Motors Corp.,*[34] where the court held that concerted action by dealers and GM not to supply discounters was a horizontal conspiracy among dealers and that they had enlisted the manufacturer into joining the conspiracy. For example, in *Lovett v. General Motors Corp.,*[35] plaintiffs alleged that various competing dealers conspired with GM to reduce the number of cars GM supplied to the plaintiff. The district court reasoned that the *Sharp* rule (Rule of Reason analysis) applied only in vertical restraint cases, in contrast to the horizontal conspiracy it believed existed between GM and the competing dealers. It concluded, therefore, that *Sharp* was inapplicable and that the *per se* rule was properly applied. Without addressing whether the arrangement was horizontal (*per se* analysis) or vertical (Rule of Reason analysis), the Eighth Circuit reversed the district court's denial of GM's motion, on the grounds that the dealer failed to produce evidence showing that GM's conduct was as consistent with permissible competition as with illegal conspiracy, for judgment notwithstanding the verdict. In a similar case, the Eighth Circuit also held that car dealers who collectively pressured car manufacturers to preclude competing dealers from building an automall were acting pursuant to a *per se* illegal horizontal conspiracy.[36]

In *Big Apple BMW v. BMW of North America, Inc.,*[37] the Third Circuit relied in part on proof of a horizontal conspiracy among competing BMW dealers to deny the plaintiff a BMW franchise because of the plaintiff's reputation as a discount and high-volume dealer. In the court's view, this made *Sharp* irrelevant. Similarly, in *Alvord Polk, Inc. v. F. Schumacher & Co.,*[38] the Third Circuit reversed a grant of summary judgment based on its conclusion that a reasonable jury could find a horizontal conspiracy among members of an association of full-service wallpaper dealers to compel manufacturers to boycott discount wall-

34. 384 U.S. 127 (1966).

35. 769 F. Supp. 1506 (D. Minn. 1991), *aff'd on certain grounds*, 975 F.2d 518 (8th Cir. 1992), *rev'd on certain grounds*, 998 F.2d 575 (8th Cir. 1993), *cert. denied*, 114 S. Ct. 1058 (1994).

36. ES Development Inc. v. RWM Enterprises, Inc., 939 F.2d 547 (8th Cir. 1991).

37. 947 F.2d 1358 (3d Cir. 1992), *cert. denied*, 113 S. Ct. 1262 (1993).

38. 37 F.3d 996 (3d Cir. 1994), *cert. denied*, 63 U.S.L.W. 3583 (U.S. April 17, 1995). *Accord, e.g.*, Denny's Marina, Inc. v. Renfro Productions, Inc., 8 F.3d 1217 (7th Cir. 1993) (the court found a horizontal agreement by boat dealers to exclude a discounting dealer from two boat shows was a per se unlawful agreement to fix prices; the participation of the operator of the boat shows in the conspiracy did not make it a vertical conspiracy); AAA Venetian Blind Sales, Inc. v. Beaulieu of America, 1995 U.S. Dist. LEXIS 11243 (W.D. Mich. 1995) (district court denied defendants' motion for summary judgment on the ground that there was sufficient evidence of conspiracy among competing dealers and the manufacturer to cut off supplies to the plaintiff/dealer).

A recent FTC consent decree also involved an attempted boycott of a discounter organized by retailers. In the Matter of New England Juvenile Retailers Ass'n, 5 Trade Reg. Rep. (CCH) ¶ 23,689 (FTC 1995).

paper dealers. The Third Circuit considered whether the actions of the association's officers could be imputed to the association as a whole and constitute collective action by the retail dealers. The court concluded that a jury could find that a statement by one of the association's officers constituted a threat by the association (and its members) to boycott manufacturers who supplied the discounting dealers.

By contrast, in *Thompson Everett, Inc. v. National Cable Advertising L.P.,*[39] the court found that "frequent business contact" among the defendants who were horizontal competitors, including joint presentations to industry trade groups, was insufficient evidence of concerted action.

Agreement between Plaintiff and Defendant. A contract between the plaintiff and defendant constitutes sufficient "agreement" to satisfy the concerted action requirement.[40]

Coerced Agreement between Plaintiff and Defendant. Similarly, the plaintiff's acquiescence in a course of conduct imposed by the defendant may satisfy the concerted action requirement.[41] If the plaintiff does not acquiesce, however, there may be no agreement within the meaning of Section 1.[42]

Agreement between Defendant and Other Complying Distributors. If the plaintiff's termination is used to coerce the agreement of other distributors, an agreement may be found between the defendant and those distributors.[43] However, as noted earlier, termination of a price cutter at the request of other higher pricing distributors does not constitute a *per se* violation, absent an agreement to set specific prices or price levels.[44]

---

39. 850 F. Supp. 470, 480 (E.D. Va. 1994).

40. Perma Life Mufflers, Inc. v. International Parts Corp., 392 U.S. 134, 136–37 (1968) (tying and territorial restrictions in franchise agreement); Hobart Bros. Co. v. Malcolm T. Gilliland, Inc., 471 F.2d 894, 899 (5th Cir.), *cert. denied*, 412 U.S. 923 (1973).

41. Albrecht v. Herald Co., 390 U.S. 145, 150 n.6 (1968); *see also* Arnott v. American Oil Co., 609 F.2d 873, 884–85, Bus. Franchise Guide (CCH) ¶¶ 1620.30, 1635.75 (8th Cir. 1979), *cert. denied*, 446 U.S. 918 (1980); World of Sleep, Inc. v. La-Z-Boy Chair Co., 756 F.2d 1467 (10th Cir.), *cert. denied*, 474 U.S. 823 (1985). *But see* Curry v. Steve's Franchise Co., Bus. Franchise Guide (CCH) ¶ 8475, 1985-2 Trade Cas. (CCH) ¶ 66,877 (D. Mass. 1985) (franchisee's accession to suggested resale prices, after only one alleged act of coercion, insufficient to create illegal combination; franchisee acceded too easily to complain about a pricing scheme); The Jeanery, Inc. v. James Jeans, Inc., 849 F.2d 1148 (9th Cir. 1988).

42. Quinn v. Mobil Oil Corp., 375 F.2d 273, 276 (1st Cir.), *cert. dismissed*, 389 U.S. 801 (1967).

43. *See* Albrecht v. Herald Co., 390 U.S. 145, 150 n.6 (1968); Black Gold, Ltd. v. Rockwool Indus., Inc., 729 F.2d 676, 686–87 (10th Cir.), *cert. denied*, 469 U.S. 854 (1984); Yentsch v. Texaco, Inc., 630 F.2d 46, 52–53 (2d Cir. 1980).

44. Center Video Indus. Co. v. United Media, Inc., 995 F.2d 735 (7th Cir. 1993) (finding no evidence that defendant and competing distributor agreed to set prices within a given range in return for terminating plaintiff-distributor); Ben Elfman and Son, Inc., v. Criterion Mills, Inc., 774 F. Supp. 683 (D. Mass. 1991) (without manufacturer-dealer agreement as to price level, termination of a "price-cutter" does not necessarily tend to restrict

Use of "Outside Entities" by Defendant. The question of when use of outside entities results in concerted action has arisen in a number of cases. In *Albrecht v. Herald Co.,*[45] the Supreme Court suggested that the defendant newspaper's use of outside agents to solicit and take over the plaintiff's paper-route customers constituted concerted action because those agents knew of the purpose for which they were used by the defendant. Some courts have read *Albrecht* to apply only in circumstances in which the outside agent shared in the anticompetitive purpose.[46]

Vertical Price Restraints

Definition

A vertical price agreement (or "resale price maintenance") is an agreement between persons at different market levels (e.g., franchisor and franchisee) establishing the resale price or range of prices for products or services.

General Principle

Resale price maintenance has long been held *per se* unlawful.[47]

Under current case law, the *per se* rule applies to agreements aimed at establishing maximum resale prices as well as those that fix minimum prices.[48] Although the *per se* rule against maximum resale price restraints has not been overturned, the practical effect of the "antitrust injury" requirement is to limit the type of plaintiffs who may succeed under a theory of maximum resale price maintenance. Thus, the Supreme Court has held that injuries inflicted on a competitor as a result of a vertical, nonpredatory maximum resale price maintenance agreement does not constitute antitrust injury, that is, injury of the type the antitrust laws were meant to prevent.[49] The Court reasoned that any loss suffered by

---

competition or reduce output; resulting arrangement is like exclusive territory arrangement, to which *per se* rule does not apply); *Cf.* Delong Equip. Co. v. Washington Mills Electro Minerals Corp., 990 F.2d 1186, Bus. Franchise Guide (CCH) ¶ 10,229 (11th Cir. 1993), *cert. denied*, 114 S. Ct. 604 (1993) (upholding jury verdict of conspiracy between manufacturer and favored distributor to raise wholesale prices to other distributors).

45. 390 U.S. 145 (1968).

46. *See* Harold Friedman, Inc. v. Kroger Co., 581 F.2d 1068, 1073 (3d Cir. 1978); Contractor Util. Sales Co. v. Certain-Teed Prods. Corp., 638 F.2d 1061, 1074 (7th Cir. 1981), *cert. denied*, 470 U.S. 1029 (1985) (outside parties must have participated for anticompetitive reasons); Spectrofuge Corp. v. Beckman Instruments, Inc., 575 F.2d 256, 289 (5th Cir. 1978), *cert. denied*, 440 U.S. 939 (1979) (supplier who changes distribution system does not "combine" with new distributors merely by entering into distribution agreements with them).

47. Dr. Miles Medical Co. v. John D. Park & Sons Co., 220 U.S. 373 (1911); California Retail Liquor Dealers Ass'n v. Midcal Aluminum, Inc., 445 U.S. 97, 102–03 (1980); United States v. Parke, Davis & Co., 362 U.S. 29 (1960). *See also* World of Sleep, Inc. v. La-Z-Boy Chair Co., 756 F.2d 1467, 1477 (10th Cir.), *cert. denied*, 474 U.S. 823 (1985) (*per se* rule applied even though manufacturer never set a specific fixed price; "independent judgment is eliminated"); State v. Lawn King, Inc., 84 N.J. 179, 417 A.2d 1025 (1980) (criminal convictions for resale price maintenance and tie-in activities reversed).

48. Albrecht v. Herald Co., 390 U.S. 145, 152 (1968).

49. Atlantic Richfield Co. v. USA Petroleum Co., 495 U.S. 328, Bus. Franchise Guide (CCH) ¶ 9610 (1990).

a competitor in that situation is not antitrust injury because the underlying harm, the inability of the competitor to raise prices, actually benefits consumers and does not threaten competition.[50] Consequently, it may be that only the dealers of a supplier who establishes a maximum resale price policy (and the government enforcement agencies) may challenge that policy.[51]

As noted earlier, the Supreme Court has held that a price-fixing (or other *per se* illegal) agreement is not established merely by proof that a franchisor agrees to terminate a price-cutting franchisee in the face of a demand by another complaining franchisee that he or she do so. There must also be proof that the franchisor and the remaining franchisee (the complaining one) had agreed on prices or price levels.[52]

Permissible Suggestion of Resale Prices versus Coercion

A supplier may suggest list prices; no violation occurs if distributors independently decide to observe specified resale prices. Suppliers are entitled to engage in "exposition, persuasion and argument."[53]

Providing suggested prices or price lists to distributors is permissible.[54] However, a supplier who goes beyond proper communication through exposition or persuasion and uses "coercive" tactics that interfere with the distributor's pricing independence runs the risk that an agreement between itself and the distributor might be found. Interference with pricing independence includes not only

---

50. *Id.* at 340; *see* Feirman & Cantor, *"Antitrust Injury: Breaches in the Shield,"* 3 FRANCHISE LEGAL DIGEST 20 (May/June 1989).

51. Slowiak v. Land 'O Lakes, Inc., 987 F.2d 1293 (7th Cir. 1993) (affirming summary judgment for manufacturer because distributor failed to present evidence of lost profits or other injury caused by his adherence to suggested price list); *but see* Caribe BMW, Inc. v. Bayerische Motoren Werke Aktiengesellschaft, 19 F.3d 745 (1st Cir. 1994) (finding plaintiff could have suffered an antitrust injury through maximum resale price maintenance scheme if customers would have preferred higher prices accompanied by better product quality or greater service).

52. Business Elecs. Corp. v. Sharp Elecs. Corp., 485 U.S. 717 (1988).

53. Gray v. Shell Oil Co., 469 F.2d 742, 748 (9th Cir. 1972), *cert. denied*, 412 U.S. 943 (1973). *See also* General Cinema Corp. v. Buena Vista Distrib. Co., 681 F.2d 594 (9th Cir. 1982) (film distributor's setting of rental rates based on percentage of ticket sales or a percentage of minimum price set in license agreement, whichever was greater, was not price fixing since exhibitor was free to establish prices); Knutson v. Daily Review, Inc., 548 F.2d 795, 806 (9th Cir. 1976), *cert. denied*, 433 U.S. 910 (1977) (strong recommendations do not amount to coercion); Yentsch v. Texaco, Inc., 630 F.2d 46, 53 (2d Cir. 1980) (evidence of exposition, persuasion, argument, or pressure alone insufficient to establish coercion to achieve resale price maintenance).

54. Martindell v. News Group Publications, Inc., 621 F. Supp. 672, Bus. Franchise Guide (CCH) ¶ 8476 (E.D.N.Y. 1985) (advertisement of a newspaper's suggested price of home delivery did not constitute resale price maintenance, as has advertising of suggested resale prices); Engbrecht v. Dairy Queen Co., 203 F. Supp. 714, 719 (D. Kan. 1962) (price advertisements for Dairy Queen products in Life magazine).

setting prices at a specific level but also requiring distributors to set prices within a certain range, if that range is above the competitive price in the market.[55]

Whether coercion exists is a question of fact. Strong exhortation in some cases has been held not to amount to coercion.[56] Evidence of coercion includes (1) threats of sanctions for noncompliance with suggested prices;[57] (2) use of sanctions;[58] (3) policing;[59] and (4) use of short-term leases and contracts.[60]

Although not directly on point, cases applying the standard of coercion contained in the Automobile Dealers Day in Court Act[61] may be helpful. Under those cases, "coercion" implies a wrongful demand that, absent compliance, results in sanctions.[62] Whether it is a "wrongful" demand depends on all the circumstances, including the manufacturer's reason for bringing pressure. Recommendation, endorsement, exposition, persuasion, urging, or argument normal in competitive commercial relationships will not lead to liability.[63]

---

55. Center Video Indus. Co. v. United Media, Inc., 995 F.2d 735, 739 n.6 (7th Cir. 1993) (noting that a restraint requiring retailers to set prices within a certain range above the competitive price is functionally equivalent to a restraint setting a specific price because retailers will set the price at the lowest possible level within the price range in order to maximize revenue).

56. *See* Sargent-Welch Scientific Co. v. Ventron Corp., 567 F.2d 701, 707 (7th Cir. 1977), *cert. denied*, 439 U.S. 822 (1978); Curry v. Steve's Franchise Co., 1985-2 Trade Cas. (CCH) ¶ 66,877 (D. Mass. 1985).

57. Yentsch v. Texaco, Inc., 630 F.2d 46, 53 (2d Cir. 1980); Bowen v. New York News, Inc., 522 F.2d 1242, 1254 (2d Cir. 1975), *cert. denied*, 425 U.S. 936 (1976); Girardi v. Gates Rubber Co. Sales Div., Inc., 325 F.2d 196, 198 (9th Cir. 1963).

58. Lehrman v. Gulf Oil Corp., 464 F.2d 26, 38 (5th Cir.), *cert. denied*, 409 U.S. 1077 (1972).

59. Interphoto Corp. v. Minolta Corp., 295 F. Supp. 711, 716 (S.D.N.Y.), *aff'd per curiam*, 417 F.2d 621 (2d Cir. 1969).

60. Sahm v. V-1 Oil Co., 402 F.2d 69, 71–72 (10th Cir. 1968). *But see* Empire Volkswagen, Inc. v. World-Wide Volkswagen Corp., 627 F. Supp. 1202, Bus. Franchise Guide (CCH) ¶ 8508 (S.D.N.Y. 1986), *aff'd*, 814 F.2d 90 (2d Cir. 1987) (conspiracy to fix retail prices not shown as a result of threats to take harsh actions against discounting dealers, decrease of allotments to discounters, or dealer's letter to defendant complaining of competitor's discounts). *See also* Bender v. Southland Corp., 749 F.2d 1205, Bus. Franchise Guide (CCH) ¶ 8269 (6th Cir. 1984) (summary judgment for defendant reversed; allegation that Southland's retail inventory accounting system had the effect of forcing franchisees to purchase from recommended vendors and to charge Southland's suggested retail price; reasonable jury could infer that Southland had imposed its accounting requirements, which involved a "substantial paperwork burden," with the intent to discourage deviations from the suggested retail prices).

61. 15 U.S.C. §§ 1221–1225.

62. *See, e.g.*, Empire Volkswagen, Inc. v. World-Wide Volkswagen Corp., 814 F.2d 90, 96 (2d Cir. 1987); R.D. Imports Ryno Indus., Inc. v. Mazda Distribs. (Gulf), Inc., 807 F.2d 1222, 1227, Bus. Franchise Guide (CCH) ¶ 8740 (5th Cir.), *cert. denied*, 484 U.S. 818 (1987).

63. *See, e.g.*, Autohaus Brugger, Inc. v. Saab Motors, Inc., 567 F.2d 901, 909–10 (9th Cir.), *cert. denied*, 436 U.S. 946 (1978). In South End Oil Co. v. Texaco, Inc., 237 F. Supp. 650, 654 (N.D. Ill. 1965), the court characterized proper communication as "informational" and "not directed toward securing any agreement." However, no bright line between threat and suggestion exists.

Special Situations: Price Promotions and Temporary Distributor Assistance, Cooperative Advertising Programs, and National Accounts Programs

Promotional allowances that reduce wholesale prices to distributors have been found lawful in circumstances in which the distributors are free to determine whether to reduce their resale prices.[64] Distributor assistance programs involving price reductions of a temporary nature to enable a distributor to meet price competition with distributors of another brand likewise are not *per se* unlawful if the price reductions are provided without regard to the resale prices charged by the distributor.[65]

What about promotional allowances or distributor assistance allowances that are conditioned on the distributor's agreement correspondingly to reduce prices?[66] The recent trend has been to permit such a condition.

Cooperative advertising programs involving price-related restrictions have been addressed in various cases.[67]

In *The Advertising Checking Bureau, Inc.*,[68] the FTC announced that it would analyze price-restrictive cooperative advertising programs under the Rule of Reason, reversing its previous policy of treating such programs as *per se* unlawful vertical price-fixing. This new policy has been reflected in several cases in

---

64. FLM Collision Parts, Inc. v. Ford Motor Co., 543 F.2d 1019 (2d Cir. 1976), *cert. denied*, 429 U.S. 1097 (1977); Hanson v. Shell Oil Co., 541 F.2d 1352, 1356 (9th Cir. 1976), *cert. denied*, 429 U.S. 1074 (1977).

65. *See* Butera v. Sun Oil Co., 496 F.2d 434, 437–38 (1st Cir. 1974).

66. *Compare* Pearl Brewing Co. v. Anheuser-Busch, Inc., 339 F. Supp. 945, 955 (S.D. Tex. 1972) ("a practice of conditioning a price reduction on the acquiescence or cooperation of the recipient to reduce its price can only be viewed as imposing restrictions on the reseller's freedom of decision and, as such, is an unlawful price fixing [scheme]") *with* AAA Liquors, Inc. v. Joseph E. Seagram & Sons, Inc., 705 F.2d 1203, 1206 (10th Cir. 1982), *cert. denied*, 461 U.S. 919 (1983) ("[a] supplier who grants discounts to a retailer to permit the retailer to charge competitive prices has a legitimate interest in making sure the retailer receiving the discount is 'not pocketing the price support instead of passing it on to consumers'"); Lewis Serv. Ctr. Inc. v. Mack Trucks, Inc., 714 F.2d 842, 846, Bus. Franchise Guide (CCH) ¶ 8034 (8th Cir. 1983), *cert. denied*, 467 U.S. 1226 (1984); Bryant Heating and Air Conditioning Corp. v. Carrier Corp., 597 F. Supp. 1045 (S.D. Fla. 1984). Note that *AAA Liquors* and *Lewis Serv. Ctr.* involved price reductions by the supplier. *Compare* Lehrman v. Gulf Oil Corp., 464 F.2d 26, 37–41 (5th Cir.), *cert. denied*, 409 U.S. 1077 (1972) (denial of competitive allowance in retaliation for distributor's failure to adhere to *minimum* suggested prices was unlawful coercive conduct and appeared to be the quid pro quo for Lehrman's receiving Gulf's allowances).

67. *Compare In re* Nissan Antitrust Litigation, 577 F.2d 910, 914–15 (5th Cir. 1978), *cert. denied*, 439 U.S. 1072 (1979) (affirming a jury verdict upholding a cooperative advertising program under which a distributor received some reimbursement only if the distributor's advertisement used the supplier's suggested resale price or no price at all) *with* United States v. Serta Assocs., Inc., 296 F. Supp. 1121, 1125–27 (N.D. Ill. 1968), *aff'd per curiam*, 393 U.S. 534 (1969) (violation found; distributor not "allowed to participate . . . unless all of his advertisements contained Serta's suggested-retail prices;" this was combined with surveillance of all distributor advertising).

68. 109 F.T.C. 146 (1987).

which the FTC has set aside or modified orders that prohibited cooperative advertising programs that affected the pricing freedom of retailers.[69] Notwithstanding this policy, the FTC reportedly is investigating whether it is a *per se* violation when a retailer, as a matter of economic necessity, is trapped into accepting a large promotional allowance where the allowance is conditioned upon the retailer advertising a product at the supplier's suggested resale price.[70]

In *Jack Walters & Sons Corp. v. Morton Buildings, Inc.*,[71] the Seventh Circuit stated that because it concededly was lawful for a supplier to advertise its product to ultimate consumers and to mention the retail price of the product, it also was lawful to take minimum steps necessary to make the advertising beneficial, including trying to persuade distributors to adhere to advertised price and checking around to ensure adherence.[72]

The propriety of a supplier preticketing packages with its suggested prices is well established.[73]

There is also the issue of national accounts programs. Vertical price-fixing issues are raised when a supplier negotiates price terms with a large buyer on behalf of its independent distributors, who each sell its products or services to different outlets or offices of the buyer. Such programs are increasingly common in franchise systems, where a buyer desires that purchase contracts be centrally negotiated and approved and where individual franchisees may be ill-equipped or unable to "deliver the system" to a geographically dispersed buyer.

National accounts programs are *per se* unlawful resale price maintenance when the supplier requires its independent distributors to participate and precludes the distributors from negotiating price terms directly with the national accounts.[74] However, such programs may be given a Rule of Reason analysis if the prices negotiated with the national accounts vary among the national cus-

---

69. *See In re* Clinique Laboratories, Inc., No. C-3027 (F.T.C. Feb. 8, 1993); U.S. Pioneer Electronics Corp., No. C-2755 (Apr. 8, 1992 and May 19, 1992); Magnavox Company, No. 8822 (Mar. 12, 1990).

70. FTC: WATCH, March 22, 1993, at p.7.

71. 737 F.2d 698 (7th Cir.), *cert. denied*, 469 U.S. 1018 (1984).

72. In Murphy v. White Hen Pantry, Bus. Franchise Guide (CCH) ¶ 7716, 1982-2 Trade Cas. (CCH) ¶ 64,845 (E.D. Wis. 1981), *aff'd*, 691 F.2d 350 (7th Cir. 1982), the court recognized the franchisor's right to advertise suggested retail prices with appropriate qualifier—such as "at participating stores"—notwithstanding the acknowledged effect of causing consumers to expect to be able to buy at prices no higher than suggested prices. Note that promotional monies from franchisors were used to pay for the advertisements in question. *See also* United States v. B. F. Goodrich Co., 1981-1 Trade Cas. (CCH) ¶ 63,898 (N.D. Cal. 1981) (consent decree permitting cooperative tire advertising on condition that any joint advertisement contain a statement that the advertised prices are those offered by Goodrich and not necessarily by participating Goodrich dealers).

73. Mesirow v. Pepperidge Farms, Inc., 703 F.2d 339 (9th Cir.), *cert. denied*, 464 U.S. 820 (1983); Klein v. American Luggage Works, Inc., 323 F.2d 787 (3d Cir. 1963).

74. *See* Greene v. General Foods Corp., 517 F.2d 635, 658 (5th Cir. 1975), *cert. denied*, 424 U.S. 942 (1976); *accord*, Bostick Oil Co. v. Michelin Tire Corp., 702 F.2d 1207, 1216–17, Bus. Franchise Guide (CCH) ¶ 8088 (4th Cir. 1983), *cert. denied*, 464 U.S. 894 (1983).

tomers and the negotiation of such accounts creates increased interbrand competition.[75]

The same conclusion has been reached when distributors are not compelled to participate and they may solicit business from national accounts apart from the program.[76] Alternatively, a national accounts program can be structured so that the supplier sells directly to the national accounts at its own prices and uses its distributors as agents or consignees to deliver its products.[77] Under this latter structure, the distributors presumably could be required to participate in the national accounts program without antitrust consequences, since the supplier, who is setting the price to the customer, is in fact the seller. The distributor is not the seller but is merely performing a delivery service for the supplier.

Vertical Non-Price Restraints

Overview

A vertical non-price agreement is one between persons at different market levels (e.g., supplier and distributor) establishing the areas in which, places from which, or customers to whom the distributor may sell.

Non-price restraints limiting the freedom of the franchisee or distributor to resell products or services of its supplier include: (1) exclusive distributorships; (2) location clauses; (3) areas of primary responsibility; (4) profit passover arrangements; and (5) territorial and customer restrictions.

Non-price restraints limiting the freedom of the franchisee or distributor to sell products or services of other suppliers include: (1) exclusive dealing requirements; (2) requirements contracts; (3) full line forcing; and (4) sales quotas, inventory requirements, and other de facto partial exclusive dealing practices. The competitive impact of such restrictions is solely on interbrand competition by foreclosing other suppliers from distribution channels.

Resale price maintenance affects only one aspect of competition—pricing—but affects both intrabrand competition (by limiting a supplier's distributors from engaging in price competition with each other) and interbrand competition (by restricting a supplier's distributors from adjusting their prices to compete with distributors of other brands). Vertical non-price restraints limit or eliminate all forms of *intrabrand* competition but do not restrict a supplier's distributors' ability to compete with *interbrand* competitors and, in fact, may foster such competi-

---

75. Wisconsin Music Network v. Muzak Ltd. Partnership, 5 F.3d 218 (7th Cir. 1993) (no resale price maintenance violation where licensor of subscription music service negotiated contracts with nationwide subscribers without going through local licensees because contract prices varied among the national customers and the contracts allowed the licensor to compete with other national licensors).

76. *See* Mesirow v. Pepperidge Farm, Inc., 703 F.2d 339, 343 (9th Cir.), *cert. denied*, 464 U.S. 820 (1983).

77. *See* Ryko Mfg. Co. v. Eden Servs., 823 F.2d 1215 (8th Cir. 1987), *cert. denied*, 484 U.S. 1026 (1988).

tion by encouraging a supplier's distributors to concentrate their efforts on capturing sales from distributors of other brands.

Exclusive Dealing Requirements

Such restrictions are common in franchise arrangements, often in the form of an in-term covenant by the franchisee not to engage in a competing business. Antitrust challenges to exclusive dealing clauses require Rule of Reason analysis and have been generally unsuccessful.[78]

The leading Supreme Court cases, *Tampa Electric v. Nashville Coal Co.* and *Jefferson Parish Hospital Dist. No. 2 v. Hyde,*[79] emphasize the percentage of the market foreclosed by the arrangement. In *Tampa Electric,* the Court asked whether the amount of competition foreclosed by the electric company's agreement to buy all of its coal needs from one supplier constituted a substantial percentage of the relevant market. It concluded that a foreclosure of less than 1 percent of the market did not offend Section 3 of the Clayton Act, even in a twenty-year contract.

In *Jefferson Parish,* the majority analyzed the exclusive contract as a tie-in and limited its exclusive dealing analysis to a one-paragraph footnote, finding no proof that the contract foreclosed competing anesthesiologists from a share of the market for anesthesiological services sufficient to restrain competition unreasonably.[80] The hospital in question, which the arrangement foreclosed to competing anesthesiologists, held a 30 percent share of the New Orleans metropolitan area market. A four-Justice concurrence, after carefully analyzing the exclusive contract as an exclusive dealing arrangement, agreed with the majority that the contract survived scrutiny under the Rule of Reason. As Justice O'Connor stated, "Exclusive dealing is an unreasonable restraint on trade only when a significant fraction of buyers or sellers are frozen out of a market by the exclusive deal."[81] The contract at issue in *Jefferson Parish* foreclosed "only a small fraction of the markets in which anesthesiologists may sell their services, and a still smaller fraction of the market in which hospitals may secure anesthesiological services."[82]

Other factors relevant to exclusive dealing analysis under *Tampa Electric, Jefferson Parish,* and the Rule of Reason, in addition to the percentage of the market foreclosed, are as follows:

---

78. *See, e.g.,* American Motor Inns, Inc. v. Holiday Inns, Inc., 521 F.2d 1230, 1245-52 (3d Cir. 1975); McElhenney Co. v. Western Auto Supply Co., 269 F.2d 332 (4th Cir. 1959); Joyce Beverages of New York, Inc. v. Royal Crown Cola Co., 555 F. Supp. 271, Bus. Franchise Guide (CCH) ¶ 7922 (S.D.N.Y. 1983).

79. Tampa Elec. Co. v. Nashville Coal Co., 365 U.S. 320 (1961) (a requirements contract case), and Jefferson Parish Hosp. Dist. No. 2 v. Hyde, 466 U.S. 2 (1984) (involving a hospital's exclusive contract with a group of anesthesiologists).

80. 466 U.S. at 30 n.51.

81. *Id.* at 45.

82. *Id.* at 46–47.

1. The duration of the agreement
2. The prevalence of exclusive arrangements in the industry
3. The ease with which alternative outlets may be obtained and the extent to which the exclusive contract(s) deter new entrants
4. The dominance of the seller
5. The relative strength of the parties
6. The state of competition in the market
7. The purposes and justifications for entering into the arrangement and its effects on competition.

Older leading cases emphasize the prevalence of exclusive contracts throughout the industry and the cumulative effect of foreclosing a significant number of outlets.[83]

Post-*Jefferson Parish* decisions have emphasized the need for a plaintiff to show that the defendant's exclusivity requirements prevent competitors from finding effective distributors for their products.[84]

Courts are increasingly considering the competitive health of the market in which an exclusive dealing arrangement arises.[85]

Exclusive dealing requirements imposed by a trademark licensor-franchisor on a franchisee may be justifiable to protect the goodwill of the trademark.[86]

---

83. *See* Brown Shoe Co., 62 F.T.C. 679 (1963), *rev'd*, 339 F.2d 45 (8th Cir. 1964), *rev'd*, 384 U.S. 316 (1966) (650 franchised outlets); Standard Oil Co. v. United States, 337 U.S. 293, 295 (1949) (defendant had exclusive contracts with independent dealers representing 6.7 percent of the market; other major competitors used similar arrangements); American Motor Inns, Inc. v. Holiday Inns, Inc., 521 F.2d 1230 (3d Cir. 1975) (court suggests that a non-Holiday Inn clause foreclosing Holiday Inns' competitors from 14.7 percent of the market may be unlawful; district court so held).

84. *See, e.g.*, Seagood Trading Corp. v. Jerrico, Inc., 924 F.2d 1555, Bus. Franchise Guide (CCH) ¶ 9770 (11th Cir. 1991) (foreclosed suppliers had ample access to other distribution channels; exclusive agreement with most desirable distributor upheld); Ryko Mfg. Co. v. Eden Servs., 823 F.2d 1215, 1234–35 (8th Cir. 1987), *cert. denied*, 484 U.S. 1026 (1988) (prohibition against selling competing products upheld despite defendant's 8–10 percent market share); Roland Mach. Co. v. Dresser Indus., Inc., 749 F.2d 380, 394–95 (7th Cir. 1984). *See also* G.A Imports, Inc. v. Subaru Mid-America, Inc., 799 F.2d 1200, Bus. Franchise Guide (CCH) ¶ 8654 (8th Cir. 1986) (court states that it would have been unreasonable for defendant to enforce a showroom square footage exclusivity requirement where it was unable to supply a sufficient inventory of Subaru vehicles to allow the dealer to operate profitably as a single-line dealership. Such a requirement would put the plaintiff at a competitive disadvantage to other Subaru dealers which carry more than one line).

85. *See* U.S. Healthcare, Inc. v. Healthsource, Inc., 986 F.2d 589, 595 (1st Cir. 1993) (attack on exclusivity clause requires proof of "probable immediate and future effects"); Joyce Beverages of New York, Inc. v. Royal Crown Cola Co., 555 F. Supp. 271 (S.D.N.Y. 1983) (exclusive dealing arrangement upheld where market was characterized by fierce interbrand competition).

86. *See* Susser v. Carvel Corp., 332 F.2d 505, 516–17 (2d Cir. 1964), *cert. dismissed*, 381 U.S. 125 (1965) (sustaining requirement that Carvel ice cream franchises sell only Carvel or Carvel-approved products and not "Christmas trees or hamburgers"). *But see* Sulmeyer v. Seven-Up Co., 411 F. Supp. 635 (S.D.N.Y. 1976) (limiting *Carvel* to cases in which franchisees sell directly to the public).

Covenants Not to Compete

Franchise agreements often contain provisions limiting the franchisee's right to engage in competitive activities during and after the term of the franchise agreement. These restrictions, whether they are "in-term" covenants against competition or "post-term" covenants against competition, are vertical nonprice restraints that are judged under the Rule of Reason.[87] Covenants against competition typically prohibit a franchisee from competing with its own franchised unit, with other franchised units, and with the franchisor. Where the franchisor is in competition with the franchisee (such as where a franchisor operates company-owned units of the system), covenants against competition generally are not treated as a horizontal market division, which would be *per se* unlawful. Rather, even in that setting, covenants against competition are usually characterized as vertical nonprice restraints subject to the Rule of Reason.

Courts have generally been quick to recognize the important business justifications served by covenants against competition in franchise agreements and have generally found them to be valid under antitrust laws.[88] To be enforceable under state law, a covenant against competition in a franchise setting must meet two tests: (1) it must be designed to protect a legitimate interest of the franchisor; and (2) the scope of the restriction must be reasonable with respect to time, area, and activity.[89]

Full Line Forcing

The issue of full line forcing arises when a supplier requires a franchisee, dealer, or other customer to carry a complete line of products. This type of restraint has been analyzed under the same standards as tie-in arrangements,[90] although some recent cases have applied a Rule of Reason standard to full line forcing.[91]

Allocation Systems

Allocation systems have been challenged in a number of recent cases as the tying of less popular models to fast-selling ones. In *Southern Pines Chrysler-Plymouth, Inc. v. Chrysler Corp.*,[92] the court rejected the theory that one Chrysler LeBaron with certain optional equipment was a separate product from a differently equipped LeBaron. However, in *Barber & Ross Co. v. Lifetimes Doors, Inc.*,[93] the

87. *See* Ungar v. Dunkin' Donuts of Am., Inc., 531 F.2d 1211 (3d Cir.), *cert. denied*, 429 U.S. 823 (1976); Capital Temporaries, Inc. v. Olsten Corp., 506 F.2d 658 (2d Cir. 1974).

88. *See* Postal Instant Press v. Jackson, 658 F. Supp. 739, Bus. Franchise Guide (CCH) ¶ 8844 (D. Colo. 1987); Joyce Beverages of New York, Inc. v. Royal Crown Cola Co., 555 F. Supp. 271 (S.D.N.Y. 1983).

89. For a state-by-state compendium of the law on noncompete covenants, *see* Covenants Against Competition in Franchise Agreements (Peter J. Klarfeld, ed., ABA 1992).

90. *See, e.g.,* Trans Sport, Inc. v. Starter Sportswear, Inc., 964 F.2d 186, 191–92 (2d Cir. 1992); Pitchford v. Pepi, Inc., 531 F.2d 92, 101 (3d Cir. 1975), *cert. denied*, 426 U.S. 935 (1976).

91. *See* Smith Mach. Co. v. Hesston Corp., 878 F.2d 1290, Bus. Franchise Guide (CCH) ¶ 8324 (10th Cir. 1989), *cert. denied*, 493 U.S. 1073 (1990).

92. 826 F.2d 1360, Bus. Franchise Guide (CCH) ¶ 8927 (4th Cir. 1987).

93. 810 F.2d 1276 (4th Cir.), *cert. denied*, 484 U.S. 823 (1987).

court upheld a tying challenge to a manufacturer's allocation system that allegedly forced the plaintiff to buy doors it would not otherwise have bought.[94]

Exclusive Distributorships

Overview

Exclusive distributorships reflect a commitment by the supplier to make a distributor the sole outlet for the supplier's products or services in an area and not to compete either directly by establishing a company-owned outlet or indirectly by appointing another independent distributor. From a practical standpoint, exclusive distributorships may insulate a distributor from intrabrand competition. However, they have been upheld routinely in antitrust challenges.[95]

Some courts have recognized the elimination of the "free rider" problem, which discourages capital investment and product innovation,[96] as a valid reason for exclusive contracts. Although the "free rider" defense may not be available to a monopolist who refuses to provide parts to a competitor,[97] recent cases continue to allow suppliers to assert the "free rider" defense as a justification for vertical restraints.[98]

Exclusive distributorships may be subject to challenge if (1) their geographic scope is unreasonably broad;[99] (2) their duration is excessive;[100] (3) the distributor also has exclusive distributorships with other suppliers;[101] or (4) the

94. *But see* Fox Motors, Inc. v. Mazda Distribs., (Gulf), Inc., 806 F.2d 953, Bus. Franchise Guide (CCH) ¶ 8712 (10th Cir. 1986) (car importer's allocation system that encouraged dealers to buy more of the less popular models in order to get the popular RX-7 was not unlawful tying, since the defendant was merely trying to boost its sales of the less popular models and thereby promote price competition).

95. *See, e.g.*, United States v. Arnold, Schwinn & Co., 388 U.S. 365, 376 (1967) (noting in *dicta* that a supplier may utilize exclusive distributors "if competitive products are readily available to others"); GTE Sylvania, Inc. v. Continental T.V., Inc., 537 F.2d 980, 997 (9th Cir. 1976) (*en banc*), *aff'd*, 433 U.S. 36 (1977); Packard Motor Car Co. v. Webster Motor Car Co., 243 F.2d 418, 420 (D.C. Cir.), *cert. denied*, 355 U.S. 822 (1957); ABA Antitrust Section, Monograph No. 9, Refusals to Deal and Exclusive Distributorship 25 (1983) (collecting cases); *cf.* Department of Justice, Vertical Restraints Guidelines ¶ 2.5 (Jan. 23, 1985) (classifying exclusive distributorship as restraints that are "always legal").

96. Monsanto Co. v. Spray-Rite Serv. Corp., 465 U.S. 752 (1984).

97. Eastman Kodak Company v. Image Technological Serv., Inc., 504 U.S. 451 (1992), Bus. Franchise Guide (CCH) ¶ 10,017.

98. Picker Int'l, Inc. v. Leavitt, 865 F. Supp. 951 (D. Mass. 1994) (exclusive arrangement between defendant and its manufacturer/supplier designed to prevent free riding of supplier selling directly to defendant's customers for lower price was a valid vertical restraint because other sources existed for the plaintiff to obtain the product).

99. United States v. Chicago Tribune-New York News Syndicate, Inc., 309 F. Supp. 1301, 1308–09 (S.D.N.Y. 1970).

100. Quality Mercury, Inc. v. Ford Motor Co., 542 F.2d 466, 471–72 (8th Cir. 1976), *cert. denied*, 433 U.S. 914 (1977).

101. United States v. Bitz, 179 F. Supp. 80 (S.D.N.Y. 1959), *rev'd in part on other grounds*, 282 F.2d 465 (2d Cir. 1960).

supplier and its dealers are engaging in a conspiracy to exclude others from competition.[102]

Location Clauses

Location clauses regulate the place from which the distributor is authorized to sell a supplier's products or services. Such restrictions are useful primarily for distributors engaged in on-premises sales and not with respect to products sold door to door or through the mail.

Location clauses establishing the physical site from which a distributor may sell a supplier's products or services, standing alone, uniformly have been upheld, frequently as a matter of law.[103] If a distributor is authorized to sell a supplier's products or services from a particular location, the supplier is not required to authorize the distributor to sell at other locations,[104] or to drop ship products to customers at the distributor's request.[105]

Area of Primary Responsibility Clauses

An area of primary responsibility (APR) clause obligates a distributor satisfactorily to market the supplier's products in a defined geographic area and, as long as the distributor continues to do so, it is not contractually restricted from selling the supplier's products outside such area. Such APR clauses are less restrictive on intrabrand competition than are exclusive territories. APR clauses regularly have been upheld.[106]

If a distributor does not adequately promote the supplier's products within the APR under the terms of the distribution agreement, a supplier acting in good

---

102. Big Apple BMW, Inc. v. BMW of North Am., Inc., 974 F.2d 1358, Bus. Franchise Guide (CCH) ¶ 10,063 (3rd Cir. 1992), *cert. denied*, 113 S. Ct. 1262 (1993) (denying defendant's summary judgment motion because evidence tended to show that defendant and its dealers conspired to exclude plaintiff from competition and that defendant's alleged reasons for rejecting plaintiff's franchise applications were pretextual).

103. *See* Continental T.V., Inc. v. GTE Sylvania, Inc., 461 F. Supp. 1046 (N.D. Cal. 1978), *aff'd*, 694 F.2d 1132 (9th Cir. 1982); Golden Gate Acceptance Corp. v. General Motors Corp., 597 F.2d 676 (9th Cir. 1979); Salco Corp. v. General Motors Corp., 517 F.2d 567 (10th Cir. 1975); Kaiser v. General Motors Corp., 396 F. Supp. 33, 40 (E.D. Pa. 1975), *aff'd per curiam without opinion*, 530 F.2d 964 (3rd Cir. 1976); Muenster Butane, Inc. v. Stewart Co., 651 F.2d 292, Bus. Franchise Guide (CCH) ¶ 7690 (5th Cir. 1981).

104. *See* GTE Sylvania, Inc. v. Continental T.V., Inc., 537 F.2d 980 (9th Cir. 1976) *(en banc), aff'd,* 433 U.S. 36 (1977), *on remand*, 461 F. Supp. 1046 (N.D. Cal. 1978), *aff'd*, 694 F.2d 1132 (9th Cir. 1982).

105. Dart Indus., Inc. v. Plunkett Co., 704 F.2d 496, 499 (10th Cir. 1983).

106. *See, e.g.,* Kestenbaum v. Falstaff Brewing Corp., 575 F.2d 564, 572–73 (5th Cir. 1978), *cert. denied*, 440 U.S. 909 (1979); Knutson v. Daily Review, Inc., 548 F.2d 795, 807–10 (9th Cir. 1976), *cert. denied*, 433 U.S. 910 (1977); Colorado Pump & Supply Co. v. Febco, Inc., 472 F.2d 637 (10th Cir.), *cert. denied*, 411 U.S. 987 (1973); Kaiser v. General Motors Corp., 396 F. Supp. 33, 39–41 (E.D. Pa. 1975), *aff'd per curiam without opinion*, 530 F.2d 964 (3d Cir. 1976); Superior Bedding Co. v. Serta Assocs., Inc., 353 F. Supp. 1143, 1147–49 (N.D. Ill. 1972).

faith may terminate the distributor.[107] However, if the sales quota in the APR is so high that it effectively prevents the distributor from handling the products of a competing supplier, it may be susceptible to challenge as a de facto exclusive dealing arrangement.

APR clauses may be treated as the equivalent of de facto exclusive territories if they operate or are enforced in a way that precludes extraterritorial sales. An APR may also be found unlawful if it is part of a broader scheme to restrict competition involving other restraints.[108]

Profit Passover Arrangements

Profit passover requirements do not restrict a distributor from selling outside of its APR. Such clauses, however, require a distributor who makes sales in another distributor's area to pay over a portion of the profits from such sales to compensate the distributor in whose area the sale was made for its presale marketing and promotional efforts and its postsale services activities in the area. Such a payment is designed to prevent "free riding."

The reasonableness of the compensation paid in relation to the services actually performed or reasonably expected to be performed by the nonselling distributor is a critical inquiry in evaluating profit passover arrangements under the Rule of Reason.[109]

Territorial and Customer Restrictions

Exclusive territories and restrictions on sales to particular customers (e.g., supplier's reservation of the exclusive right to sell national, fleet, and government accounts; prohibitions on selling to certain types of outlets or to unauthorized dealers) preclude, rather than merely limit, intrabrand competition.

Before 1967, such restrictions were judged under the Rule of Reason.[110] For a decade following the Supreme Court's 1967 decision in *United States v. Arnold, Schwinn & Co.*,[111] territorial and customer restrictions imposed in resale transactions in which the supplier parted with dominion over the product were viewed as *per se* unlawful.[112] During the same period, territorial and customer restrictions imposed on distributors in agency and consignment arrangements in which the supplier retained title, dominion, and risk of loss with respect to its products

---

107. *See, e.g.,* Joe Regueira, Inc. v. American Distilling Co., 642 F.2d 826 (5th Cir. 1981); Frank Chevrolet Co. v. General Motors Corp., 419 F.2d 1054 (6th Cir. 1969).

108. *See* Ohio-Sealy Mattress Mfg. Co. v. Sealy, Inc., 585 F.2d 821 (7th Cir. 1978), *cert. denied*, 440 U.S. 930 (1979).

109. *Compare* Superior Bedding Co. v. Serta Assocs., Inc., 353 F. Supp. 1143, 1150–51 (N.D. Ill. 1972) (upholding passover fee of 7 percent of gross sales to compensate non-selling distributor for marketing expenses) *with* Eiberger v. Sony Corp. of Am., 622 F.2d 1068, 1076–81 (2d Cir. 1980) (passover fee designed to compensate non-selling distributors for providing warranty service held unlawful as being an unreasonable attempt to restrain intrabrand competition by penalizing extraterritorial sales).

110. *See* White Motor Co. v. United States, 372 U.S. 253 (1963).

111. 388 U.S. 367 (1967).

112. *Id.* at 378–79.

and distributors that were "indistinguishable in function from agents or sales-men" were evaluated under the Rule of Reason.[113]

In 1977, in *Continental T.V., Inc. v. GTE Sylvania, Inc.,*[114] the Supreme Court overruled *Schwinn* and mandated a "return to the Rule of Reason that governed vertical restrictions prior to Schwinn."[115] In so doing, the Court criticized as "for-malistic line drawing" the distinction made in *Schwinn* between restrictions im-posed in sales and consignment or agency transactions, noting that no sound ba-sis existed in terms of the effect on competition to support the distinction.[116] (Note, however, that the distinction remains in the case of vertical resale price maintenance.)

The clear trend in post-*Sylvania* decisions is to uphold vertical territorial and customer restrictions under the Rule of Reason.[117]

The fact that the Supreme Court in *Sylvania* did not indicate how to weigh the various factors relevant to a Rule of Reason analysis and the difficulty in bal-ancing a loss of *intrabrand* competition against a stimulation of *interbrand* com-petition makes it difficult to predict how a court or jury will assess a given re-straint under the Rule of Reason.[118] Nevertheless, several conclusions can be distilled from the post-*Sylvania* decisions applying the Rule of Reason.

113. *Id.* at 381–82.
114. 433 U.S. 36 (1977).
115. *Id.* at 59.
116. *Id.* at 52–54, 57.
117. *See, e.g.,* Murrow Furniture Galleries, Inc. v. Thomasville Furniture Indus., Inc., 889 F.2d 524 (4th Cir. 1989) (denying preliminary injunction against ban on mail and phone orders and advertising outside of area of responsibility); Murphy v. Business Cards Tomorrow, Inc., 854 F.2d 1202, 1204, Bus. Franchise Guide (CCH) ¶ 9194 (9th Cir. 1988), *overruled in part*, 914 F.2d 1136 (territorial restrictions); O.S.C. Corp. v. Apple Computer, Inc., 792 F.2d 1464, Bus. Franchise Guide (CCH) ¶ 8608 (9th Cir. 1986) (ban on mail-order sales upheld); Dart Indus., Inc. v. Plunkett Co., 704 F.2d 496, 499 (10th Cir. 1983) (restric-tion on shipments to customers outside distributor's territory); JBL Enters., Inc. v. Jhirmack Enters., Inc., 698 F.2d 1011, 1016–17 (9th Cir.), *cert. denied*, 464 U.S. 829 (1983) (territorial restrictions); Mesirow v. Pepperidge Farm, Inc., 703 F.2d 339 (9th Cir.), *cert. denied*, 464 U.S. 820 (1983) (territorial restrictions); Maykuth v. Adolph Coors Co., 690 F.2d 689, Bus. Franchise Guide (CCH) ¶ 7889 (9th Cir. 1982) (territorial restrictions); Sports Ctr., Inc. v. Riddell, Inc., 673 F.2d 786 (5th Cir. 1982) (customer restrictions); Davis-Watkins Co. v. Ser-vice Merchandise, 686 F.2d 1190 (6th Cir. 1982), *cert. denied*, 466 U.S. 931 (1984) (territo-rial restrictions); Mendelovitz v. Adolph Coors Co., 693 F.2d 570, 575–76 (5th Cir. 1982) (territorial restrictions); Donald B. Rice Tire Co. v. Michelin Tire Corp., 638 F.2d 15 (4th Cir.), *cert. denied*, 454 U.S. 864 (1981) (customer and territorial restrictions); Muenster Bu-tane, Inc. v. Stewart Co., 651 F.2d 292 (5th Cir. 1981) (territorial restrictions); Red Diamond Supply, Inc. v. Liquid Carbonic Corp., 637 F.2d 1001 (5th Cir.), *cert. denied*, 454 U.S. 827 (1981) (customer and territorial restrictions).
118. *See* Graphic Prods. Distribs. v. Itek Corp., 717 F.2d 1560, 1568, n.10 (11th Cir. 1983).

At least one court has employed a balancing test to determine the effect on interbrand and intrabrand competition caused by territorial restraints imposed on distributors.[119]

First, the fact that a territorial or customer restriction eliminates intrabrand competition ordinarily is insufficient by itself to prove an unreasonable restraint of trade.[120]

Second, a showing of an adverse effect on interbrand competition in a relevant product and geographic market ordinarily is required.[121]

Third, to establish that the supplier imposing the restrictions has the market power to bring about the required adverse effect on competition, courts increasingly have required plaintiffs to make a threshold showing that the supplier's market share (used as a proxy for market power) is sufficiently high so that the overall market could be affected.[122] If the supplier imposing the restrictions has only a small share of the market, such restrictions ordinarily will be upheld.[123] Although the level of market share required to possess market power varies, at least one court has found that "there do not appear to be any vertical restraint cases in which a possessor of less than 70% of the relevant market possessed market power."[124] To show that a supplier has market power, the plaintiff must also establish the relevant market for products in which the seller is imposing re-

---

119. New York by Abrams v. Anheuser-Busch Inc., 811 F. Supp. 848 (E.D.N.Y. 1993) (the benefits of the territorial restraints outweighed their anticompetitive effects, resulting in dismissal of the complaint); *Cf.* Eiberger v. Sony Corp of America, 622 F.2d 1068 (2nd Cir. 1980) (no procompetitive interbrand benefits existed to outweigh the significant intrabrand harms).

120. *See, e.g.*, Davis-Watkins Co. v. Service Merchandise, *supra* note 117, 686 F.2d at 1200; Valley Liquors, Inc. v. Renfield Importers, Ltd., 678 F.2d 742, 745 (7th Cir. 1982). *But see* Eastman Kodak Co. v. Image Technical Services, Inc., 504 U.S. 451 (1992).

121. *See, e.g.*, JBL Enters., Inc. v. Jhirmack Enters., Inc., 698 F.2d 1011, 1017 (9th Cir.), *cert. denied*, 464 U.S. 829 (1983); Hornsby Oil Co. v. Champion Spark Plug Co., 714 F.2d 1384, 1394 (5th Cir. 1983). *But see* Eastman Kodak Co. v. Image Technical Servs., Inc., 504 U.S. 451 (1992).

122. Graphic Prods. Distribs., Inc. v. Itek Corp., *supra* note 112, 717 F.2d at 1568; JBL Enters., Inc. v. Jhirmack Enters., Inc., *supra* note 111, 698 F.2d at 1017; Valley Liquors, Inc. v. Renfield Importers, Ltd., *supra* note 120, 678 F.2d at 745; Davis-Watkins Co. v. Service Merchandise Co., *supra* note 117, 686 F.2d at 1202; Muenster Butane, Inc. v. Stewart Co., *supra* note 117, 651 F.2d at 295, 298.

123. *See, e.g.*, JBL Enters., Inc. v. Jhirmack Enters., Inc., 698 F.2d at 1017 (2 percent–4 percent share too insignificant to adversely affect competition); Carlson Mach. Tools, Inc. v. American Tool, Inc., 678 F.2d 1253, 1259 (5th Cir. 1982) (supplier's share below 10 percent); Copy-Data Sys., Inc. v. Toshiba America, Inc., 663 F.2d 405, 410–11 (2d Cir. 1981) (insignificant market share minimized anticompetitive effect); Donald B. Rice Tire Co. v. Michelin Tire Corp., 483 F. Supp. 750, 761 (D. Md. 1980), *aff'd per curiam*, 638 F.2d 15 (4th Cir.), *cert. denied*, 454 U.S. 864 (1981) (7.9 percent share does not confer "market power to restrain competition"); Beltone Elecs. Corp., 100 F.T.C. 68, 209–10 (1982) (declining market share from 21 percent to 16 percent indicates lack of market power).

124. New York by Abrams v. Anheuser-Busch, Inc., 811 F. Supp. 848, 873 n.70 (E.D.N.Y. 1993).

strictions. The definition of the relevant market must be broad enough to ensure that all affected products are included.[125]

Fourth, vigorous interbrand competition negating the supplier's ability to insulate its distributors from price competition through the imposition of territorial and customer restrictions has been a factor leading courts to uphold such restrictions under the Rule of Reason.[126]

Fifth, if a supplier can demonstrate that restrictions enhance interbrand competition, courts are required to engage in the balancing analysis mandated by *Sylvania,* which makes an ultimate determination of the reasonableness of the restrictions easier to obtain. Territorial and customer restrictions are more likely to be upheld when the supplier is able to demonstrate that such restrictions enhance interbrand competition.[127]

Sixth, if interbrand competition is not enhanced by the restrictions, the loss of intrabrand competition may take on greater significance.[128]

---

125. Smalley & Co. v. Emerson & Cuming, Inc., 13 F.3d 366, Bus. Franchise Guide (CCH) ¶ 10,339 (10th Cir. 1993) (definition of relevant market for purposes of supplier imposing customer restrictions and terminating dealer for failing to follow them could not be so narrow as to include only the sale of one product to one customer).

126. *See, e.g.,* Mendelovitz v. Adolph Coors Co., 693 F.2d 570, 576 n.10 (5th Cir. 1982) (*interbrand* competition significant); Muenster Butane, Inc. v. Stewart Co., 651 F.2d at 297–98 (stiff interbrand competition and lack of market power); Copy-Data Sys., Inc. v. Toshiba America, Inc., 663 F.2d at 410 (supplier's competitors were "industry giants").

127. *See, e.g.,* Red Diamond Supply, Inc. v. Liquid Carbonic Corp., 637 F.2d at 1005–07 (upholding restrictions that did not harm and "may have improved" interbrand competition); Krehl v. Baskin-Robbins Ice Cream Co., 664 F.2d 1348, 1356 (9th Cir. 1982) (restrictions facilitated entry into new markets and wider availability of supplier's products); Muenster Butane, Inc. v. Stewart Co., 651 F.2d 292 (5th Cir. 1981) (restrictions designed to promote interbrand competition by increasing product advertising); Orson, Inc. v. Miramax Film Corp., 862 F. Supp. 1378 (E.D. Pa. 1994) (exclusive license of art films was a valid non-price vertical restraint because the interbrand competition was enhanced by creating a larger choice to consumers since the exclusively licensed film would not be showing at more than one location); *but see* El Cajon Cinemas, Inc. v. American Multi-Cinema, Inc., 1993-1 Trade Cas. (CCH) ¶ 70,158 (S.D. Cal. 1993) (holding that distributor contract with exhibitor to show films at only one chain of theaters could be an unreasonable restraint of trade if clearance was needed to show films at another theater).

128. *See* Eiberger v. Sony Corp. of Am., 622 F.2d 1068 (2d Cir. 1980) (restrictions imposed by a supplier with a 12 percent market share found unreasonable when court determined they had no valid business purpose and there was no enhancement of interbrand competition to offset loss of intrabrand competition); Graphic Prods. Distribs., Inc. v. Itek Corp., 717 F.2d at 1578 n.32 (restrictions found unreasonable where "[there was no] evidence indicating the existence of, or potential for, a free-rider problem requiring territorial restrictions to ensure [improved service coverage]"). And of greater significance Wallace Oil Co. v. Michaels, 839 F. Supp. 1041, Bus. Franchise Guide (CCH) ¶ 10,414 (S.D.N.Y. 1993) (in exclusive dealing contracts, court must weigh the foreclosure of competition and increase in consumer prices against the economies of scale and the ability to plan in advance in long-term contracts to determine whether or not there is an unreasonable restraint on competition).

Seventh, a supplier does not have to establish that vertical territorial and customer restrictions are the least restrictive means to achieve its business objectives.[129] However, if they are more restrictive than "reasonably necessary," this fact may be relevant under a Rule of Reason analysis.[130]

Selling to Franchisees: Antitrust Tie-In Issues

Common Interest

Franchisors and franchisees both have a significant interest in maintaining quality, standardization, and continuity of supply for raw materials used to produce products that are sold in a franchised operation identified in the public mind with the franchisor, its trademark or service mark, and its entire franchise system.

Key Elements

Stringent quality control, uniformity, and regular supply are key elements of any nationwide franchising system. The franchisor will seek effective control over the quality and uniformity of products and services that are important to the image and integrity of the franchise system. The franchisor also has obligations to control use of its trademark pursuant to its duties as trademark owner.[131]

The Basic Choices: Controlling Where, What, and From Whom Franchisee Purchases May Be Made

The franchisor itself may be the seller to franchisees of separate and distinct products or supplies, raising antitrust "tie-in" issues. The franchisor may designate sources of supply in which it has some ownership interest or from which it receives some type of commission or similar payment. Such arrangements also raise tie-in issues.

Use of approved or designated suppliers from which the franchisor receives no commission or equivalent presents fewer antitrust risks than either of the foregoing approaches. An "approved supplier program" involves setting standards

---

129. *See, e.g.,* Graphic Prods. Distribs., Inc. v. Itek Corp., 717 F.2d at 1577 & n.31 (rejecting least restrictive alternative test); American Motor Inns, Inc., v. Holiday Inns, Inc., 521 F.2d 1230, 1249 (3rd Cir. 1975) (same); Newberry v. Washington Post Co., 438 F. Supp. 470, 475 (D.D.C. 1977) (same); Beltone Elec. Corp., 100 FTC 68,209 (1982) (same).

130. *See* Graphic Prods. Distribs., Inc. v. Itek Corp., 717 F.2d at 1577 (noting, in striking down territorial restraints, that "there was no showing—nor any serious attempt to show—that the territorial restrictions were reasonably necessary to achieve [the] legitimate purpose" advanced as the rationale for such restrictions); Coca-Cola Co., 91 FTC. 517 (1978), *remanded for dismissal,* 642 F.2d 1387 (D.C. Cir. 1981) (territorial restrictions found unlawful when more restrictive than necessary to provide product source identification to maintain quality control).

131. 15 U.S.C. §§ 1055, 1127, McAlpine v. AAMCO Automatic Transmissions, Inc., 461 F. Supp. 1232, 1239–40 (E.D. Mich. 1978) ("For a licensor, through the relaxation of quality control, to permit inferior products to be presented to the public under its licensed [trademark] might well constitute a misuse of the mark.").

and specifications for products or services necessary to the operation of the franchised outlet and initially approving and thereafter monitoring the suppliers (i.e., manufacturers and distributors of these products and services).

"Tying" Arrangements in the Franchising Context

Definition

A tying arrangement involves the sale of "one product but only on the condition that the buyer also purchases a different (or tied) product."[132]

The prevailing view is that the defendant must sell the tied product, or have an ownership interest in the seller of the alleged "tied" product, or receive commissions or their equivalent on sales of the alleged tied product by some other third party.[133]

However, a Second Circuit case takes the view that the unlawfulness of a tie-in agreement does not hinge upon a showing that the tying seller has an economic interest in the tied market.[134]

Purported Vices of Tying Arrangements

The "essence of illegality in tying agreements is the wielding of monopolistic leverage; a seller exploits his dominant position in one market to expand his empire into the next."[135] Tying arrangements "deny competitors free access to the market for the tied product, not because the party imposing the tying require-

---

132. Northern Pac. Ry. v. United States, 356 U.S. 1, 5 (1958). While courts have recognized that a Section 1 contract, combination or conspiracy may be formed between the seller and its customers subjected to the tie-in, the Tenth Circuit has taken the position that a contract between a customer and the seller does not establish a Section 1 conspiracy. *See* McKenzie v. Mercy Hosp. of Independence, Kansas, 854 F.2d 365, 368 (10th Cir. 1988); Chanute v. Williams Natural Gas Co., 955 F.2d 641 (10th Cir.), *cert. denied*, 113 S. Ct. 96 (1992); Systemcare, Inc. v. Wang Lab., Inc., 787 F. Supp. 179 (D. Colo. 1992).

133. *See, e.g.*, Midwestern Waffles, Inc. v. Waffle House, Inc., 734 F.2d 705, 712 (11th Cir. 1984); Robert's Waikiki U-Drive, Inc. v. Budget Rent-A-Car Sys., Inc., 732 F.2d 1403, 1407–08 (9th Cir. 1984); Olmstead v. Amoco Oil Co., 725 F.2d 627, 629–30, Bus. Franchise Guide (CCH) ¶ 8133 (11th Cir. 1984); Ohio-Sealy Mattress Mfg. Co. v. Sealy Inc., 585 F.2d 821, 834–835 (7th Cir. 1978), *cert. denied*, 440 U.S. 930 (1979) (Sealy received secret rebates from supplier in return for creating a "captive market"); Roberts v. Elaine Powers Figure Salons, Inc., 708 F.2d 1476 (9th Cir. 1983), Bus. Franchise Guide (CCH) ¶ 8002 (sufficient economic interest shown in bookkeeping services supplier); Shaeffer v. Collins, Bus. Franchise Guide (CCH) ¶ 7578 (E.D. Pa. 1980); Moore v. Jas. H. Matthews & Co., 550 F.2d 1207, 1216 (9th Cir. 1977); Martino v. McDonald's Sys., Inc., 625 F. Supp. 356, Bus. Franchise Guide (CCH) ¶ 8477 (N.D. Ill. 1985) (payment by supplier of advertising allowances; franchisor did not have any substantial access to the allowance and did not use the funds to fulfill its responsibilities; no *per se* argument).

134. Gonzalez v. St. Margaret House Housing Dev. Fund Corp., 880 F.2d 1514, 1517 (2d Cir. 1989). *See also* Beauford v. Helmsley, 740 F. Supp. 201, 208 (S.D.N.Y. 1990); Action Ambulance Service, Inc. v. Atlanticare Health Services, Inc., 815 F. Supp. 33 (D. Mass. Feb. 5, 1993) (plaintiffs not required to prove that the same defendant participated in the markets for both the tying and tied products).

135. Times-Picayune Publishing Co. v. United States, 345 U.S. 594, 611 (1953).

ments has a better product or a lower price but because of his power or leverage in another market. At the same time buyers are forced to forgo their free choice between competing products."[136]

Methods of Attacking Tie-Ins

In the federal law context, tying arrangements may be challenged under Section 1 of the Sherman Act, Section 3 of the Clayton Act, or Section 5 of the FTC Act.[137] However, the trademark, franchise system, and logo of a defendant-franchisor do not constitute "goods, wares, merchandise, machinery, supplies, or other commodities" within the meaning of Section 3 of the Clayton Act, so that Section 3 would be inapplicable if the alleged tying product is the trademark or logo.[138] The state antitrust laws of many states also could be used to attack tie-in arrangements.

Per Se Illegality

The elements of a cause of action for *per se* unlawful tying, under the Supreme Court's decision in *Jefferson Parish*,[139] are as follows:

1. The sale or lease of one product (the tying product) is conditioned on the purchase of another product (the tied product), that is, the existence of a tying arrangement
2. The tying product and the tied product are separate and distinct
3. The seller's possession of "market power" over the tying product is sufficient to enable it to "force" the buyer to purchase the tied product
4. A "not insubstantial" amount of interstate commerce is affected.

As discussed later, notwithstanding the rule of *per se* illegality, a tying arrangement that otherwise satisfies the foregoing test may not be unlawful if implemented for a legitimate business reason and no less restrictive alternative is available.[140]

If a tying arrangement does not satisfy the test for *per se* illegality, it may still be analyzed under the Rule of Reason. The court may still scrutinize the effects of the tie on competition for the tied product and find it unreasonable, but

---

136. Northern Pac. Ry. v. United States, 356 U.S. 1, 6 (1958); United States v. Loew's, Inc., 371 U.S. 38 (1962). *See also* Hirsh v. Martindale-Hubbell, Inc., 674 F.2d 1343 (9th Cir. 1982), *cert. denied*, 459 U.S. 973 (1982) (tying arrangements thought to facilitate price discrimination and to erect artificial barriers by requiring competitors to enter two separate markets simultaneously).

137. 15 U.S.C. § 1 (Sherman Act); 15 U.S.C. § 14 (Clayton Act); 15 U.S.C. § 45 (Federal Trade Commission Act).

138. *See* Webb v. Primo's, Inc., 706 F. Supp. 863, 869–70, Bus. Franchise Guide (CCH) ¶ 9486 (N.D. Ga. 1988); Shaeffer v. Collins, 1980-81 Trade Cas. (CCH) ¶ 63,666, at 77,576 (E.D. Pa. 1980).

139. Jefferson Parish Hosp. Dist. No. 2 v. Hyde, 466 U.S. 2, 12–13 (1984).

140. *See, e.g.,* International Salt Co. v. United States, 332 U.S. 392, 398 (1947); International Business Machs. Corp. v. United States, 298 U.S. 131, 139–40 (1936).

"only when its anticompetitive impact outweighs its contribution to efficiency."[141]

Plaintiffs have generally been unsuccessful in proving the existence of unlawful tying in a Rule of Reason analysis.[142]

Relationship between Tie-Ins and Exclusive Dealing

An exclusive dealing arrangement is an agreement in which a seller conditions the sale or lease of products or services upon a buyer's agreement not to obtain those products or services from any competitive source, or in which a buyer agrees to purchase its needs for an item from a particular seller (a "requirements" contract). Exclusive dealing arrangements are tested under the Rule of Reason rather than the *per se* rule. Tying arrangements and exclusive dealing arrangements both place an obligation upon the purchaser to buy a commodity or service. The distinction between the two is whether the requisite market power to obtain the agreement flows from the attractiveness of the single item subject to the exclusive condition (exclusive dealing) or from an attractive item that is used as a lever to induce buyers to purchase a second, separate item (tie-in).

The Requirement of Two Separate and Distinct Products

The existence of two separate and distinct products is a necessary prerequisite to establishing an unlawful tying arrangement.[143]

The *Jefferson Parish* Formulation

In *Jefferson Parish,*[144] the Supreme Court analyzed the legality of East Jefferson Hospital's contract with a firm of anesthesiologists requiring all anesthesiological services to be performed by that firm. The Court rejected the hospital's argument that no tie-in was involved because the hospital was only providing a "functionally integrated package of services." The Court held that the relevant test is not based "on the functional relation[ship] between [the products], but rather on the character of the demand for the two items."[145]

The majority framed the test for finding two separate and distinct products to be whether there exists "a sufficient demand for the purchase of [the tied product] separate from [the tying product] to identify a distinct product market in which it is efficient to offer [the tied product] separately from [the tying prod-

---

141. Jefferson Parish, 466 U.S. at 42 (O'Connor, J., concurring). *See also* Fortner Enters., Inc. v. United States Steel Corp., 394 U.S. 495, 499–500 (1969) ("Fortner I"); Electroglas, Inc. v. Dynatex Corp., 497 F. Supp. 97 (N.D. Cal. 1980).

142. *See, e.g.,* Town Sound & Custom Tops, Inc. v. Chrysler Motors Corp., 950 F.2d 468, Bus. Franchise Guide (CCH) ¶ 9983 (3d Cir.), *cert. denied*, 113 S. Ct. 196 (1992) (rejected *per se* and Rule of Reason tie-in claims based on Chrysler's alleged conditioning of the sale of Chrysler automobiles on the purchase of Chrysler-supplied auto sound systems).

143. *See* Fortner Enters., Inc. v. United States Steel Corp., 394 U.S. 495, 507 (1969).

144. Jefferson Parish Hosp. Dist. No. 2 v. Hyde, 466 U.S. 2 (1984).

145. *Id.* at 19.

uct]."[146] The majority found that the record amply supported the conclusion that two separate items existed (e.g., patients differentiated between hospital services and anesthesiological services; the latter were frequently separately arranged for and paid for).[147]

The *Kodak* Case and the Two-Product Issue

In *Eastman Kodak Co. v. Image Technical Services, Inc.,*[148] the plaintiff independent service organizations (ISOs) alleged that Kodak tied service of its photocopier and micrographic equipment to parts for that equipment. The district court judge ruled that there was no tie-in at all: "Kodak does not require the buyer to agree to purchase parts or service from Kodak. A Kodak customer can buy equipment without having to buy parts; and he can buy parts if he simply owns Kodak equipment."[149] The court of appeals wrote that the district court had misunderstood the claims and that Kodak allegedly tied parts to service, and not just equipment to parts, since Kodak conditioned receipt of parts on a promise not to purchase service from ISOs. "A tying arrangement is 'an agreement by a party to sell one product but only on the condition that the buyer also purchase a different (or tied) product, *or at least agrees that he will not purchase that product from any other supplier.*' "[150]

The Supreme Court applied the *Jefferson Parish* test of whether consumer demand is such that it is efficient to provide service separately from parts. The Court found sufficient evidence to put the question to the jury. The evidence included the fact that Kodak had sold service and parts separately in the past (and still did so in the case of equipment owners who serviced their own equipment). On the basis of *Jefferson Parish,* the Court rejected Kodak's argument that, since there is no demand for parts separate from service, there cannot be separate markets for service and parts. The Court stated: "We have often found arrangements involving functionally linked products at least one of which is useless without the other to be prohibited tying devices."[151] The Court did not rule that, as a matter of law, two products did exist, but only that the trier of fact should resolve the issue.

The "Two-Product Tests" in Pre-*Jefferson Parish* Cases

In cases before *Jefferson Parish,* courts of appeals had applied variously framed "tests" for determining whether one or two products existed.

Courts generally examined whether separate products existed on a case-by-case basis. Among the pre-*Jefferson Parish* factors that were considered were (1) whether the sales practices of other members of the market were to sell the

146. *Id.* at 21.

147. *Id.* at 19–21.

148. 504 U.S. 451 (1992).

149. *See* Image Technical Servs., Inc. v. Eastman Kodak Co., 1989-1 Trade Cas. (CCH) ¶ 68,402 at 60,212 (N.D. Ca. 1988), *rev'd, remanded,* 903 F.2d 612 (9th Cir. 1990).

150. 903 F.2d at 615 (quoting Northern Pac. Ry v. United States, 356 U.S. 1, 5–6 (1958)).

151. Jefferson Parish, 466 U.S. at 21 n.30.

products separately or together; (2) whether versions of the product at issue differed in significant respects; (3) whether any efficiencies were gained by the combination; (4) whether the two alleged products were sold separately; and (5) whether the two products were regularly sold or used as a unit with fixed proportions.[152]

In *Anderson Foreign Motors, Inc. v. New England Toyota Distributors, Inc.,*[153] the district court used a multipronged analysis, looking at the product structure itself, the defendant's product marketing practices, the practices of competitors, and the efficiencies gained by, and justification for, the combination, to find that new automobiles and delivery services provided to dealers were separate products. In that case, the court indicated that the fact finder essentially evaluates the facts to determine whether the seller should be forced to market two alleged products separately.

In the franchising area, a number of pre-*Jefferson Parish* cases analyzed whether a franchisor's trademark license was a separate product from food, equipment, supplies, real estate, and the like sold or leased by the franchisor to its franchisees. A seminal case was *Siegel v. Chicken Delight, Inc.*[154] It involved a "business format" franchise. There the Ninth Circuit looked to the "function of the aggregation" and held that cooking equipment, dry-mix food items, and packaging constituted separate and distinct products from the license of the trademark. The court stated that "attempts by tie-in to extend the trademark protection to common articles (which the public does not and has no reason to connect with the trademark) simply because they are said to be essential to production of that which is the subject of the trademark, cannot escape antitrust scrutiny."

Subsequently, in *Krehl v. Baskin-Robbins Ice Cream Co.,*[155] the Ninth Circuit revisited *Siegel.*[156] It stated that, in determining whether a trademark is a separate product, the relevant inquiry focuses on the "relationship between the trademark and the products allegedly tied to its sale" and on "the type of franchising system involved." The court stated that in a "distribution" type of system, such as that employed by Baskin-Robbins, as distinguished from a "business format" franchise, "the franchised outlets serve merely as conduits through which the trademarked goods . . . manufactured by the franchisor or . . . by its licensees according to detailed specifications 'flow to the ultimate consumer.' "

---

152. *See, e.g.,* Associated Press v. Taft-Ingalls Corp., 340 F.2d 753, 759–64 (6th Cir.), *cert. denied*, 382 U.S. 820 (1965); *In re* Data Gen. Corp. Antitrust Litig., 490 F. Supp. 1089, 1104–05 (N.D. Cal. 1980), and 529 F. Supp. 801, 806 (N.D. Cal. 1981), *aff'd in relevant part and rev'd in part on other grounds sub nom.* Digidyne Corp. v. Data Gen. Corp., 734 F.2d 1336 (9th Cir. 1984), *cert. denied*, 473 U.S. 908 (1985); Washington Gas Light Co. v. Virginia Elec. & Power Co., 438 F.2d 248, 253 (4th Cir. 1971).

153. 475 F. Supp. 973, 982 (D. Mass. 1979).

154. 448 F.2d 43, 49 (9th Cir. 1971), *cert. denied*, 405 U.S. 955 (1972).

155. 664 F.2d 1348, 1353–54 (9th Cir. 1982).

156. Other cases questioning the soundness of the *Siegel* approach include Capital Temporaries, Inc. v. Olsten Corp., 506 F.2d 658, 663–64 (2d Cir. 1974); Redd v. Shell Oil Co., 524 F.2d 1054, 1057 (10th Cir. 1975), *cert. denied*, 425 U.S. 912 (1976) (court did "not necessarily agree with [*Siegel's*] analysis of the problem" of a trademark as a separate product); and Ungar v. Dunkin' Donuts of Am., Inc., 531 F.2d 1211, at 1214 n.4, 1215–16 n.5 (3d Cir.), *cert. denied*, 429 U.S. 823 (1976).

In the context of the Baskin-Robbins system, the court found that the trademark "serves merely as a representation of the end product [i.e., ice cream] marketed by the system" and that the "sale of substandard products under the mark would dissipate this goodwill and reduce the value of the trademark." In such circumstances, "[t]he desirability of the trademark and the quality of the product it represents are so inextricably interrelated in the mind of the consumer as to preclude any finding that the trademark is a separate item for tie-in purposes."[157] On the other hand, in a "business format franchise," where the "franchisor merely provides the trademark and, in some cases, supplies used in operating the franchised outlet and producing the system's products," the Ninth Circuit believes there is "generally only a remote connection between the trademark and the products the franchisees are compelled to purchase . . . because consumers have no reason to associate with the trademark, those component goods used either in the operation of the franchised store or in the manufacture of the end product." In that type of situation, the court found that a trademark could be a separate product for tie-in purposes.

In another leading pre-*Jefferson Parish* case, *Principe v. McDonald's Corp.*,[158] the Fourth Circuit found that the trademark license, lease of restaurant premises, and security deposit paid by the franchisee to McDonald's constituted "integral components of the business method being franchised" and the "challenged aggregation is an essential ingredient" of the franchised system's formula for success.[159]

---

157. Redd v. Shell Oil, 524 F.2d 1054 (10th Cir. 1975), *cert. denied*, 425 U.S. 912 (1976).

158. 631 F.2d 303, Bus. Franchise Guide (CCH) ¶ 7553 (4th Cir. 1980), *cert. denied*, 451 U.S. 970 (1981).

159. *Id.* at 309. Other decisions in which trademark licenses have been considered as separate items from food, supplies, and equipment sold by the licensor: Roberts v. Elaine Powers Figure Salons, Inc., 708 F.2d 1476, 1482 (9th Cir. 1983) (franchise and bookkeeping services could be considered to be two products); Carpa, Inc. v. Ward Foods, Inc., 536 F.2d 39, 43 (5th Cir. 1976) (franchise agreement contained clauses requiring "franchisees to purchase all food, supplies and equipment" from affiliated corporation); Warriner Hermetics, Inc. v. Copeland Refrig. Corp., 463 F.2d 1002 (5th Cir.), *cert. denied*, 409 U.S. 1086 (1972); Northern v. McGraw-Edison Co., 542 F.2d 1336 (8th Cir. 1976), *cert. denied*, 429 U.S. 1097 (1977) (tied items of dry cleaning equipment and incidental equipment).

Other pre-*Jefferson Parish* decisions that did *not* find the trademark to be a separate and distinct product or which have questioned such an analysis: Kugler v. AAMCO Automatic Transmissions, Inc., 460 F.2d 1214 (8th Cir. 1972) (national, as well as local, advertising services "became an integral and inseparable aspect" of the "single package" agreement); In re 7-Eleven Franchise Antitrust Litigation, 1974-2 Trade Cas. (CCH) ¶ 75,429 (N.D. Cal.) ("The only thing [defendant has] for sale is an overall package, which includes the franchise and a group of services which constitute an integral part of the total package."). *But see* United States v. Mercedes-Benz of North Am., Inc., 517 F. Supp. 1369 (N.D. Cal. 1981), and Metrix Warehouse, Inc. v. Daimler-Benz Aktiengesellschaft, 555 F. Supp. 824 (D. Md. 1983) (distinguishing *Principe* and finding that Mercedes-Benz automobiles and replacement parts for them are separate products capable of being unlawfully tied).

Post-*Jefferson Parish* Analysis of the Separate Product Issue

The impact of the *Jefferson Parish* two-product test on cases involving franchising remains unclear.

In *Casey v. Diet Center, Inc.,*[160] the court thought that *Jefferson Parish* overrules the "distribution v. business format" distinction discussed by the Ninth Circuit in *Krehl*. Nonetheless, in that case, the court found that the nutritional tablet that Diet Center clients must take is not separate from the system to promote weight loss and control for individual clients, stating that "the demand for the Diet Supp is not separate from that for the franchise: it is generated wholly by the franchisee's operation of the franchise." Where "franchisees bargain for the right to use a package of products and services none of which represents a market distinct from that of the franchise itself, the competitive purposes of the rule against tying are not served by fractionating the franchise into separate components."

In *Jack Walters & Sons Corp. v. Morton Buildings, Inc.,*[161] the Seventh Circuit held that a building components manufacturer did not illegally tie prefabricated buildings to its trademark. The court indicated that the "practice has been to classify a product as a single product if there are rather obvious economies of joint provision, as in the left-shoe-right-shoe example."[162] The court stated, "Only time will tell how far the 'separate markets' approach of Jefferson Parish will be pushed."[163] In the *Jack Walters* decision, Judge Posner suggests that the Supreme Court's emphasis on whether there are separate markets for each product is not a total rejection of the cases that look at the economies of jointly providing the two items in question.

Cases such as *Jack Walters* and *Casey* can be read to indicate that there is room—even after *Jefferson Parish*—to recognize the functional utility of the combination as proof of one product, at least when such functional utility is consistent with *Jefferson Parish*'s emphasis on the character of the demand and on the requirement of a market where it is efficient to offer separate products.[164]

---

160. 590 F. Supp. 1561, 1563–66, Bus. Franchise Guide (CCH) ¶ 8210 (N.D. Cal. 1984).

161. 737 F.2d 698 (7th Cir.), *cert. denied*, 469 U.S. 1018 (1984).

162. *Id.* at 703.

163. *Id.* at 703–04.

164. Other post-*Jefferson Parish* cases of note on the two-product issue: Service & Training, Inc. v. Data Gen. Corp., 737 F. Supp. 334 (D. Md. 1990), *aff'd*, 963 F.2d 680 (4th Cir. 1992) (no tie-in of customer access to copyrighted diagnostic software to unwanted computer maintenance and repair services; there was only one legitimate purpose for which customers would use the software: to maintain and repair the computer systems, and the software was only one feature of the manufacturer's integrated and unified "product," *i.e.*, computer servicing); KFC Corp. v. Marion-Kay Co., 620 F. Supp. 1160, Bus. Franchise Guide (CCH) ¶ 8456 (S.D. Ind. 1985) (Kentucky Fried Chicken franchise trademarks and the Colonel's secret seasoning were so interrelated that they formed a single product for purposes of tying analysis; seasoning was an integral part of the franchise); Power Test Petroleum Distribs., Inc. v. Calcu Gas, Inc., 754 F.2d 91, 86–98, Bus. Franchise Guide (CCH) ¶ 8306 (2d Cir. 1985) (franchisor's gasoline and trademark did not constitute separate products in the consumer's eyes; even though franchisor did not refine the gasoline, it applied its own standards for octane, viscosity and impurities before distributing under its

The history of *Faulkner Advertising Associates, Inc. v. Nissan Motors Corp.*[165] demonstrates the difficulty of applying the *Jefferson Parish* "distinct markets" test in the franchise context. In that case, a local advertising agency alleged that Nissan unlawfully tied advertising services to automobiles by using a centralized advertising agency to produce local advertising for its dealers and by financing such centralized advertising by (1) charging its dealers higher whole-

own mark; it thus guaranteed the contents and standards of the gasoline, thereby rendering it nonfungible with other gasoline); Smith v. Mobil Oil Corp., 667 F. Supp. 1314, 1322–24, Bus. Franchise Guide (CCH) ¶ 8915 (W.D. Mo. 1987) (oil company's standard contracts and lease for its franchised service stations did not unlawfully require the purchase of any gasoline (or oil) from the company as a condition to obtaining the oil company's franchise package; when a trademarked product is sold in a distribution-type franchise system, as distinguished from a business-format franchise system, the trademark and the product are not separate products for antitrust tie-in purposes; rejects suggestion in *Casey* that *Jefferson Parish* overruled "business format vs. distribution" distinction); William Cohen & Son, Inc. v. All-American Hero, Inc., 693 F. Supp 201 (D.N.J. 1988) (fast food trademark and steak meat portions were separate products, since the franchise system at issue was a "business format system" under which the franchise or trademark itself serves as nothing more than a representation of the end product marketed by the system; it was unlikely that consumers would associate the "All American Hero" franchise with the steak meat portions); Genna v. Lady Foot Int'l, Inc., Bus. Franchise Guide (CCH) ¶ 8694, 1986-2 Trade Cas. (CCH) ¶ 67,317 at 61,636 (E.D. Pa. 1986) (trademark, logo and franchise system not separate products); Southern Pines Chrysler-Plymouth v. Chrysler Corp., 826 F.2d 1360, 1363 (4th Cir. 1987) (two different models of automobiles manufactured by Chrysler are not separate products because they do not involve the linking of separate product markets); Mozart Co. v. Mercedes-Benz of N. Am., Inc., 593 F. Supp. 1506, 1515, Bus. Franchise Guide (CCH) ¶ 8239 (N.D. Cal. 1984) (demand for repair parts separate from automobiles compels finding of separate products); Parts and Elec. Motors, Inc. v. Sterling Elec., Inc., 826 F.2d 712, 720, Bus. Franchise Guide (CCH) ¶ 9283 (7th Cir. 1987) (evidence of differences in distribution channels, markup, margins, industry treatment, and sources of demand for electric motors and parts supported jury's finding that they represented two separate product markets); Midwest Communications, Inc. v. Minnesota Twins, Inc., 779 F.2d 444 (8th Cir. 1985) (telecast rights of baseball team and of hockey team held to be separate products), *cert. denied*, 476 U.S. 1163 (1986); R & G Affiliates, Inc. v. Knoll Int'l, Inc., 587 F. Supp. 1395, 1403 (S.D.N.Y. 1984); Metro Media Broadcasting Corp. v. MGM/UA Entertainment Co., 611 F. Supp. 415, 422–24 (C.D. Cal. 1985) (syndicated first runs of television series and reruns of same series were not separate products); Cia. Petroleum Caribe, Inc. v. Avis Rental Car Corp., 576 F. Supp. 1011, 1015–16 (D.P.R. 1983), *aff'd*, 753 F.2d 636 (1st Cir. 1984) (rental car and gasoline provided in it are not separate products); Klo-Zik Co. v. General Motors Corp., 677 F. Supp. 499 (E.D. Tex. 1987) (sale of tractor-trailer truck engines with warranties did not constitute an illegal tying arrangement; engines and warranties were not separate products since it was not shown that there was sufficient demand for the purchase of the warranties from someone other than the manufacturer or that it would be efficient for warranties to be provided separately from the engines themselves); Service & Training, Inc. v. Data General Corp., 963 F.2d 680 (4th Cir. 1992) (diagnostic software program of Data General and Data General's repair services were separate products; however, there was no tie-in).

165. 905 F.2d 769 (4th Cir. 1990) (reversing district court decision), *on reh'g en banc*, 945 F.2d 694 (4th Cir. 1991) (*per curiam*) (affirming district court's decision by an equally divided court).

sale prices and (2) subsidizing such advertising with funds that Nissan previously had contributed to dealers' independent local advertising efforts. A Fourth Circuit panel held that the district court had erred in dismissing the claim for failure to allege two separate products,[166] but an equally divided *en banc* court affirmed the district court's dismissal of the action, effectively reversing the three-judge panel's decision.[167]

Sufficient Economic Power over the Tying Product

Fortner II

In *United States Steel Corp. v. Fortner Enterprise, Inc.* (Fortner II),[168] in a non-franchise context, the Supreme Court addressed the question of what evidence would be necessary to prove sufficient economic power over the tying product to compel purchase of the tied product. The Court found no tie-in violation.

The Court stated that "the question [is] whether the seller has the power, within the market for the tying product, to raise prices or to require purchasers to accept burdensome terms that could not be exacted in a completely competitive market" or "whether the seller has some advantage not shared by his competitors in the market for the tying product."

Jefferson Parish

In *Jefferson Parish,* the five-Justice majority opinion written by Justice Stevens began with the premise that certain tying arrangements remain *per se* illegal, while others should be judged under the Rule of Reason. The majority requires that there must be "forcing," which occurs when a seller uses its market power "to force the buyer into the purchase of a tied product that the buyer either did not want at all, or might have preferred to purchase elsewhere on different terms."[169]

However, "[p]er se condemnation . . . is *only* appropriate if the existence of forcing is probable [or likely]." Forcing is considered "likely" only if the seller possesses "market power," as demonstrated by one of three specified indicators: (1) a patent monopoly or similar monopoly, (2) a high market share, or (3) a unique product that others cannot offer.[170] The majority found that the only evidence of market power was consumer "preference" for the hospital, but that "a preference of this kind . . . is not necessarily probative of significant market power."[171] Moreover, the majority concluded that the hospital's market share, 30 percent, was insufficient to infer market power by itself.[172]

---

166. 905 F.2d at 773–74.
167. 945 F.2d 696 (4th Cir. 1991).
168. 429 U.S. 610, 620 (1977).
169. 466 U.S. at 12.
170. *Id.* at 15–17.
171. *Id.* at 26.
172. *Id.* at 27.

Kodak

The 1992 *Kodak* decision has already been the subject of much discussion and analysis. As noted earlier, the case focused on policies that Kodak adopted to prevent ISOs from obtaining "aftermarket" replacement parts for Kodak copying equipment, making it difficult or impossible for ISOs to compete with Kodak in providing service to end-users. The ISOs claimed that by controlling the supply of parts and requiring end-users to purchase both service and parts from Kodak, Kodak had unlawfully tied service to parts in violation of Section 1 of the Sherman Act. The plaintiffs also claimed that Kodak had unlawfully monopolized and attempted to monopolize the sale of service and parts in violation of Section 2 of the act.

After concluding (as noted) that a reasonable trier of fact could find that parts and service are two distinct products for purposes of tying under Section 1, the Court found enough evidence that Kodak had sufficient power over parts to force customers into unwanted purchases of Kodak's service.[173] Such evidence included Kodak's control of virtually 100 percent of the "tying" market (Kodak-compatible replacement parts). There was also evidence that customers had been forced to buy Kodak's service. The plaintiffs also claimed that Kodak's service was inferior in quality and more expensive than ISO service.[174]

Kodak's theory (at least as stated by the Court) was an assertion that Kodak clearly lacked market power in the "primary equipment market" and that this precluded—as a matter of law—the possibility of its exercising any market power in "derivative aftermarkets" for parts or service. The Court assumed that the primary equipment market was competitive, but it rejected the proposed conclusion argued by Kodak because Kodak had failed to come forward with "any actual data on the equipment, service, or parts markets."[175]

According to the Court, Kodak's theory rested on the factual assumption that if it had raised its prices for parts or service above competitive levels, potential customers would have simply stopped buying its primary equipment. However, there was no evidence or assertion that Kodak had actually lost equipment sales after it raised its service prices.[176] As a second counter to Kodak's theory, the Court observed that exorbitant aftermarket pricing could depress Kodak's sales in the primary market only if consumers "inform themselves of the total cost of the 'package'—equipment, service, and parts—at the time of purchase; that is, consumers must engage in accurate lifecycle pricing."[177] As a third response to Kodak's theory, the Court also cited "lock-ins" as potentially insulating the primary market from price increases in the service aftermarket; that is, if the cost of switching to another brand of basic equipment is high, consumers who have al-

173. 504 U.S. at 459.
174. *Id.* at 460.
175. *Id.* at 466.
176. *Id.* at 452.
177. *Id.* at 473.

ready purchased the basic equipment, and are thus "locked-in," "will tolerate some level of service-price increases before changing equipment brands."[178]

The "Market Power" Inquiry in Franchising Cases

Since the *Chicken Delight* decision in 1971, franchise cases have often involved the question of the extent to which the "uniqueness" of the franchisor's trademark (with or without other factors or evidence) is sufficient to establish the sufficient economic power requirement. In light of *Fortner II* and *Jefferson Parish,* courts have generally moved toward imposing higher thresholds of proof for franchisees seeking to establish this crucial element in tie-in cases—although the cases are somewhat difficult to reconcile. The following sections trace developments in this area, from pre-*Fortner II* cases to recent cases decided in light of *Jefferson Parish.* There is also some discussion of the possible impact of *Kodak* in franchising cases.

Pre-*Fortner II* Cases Addressing Power of Trademark

In a number of cases in the early 1970s courts addressed the extent to which a trademarked product or service could possess sufficient economic power to compel purchases of tied products.[179]

---

178. *Id.* at 476. The Court also found sufficient issues for trial as to whether Kodak had violated Section 2 of the Sherman Act. Evidence that Kodak had controlled nearly 100 percent of the parts market and 80–95 percent of the service market, with no readily available substitutes, was enough to defeat summary judgment on the issue of monopoly power. *Id.* at 469. As to the second element of a Section 2 claim, the willful use of monopoly power, the Court found sufficient evidence that Kodak had taken exclusionary action to maintain its parts monopoly and used its control over parts to strengthen its monopoly share of the service market. Thus, liability under Section 2 turned on whether valid business reasons could justify Kodak's actions. Kodak's asserted business justifications—a need to ensure quality service, a need to control inventory costs, and a desire to prevent ISOs from "free-riding"—were held insufficient to prove that Kodak was entitled to judgment as a matter of law. *Id.* at 470.

179. *See, e.g.,* Siegel v. Chicken Delight, Inc., 448 F.2d 43, 50 (9th Cir. 1971), *cert. denied,* 405 U.S. 955 (1972) (unique registered trademark, in combination with demonstrated power to impose a tie-in; "we see no reason why the presumption [of sufficient economic power] that exists in the case of the patent and copyright does not equally apply to the trademark"); Capital Temporaries, Inc. v. Olsten Corp., 506 F.2d 658, 663 (2d Cir. 1974) ("trademark *qua* trademark is not a sufficient indication of dominance over the tying product to qualify for *per se* treatment"); Warriner Hermetics, Inc. v. Copeland Refrig. Corp., 463 F.2d 1002 (5th Cir.), *cert. denied,* 409 U.S. 1086 (1972) (could be little doubt that the designation of a wholesaler as an "authorized" outlet is of great economic value and that designation of a rebuilder as "authorized" was highly regarded as a competitive advantage; franchisor's trademark highly regarded as competitive advantage in the rebuilding field); Northern v. McGraw-Edison Co., 542 F.2d 1336, 1346 (8th Cir. 1976), *cert. denied,* 429 U.S. 1097 (1977) ("attributes of uniqueness and desirability, coupled with power of defendant to impose the tying arrangement on buyers at an artificially enhanced price, constitute sufficient economic power"); Carpa, Inc. v. Ward Foods, Inc., 536 F.2d 39 (5th Cir. 1976) (although legally unique name alone cannot demand a presumption of economic power, jury could have found that franchisor with five franchisees had sufficient economic power; court refers to franchisor's advertising itself throughout Southwest and characterization of itself to potential buyers as enjoying a growth trend in sales and earnings).

Cases Decided After *Fortner II* and Before *Jefferson Parish*

In *Krehl v. Baskin-Robbins Ice Cream Co.*,[180] the court found that an ice cream store chain's trademark was coupled with such nationwide preeminence in the retail sale of ice cream that economic power in the trademark was present as a matter of law. On the other hand, in *Cash v. Arctic Circle, Inc.*,[181] the court refused to presume economic power solely from the fact that the tying product is a trademark owned by the defendant.[182]

In a number of other cases where the tying product was other than a trademark, courts frequently found in favor of defendants.[183]

Cases Decided After *Jefferson Parish*

The general trend in cases after *Jefferson Parish* has been to stiffen the requirements for proof of economic power over the tying product. However, there are no clear guidelines, and the degree to which "market share" will become the primary focus is unclear.

A leading case in the franchise area is *Will v. Comprehensive Accounting Corp.*[184] The Seventh Circuit (Judge Easterbrook) found that the plaintiffs had failed to show that the price of the tied package was higher than the price of components sold in competitive markets or that the franchisor enjoyed a significant market share. Nor did plaintiffs demonstrate that the franchise system was "unique." "Uniqueness" occurs only where a franchisor has cost advantages over

---

180. 78 F.R.D. 108 (C.D. Cal. 1978).

181. 85 F.R.D. 618 (E.D. Wash. 1979).

182. *See also* Esposito v. Mister Softee, Inc., 1980-1 Trade Cas. (CCH) ¶ 63,089 (E.D.N.Y. 1979).

183. *See, e.g.*, Phillips v. Crown Cent. Petroleum Corp., 602 F.2d 616 (4th Cir. 1979), *cert. denied*, 444 U.S. 1074 (1980); Bell v. Cherokee Aviation Corp., 660 F.2d 1123 (6th Cir. 1981); Gowdish v. Eaton Corp., Bus. Franchise Guide (CCH) ¶ 7622 1981-1 Trade Cas. (CCH) ¶ 63,913 (M.D.N.C.) (lack of evidence that the supplier possessed sufficient economic power in the market for lift trucks to restrain competition for credit); JBL Enters., Inc. v. Jhirmack Enters., Inc., 509 F. Supp. 357 (N.D. Cal. 1981), *aff'd*, 698 F.2d 1011 (9th Cir. 1983), *cert. denied*, 464 U.S. 829 (1983) (manufacturer's 5 percent share of relevant market did not give it sufficient economic power to impose significant restrictions in the tied product market); Spartan Grain & Mill Co. v. Ayers, 581 F.2d 419, 425 (5th Cir. 1978), *cert. denied*, 444 U.S. 831 (1979) (the inquiry is whether the seller "had sufficient economic power in the relevant market"); Blackwell v. Power Test Corp., 540 F. Supp. 802 (D.N.J. 1981), *aff'd without opinion*, 688 F.2d 818 (3d Cir. 1982) (no violation; defendant-distributor controlled only 6 percent of the retail sales in the market, the product was not unique, and the distributor possessed no advantage not shared by competitors); Yentsch v. Texaco, Inc., 630 F.2d 46 (2d Cir. 1980) (oil company did not dominate the regional market nor control the best station sites); United States v. Mercedes-Benz of North Am., Inc., 517 F. Supp. 1369, 1387 (N.D. Cal. 1981) (extensive discussion of economic power issue; Mercedes-Benz trademark may be a factor in determining its leverage but alone is not sufficient; "uniqueness" of Mercedes automobiles "must be based largely on objective market factors and partially on subjective impression").

184. Will v. Comprehensive Accounting Corp., 776 F.2d 665, Bus. Franchise Guide (CCH) ¶ 8450 (7th Cir. 1985), *cert. denied*, 475 U.S. 1129 (1986).

potential rivals, where there are barriers to entry, or where rivals could not produce a similar package for a similar cost.

Will expressly refused to follow the much-discussed decision of the Ninth Circuit in *Digidyne v. Data General Corp.*[185] In *Digidyne* the court found that market power could be presumed when the tying product (software) is protected by copyright. The court concluded that when the product is sufficiently distinctive and "attractive to enable the seller by tying arrangements to foreclose a part of the market for a tied product, the adverse impact on competition in the tied product is not diminished by the fact that other sellers may be selling products similar to the tying products." The Ninth Circuit's subsequent decision in *Mozart Co. v. Mercedes-Benz of North America, Inc.*[186] may cast some doubt on the viability of *Digidyne,* at least in franchising situations.

In a number of cases involving trademarked products (whether or not sold through a product distribution type of franchise), courts rejected plaintiff's arguments of sufficient economic power.[187]

While it may be more difficult to prove "uniqueness" as a source of economic power, the extent to which a product can be "unique" (even with a small

185. 734 F.2d 1336 (9th Cir. 1984), *cert. denied,* 473 U.S. 908 (1985).

186. 833 F.2d 1342, 1346 n.4 (9th Cir. 1987), *cert. denied,* 488 U.S. 870 (1988).

187. *See, e.g.,* Webb v. Primo's Inc., 706 F. Supp. 863 (N.D. Ga. 1988) (franchisor lacked economic power; there were many other pizza, sub and Italian restaurants in the market, and the franchisor's position in the market did not create a disincentive for competition in the market; mere existence of trademark insufficient); Hudson's Bay Co. Fur Sales v. American Legend Coop., 651 F. Supp. 819, 841–42 (D.N.J. 1986) (trademark for high quality mink which accounted for one-ninth of U.S. market, which in turn accounted for one-eighth of worldwide market, insufficient economic power; trademark for high quality mink not unique since any competitor could develop its own trademark for marketing a similar product); Casey v. Diet Center, Inc., 590 F. Supp. 1561, 1567 (N.D. Cal. 1984); Mozart Co. v. Mercedes-Benz of N. Am. Inc., 833 F.2d 1342, 1346–47 (9th Cir. 1987), *cert. denied,* 488 U.S. 870 (1988) (uniqueness of automobile to consumers does not establish uniqueness in the market for dealership franchises, the relevant market) (dictum); Klo-Zik Co. v. General Motors Corp., 677 F. Supp. 499 (E.D. Tex. 1987) (tractor-trailer manufacturer did not possess power in the market for engines; engines were not significantly different from other engines in the market to be "unique"; although the engines were patented, it was not shown what effect the patents had on the product's interchangeability with competing products); Homeware, Inc. v. Rexair, Inc., Bus. Franchise Guide (CCH) ¶ 9147, 1988-1 Trade Cas. (CCH) ¶ 68,035 at 58,593 (E.D. Mich. 1988) (manufacturer's 3 percent share of vacuum cleaner market did not constitute sufficient power in the market); *see also* William Cohen & Son, Inc. v. All American Hero, Inc., 693 F. Supp. 201 (D.N.J. 1988) (the court could not conclude on the record before it either that the franchisor had sufficient economic power in the tying product to impose an appreciable restraint on free competition in the tied product or even which of two alleged relevant markets—the wholesale steak market or the market for all steak-sandwich-centered restaurant franchises—was the appropriate one for market power analysis). *See also* Town Sound & Custom Tops, Inc. v. Chrysler Motors Corp., 959 F.2d 468 (3d Cir. 1992), *cert. denied,* 113 S. Ct. 196 (1992) (alleged conditioning of sale of Chrysler automobiles on purchase of Chrysler-supplied auto sound systems; *per se* tying claim rejected since Chrysler lacked market power in both the tying product market (all domestic autos) and the tied product market (all auto sound systems sold domestically).

amount of market power in a properly defined market) and the contours of the "uniqueness" concept remain unclear.[188]

Possible Impact of *Kodak* on the Market Power Issue

A business format franchisor that pressures its franchisees to purchase one or more collateral, after-market, products as a condition of obtaining, or retaining, the franchise may well face arguments on its "market power" based on *Kodak.*

Cases brought after the *Kodak* decision have developed the arguments along the following lines.

The analogy between the fact situation in *Kodak,* and the after-market in a business format franchise system is sufficiently close to warrant caution. In *Kodak*, the alleged tying product was not the original sale of the Kodak copier, but the after-market sale of proprietary Kodak parts. In a business format franchise, the plaintiff would allege that the tying product is not the original grant of the franchise (the license of the bundle of intellectual property comprising the franchise, as was the case in *Chicken Delight*), but some after-market "product" such as forbearance from terminating the franchise, or the explicit or implicit promise of renewal of the existing franchise when its term expires, or perhaps the opportunity to acquire additional franchises, but only to franchisees who "go along" with the franchisor's captive sourcing mechanism.

---

188. *See, e.g.,* Montvale Management Group, Inc. v. Snowshoe Co., 1984-1 Trade Cas. (CCH) ¶ 65,990 at 68,374 (N.D. W.Va. 1984) (insufficient showing of uniqueness; plaintiff did not show defendant possessed skiing facilities superior to those of competitors); Parts and Elec. Motors, Inc. v. Sterling Elec., Inc., 826 F.2d 712 (7th Cir. 1987) (sufficient market power in the tying market for replacement parts; manufacturer conceded that it had 100 percent dominance in the market for the parts to its own electric motors, the parts were not fabricated by any other manufacturer, the parts could not be used on any other brands of electric motors, there were substantial barriers to entry because of level of demand for parts would accommodate one manufacturer, and there was a general acceptance of the tie among the distributors); Microbyte Corp. v. New Jersey State Golf Ass'n, 1986-2 Trade Cas. (CCH) ¶ 67,228 at 61,163 (D.N.J. 1986) (defendant-sponsored golf tournaments were unique product because of association prestige and tradition); Ringtown Wilbert Vault Works v. Schuylkill Memorial Park, Inc., 650 F. Supp. 823, 825–26 (E.D. Pa. 1986) (unique nature of cemetery lots and defendant's 10 percent market share sufficient to demonstrate market over cemetery lots); Tic-X-Press, Inc. v. Omni Promotions Co. of Ga., 815 F.2d 1407, 1420 (11th Cir. 1987) (defendant controlled only enclosed concert facility capable of seating more than 4000 people); R & G Affiliates, Inc. v. Knoll Int'l Inc., 587 F. Supp. 1395, 1403–04 (S.D.N.Y. 1984) (fact that reputation of product was such that some customers asked for it by name did not alone establish that the manufacturer had the "special ability" to force a tying arrangement upon dealers; moreover, fact that some of defendant's furniture is patented does not in itself establish requisite market power); Seaward Yacht Sales, Ltd. v. Murray Chris-Craft Cruisers, Inc., 701 F. Supp. 766 (D. Ore. 1988) (fact that manufacturer of boats had only a less than 5 percent market share did not preclude the possibility of market power over the allegedly tying product in full line forcing case, since market power can be inferred from a tying product's desirability to consumers or its unique attributes; nonetheless, there was no evidence that the manufacturer's boats were unique or especially desirable to consumers or that the desired type of boats were not available from other dealers).

In denying Kodak summary judgement, the Court faced a situation where Kodak was essentially the sole supplier of the alleged tying product (Kodak-compatable replacement parts) and there was inadequate proof that Kodak's power was disciplined by other market factors. Kodak's argument that competition in the market for photocopiers precluded the possibility of market power in the after-market for parts was rejected by the Court. Therefore, franchisors who argue that competition for franchises generally, or for franchises in their particular industry segement, precludes the possibility of the franchisor having "market power" in their franchise offering, or system, miss the point of *Kodak*. Instead, the plaintiff will argue that the tying product is something unique to that franchisor which its competitors absolutely cannot offer, such as renewal, or additional franchises, in the same brand or even just the right to continue operating the franchise.

To escape such an attack on a coercive, hence "tied," after-market sourcing arrangement, the franchisor might try to establish one or more of the following defenses in an attempt to take the franchise case out of the analogy to *Kodak*:

1. Franchisees had notice of or access to the full cost of the allegedly tied products at the time they entered into the franchise agreements, possibly from presale disclosure in the franchisor's offering circular;
2. Franchisees have, in fact, competitively sourced the allegedly tied product lines; and
3. The franchisor continues to enjoy brisk sales of new franchises, defeating the implication that the after-market tie is disadvantageous, or priced above the combined market value of the tied and tying items.

The franchisee, or competitive vendor, who is the plaintiff in such a case will rely heavily on the argument that, by analogy to *Kodak*, no one is more "locked in" to a single brand, hence facing impossibly high "switching costs," than the franchisee who is party to a 10- or 20-year franchise agreement, replete with post-term covenents and vulnerable to a lawsuit for damages for breach of the contract should he or she break away. The plaintiff's case might be especially strong if the facts support a claim that the franchisor first imposed or enforced the tie-in after the franchisee (or a sizable number of franchisees) had purchased the franchise, or if the franchisor's offering circular either was silent on this subject, or perhaps misdescribed the actual sourcing environment in the system, based on the facts shown in *Kodak* that Kodak had imposed its refusal to sell parts to independent service providers only long after it had begun selling the photocopiers.

---

189. *See* Tominaga v. Shepherd, 682 F. Supp. 1489, 1494–1495, Bus. Franchise Guide (CCH) ¶ 9105 (C.D. Cal. 1988) (precontract competition among franchisors prevented the franchisor from exercising any economic power in setting contract terms with potential franchisees: "Nothing in the record shows that El Centro had the power (precontract) to 'force' potential franchisees to purchase the tied goods. Such power could only be exercised by El Centro if the relevant market for the tying product were Pizza Man franchises. No such showing has been made, nor could such a showing be made.").

Post-*Kodak* Decisions

Subsequent to *Kodak,* the Sixth Circuit reevaluated its earlier decision in *Virtual Maintenance, Inc. v. Prime Computer, Inc.*[190] The defendant, a computer marketer, tied a hardware maintenance service contract to computer-aided design and computer-aided manufacturing software that it licensed exclusively from an automobile manufacturer, which required use of the most recent version of the software sold by all automotive design firms that dealt with it. In light of *Kodak,* the court found that the arrangement could be *per se* illegal in the derivative aftermarket for the manufacturer-required software support. The marketer was able to control the sale of software because of its exclusive license and the manufacturer's requirement to force buyers to purchase an unwanted tied product. The tying product market alleged by the plaintiff, a complaining firm that was unable to enter into hardware maintenance agreements with owners of related computers, was not improper as a matter of law.

However, the court found that the arrangement did not violate the Rule of Reason because the defendant lacked market power. Even with the manufacturer-required software support as the tying product, there was no substantial threat that the marketer would acquire market power in the most narrowly defined tied product market of its own hardware systems.[191]

Coercion

Some "conditioning" of the availability of one product or service upon the purchase of another is a necessary element of an illegal tie-in. "[W]here the buyer is free to take either product by itself there is no tying problem."[192] Thus, if the tying product is separately available, no tie-in violation will be found.[193] Different standards of proof have been used by different courts on the issue of what proof is required to establish the necessary "conditioning."

Several courts have required that the plaintiff show some degree of "coercion" to establish that a sale has been conditioned—defining "coercion" to mean

---

190. 1993-2 Trade Cas. (CCH) ¶ 70,446 (6th Cir. 1993).

191. *Compare* Lee v. Life Ins. Co. of N. Am., 1993-2 Trade Cas. (CCH) ¶ 70,366 (D.R.I. 1993) (a university charged with illegally tying a university education to mandatory health clinic coverage; claim dismissed because, among other things, the university lacked sufficient economic market power to impose a tie; students were not "locked in" to an education at the university; the health insurance requirements were not a hidden cost; students who did not want to buy health insurance had enough information before enrolling to matriculate at the university or to choose another school) *with* Forsyth v. Humana, Inc., 827 F. Supp. 1498 (D. Nev. 1993) (insurer never possessed market power within the group health insurance market; during the relevant time period, the insurer's share of the market ranged from 4 percent to 24 percent).

192. Northern Pac. Ry. v. United States, 356 U.S. 1, n.4 (1958). *Accord* Jefferson Parish Hosp. Dist. No. 2 v. Hyde, 466 U.S. 2, 12 n.7 (1984).

193. *See* General Motors v. Gibson Chem. & Oil Corp., 661 F. Supp. 567, 570 (E.D.N.Y. 1987) (buyers could purchase allegedly tied product from other sellers; seller merely recommended purchase of tied product).

that the buyer was forced or compelled to purchase a product that it did not want. A leading case for this view is *Ungar v. Dunkin' Donuts of America, Inc.,*[194] where the court stated:

> We believe that coercion is implicit—both logically and linguistically—in the concept of leverage upon which the illegality of tying is premised: the seller with market power in one market uses that power as a "lever" to force acceptance of his product in another market. If the product in the second market would be accepted anyway, because of its own merit, then, of course, no leverage is involved; in the language of the district court, there is no use of the seller's market power.[195]

The standards for proving coercion have been enunciated in different ways.[196]

Where there is express contractual evidence of a tie-in, some cases have indicated it may be unnecessary to show actual coercion to purchase an unwanted product.[197]

---

194. 531 F.2d 1211 (3d Cir.), *cert. denied*, 429 U.S. 823 (1976).

195. *Id.* at 1218. *Cf. Jefferson Parish:* "Our cases have concluded that the essential characteristic of an invalid tying arrangement lies in the seller's exploitation of its control over the tying product to force the buyer into the purchase of a tied product that the buyer either did not want at all, or might have preferred to purchase elsewhere on different terms." 466 U.S. at 12. *See also* Ogden Food Serv. Corp. v. Mitchell, 614 F.2d 1001 (5th Cir. 1980) (coercion an element of an illegal tie-in); Lupia v. Stella D'Oro Biscuit Co., 586 F.2d 1163 (7th Cir. 1978), *cert. denied*, 440 U.S. 982 (1979) (plaintiff alleges no instance where defendant forced him to purchase one product as a condition of buying another); Capital Temporaries, Inc. of Hartford v. Olsten Corp., 506 F.2d 658 (2d Cir. 1974) (no tying arrangement can exist unless the complaining party can establish that he has been coerced into purchasing something that he does not want); Tire Sales Corp. v. Cities Serv. Oil Co., 637 F.2d 467 (7th Cir. 1980), *cert. denied*, 451 U.S. 920 (1981); Response of Carolina, Inc. v. Leasco Response, Inc., 537 F.2d 1307 (5th Cir. 1976) (franchisees must establish that decision to lease computer hardware from franchisor was not voluntary but, rather, was coerced); Photovest Corp. v. Fotomat Corp., 606 F.2d 704, 723 (7th Cir. 1979), *cert. denied*, 445 U.S. 917 (1980) ("tying arrangement requires that the defendant use his economic power in the tying product to coerce the plaintiff to purchase the tied product on terms the plaintiff would not otherwise accept but for his desire to obtain the tying product"). *But see* Bell v. Cherokee Aviation Corp., 660 F.2d 1123 (6th Cir. 1981) (coercion is not an essential element of an illegal tying arrangement).

196. *Compare* Ungar v. Dunkin' Donuts of Am., Inc., 531 F.2d 1211, 1226 (3d Cir.), *cert. denied*, 429 U.S. 823 (1976) ("Where, as here, plaintiff franchisees place no reliance on express contractual tie-ins, each, individually, must prove that his purchases were coerced as an element of establishing a prima facie case of illegal tying"); Bob Maxfield, Inc. v. American Motors Corp., 637 F.2d 1033 (5th Cir.), *cert. denied*, 454 U.S. 860 (1981) (actual coercion required) *with* Moore v. Jas. H. Matthews & Co., 550 F.2d 1207, 1216–17 (9th Cir. 1977) ("some modicum of coercion [must be] shown"; "coercion may be implied from a showing that an appreciable number of buyers have accepted burdensome terms, such as a tie-in, and there exists sufficient economic power in the tying product market"); Hill v. A-T-O, Inc., 535 F.2d 1349, 1355 (2d Cir. 1976).

197. *See, e.g.*, Bogosian v. Gulf Oil Corp., 561 F.2d 434, 452 (3d Cir. 1977), *cert. denied*, 434 U.S. 1086 (1978) ("If plaintiffs are able to show that the lease agreements in use

Extrinsic evidence of coercion might also be used. Thus, in *Tire Sales Corp. v. Cities Service Oil Co.,*[198] the court found that direct threats of lease cancellation and of termination of credit card services, in addition to a precipitous decline in the plaintiff's business with the dealers, were sufficient to establish coercion. However, in a number of cases where there was no express contractual language conditioning purchase of the tied products, coercion was not found from extrinsic evidence.[199]

"Not Insubstantial" Effect on Commerce and Proof of Actual Market Foreclosure

Relevant Factor: Substantiality

The final requirement in proving an unlawful tying arrangement is showing that a "not insubstantial effect on commerce" resulted. As the Supreme Court has noted, "[T]he relevant figure is the total volume of sales tied by the sales policy under challenge, not the portion of this total accounted for by the particular plaintiff."[200] The question is "whether a total amount of business, substantial enough in terms of dollar-volume so as not to be merely *de minimis,* is foreclosed to competitors by the tie."[201] The Supreme Court has noted that $200,000 could hardly be called "insubstantial."[202]

by all defendants have similar clauses which have the practical economic effect of precluding sale of other than the lessor's gasoline, they will have shown that the purchase of gasoline was tied in to the lease of the service station"); United States v. Mercedes-Benz of N. Am., Inc., 517 F. Supp. 1369, 1384 n.22 (N.D. Cal. 1981); Bogus v. American Speech & Hearing Ass'n, 582 F.2d 277 (3d Cir. 1978); Anderson Foreign Motors, Inc. v. New England Toyota Distributors, Inc., 475 F. Supp. 973, 988 (D. Mass. 1979) (where "tie" is manifest in the express terms of a standard form contract, independent proof of individual coercion entirely unnecessary).

198. 637 F.2d 467 (7th Cir. 1980), *cert. denied*, 451 U.S. 920 (1981).

199. *See, e.g.,* Belliston v. Texaco, Inc., 455 F.2d 175 (10th Cir.), *cert. denied*, 408 U.S. 928 (1972); LaMar Printing, Inc. v. Minuteman Press Int'l, Inc., 1981-1 Trade Cas. (CCH) ¶ 64,034 (N.D. Ga. 1981) (franchise agreement clause that franchisee had no express obligation to purchase or lease equipment from franchisor or equipment manufacturer contradicted tie-in claim); Roberts v. Elaine Powers Figure Salons, Inc., 1981-1 Trade Cas. (CCH) ¶ 63,976 (E.D. Cal. 1980), *rev'd on other grounds*, 708 F.2d 1476 (9th Cir. 1983) (mere offering of a turnkey franchise package did not establish a tie-in; franchisee failed to rebut presumption that he bought turnkey operation because of the economic advantages of such an operation); McAlpine v. AAMCO Transmissions, Inc., 461 F. Supp. 1232 (E.D. Mich. 1978) (even though plaintiffs may have felt harassed and frustrated in their inability to be free from the franchisor's sales pressure, there had been no unlawful coercion); Unijax, Inc. v. Champion Int'l, Inc., 516 F. Supp. 941 (S.D.N.Y. 1981), *aff'd*, 683 F.2d 678 (2d Cir. 1982); Gowdish v. Eaton Corp., 1981-1 Trade Cas. (CCH) ¶ 63,913 (M.D.N.C.); World-Wide Volkswagen Corp. v. Autobahn Motors Co., 1980-81 Trade Cas. (CCH) ¶ 63,601 (S.D.N.Y.); E.B.E., Inc. v. Dunkin' Donuts of Am., Inc., 387 F. Supp. 737 (E.D. Mich. 1971).

200. Fortner Enters., Inc. v. United States Steel Corp., 394 U.S. 495, 502 (1969).

201. *Id.* at 501.

202. *See also* United States v. Loew's, Inc., 371 U.S. 38, 49 (1962) ($60,800 not insubstantial).

The courts have usually held, consistent with a *per se* analysis, that proof of anticompetitive effects in the tied market is unnecessary.[203] However, in certain circumstances, courts have required proof of anticompetitive effects in the tied market.[204]

Seventh Circuit Decisions

Some decisions, particularly in the Seventh Circuit, have suggested that, for a tie to be *per se* illegal, the seller must not only have market power in the tying product but must use that power to acquire market power in the tied product market.[205] The most recent pronouncements on this issue from courts in the Seventh Circuit, however, appear to have rejected this additional threshold for *per se* liability, holding that there need only be a sufficient impairment of competition in the tied product market so that a not insubstantial volume of commerce is foreclosed by the tie.[206]

Defenses or "Justifications"

Courts have suggested that tying arrangements might be lawful if the tying product must be used with the tied product and the specifications for possible substi-

---

203. *See, e.g.*, Ohio-Sealy Mattress Mfg. Co. v. Sealy, Inc., 585 F.2d 821, 835 (7th Cir. 1978), *cert. denied*, 440 U.S. 930 (1979) (rejecting need to prove anticompetitive effects except for limited circumstances in which "a given tying arrangement has no potential to foreclose access to the tied product market," *e.g.*, where seller already has a monopoly in tied market); Northern v. McGraw-Edison Co., 542 F.2d 1336, 1346 (8th Cir. 1976), *cert. denied*, 429 U.S. 1097 (1977).

204. Gonzalez v. St. Margaret's House Housing Dev. Fund Corp., 880 F.2d 1514 (2d Cir. 1989) (requiring proof of both anticompetitive effects in the tied product market and the foreclosure of a not insubstantial volume of commerce); Driskill v. Dallas Cowboys Football Club, Inc., 498 F.2d 321 (5th Cir. 1974) (no possible foreclosure of competition in market for "exhibition game tickets" for football games; failure to show any anticompetitive effects in the tied market for long term bonds); Yentsch v. Texaco. Inc., 630 F.2d 46 (2d Cir. 1980) (plaintiff testified that he would not have purchased alleged tied products—promotional items—from anyone if he did not have to buy them from Texaco; jury could assume that other Texaco dealers would have reacted the same; consequently, other suppliers of promotional items not actually foreclosed and there was no anticompetitive effect in tied market); Kingsport Motors, Inc. v. Chrysler Motors Corp., 644 F.2d 566, Bus. Franchise Guide (CCH) ¶ 7611 (6th Cir. 1981) (court required proof of a "not insubstantial" anticompetitive impact on the relevant market; no proof that alleged tie had anticompetitive effect in the market for land and facilities used for retail car sales; no proof of a general pattern requiring dealers to do business with Chrysler Realty); Community Builders, Inc. v. Phoenix, 652 F.2d 823 (9th Cir. 1981).

205. *See* Will v. Comprehensive Accounting Corp., 776 F.2d 665, 674 (7th Cir. 1985), *cert. denied*, 475 U.S. 1129 (1986); Carl Sandberg Village Condominium Ass'n No. 1 v. First Condominium Dev. Co., 758 F.2d 203, 210 (7th Cir. 1985).

206. Parts & Elec. Motors, Inc. v. Sterling Elec., Inc., 826 F.2d 712, 718 (7th Cir. 1987), *appeal dismissed after remand*, 866 F.2d 228 (7th Cir. 1988), *cert. denied*, 493 U.S. 847 (1989); A.O. Smith Corp. v. Lewis, Overbeck & Furman, 777 F. Supp. 1405, 1416 (N.D. Ill. 1991), *rev'd on other grounds*, 979 F.2d 546 (7th Cir. 1992).

tutes for the tied product cannot practicably be set forth because they would be too detailed or because disclosure of specifications would reveal trade secrets.[207]

However, quality control or superior service is not a justification for an otherwise illegal tie-in if a less restrictive way exists to ensure quality, such as product specifications or reasonable grant of approval to outside suppliers after testing of products.[208]

In one Mercedes-Benz case, the "quality control" defense was rejected where the defendant failed to prove that a less restrictive alternative did not exist.[209] However, a jury's finding in favor of the defendant was upheld in another Mercedes-Benz case.[210]

In *Kodak,* one of the "valid business justifications" proffered by the defendant for its restrictive parts policy was "to promote interbrand equipment competition by allowing Kodak to stress the quality of its service." The *Kodak* majority, however, found a triable issue of fact based on "evidence that ISOs provide quality service and are preferred by some Kodak equipment owners."

A limited "new entrant" defense has been recognized when the seller is launching a new business or is attempting to break into the market.[211] This "new

207. *See, e.g.,* Standard Oil Co. v. United States, 337 U.S. 293, 306 (1949); Siegel v. Chicken Delight, Inc., 448 F.2d 43, 51 (9th Cir. 1971), *cert. denied,* 405 U.S. 955 (1972); Susser v. Carvel Corp., 332 F.2d 505, 514–15 (2d Cir. 1964), *cert. dismissed,* 381 U.S. 125 (1965); Northern v. McGraw-Edison Co., 542 F.2d 1336 (8th Cir. 1974), *cert. denied,* 429 U.S. 1097 (1974) (goodwill-product quality defense limited to those situations in which substitutes for the tied product had to comply with such precise and detailed specifications that other manufacturers might not be able to market a product); Chock Full O'Nuts Corp., 83 FTC 570, 1973–76 Transfer Binder (CCH) ¶ 20,441 (FTC 1973) (but only as to Chock's coffee and certain baked goods actually manufactured by Chock).

208. *See, e.g.,* International Salt Co. v. United States, 332 U.S. 392, 397–98 (1947); International Business Machs. Corp. v. United States, 298 U.S. 131, 138–40 (1936) (the Court rejected defendant's argument that the tied card was necessary to the functioning of the tabulating machine, since other companies could manufacture cards meeting the necessary specifications); Kentucky Fried Chicken Corp. v. Diversified Packaging Corp., 549 F.2d 368, 376 (5th Cir. 1977) ("the franchisor must establish that the tie constitutes the method of maintaining quality that imposes the least burden on commerce").

209. Metrix Warehouse, Inc. v. Daimler-Benz Aktiengesellschaft, 828 F.2d 1033 (4th Cir. 1987), *cert. denied,* 486 U.S. 1017 (1988) (less restrictive means than the tie-in of replacement parts to new cars existed to insure quality of the replacement parts). *See also* Carpa, Inc. v. Ward Foods, Inc., 536 F.2d 39, 47 (5th Cir. 1976) ("otherwise illegal tie will not be excused if there is some less restrictive way to insure product quality such as product specifications or reasonably granting approval of outside suppliers after testing products"); Siegel v. Chicken Delight, Inc., 448 F.2d 43, 51 (9th Cir. 1971), *cert. denied,* 405 U.S. 955 (1972) (alternative of specifications is available); Moore v. Jas. H. Matthews Co., 550 F.2d 1207, 1217 (9th Cir. 1977).

210. *See* Mozart Co. v. Mercedes-Benz of N. Am., Inc., 833 F.2d 1342 (9th Cir. 1987), *cert. denied,* 488 U.S. 870 (1988) (MBNA's tie of the sale of replacement parts to sale of new cars had a sufficient business justification, *i.e.,* assuming quality control and protecting goodwill; jury's finding that no less restrictive alternative to the tie-in existed was upheld).

211. *See* United States v. Jerrold Elecs. Corp., 187 F. Supp. 545 (E.D. Pa. 1960), *aff'd per curiam,* 365 U.S. 567 (1961); *but see* Carpa, Inc. v. Ward Foods, Inc., 536 F.2d 39, 47 (5th Cir. 1976) ("once there is a competitor who can supply the tied items in the same

entrant" defense is, in any event, not available to a company that has survived its infant years.[212]

Proof of Injury

An unlawful tying arrangement may result in antitrust injury both to purchasers of the tied product and to competitors in the tied product market. Plaintiffs outside of these groups are unlikely to have standing to pursue a claim for tying damages.[213]

Some courts have measured a buyer's tying damages as "the difference between the price actually paid for the tied product and the price at which the product could have been obtained in the open market."[214] Other courts have held that a buyer can recover tying damages only by demonstrating that the combined price of the tying and tied products exceeded their combined fair market value.[215]

An increased reluctance to award damages to plaintiff-franchisees in tie-in cases has appeared. However, as the court noted in *Casey,*[216] this will not necessarily immunize conduct violative of the antitrust laws, since the "franchisor who illegally ties separate products to his trademark may still be subject to challenge not only by the government but also by potential competitors in the tied product market who can establish market foreclosure generated by the tying arrangement." Damages on a tying claim brought by a competitor of the supplier

---

quality class as the original vendor, the justification for a tying arrangement to protect the industry name evaporates"); Northern v. McGraw-Edison, 542 F.2d 1336 (8th Cir. 1976), *cert. denied,* 429 U.S. 1097 (1977).

212. *See* Siegel v. Chicken Delight, Inc., 448 F.2d at 51.

213. *See* Eureka Urethane, Inc. v. PBA, Inc., 746 F. Supp. 915, 929–30 (E.D. Mo. 1990), *aff'd,* 935 F.2d 990 (8th Cir. 1991).

214. Bell v. Cherokee Aviation Corp., 660 F.2d 1123, 1133 (6th Cir. 1981); Northern v. McGraw-Edison Co., 542 F.2d 1336, 1347 (8th Cir. 1976), *cert. denied,* 429 U.S. 1097 (1977); Gray v. Shell Oil Co., 469 F.2d 742, 751 (9th Cir. 1972), *cert. denied,* 412 U.S. 943 (1973).

215. Kypta v. McDonald's Corp., 671 F.2d 1282, Bus. Franchise Guide (CCH) ¶ 7812 (11th Cir.), *cert. denied,* 459 U.S. 857 (1982) (plaintiff must show violation caused him concrete economic injury; injury must be shown by establishing that payments for both the tied and tying product exceed their combined fair market value); Siegel v. Chicken Delight, Inc., 448 F.2d 43 (9th Cir. 1971), *cert. denied,* 405 U.S. 955 (1972); Midwestern Waffles, Inc. v. Waffle House, Inc., 734 F.2d 705 (11th Cir. 1984) (plaintiff failed to prove that it could have obtained equivalent equipment at a lower price from other sources or that value of franchise and allegedly tied equipment was less than price paid); Casey v. Diet Ctr., Inc., 590 F. Supp. 1561, 1571–74 (N.D. Cal. 1984) (franchisee does not suffer economic harm from inflated price of tied product where seller might simply have reduced that price to a competitive level and correspondingly increased price of tying product; bare comparison of royalties charged other franchisees of system did not establish noncompetitiveness of package price, absent proof that initial price of arrangement was somehow disguised); Olmstead v. Amoco Oil Co., 725 F.2d 627 (11th Cir. 1984) (following *Kypta:* no evidence existed of the fair market value of the tying and tied products combined, which is needed to determine damages).

216. 590 F. Supp. at 1573–74.

in the tied product market, whose sales were reduced or eliminated as a result of unlawful tying, will be measured by his or her lost profits.[217]

Approved Supplier

A franchise agreement that required franchisees to buy supplies from approved sources did not constitute an illegal tying arrangement, especially when the franchisor had not refused a request to approve a supplier. The franchisor did not engage in any coercive tactics leading to purchases from its affiliate, and its approved source provision was not a *per se* violation.[218] Nor did the agreement contravene the Rule of Reason because the plaintiff "failed to demonstrate adverse competitive impacts and because it . . . failed to show that Kentucky Fried's system is not a reasonable method for achieving quality control." In *Kentucky Fried Chicken,* one of the approved suppliers was an affiliate of Kentucky Fried Chicken. If there had been coercion of franchisees into purchasing the supplies in question from Kentucky Fried Chicken, there would have been a tie-in. No proof of coercion existed.[219]

However, as noted earlier, in the Second Circuit and the District of Massachusetts, it appears that a *per se* tying violation may be found even when the seller of the tying product does not have a direct financial interest in the sale of the tied product.[220]

Enforcement of an approved source of supply clause in a franchise agreement was found lawful despite injury to a potential supplier where there was no showing of adverse effect on competition.[221]

217. *See* Tic-X-Press, Inc. v. Omni Promotions Co., 815 F.2d 1407 (11th Cir. 1987); Moore v. Jas. H. Matthews & Co., 682 F.2d 830 (9th Cir. 1982).

218. Kentucky Fried Chicken Corp. v. Diversified Packaging Corp., 549 F.2d 368 (5th Cir. 1977).

219. *See also* Keener v. Sizzler Family Steak Houses, 597 F.2d 453 (5th Cir. 1979) (defendant had no ownership interest in contractor's business and received no commissions from contractor, so that its insistence on use of the contractor did not amount to illegal tying arrangement); Rodrigue v. Chrysler Corp., 421 F. Supp. 903 (E.D. La. 1976); Shaeffer v. Collins, 1980-81 Trade Cas. (CCH) ¶ 63,666 (E.D. Pa. 1980).

220. *See* Gonzalez v. St. Margaret's House Housing Dev. Fund Corp., 880 F.2d 1514, 1518 (2d Cir. 1989); Action Ambulance Serv., Inc. v. Atlanticare Health Serv. Inc., 815 F. Supp. 33 (D. Mass. 1993).

221. Fast Food Fabricators v. McDonald's Corp. (9th Cir., December 21, 1981, unpublished opinion). *See also* Martino v. McDonald's Sys., Inc., 625 F. Supp. 356 (N.D. Ill. 1985) (McDonald's requirement that franchisees buy and use Coca-Cola as their only sugar-sweetened cola upheld under Rule of Reason and *per se* analysis; no showing that the restraint lessened competition in the overall sugar-sweetened cola syrup business; "[d]esignating menu selections and specifications, without more, does not implicate the antitrust laws"); Seagood Trading Corp. v. Jerrico, Inc., 924 F.2d 1555 (11th Cir. 1991) (even if a restaurant food distributor, Martin-Brower, and a seafood shop franchisor, Long John Silver, agreed that the distributor would refuse to deal with wholesalers competing with Long John Silver in the sale of foodstuffs to franchisees, the agreement had no anticompetitive effect in the market for the sale of food to the franchisor's franchisees; two wholesale food suppliers that competed for the franchisees' business were merely seeking a "free ride" on the economics and the efficiency of the challenged arrangement).

Full Line Forcing

A variation of tying, full line forcing is an arrangement whereby a manufacturer of a line of products requires its dealers to offer for sale the manufacturer's complete line of products. It differs from exclusive dealing in that the dealer is not expressly prohibited from selling competing product lines. Full line forcing is not *per se* unlawful. It has generally been upheld under the Rule of Reason because dealers are free to handle competing product lines. Consequently it is difficult for plaintiffs to prove the amount of competition foreclosed or even that any competition was foreclosed at all.[222]

A key factor in the analysis is whether the dealer is contractually restricted from handling competitive products. In most cases, courts have used a tie-in analysis in addressing full line forcing. Using that approach, cases have upheld full line forcing because of the lack of evidence that the dealer's right to distribute competing products was restricted. "The mere existence of the requirement that the full line be stocked, without additional information about its competitive impact, does not suffice to establish an unreasonable restraint of trade."[223] "Regardless of the manufacturer's economic power, there can be no liability under a full line forcing count absent a showing of foreclosure of competition in a substantial amount of commerce under the rule in Northern Pacific."[224]

Where a full line forcing policy contains purchase requirements, it may effectively preclude a dealer from selling competitive products and therefore warrant more serious antitrust scrutiny.[225] However, a requirement to carry a representative amount of trademarked products or parts will probably be upheld.[226]

Full line forcing has also been upheld on the ground that the manufacturer did not have sufficient economic power.[227]

---

222. *See, e.g.,* Pitchford v. Pepi Inc., 531 F.2d 92, 100–01 (3d Cir. 1975); *cert. denied,* 426 U.S. 935 (1976); Colorado Pump & Supply Co. v. Febco, Inc., 472 F.2d 637, 641 (10th Cir.), *cert. denied,* 411 U.S. 987 (1973).

223. Colorado Pump & Supply v. Febco, Inc., 472 F.2d at 641.

224. Pitchford v. Pepi, 531 F.2d at 101. *See* Smith Mach. Corp. v. Hesston Corp., 878 F.2d 1290 (10th Cir. 1989), *cert. denied,* 493 U.S. 1073 (1990) (farm equipment manufacturer's full line forcing did not constitute a *per se* illegal tie-in and had to be evaluated under the Rule of Reason; because a complaining retailer was not prohibited from carrying competing equipment lines, the forcing enhanced interbrand competition by making the manufacturer's tractor, which the retailer did not want to carry, available for sale to the public; in any event, it would have to be shown that the forcing so restricted the marketing of the competitor's tractors that it impeded competition in the consumer market; even if a traditional tying analysis were applied to the forcing, the likelihood that it would cause anticompetitive forcing was virtually nil). *See also* McElhenney Co. v. Western Auto Supply Co., 269 F.2d 332, 338 (4th Cir. 1959).

225. *See, e.g.,* Miller Motors, Inc. v. Ford Motor Co., 252 F.2d 441, 449 (4th Cir. 1958) (if a requirement to carry a stock of Ford-manufactured parts to meet current demand meant current demand for all parts, then it would raise "serious antitrust questions" because it would interfere with the dealer's ability to stock rival replacement parts).

226. *See, e.g.,* Magnavox Co., 78 F.T.C. 1183 (1971) (FTC consent order permits Magnavox to require dealers to purchase, display, and maintain in inventory a representative line of its products).

227. *See* Colorado Pump & Supply Co. v. Febco, Inc., 472 F.2d 637 (10th Cir.), *cert. denied,* 411 U.S. 987 (1973).

CHAPTER 7

Counseling Franchisees

Rupert M. Barkoff and Andrew C. Selden

Contents

The complexity of legal counseling of franchisees is often overlooked. The challenge is multiplied by the comparative inability of many start-up franchisees to pay substantial legal fees. Counseling of different kinds will be needed at different stages of the franchise relationship. The lawyer will be called on as a business counselor as well as a legal advisor.

There are four stages of franchisee counseling. The first stage occurs at the time of purchase. At this point, the franchisee needs someone who is familiar with investments in business but who also has some knowledge of the idiosyncrasies of franchising. Counsel should be offered on whether a franchise is actually an appropriate investment vehicle and, if so, on comparatively evaluating different offerings.

During the ownership stage, business counseling is often required. If important franchisee-franchisor disputes arise, more traditional legal counseling is called for regarding the franchisee's legal rights to protect his or her business interests and if, when, and where it is appropriate to turn to the courts or to alternative dispute resolution for issue resolution. Negotiating skills are always a plus.

Problems may surface in a franchise system that are not peculiar to a particular franchisee but, instead, are systemwide. In these instances, the counselor must be familiar with the business arrangements within the system and understand what the bargaining positions of franchisees may be. In addition, the counselor must have an understanding of how to organize the affected franchisees and to channel those collective efforts in an effective manner. In part, the counselor will not only be playing the role of a traditional business lawyer but will to some degree be acting as a diplomat. That is, the counselor will be trying to take a diverse group (the franchisees), often with different agendas, and find common grounds on which to negotiate a mutually agreeable solution to a common problem. Once that task has been achieved, the counselor will frequently play a role, trying to negotiate a collective agreement with the franchisor.

Lastly, when a dispute has arisen and diplomacy has failed, the counselor must be skilled in dispute resolution. The dispute might be a traditional one before a court, or it might be resolved through various alternative dispute resolution procedures. Arbitration in particular has made a strong presence on the franchise scene in recent years.

This chapter addresses the problems that will be encountered in each of these situations. This focus does not lend itself to detailed discussions of legal principles, with case and statutory citations, for little on this subject exists in the cases or statutes. Rather, most of what follows is based on experience. While there are often common fact patterns, franchising is sufficiently complicated, diverse, and fluid that sound but inherently subjective judgment is called for, rather than a "right" answer. Needs, circumstances, and resources differ from one system to another, sometimes substantially. For example, as noted later, negotiating a franchise agreement with an industry leader will be a markedly different experience from negotiating with a start-up organization.

Counseling the Prospective Franchisee

The Often Limited Role of the Lawyer

Often there truly is no counseling of prospective franchisees.

Many franchisees never involve a lawyer in the process. They believe, or are told, that a lawyer will be costly and will only slow down the process or kill the deal.

In other circumstances, the franchisee has made up his or her mind long before seeking legal counseling. Here, the lawyer is being asked simply to "bless" the franchise agreement and may be further hand-tied by the client's statement that the franchisor has announced that the agreement is nonnegotiable. Therefore, the client is not willing to pay significant sums for what the client perceives to be useless advice.

Accepting engagements under these restrictions can place the lawyer in a precarious position. Franchise agreements are lengthy, complex, and subtle. They usually involve considerable investments, and they are typically one-sided documents. At best, under these circumstances, the lawyer can simply tell the client the obvious, and there is no true counseling. At worst, the lawyer may not explain in understandable terms all of the subtleties of a franchise relationship and may find out later that the client's expectations of the lawyer in the counseling process were greater than those communicated at the time of the first client-lawyer meeting.

In any case, it is important for the lawyer to carefully record the advice given to the client, while also noting any constraints put on the representation (e.g., the franchisee has already decided to buy a particular franchise, the franchisee is not interested in negotiation strategies, the deal must be signed by tomorrow).

The Counseling Process

Ideally, the lawyer is brought into the franchise acquisition at an early stage—that is, at a time when the lawyer can provide value to the client.

Know the Client

The first step in the process is to get to know your client.

1. What is the client's background?
2. What financial resources are available to the client?
3. What particular skills does the client possess or lack?
4. What are the client's objectives (i.e., why is he or she buying a franchise)?
5. Are there any time constraints on the acquisition?
6. Is the client interested in any particular industry?
7. Is the client's personality well suited to the unusual decision-making constraints of a franchise?
8. Does the client have any history with this, or any other, franchise?

Educate the Client

Next, you must educate your client on franchising generally and specifically.

1. Advise the client of written materials that he or she can purchase that will explain what franchising is all about, and encourage the client to read these.
2. Give the client a "Miranda warning" about franchising (i.e., it is a long-term relationship; to become an independent businessperson, the client must give up a significant amount of independence; there are no guarantees; owning a franchise frequently involves long hours and hard work).
3. Help the client understand the shortcomings of industry propaganda touting franchising as the world's greatest business format.
4. Advise the client of uncontrollable risks that are unique to the status of being a franchisee (e.g., your franchisor goes bankrupt or is taken over by a competitor; your franchisor stops granting renewal franchises; the franchisor's charismatic founder or CEO dies; technology leapfrogs your chain's format and the chain's systems do not evolve; the location

of your outlet becomes untenable, but your franchisor won't let you re-locate).

Clients must also educate themselves on the particular industry in which they may be interested. Encourage them to read materials about market trends and other developments in that area and point them to the directories that list franchise opportunities. These books will allow clients to get a feel for the economics of a particular industry. For example, these materials can explain what a common up-front franchise fee is, what the range of royalty and advertising fees will be, and what type of capital investment will be necessary.

Develop a Game Plan

Once the client has focused on a small number of franchise opportunities, you should help the client develop a game plan for investigating each.

First, review the offering circulars with the client. From an informational standpoint, these documents often should be viewed only as the starting point of the investigation. Focus the client's attention on things that will directly affect operating profit, equity in the business, and the system climate, such as:

1. Litigation and bankruptcy history
2. Fee structure
3. Depth of management
4. The franchisor's track record. (How many franchise failures have there been? What is the trend in new franchise sales?)
5. The financial statements (Is the franchisor making money as franchisor? Are the company units, if any, making money? Does the franchisor have staying power? What happens if sales of new franchises slow down?)
6. Availability of independent, competitive sources of supply
7. Growth opportunities, if the business is lucrative
8. Vulnerability to same-brand competitive encroachment
9. The franchise's reliability and genuine renewability (Or does an "on the then current contract" clause make transfer or "renewal" really an option on an unknown and possibly horrible *new* franchise contract, with a post-term covenant not to compete acting as a gun to the owner's head?)
10. The franchisor's readiness to participate in the National Franchise Mediation Program.

You should also encourage the client to speak with as many franchisees as possible, and perhaps even assist him or her in developing a list of questions. In particular, try to get financial performance information from the franchisees, but examine these numbers with skepticism. Ask the franchisees what other opportunities they considered, and why they made their particular choices. Also ask the franchisees if, knowing what they do now, they would again invest in the same franchise.

It is also helpful to check with regulatory officials in those states that regulate franchise sales and to determine whether there have been any complaints lodged against the franchisor. Check with the Better Business Bureau or other consumer-oriented groups to assess the reputation of the franchisor and its franchisees with customers.

If your client is discussing franchise opportunities with more than one franchisor in a particular industry (something you should encourage), ask each franchisor to identify the weaknesses and strengths of its competitors.

Frequently your clients will not be sophisticated in business. Accordingly, encourage the prospective franchisee to develop a business plan, and, if appropriate, encourage engagement of a good accountant or other financial advisor. Perhaps the most frequent cause of franchisee failures is lack of capital. Therefore, the franchisee should understand at the outset what the capital needs will be and where those needs will be accommodated.

Also, review the franchise agreement carefully with your client. Make sure that he or she has read it in its entirety (something prospective franchisees hate to do). Among other provisions, focus attention on the following:

1. All fee payments
2. The term and renewal rights
3. Whether the agreement requires the client to devote full time to the endeavor
4. Whether the client is required to purchase from designated sources, some of whom may be affiliates of the franchisor
5. Noncompetition provisions, both in-term and post-term
6. Events of default and whether adequate cure periods have been provided.
7. Any restrictions on transfer and how these affect the franchisee's estate planning
8. The protections the franchisee has against encroachment
9. The *firm* commitments of services the franchisee obtains from the franchisor before and after start-up (One of the most common complaints of franchisees is that franchisors are unclear with respect to the level and types of services they will provide once a franchisee has opened for business.)
10. The assurances the franchisee receives as to the validity of the trademark, and what happens if the franchisor loses the mark
11. Whether the franchisor has the right to impose additional fees on the franchisee unilaterally subsequent to the execution of the franchise agreement
12. The restrictions imposed on the franchisor's use of funds earmarked for advertising or marketing.

Every franchise involves tradeoffs of risk and reward (or at least opportunity). The bottom-line inquiry with any franchise offering (assuming a franchise is an appropriate investment for the particular client in the first place) is: Does *this* franchise represent a reasonable price-value relationship, viewing "price" as a combination of the fees, contractual restraints, inherent franchise risks, and system climate and "value" as a combination of economic opportunities and leveraging value of system brands, training, operating support, advertising, and the like?

The Negotiability of Franchise Agreements

Is a Franchise Agreement Negotiable?

One of the partial myths in franchising is that franchise agreements are not negotiable. As in any other area of life, negotiability is a function of many factors, and it is a mistake simply to assume that the franchisor's form of franchise agreement is fixed in concrete. As a general principle, assume that *every* franchise agreement is negotiable, giving due regard to the franchisor's economic and legal interests.

There can be some legal impediments to negotiation of a franchise agreement. Some states have statutes that prohibit a franchisor from discriminating among franchisees on various economic grounds, without objective business justification. New York franchise registration authorities used to take the position that a franchise could not be sold in that state except strictly in accordance with the terms set forth in the offering circular. This interpretation of the state's General Business Law was not upheld.[1] California requires the franchisor to jump through certain hoops if it wants to negotiate a franchise agreement.[2] Otherwise, there are no legal prohibitions on franchise agreement negotiations.

There are often sound business reasons why a franchisor does not want to negotiate a franchise agreement (in addition to the obvious one). For example, a system that has different forms of agreements in effect will be more difficult to administer. Moreover, franchisees frequently become resentful when they find that another franchisee has negotiated a "better" deal.

Negotiability will normally be a function of bargaining power, which, in turn, will be a function of supply and demand.

A highly respected, successful franchisor can write its own ticket. It will have prospective franchisees lined up outside its door and will be able to pick and choose from among them. In this circumstance, there is little reason for the franchisor to sit down at the negotiating table. Even here, however, the franchisor will often be willing to discuss matters that are peculiar to the franchisee or market. For example, if the franchise agreement for a restaurant prohibits ownership of a competing operation and the prospective franchisee already owns such an operation, the franchisor may be willing to waive this prohibition. You will not know that, however, unless you assume that some degree of "fine-tuning," "clarification," "local adaptation," or the like is possible and *ask* for it. In other words, some franchisors will not "negotiate" but they may "refine" or "clarify" the terms

---

1. The Southland Corp. v. Attorney General of New York, Bus. Franchise Guide (CCH) ¶ 9661 (N.Y. Sup. Ct. 1990).

2. 10 Cal. Code Regs. § 310.100.2, Bus. Franchise Guide (CCH) ¶ 5050.071.

of their franchise in a side agreement. Beware in these cases, though, of the franchise agreement's integration clause.

It is very common, however, for the franchisor to be of the start-up variety. Indeed, of the two thousand to three thousand franchisors in the United States, more than 90 percent are very small or very new businesses, or both. The franchisor may have sold few, or even no, franchises; start-up costs may have exceeded projections; and cash (especially your client's) may be very attractive. In this case, the franchisee may have significant leverage, especially if he or she is well-heeled financially or exploring developing several units. It will be difficult for the franchisor to turn down reasonable requests when there is cash on the table.

Most often, the facts lie somewhere between these two extremes. Some elements of a franchise probably represent core values that the franchisor, or its lawyers, just will not sacrifice.

What franchisees often do not realize is that they may bring many things to the bargaining table, financial resources being only one. Another is reputation. A franchisee who is known for his or her success as a businessperson can be an attractive catch to a new franchisor. A celebrity, too, can be a good find. Often numbers in themselves can be attractive to a franchisor, so that a commitment to enter into a multiunit development contract can be a strong attraction to a franchisor to negotiate various points. Willingness to "pioneer" a new or remote market may carry some weight. Fluency in Spanish could be important to a company seeking to develop franchises in, for example, southern California.

What May Be Negotiable?

What to negotiate for is always a question of importance, and there is no pat answer.

Fees are often difficult to negotiate. Payment terms, on the other hand, are common subjects of discussion and compromise. Many franchisors will be more flexible on initial fees than royalties.

A limitation on personal liability is often a subject ripe for compromise. The more capital a prospective franchisee is willing to inject into the business, the less likely the franchisor will be to demand personal liability, which is generally the rule and not the exception. Also, watch for indemnity clauses that have the franchisee indemnifying the franchisor for the consequences of the franchisor's acts or omissions.

Territorial protection is often negotiable, and the possible avenues to follow are numerous. Protection can include a protected radius or trade area, a right of first refusal on future neighboring units, an economic adjustment if the franchisee's unit is "cannibalized," or a "put" to the franchisor with respect to the franchise and related property if the franchisee is encroached.

Many franchise agreements require the franchisee to devote full time to the operation. Often the franchisor is simply concerned that a qualified person will run the operation, and it need not be the franchisee personally.

Forum selection and consent to jurisdiction clauses are often negotiated. If the governing law clause designates another state's law but *your* state has a franchise relationship law, you can frequently negotiate a qualifier preserving applicability of your relationship law.

Default provisions, particularly right to cure provisions, often are discussed, especially when the franchisor has written extreme positions into its agreement.

Renewal provisions, including the conditions for renewal and the term of renewal, can be negotiated. These are non-cash items and often are not viewed as having any economic costs to the franchisor in the short run. Beware of the coercive effect of the combination of a "then current contract" clause, which is a *very* blank check in the franchisor's favor, and a post-term covenant. If the "renewal" contract is unacceptable, the franchisee cannot simply allow the old deal to expire and then go his or her way but instead will face a sign-or-sell choice.

Other issues to consider are: Do the transfer provisions allow disposition to a child or to an estate planning trust? Can co-owners sell equity to each other? Can the franchisee realistically get approval for independent, competitive sources of supply?

One should be careful about a franchisor who is too willing to negotiate or who is willing to negotiate items of systemwide importance. For example, a franchisor who is willing is bargain away some of its rights to protect its trademark may be turning its system into an accident waiting to happen.

The only definitive statement that can be made about negotiating franchise agreements is that if you do not ask, you can be guaranteed that you will not get it.

Franchisee Associations

The Evolution of Franchisee Associations

Benjamin Franklin said, "We must all hang together, or assuredly we shall all hang separately."

Franchisee associations are a growing phenomenon.[3] Some associations date from the 1960s, but in a growing number of systems, associations have been formed only in the 1990s. Most associations appear to have been created at times of strife within a chain (e.g., when the franchisor suffers from financial difficulties or tries to introduce some type of change into the system).

The collective representation of franchisees within a system can take several shapes. At one extreme are franchisee advisory councils. The representatives are often handpicked by the franchisor, and the franchisor controls the group's agenda as well as the financing and flow of information. The franchisor will often pay for the travel and meeting costs of the council but rarely for the cost of inde-

---

3. There is little written about franchisee associations, the most comprehensive piece being, Gerald T. Aaron et al., *Dynamics of Franchisee Associations, in* BUILDING FRANCHISE RELATIONSHIPS: A GUIDE TO ANTICIPATING PROBLEMS, RESOLVING CONFLICTS, AND REPRESENTING CLIENTS 355 (Ann Hurwitz and Rochelle Buchsbaum Spandorf, eds., ABA 1996).

pendent professional advisors for the council. Many franchisees will view being on the council as an honor. Others may view the council members as "lackeys."

At the other extreme is the independent franchisee association that is formed by and paid for by franchisees. It sets its own agenda. Often this type of organization is feared by the franchisor because of its independence—it represents a potential limit to the franchisor's otherwise nearly absolute autonomy in managing the system in pursuit of its own economic interests.

There are various hybrids. Some associations are formed by franchisors but may truly be independent. Others may be independently created, but the franchisor may control the finances or meeting agendas. In some groups the franchisor may even be a member of the franchisee association or have rights to attend and participate in association meetings.

From the franchisor's perspective, there are two clearly different views toward associations. One school views them with a high level of suspicion. They are characterized as being analogous to unions. They are there to change the split of the pie and interfere with the franchisor's "right" to operate its system in its own unfettered discretion.

The other school views them somewhat more neutrally, recognizing that an association can be a source of consternation but that it can also be useful in furthering the system's and even the franchisor's objectives. For example, an association can provide an effective means for disseminating information to and from the franchisor; it can be used to build franchisee support for franchisor initiatives; and it can be an effective means of negotiating widespread change in franchise agreements or system direction.

Structuring an Association

Organizing an association is no easy task. Those franchisees who are content with the system will always ask why an association is necessary. Historically a common peril was a prerequisite for forming an association. Today there are several major groups that have developed more proactively out of concerns for the health or direction of their systems rather than reactively as the result of a perceived or actual threat.

From a structural standpoint, most franchisee associations are incorporated under some state's nonprofit corporation statute. This limits the liability of individual members. For federal tax purposes, a franchisee association will not qualify as a tax-exempt entity pursuant to Section 501(c)(6) of the Internal Revenue Code.[4] This means that the association must be careful in structuring its revenues and expenditures to minimize its tax liabilities.

Critical issues that must be considered when drafting the governance documents of an association include the following:

- *The basis for voting.* This can be structured on a per-unit basis, a one member–one vote basis, or some other, perhaps blended, basis.

---

4. National Mufflers Dealers Ass'n v. United States, 440 U.S. 472 (1979).

- *The definition of a member.* Will the member be the legal entity that owns the franchise, or an officer, director, or designated representative of the entity? How do you handle affiliated groups when there are overlapping but different ownership interests?
- *Dues.* Dues can be levied on a per-member basis, on the number of units owned, or as a percentage of gross revenues, among other possibilities. Sometimes maximum dues are established to encourage large franchisees to join. In other instances, hardship rules may be established to encourage participation by financially troubled franchisees.
- *Board representation.* Representation on the board of directors can be accomplished on a regional or at-large basis, or a combination of both. Sometimes provisions are drafted to ensure representation by very large or very small franchisees.

Experience suggests that it is important for the governance documents to set out a mission statement for the group and for the group to plan its activities carefully based on that statement. Some groups narrow their activities simply to communicating and negotiating with the franchisor. Other groups are more proactive and may be involved in activities such as purchasing co-ops and insurance programs and exchanging information among franchisees regarding marketing, operations, and other issues. Most groups hold conventions or other meetings on a regular basis. Sometimes these are national, and sometimes they are regional, depending in large measure on the size of the group. Sometimes these meetings will be held in conjunction with a meeting planned by the franchisor.

Because franchisee associations by their very nature may involve combinations and agreements among competitors or potential competitors, they must be careful not to run afoul of antitrust laws. Common concerns include potential claims of price-fixing and group boycotts as well as claims of market or customer market allocations.[5] Franchisee associations as such are no more or less prone to antitrust concerns than are other trade associations.

Litigation and Arbitration: When All Else Fails

The Imbalance in Judicial Remedies

Often it is not possible to settle differences of opinion between a franchisor and a franchisee amicably, and it may become necessary to resort to litigation.

Counseling the franchisee preparing for "war" is not much different from counseling any other client who is about to become embroiled in litigation. The counselor should gather the facts and perform the necessary research to assess the factual and legal strengths of the claim and the tactical considerations of where and when a claim should be asserted or if some form of alternative dispute

---

5. *See Dynamics of Franchisee Associations, in* Building Franchise Relationships, at 391–98.

resolution is desirable or perhaps mandatory. Then the franchisee must determine if he or she wants to "go to war" or simply to accept the status quo.

It must be kept in mind that a franchise relationship is an ongoing one, and there are often advantages in not rocking the boat. This may be particularly true if the franchisee wants to expand or renew and the franchisor can control whether the franchisee will be granted expansion or renewal rights. On the other hand, failure to assert rights at the appropriate moments may give off the wrong signals and lead to future overreaching by the franchisor.

The franchisee must realize that a claim against a franchisor is quite often difficult to prosecute effectively. The franchisor will often have several procedural and other advantages unrelated to the merits of the case. The franchisor may have legal counsel on retainer or experienced house counsel who handle these types of matters on a regular basis. In contrast, there is a limited number of lawyers whose practices are devoted primarily to representing franchisees. Therefore, it may be more difficult to find an experienced lawyer to represent the franchisee and, as a result, the lawyer may have to spend more time (and money) getting up to speed.

In addition, the franchise agreement may require the dispute to be resolved in a forum more favorable to the franchisor, such as one near the franchisor's headquarters, and under the laws of the franchisor's state, which may or may not include a franchise relationship law.

Frequently, the franchise agreement may have an arbitration clause in which the rules of battle have been rewritten. For example, the arbitration clause may limit the rules of discovery in a manner favorable to the franchisor or may limit the franchisee's right to recover punitive damages.

Since the franchisor (or its lawyers) drafted the franchise agreement, it is almost certainly the case that the agreement favors the franchisor. To illustrate, the franchisee's obligations in the franchise agreement are customarily spelled out in painful detail, while the franchisor's obligations are somewhat nebulous and often coupled with phrases such as "in its sole discretion" or "as the franchisor may reasonably determine."

On balance, the case law has not been very kind to franchisees. One reason is that, as noted, the franchise agreements are tilted in favor of the franchisor. Thus, when only an issue of contract interpretation is involved, the franchisee will often be at a decided disadvantage.

Common-law fraud cases, especially cases alleging that the franchisor has intentionally misled the franchisee, are possible but, as with all fraud cases, are difficult to prove. These cases require the franchisee to prove: that the franchisor made a material misrepresentation or omitted to state a material fact necessary to make the representations not misleading, where the statement was false *when made;* that the misrepresentation or omission was knowingly made or made recklessly; that the franchisee relied on the misrepresentation and the reliance was justified; and that the damages resulted from the misrepresentation. Unfulfilled promises of future performance may give rise to claims of breach of contract but not of fraud unless the plaintiff can provide that the defendant meant at the time the promise was made not to perform it.

In the 1960s and 1970s, claims against franchisors were often made on the basis of violations of federal antitrust laws, but shifts in the law over the past decade, as well as the expense of bringing these kinds of claims, have made it much more difficult for antitrust plaintiffs generally and have produced few victories for franchisees on this basis.

In the late 1970s and 1980s, claims that the franchisor owed a fiduciary duty to the franchisee were frequently asserted, but there were few franchisee victories under this theory. Today, it seems well settled that there is no general fiduciary duty of a franchisor to its franchisees, although peculiar facts could well lead a court to the opposite conclusion.

Most recently, many franchisees have asserted that a franchise agreement contains an implied covenant of good faith and fair dealing. Generally, courts have found this statement of black-letter law appealing but have been highly reluctant to use it to alter unambiguous terms of a franchise agreement.[6]

Legislative Solutions

In part, the state franchise registration or disclosure laws and the state franchise relationship laws were enacted to set a baseline, minimum level of acceptable franchisor behavior in managing franchise relations, especially in respect to ending a franchise relationship.[7]

Fifteen states have adopted laws that regulate the sale of franchises. These laws usually require the franchisor to register the franchise offering with the appropriate state administrator before the franchise can be offered or sold. The statutes also require that a disclosure statement in a prescribed form be given to the franchisee before the franchise is sold; that certain advertising materials concerning franchise sales be filed in advance with the state; that earnings claims or representations concerning the financial performance or prospects of a franchise be made in accordance with prescribed rules; and that civil and criminal remedies may exist if the statute is violated.

Nineteen states have statutes regulating to widely varying degrees various aspects of the franchise relationship. These laws often promise more than they deliver. Most were enacted in the mid-1970s in reaction to oil industry retailing retrenchment following the first OPEC oil embargo in 1973. Others responded to sporadic franchise abuses by some franchisors in the 1960s and early 1970s. The last to be enacted was the watered-down California Franchise Relations Act in 1980, until a more novel law was passed in Iowa in 1992. Except for Iowa, and to a lesser degree Indiana, Michigan, and Minnesota, these states' laws tend to address practices that were problems twenty years ago (such as unjustified termination)

---

6. An interesting case addressing this issue is Scheck v. Burger King Corp., 756 F. Supp. 543 (S.D. Fla. 1991), *on rehearing,* 798 F. Supp. 692 (S.D. Fla. 1992). The viability of *Scheck* has been called into question by Burger King Corp. v. G.R. Weaver, Bus. Franchise Guide (CCH) ¶ 10762 (S.D. Fla. 1995).

7. See the discussion of registration laws in Chapter 4 and of the relationship laws in Chapter 5.

and fail to address practices that are serious problems in some franchise systems in the 1990s (such as opportunistic abuse of franchise sourcing opportunities, encroachment, and subtle intimidation of franchisees who lead independent associations). For franchisees in states that have these laws, and whose franchises were signed, renewed, or amended after enactment of the respective law, these laws *may* afford *some* relief in *some* cases. Their effect is narrow.

In 1979 the Federal Trade Commission adopted a disclosure rule, titled "Disclosure Requirements and Prohibitions Concerning Franchising and Business Opportunity Ventures" (the FTC Rule).[8] The FTC Rule differs from the state registration and disclosure laws in that the disclosure statement is not filed with or reviewed by the FTC and there is no private cause of action if the FTC Rule is violated. The FTC Rule does not regulate the franchise relationship.

Many states have what are known as "little FTC acts," which incorporate concepts of unfair trade practices under the Federal Trade Commission Act. This kind of state law *may* allow franchisees to bring suit on what is basically a violation of the FTC Rule.[9]

Even with legislative support, litigation can be a difficult row to hoe for a franchisee. Often the aggrieved franchisee may be in a difficult financial position and may be forced to pay either his or her royalties or his or her lawyer. If the franchisee pays only the lawyer, the franchise will be in default under his or her franchise agreement, and it is vitally important in franchise litigation for the franchisee not to give the franchisor a credible basis for a sustainable retaliatory termination. Failure to pay royalties is good cause for termination regardless of the alleged provocation.

Frequently, litigation on behalf of the franchisee will be difficult for various other reasons. For example, the evidence may be based in large measure on oral exchanges between the parties, and these might not be admissible into evidence (at least in a contract dispute) if the franchise agreement contains an integration clause and if the contract is not ambiguous.[10]

It may also be difficult to get good witnesses. Other franchisees who may be similarly situated or who have relevant testimony may not be willing to be witnesses because they will have continuing relationships with the franchisor, which they might not want to jeopardize. Officers of the franchisor will be interested primarily in protecting their jobs and employers. Former officers often know where the skeletons are buried, but if they become proactive, they might be hurting their job opportunities in the industry, or they may simply want to bury the past. Because of the financial restraints that usually exist, the franchisee's lawyer will not be able to depose every witness and pursue every theory but, instead, will have to pick and choose.

One avenue the franchisee's lawyer should explore is whether there are other franchisees with similar complaints against the franchisor. An action on be-

---

8. 16 C.F.R. pt. 436.

9. *See, e.g.,* Morgan v. Air Brook Limousine, 510 A.2d 1197 (N.J. Sup. Ct., Law Div. 1986).

10. *See* Carlock v. Pillsbury Co., 719 F. Supp. 791 (D. Minn. 1989).

half of multiple franchisees can often put more pressure on the franchisor and provide a vehicle for cost sharing, thereby increasing the lawyer's ability to pursue the claims vigorously.

One alternative is a class action, but often there is not a sufficient number of similarly situated franchisees. Another obstacle to a class action is that franchise cases tend to be very fact-specific and there may be little commonality, reducing the probability of class certification. If the relief sought includes money damages, the difficulties inherent in proving the facts and amount for each class member may preclude class treatment. In addition, even if the case is ripe for a class action, it should be expected that the franchisor will aggressively oppose class certification—a fight that could easily go on for a year or more, without, in the meantime, allowing the case to proceed toward a resolution on the merits.

A second alternative is for all of the involved franchisees to be named plaintiffs. This eliminates the delays and diversion of resources over the class certification issue, but it also eliminates the leverage achieved if class certification is probable or in fact granted. A second problem with this approach is that it might destroy the franchisees' ability to proceed in federal court if any of the participating franchisees are residents of the same jurisdiction as the franchisor.

A third alternative is for the group of franchisees to choose a test case and back a volunteer lead plaintiff, in the hope that if the franchisor loses that case, it will negotiate settlements with the other franchisees, or possibly be bound by the decision in later litigation under a collateral estoppel theory.

If the franchisor is financially strapped, a fourth alternative is for the franchisees to bring actions in many jurisdictions, thereby forcing the franchisor to commit more resources to the litigation than it can afford.

Another tactic that can be successful in cases seeking *only* injunctive or declaratory relief is to bring an action in the name of the association on behalf of its members in the capacity of a representative of the members.

Conclusion

The quintessential franchise lawyer must be knowledgeable in the field of franchise law, be a business counselor, and, at times, be knowledgeable in problems of group dynamics as well as in the area of dispute resolution. When all else fails, the franchise lawyer must be expert in litigation (or know how to find a franchise-qualified litigator).

Naturally, it is difficult for any lawyer in today's society to be all these things. Therefore, it is important for counselors to be able to spot relevant issues, handle those problems within their area of expertise, and call for help when they find themselves under water.

State Franchise and Business Opportunity Statutes (as of May 1, 1997)

California

Statutes:

Franchise	Franchise Investment Law, CAL. CORP. CODE § 31000 *et seq.*, Bus. Franchise Guide (CCH) ¶ 3050.01 *et seq.*
Business Opportunity	Contracts for Seller Assisted Marketing Plans, CAL. CIV. CODE § 1812.200 *et seq.*, Bus. Franchise Guide (CCH) ¶ 3058.01.

Fees:

	Registration	Renewal	Amendment	Exemption
Franchise	$675	$450	$50	$450/$150
Business Opportunity	$100	$100	$30	N/A

State Administrator:

Franchise

Department of Corporations

Los Angeles	3700 Wilshire Boulevard Los Angeles, CA 90010 (213) 736-2741
Sacramento	1115 Eleventh Street Sacramento, CA 95814 (916) 445-7205
San Diego	1350 Front Street San Diego, CA 92101 (619) 525-4044
San Francisco	1390 Market Street San Francisco, CA 94102 (415) 557-3787

Business Opportunity   **Department of Corporations**
Office of Policy
1107 Ninth Street, 8th Floor
Sacramento, CA 95814
(916) 322-3553

Registration:

	Effective Period	Renewal Duty
Franchise	1 year	Annual. Automatically renewed if renewal application is filed 15 business days before expiration of current registration.
Business Opportunity	1 year	Annual. List of sales personnel must be updated every 6 months.

Type of Disclosure Document Accepted:

Franchise   UFOC
Business Opportunity   UFOC/FTC may be used if modified to conform to statute.

Connecticut

Statutes:

Franchise   N/A
Business Opportunity   CONN. GEN. STAT. § 36-503 *et seq.,* Bus. Franchise Guide (CCH) ¶ 3078.01 *et seq.*

Fees:

	Registration	Renewal	Amendment	Exemption
Franchise	N/A	N/A	N/A	N/A
Business Opportunity	$400	$100	N/A	N/A

State Administrator:

Franchise   N/A
Business Opportunity   Securities and Business Investment Division
Connecticut Department of Banking
44 Capitol Avenue
Hartford, CT 06106
(203) 240-8299

Registration:

	Effective Period	Renewal Duty
Franchise	N/A	N/A

Business Opportunity	Until 120 days after end of fiscal year.	Annual. Updated disclosure document must be filed within 120 days after end of fiscal year.

Type of Disclosure Document Accepted:

Franchise	N/A
Business Opportunity	UFOC/FTC

Florida

Statutes:

Franchise	FLA. STAT. § 817.416 *et seq.*, Bus. Franchise Guide (CCH) ¶ 3090.01 *et seq.* Statute limited to prohibiting misrepresentations in sale of franchises. Does not create disclosure or registration duty.
Business Opportunity	Sale of Business Opportunities Act, ch. 559, § 559.80 et seq., Bus. Franchise Guide (CCH) ¶ 3098.01 *et seq.*

Fees:

	Registration	Renewal	Amendment	Exemption
Franchise*	N/A	N/A	N/A	$100
Business Opportunity	$300	$300	$50	$100

State Administrator:

Franchise	N/A
Business Opportunity	Division of Consumer Services Department of Agriculture and Consumer Services Mayo Building, Second Floor Tallahassee, FL 32399-0800 (904) 922-2770

Registration:

	Effective Period	Renewal Duty
Franchise	1 Year	Annual
Business Opportunity	1 Year	Annual

Type of Disclosure Document Accepted:

Franchise	UFOC
Business Opportunity	UFOC/FTC

*Annual notice to claim exemption if franchisor is otherwise covered by the act.

Georgia

Statutes:

Franchise   N/A
Business Opportunity   Business Opportunity Sales Act, O.C.G.A. § 10-1-410 *et seq.,* Bus. Franchise Guide (CCH) ¶ 3108.01 *et seq.*

Fees:

	Registration	Renewal	Amendment	Exemption
Franchise	N/A	N/A	N/A	N/A
Business Opportunity	Not to exceed $100	Nonregistration state		

State Administrator:

Franchise   N/A
Business Opportunity   Office of Consumer Affairs
                         2 Martin Luther King Jr. Drive
                         Plaza Level, East Tower
                         Atlanta, GA 30334
                         (404) 656-3790

Registration:

	Effective Period	Renewal Duty
Franchise	N/A	N/A
Business Opportunity	1 Year	Annual

Type of Disclosure Document Accepted:

Franchise   N/A
Business Opportunity   UFOC/FTC

Hawaii

Statutes:

Franchise   Franchise Investment Law, HAW. REV. STAT. § 482E-1 *et seq.,* Bus. Franchise Guide (CCH) ¶ 3110.01 *et seq.*
Business Opportunity   N/A

Fees:

	Registration	Renewal	Amendment	Exemption
Franchise	$50	N/A	$50	N/A
Business Opportunity	N/A	N/A	N/A	N/A

State Administrator:

Franchise	Securities Examiner
	1010 Richards Street
	Honolulu, HI 96813
	(808) 586-2722
Business Opportunity	N/A

Registration:

	Effective Period	Renewal Duty
Franchise	1 year, registration effective 7 days after filing	On or before 90 days after fiscal year-end, franchisor must file an annual sales report (indicating number of franchises sold and proceeds derived thereupon), year-end audit, and material changes to any disclosure document.
Business Opportunity	N/A	N/A

Type of Disclosure Document Accepted:

Franchise	UFOC/FTC
Business Opportunity	N/A

Illinois

Statutes:

Franchise	Franchise Disclosure Act, III. REV. STAT., ch. 85-551, Bus. Franchise Guide (CCH) ¶ 3130.01 *et seq.*
Business Opportunity	N/A

Fees:

	Registration	Renewal	Amendment	Exemption
Franchise	$500	$100	$25/$100	N/A
Business Opportunity	N/A	N/A	N/A	N/A

State Administrator:

Franchise	Franchise Division
	Office of Attorney General
	500 South Second Street
	Springfield, IL 62706
	(217) 782-4465
Business Opportunity	N/A

Registration:

	Effective Period	Renewal Duty
Franchise	1 year	Annual. Automatically renewed if renewal application is filed 20 business days before expiration of current registration.
Business Opportunity	N/A	N/A

Type of Disclosure Document Accepted:

Franchise	UFOC/FTC
Business Opportunity	N/A

Indiana

Statutes:

Franchise	Franchise Law, IND. CODE, Title 23, § 1 *et seq.*, Bus. Franchise Guide (CCH) ¶ 3140.01 *et seq.*
Business Opportunity	Business Opportunity Transactions, IND. CODE, Title 24, § 1 *et seq.*, Bus. Franchise Guide (CCH) ¶ 3148.01 *et seq.*

Fees:

	Registration	Renewal	Amendment	Exemption
Franchise	$500	$250	$50	$50
Business Opportunity	$50	$10	$10	N/A

State Administrator:

Franchise	Franchise Section Indiana Securities Division Secretary of State Room E-111 302 West Washington Street Indianapolis, IN 46204 (317) 232-6681
Business Opportunity	Director of Consumer Protection Office of Attorney General 219 State House Indianapolis, IN 46204 (317) 232-4774

Registration:

	Effective Period	Renewal Duty
Franchise	1 year	Annual. Automatically renewed if renewal application is filed 30 days before expiration of current registration.

	Effective Period	Renewal Duty
Business Opportunity	Upon filing of disclosure documents	All material changes/amendments to disclosure documents must be filed as they occur. Annual renewal duty implied in statute (updated financials amounts to material change in disclosure).

Type of Disclosure Document Accepted:

Franchise	UFOC
Business Opportunity	UFOC/FTC may be used if modified to conform to state-required information.

Iowa

Statutes:

Franchise	N/A
Business Opportunity	Business Opportunity Promotions, IOWA CODE § 523B.1 *et seq.,* Bus. Franchise Guide (CCH) ¶ 3158.01 *et seq.*

Fees:

	Registration	Renewal	Amendment	Exemption
Franchise	N/A	N/A	N/A	N/A
Business Opportunity	$500	$250	$25	$100

State Administrator:

Franchise	N/A
Business Opportunity	Iowa Securities Bureau Second Floor Lucas State Office Building Des Moines, IA 50319 (515) 281-4441

Registration:

	Effective Period	Renewal Duty
Franchise	N/A	N/A
Business Opportunity	1 year	Annual. List of officers must be updated every 6 months.

Type of Disclosure Document Accepted:

Franchise	N/A
Business Opportunity	UFOC/FTC may be used if modified to conform to state-required information.

Kentucky

Statutes:

Franchise*	N/A
Business Opportunity	Sale of Business Opportunities, KY. REV. STAT. § 367.801 et seq., Bus. Franchise Guide (CCH) ¶ 3278.01 et seq.

Fees:

	Registration	Renewal	Amendment	Exemption
Franchise	N/A	N/A	N/A	N/A
Business Opportunity	N/A	N/A	N/A	N/A

State Administrator:

Franchise	N/A
Business Opportunity	Office of Attorney General 209 St. Clair Street Frankfort, KY 40601-1875 (502) 573-2200

Registration:

	Effective Period	Renewal Duty
Franchise	N/A	N/A
Business Opportunity	N/A	All material changes/amendments to disclosure documents must be filed as they occur. Annual renewal duty implied in statute (updated financials amounts to material change in disclosure).

Type of Disclosure Document Accepted:

Franchise	N/A
Business Opportunity	UFOC/FTC may be used if modified to conform to state-required information.

*One-time notice for franchisor claiming exemption from the act.

Maine

Statutes:

Franchise	N/A
Business Opportunity	Regulations of Sale of Business Opportunities, ME. REV. STAT. ANN. § 4691 *et seq.,* Bus. Franchise Guide (CCH) ¶ 3198.01 *et seq.*

Fees:

	Registration	Renewal	Amendment	Exemption
Franchise	N/A	N/A	N/A	N/A
Business Opportunity	$25	$10	N/A	N/A

State Administrator:

Franchise	N/A
Business Opportunity	Department of Attorney General State House Station 6 Augusta, ME 04333 (207) 626-8800

Registration:

	Effective Period	Renewal Duty
Franchise	N/A	N/A
Business Opportunity	1 year	Annual

Type of Disclosure Document Accepted:

Franchise	N/A
Business Opportunity	UFOC/FTC

Maryland

Statutes:

Franchise	Maryland Franchise Law, MD. CODE ANN. § 345 *et seq.,* Bus. Franchise Guide (CCH) ¶ 3200.01 *et seq.*
Business Opportunity	Business Opportunity Sales Act, MD. CODE ANN. § 401 *et seq.,* Bus. Franchise Guide (CCH) § 3208.01 *et seq.*

Fees:

	Registration	Renewal	Amendment	Exemption
Franchise	$500	$250	$100	$250
Business Opportunity	$250	$100	$50	N/A

State Administrator:

Franchise   Maryland Division of Securities
                   20th Floor
                   200 St. Paul Place
                   Baltimore, MD 21202
                   (410) 576-7044

Business Opportunity   Same as above.

Registration:

	Effective Period	Renewal Duty
Franchise	1 year	Annual. Automatically renewed if renewal application is filed 15 business days before expiration of current registration.
Business Opportunity	1 year	Annual

Type of Disclosure Document Accepted:

Franchise	UFOC/FTC
Business Opportunity	UFOC/FTC

Michigan

Statutes:

Franchise   Franchise Investment Law, MICH. COMP. LAWS §
                   445.1501 *et seq.*, Bus. Franchise Guide (CCH) ¶ 3220.01
                   et seq.

Business Opportunity   Consumer Protection Act, MICH. COMP. LAWS §
                   445.901 *et seq.*, Bus. Franchise Guide (CCH) ¶
                   3228.01 *et seq.*

Fees:

	Registration	Renewal	Amendment	Exemption
Franchise*	$250	$250	N/A	N/A
Business Opportunity	N/A	N/A	N/A	N/A

State Administrator:

Franchise   Consumer Protection Division
                   Antitrust and Franchise Unit
                   Michigan Department of Attorney General
                   670 Law Building
                   Lansing, MI 48913
                   (517) 373-7117

Business Opportunity   Same as above.

Registration:

	Effective Period	Renewal Duty
Franchise	1 year	Annual
Business Opportunity	N/A	N/A

Type of Disclosure Document Accepted:

Franchise	UFOC/FTC
Business Opportunity	N/A

*Requires filing of annual "notice of franchise offering."

Minnesota

Statutes:

Franchise	Minn. Stat. § 80C.01 *et seq.*, Bus. Franchise Guide (CCH) ¶ 3230.01 *et seq.*
Business Opportunity	(Treated as a "franchise" under the Franchise Law (MSA 80C.01))

Fees:

	Registration	Renewal	Amendment	Exemption
Franchise	$400	$200*	$100	N/A
Business Opportunity	(same as franchise)			

State Administrator:

Franchise	Minnesota Franchise Examiner Department of Commerce 133 East Seventh Street St. Paul, MN 55101 (612) 296-6328
Business Opportunity	(same)

Registration:

	Effective Period	Renewal Duty
Franchise	N/A	Annual report and audited financial statements must be filed within 120 days following franchisor's fiscal year-end.
Business Opportunity	N/A	(same)

Type of Disclosure Document Accepted:

Franchise	UFOC
Business Opportunity	UFOC

*Filing of annual report.

Nebraska

Statutes:

Franchise   N/A
Business Opportunity   Seller Assisted Marketing Plan Act, NEB. REV. STAT. § 59-1701 *et seq.,* Bus. Franchise Guide (CCH) ¶ 3278.01 *et seq.*

Fees:

	Registration	Renewal	Amendment	Exemption
Franchise*	N/A	N/A	N/A	$100
Business Opportunity	$100	$50	$50	$100

State Administrator:

Franchise   N/A
Business Opportunity   Department of Banking and Finance
1200 N Street
Suite 311
P.O. Box 95006
Lincoln, NE 68509
(402) 471-3445

Registration:

	Effective Period	Renewal Duty
Franchise	N/A	N/A
Business Opportunity	1 year	Annual. List of sales personnel must be updated every 6 months.

Type of Disclosure Document Accepted:

Franchise   N/A
Business Opportunity   UFOC/FTC

*One-time notice for franchisor claiming exemption from the act.

New Hampshire

Statutes:

Franchise   N/A
Business Opportunity   Distributorship Disclosure Act, N.H. REV. STAT. ANN. § 358-E.1 *et seq.,* Bus. Franchise Guide (CCH) ¶ 3298.01 *et seq.*

Fees:

	Registration	Renewal	Amendment	Exemption
Franchise	N/A	N/A	N/A	N/A
Business Opportunity	N/A	N/A	N/A	N/A

State Administrator:

Franchise	N/A
Business Opportunity	Office of Attorney General
	Consumer Protection and Antitrust Division
	25 Capitol Street
	Concord, NH 03301
	(602) 271-3641

Registration:

	Effective Period	Renewal Duty
Franchise	N/A	N/A
Business Opportunity	N/A	All material changes/amendments to disclosure documents must be immediately filed as they occur. Annual renewal duty implied in statute (updated financials amounts to material change in disclosure).

Type of Disclosure Document Accepted:

Franchise	N/A
Business Opportunity	UFOC/FTC

New York

Statutes:

Franchise	N.Y. GEN. BUS. LAW § 680.1 *et seq.*, Bus. Franchise Guide (CCH) ¶ 3320.01 *et seq.*
Business Opportunity	N/A

Fees:

	Registration	Renewal	Amendment	Exemption
Franchise	$750	$150	$150	N/A
Business Opportunity	N/A	N/A	N/A	N/A

State Administrator:

Franchise	Bureau of Investor Protection and Securities
	New York State Department of Law
	120 Broadway, 23rd Floor
	New York, NY 10271
	(212) 416-8211
Business Opportunity	N/A

Registration:

	Effective Period	Renewal Duty
Franchise	1 year	Annual sales report providing name and address of each franchise sold, date of sale, and price paid must be filed within 120 days after franchisor's fiscal year-end, plus updated disclosure documents and audited financial statements must be filed at this time.
Business Opportunity	N/A	N/A

Type of Disclosure Document Accepted:

Franchise   UFOC/FTC and New York addendum
Business Opportunity   N/A

North Carolina

Statutes:

Franchise   N/A
Business Opportunity   Business Opportunity Sales, N.C. GEN STAT. § 66-94 *et seq.*, Bus. Franchise Guide (CCH) ¶ 3338.01 *et seq.*

Fees:

	Registration	Renewal	Amendment	Exemption
Franchise	N/A	N/A	N/A	N/A
Business Opportunity	$10	N/A	N/A	N/A

State Administrator:

Franchise   N/A
Business Opportunity   Secretary of State
                       Securities Division
                       Room 302
                       300 North Salisbury Street
                       Raleigh, NC 27611

Registration:

	Effective Period	Renewal Duty
Franchise	N/A	N/A
Business Opportunity	1 year	Annual

Type of Disclosure Document Accepted:

Franchise   N/A
Business Opportunity   UFOC/FTC

North Dakota

Statutes:

Franchise   Franchise Investment Law, N. DAK. CENT. CODE § 51-19-01 *et seq., Bus. Franchise Guide (CCH)* ¶ 3340.01 *et seq.*

Business Opportunity N/A

Fees:

	Registration	Renewal	Amendment	Exemption
Franchise	$250	$100	$50	$100/$50
Business Opportunity	N/A	N/A	N/A	N/A

State Administrator:

Franchise   Franchise Examiner
Office of Commissioner of Securities
Fifth Floor
600 East Boulevard
Bismarck, ND 58505
(701) 224-4712

Business Opportunity N/A

Registration:

	Effective Period	Renewal Duty
Franchise	1 year	Annual. Automatically renewed if renewal application is filed 15 business days before expiration of current registration.
Business Opportunity	N/A	N/A

Type of Disclosure Document Accepted:

Franchise   UFOC/FTC
Business Opportunity N/A

Ohio

Statutes:

Franchise   N/A

Business Opportunity Business Opportunity Purchasers Protection Act, OHIO REV. CODE ANN. § 1334.01 *et seq.*, Bus. Franchise Guide (CHH) ¶ 3340.01 *et seq.* (Disclosure obligation only; no registration required.)

Fees:

	Registration	Renewal	Amendment	Exemption
Franchise	N/A	N/A	N/A	N/A
Business Opportunity	N/A	N/A	N/A	N/A

State Administrator:

Franchise   N/A
Business Opportunity   Office of Attorney General
                        Consumer Protection Section
                        30 East Broad Street, 25th Floor
                        Columbus, OH 43266
                        (614) 466-3910

Registration:

	Effective Period	Renewal Duty
Franchise	N/A	N/A
Business Opportunity	N/A	N/A (No filing, although disclosures must be updated as material changes occur.)

Type of Disclosure Document Accepted:

Franchise   N/A
Business Opportunity   UFOC/FTC

Oklahoma

Statutes:

Franchise   N/A
Business Opportunity   Business Opportunity Sales Act, OK. STAT., Title 71, ch. 4,
                        § 801 *et seq.*, Bus. Franchise Guide (CCH) ¶ 3368.01 *et seq.*

Fees:

	Registration	Renewal	Amendment	Exemption
Franchise	N/A	N/A	N/A	N/A
Business Opportunity	$250	$150	N/A	N/A

State Administrator:

Franchise   N/A
Business Opportunity   Oklahoma Department of Securities
                        2401 North Lincoln Boulevard
                        Will Rogers Building
                        Suite 408
                        Oklahoma City, OK 73105
                        (405) 235-0230

Registration:

	Effective Period	Renewal Duty
Franchise	N/A	N/A
Business Opportunity	1 year	Annual. In addition, registrants are required by rule to submit sales reports not later than 6 months following the effective date of registration or renewal, together with a $10 filing fee.

Type of Disclosure Document Accepted:

Franchise	N/A
Business Opportunity	UFOC/FTC

Oregon

Statutes:

Franchise	Oregon Transactions, OR. REV. STAT. § 650.005 *et seq.*, Bus. Franchise Guide (CCH) ¶ 3370.01 *et seq.* (Disclosure obligation only; no registration required.)
Business Opportunity	N/A

Fees:

	Registration	Renewal	Amendment	Exemption
Franchise	N/A	N/A	N/A	N/A
Business Opportunity	N/A	N/A	N/A	N/A

State Administrator:

Franchise	Division of Finance and Corporate Securities 21 Labor and Industries Building Salem, OR 97310 (503) 378-4387
Business Opportunity	N/A

Registration:

	Effective Period	Renewal Duty
Franchise	N/A	Disclosure statements are effective for a 12-month period only and must be updated as of January 1 of each calendar year or within 120 days of fiscal year-end. No filing requirements.
Business Opportunity	N/A	N/A

Type of Disclosure Document Accepted:

Franchise   UFOC/FTC
Business Opportunity   N/A

Rhode Island

Statutes:

Franchise   Franchise and Investment Act, General Laws of Rhode
                         Island, 1956, Title 19, ch. 28, § 19-28-1 *et seq.*, Bus.
                         Franchise Guide (CCH) ¶ 3390.01 *et seq.*
Business Opportunity   N/A

Fees:

	Registration	Renewal	Amendment	Exemption
Franchise	$500	$250	$100	$300
Business Opportunity	N/A	N/A	N/A	N/A

State Administrator:

Franchise   Securities Examiner
                         Division of Securities
                         Suite 232
                         233 Richmond Street
                         Providence, RI 02903
                         (401) 277-3048
Business Opportunity   N/A

Registration:

	Effective Period	Renewal Duty
Franchise	1 year	Annual. Automatically renewed if renewal application is filed 15 business days before expiration of current registration.
Business Opportunity	N/A	N/A

Type of Disclosure Document Accepted:

Franchise   UFOC
Business Opportunity   N/A

South Carolina

Statutes:

Franchise   N/A
Business Opportunity   Business Opportunity Sales Act, S.C. CODE § 39-57-10 *et
                         seq.*, Bus. Franchise Guide (CCH) ¶ 3408.01 *et seq.*

Fees:

	Registration	Renewal	Amendment	Exemption
Franchise	N/A	N/A	N/A	N/A
Business Opportunity	$100	N/A	N/A	N/A

State Administrator:

Franchise	N/A
Business Opportunity	Secretary of State
	Deputy Securities of Commissioner
	816 Keenan Building
	Columbia, SC 29201

Registration:

	Effective Period	Renewal Duty
Franchise	N/A	N/A
Business Opportunity	1 year	Annual

Type of Disclosure Document Accepted:

Franchise	N/A
Business Opportunity	UFOC/FTC may be used if modified to conform to state-required information.

South Dakota

Statutes:

Franchise	Franchises for Brand-Name Goods and Services, S.D. COMP. LAWS ANN. § 37-5A-1 *et seq.*, Bus. Franchise Guide (CHH) ¶ 3410.01 *et seq.*
Business Opportunity	Model Business Opportunities Act, House Bill No. 1076, Bus. Franchise Guide (CCH) ¶ 3410.01 *et seq.*

Fees:

	Registration	Renewal	Amendment	Exemption
Franchise	$250	$100*	$50	N/A
Business Opportunity	$100	$100	N/A	N/A

State Administrator:

Franchise	Franchise Administrator
	Division of Securities
	c/o 118 West Capitol
	Pierre, SD 57501
	(605) 773-4013
Business Opportunity	Same as above.

Registration:

	Effective Period	Renewal Duty
Franchise	N/A	Annual report must be filed within 120 days after franchisor's fiscal year-end. Material changes must be filed within 30 days of occurrence.
Business Opportunity	1 year, beginning 10 days after filing	Annual

Type of Disclosure Document Accepted:

Franchise	UFOC
Business Opportunity	UFOC/FTC may be used if modified to conform to state-required information.

*Filing of annual report.

Texas

Statutes:

Franchise	N/A
Business Opportunity	Business Opportunities Act, TEX. REV. CIV. STAT. Act. 16.01 *et seq., Bus. Franchise Guide (CCH)* ¶ 3438.01 *et seq.* 5430.01 *et seq.*

Fees:

	Registration	Renewal	Amendment	Exemption
Franchise*	N/A	N/A	N/A	$25
Business Opportunity	$195	$25	$25	$25

State Administrator:

Franchise	N/A
Business Opportunity	Secretary of State Statutory Document Section P.O. Box 12887 Austin, TX 78711-3563 (512) 475-1769

Registration:

	Effective Period	Renewal Duty
Franchise	N/A	N/A
Business Opportunity	N/A	Disclosure statements must be updated and filed every 6 months.

Type of Disclosure Document Accepted:

Franchise   N/A

Business Opportunity   UFOC/FTC

*One-time notice filing for franchisor claiming exemption from the act.

Utah

Statutes:

Franchise   N/A

Business Opportunity   Business Opportunity Disclosure Act, UTAH CODE ANN. § 13-15-1 *et seq.*, Bus. Franchise Guide (CCH) ¶ 3448.01 *et seq.*

Fees:

	Registration	Renewal	Amendment	Exemption
Franchise*	N/A	N/A	N/A	$100
Business Opportunity	$200	N/A	N/A	$100

State Administrator:

Franchise   N/A

Business Opportunity   Department of Commerce
Division of Consumer Protection
160 East Three Hundred South
P.O. Box 45804
Salt Lake City, UT 84145-0804
(801) 530-6601

Registration:

	Effective Period	Renewal Duty
Franchise	N/A	N/A
Business Opportunity	N/A	Annual renewal duty implied in statute (updated financials amounts to material change in disclosure).

Type of Disclosure Document Accepted:

Franchise   N/A

Business Opportunity   UFOC/FTC

*Annual notice to claim exemption if franchisor is otherwise covered by the act.

Virginia

Statutes:

Franchise	Retail Franchising Act, VA. CODE § 13.1-557 *et seq.*, Bus. Franchise Guide (CCH) ¶ 3460.01 *et seq.*
Business Opportunity	Business Opportunity Sales Act, VA. CODE § 59.1-262 *et seq.*, Bus. Franchise Guide (CCH) ¶ 3468.01 *et seq.*

Fees:

	Registration	Renewal	Amendment	Exemption
Franchise	$500	$250	$100	N/A
Business Opportunity	N/A No registration	N/A	N/A	N/A

State Administrator:

Franchise	Chief Examiner State Corporation Commission Ninth Floor 1300 East Main Street Richmond, VA 23219 (804) 371-9051
Business Opportunity	Same as above.

Registration:

	Effective Period	Renewal Duty
Franchise	1 year	Annual. Automatically renewed if renewal application is filed 30 business days before expiration of current registration.
Business Opportunity	N/A	N/A

Type of Disclosure Document Accepted:

Franchise	UFOC
Business Opportunity	UFOC/FTC may be used if modified to conform to state-required information.

Washington

Statutes:

Franchise	Franchise Investment Protection Act, WASH. REV. CODE § 19.100.010 *et seq.*, Bus. Franchise Guide (CCH) ¶ 3470.01 *et seq.*
Business Opportunity	Business Opportunity Fraud Act, WASH. REV. CODE § 19.110.010 *et seq.*, Bus. Franchise Guide (CCH) ¶ 3478.01 *et seq.*

Fees:

	Registration	Renewal	Amendment	Exemption
Franchise	$600	$100	$100	$100/$100
Business Opportunity	$200	$125	$100	N/A

State Administrator:

Franchise	Acting Administrator
	Department of Financial Institutions
	Securities Division
	P.O. Box 9033
	Olympia, WA 98507-9033
	(206) 902-8760
Business Opportunity	Same as above.

Registration:

	Effective Period	Renewal Duty
Franchise	1 year	Annual. Automatically renewed if renewal application is filed 15 business days before expiration of current registration.
Business Opportunity	1 year	Annual

Type of Disclosure Document Accepted:

Franchise	UFOC
Business Opportunity	UFOC/FTC may be used if modified to conform to state-required information.

Wisconsin

Statutes:

Franchise	Wisconsin Franchise Investment Law, WIS. STAT. § 553.01 *et seq.*, Bus. Franchise Guide (CCH) ¶ 3490.01 *et seq.*
Business Opportunity	N/A

Fees:

	Registration	Renewal	Amendment	Exemption
Franchise	$400	$200	$200	$200*
Business Opportunity	N/A	N/A	N/A	N/A

State Administrator:

Franchise	Franchise Administrator
	Securities and Franchise Registration
	Wisconsin Securities Commission

P.O. Box 1768
Madison, WI 53701
(608) 266-8559

Business Opportunity   N/A

Registration:

	Effective Period	Renewal Duty
Franchise	1 year	Annual. Automatically renewed if renewal application is filed 15 business days before expiration of current registration.
Business Opportunity	N/A	N/A

Type of Disclosure Document Accepted:

Franchise   UFOC
Business Opportunity   N/A

*For opinion confirming exemption.

Franchise Relationship Law Citations and Popular Names

Arkansas Franchise Practices Act, ARK. STAT. ANN. §§ 4-72-201 to -210 (1987).

California Franchise Relations Act, CAL. BUS. & PROF. CODE §§ 20000–20043 (West 1981).

Trading Stamps, Mail Order, Franchises, Credit Programs, Subscriptions Act, CONN. GEN. STAT. ANN. §§ 42-133e to -133h (1972).

Delaware Franchise Security Law, DEL. CODE. ANN. tit. 6 §§ 2551–2556 (1953).

Franchising Act of 1988, D.C. CODE ANN. §§ 29-1201 to -1208 (1989).

Franchise Investment Act, HAW. REV. STAT. § 482E-6 (1978).

Franchise Disclosure Act of 1987, ILL. REV. STAT. ch. 815, para. 705/18 to 705/20 (1992).

Deceptive Franchise Practices Act, IND. CODE ANN. § 23-2-2.7-1 to -7 (1987).

Franchise Act, IOWA CODE §§ 523H.1 to 523H.17 (1995).

Franchise Investment Law, MICH. COMP. LAWS § 445.1527 (1984).

Franchise Act, MINN. STAT. § 80C.14 (1986).

Pyramid Sales Scheme Act, MISS. CODE ANN. §§ 75-24-51 to -61 (1975).

Pyramid Sales Scheme Act, MO. REV. STAT. §§ 407.400 to .420 (1975).

Franchise Practices Act, NEB. REV. STAT. §§ 87-401 to -410 (1978).

Franchise Practices Act, N.J. REV. STAT. §§ 56:10–1 to :10–12 (1971).

Retail Franchising Act, VA. CODE ANN. § 13.1-564 (Michie 1993).

Franchise Investment Protection Act, WASH. REV. CODE §§ 19.100.180 to .190 (1980).

Wisconsin Fair Dealership Law, WIS. STAT. §§ 135.01 to .07 (1985).

Dealers' Contracts Law, P.R. LAWS ANN. tit. 10, § 14–278 (1964).

Franchised Business Law, V.I. CODE ANN. tit. 12A §§ 2-130 to -139 (1979).

Types of Franchise Relationship Laws

This chart shows which franchise relationship laws include in their definition of a "franchise" a trademark license, a marketing plan or community of interest, and a fee. It also shows which states regulate the relationship between franchisors and franchisees as part of their registration and disclosure laws, using the same definition of a "franchise" for both purposes, and which ones have separate registration and disclosure laws.

	Trademark License	Marketing Plan/Community of Interest	Fee	Part of Disclosure Law	Separate Disclosure Law
Arkansas	√				
California		M	√		√*
Connecticut		M			
Delaware			√		
District of Columbia	√	C	√		
Hawaii	√	C	√	√	
Illinois		M	√	√	
Indiana		M	√	√	
Iowa		M	√		
Michigan		M	√	√	
Minnesota		C	√	√	
Mississippi	√	C	√		
Missouri	√	C			
Nebraska	√	C	√		
New Jersey	√	C			
Virginia		M	√	√	
Washington	√	M	√	√	
Wisconsin		C			√

M = Marketing plan definition of "franchise."
C = Community of interest definition of "franchise."
* Same definition as in Franchise Investment Law.

The following states require franchise registration or disclosure but do not have franchise relationship laws: Maryland, New York, North Dakota, Oregon, Rhode Island, and South Dakota.

Statutory Examples of Good Cause for Termination

	Grounds	States
1.	Failure to comply with the requirements imposed by the franchisor, or breach of the franchise agreement.	Arkansas, California, Connecticut, District of Columbia, Hawaii, Illinois, Indiana, Iowa, Michigan, Minnesota, Nebraska, New Jersey, Washington, Wisconsin
2.	Voluntary abandonment of the franchise.	Arkansas, California, Connecticut, Illinois, Iowa, Minnesota, Nebraska, New Jersey, Washington
3.	Criminal conviction of the franchisee on a charge related to the franchise business.	Arkansas, California, Connecticut, Illinois, Iowa, Minnesota, Nebraska, New Jersey, Washington
4.	The franchisee's insolvency or bankruptcy, or assignment for the benefit of creditors.	Arkansas, California, Illinois, Iowa, Minnesota, Nebraska, Washington
5.	Failure of the franchisee to pay sums due to the franchisor.	Arkansas, California, Nebraska
6.	Loss of either party's right to occupy the premises.	Arkansas, Nebraska
7.	Material misrepresentation by the franchisee relating to the franchise.	California, Nebraska, Iowa
8.	Conduct by the franchisee that materially impairs the goodwill of the franchise business.	California, Minnesota
9.	The franchisee's repeated noncompliance with the requirements of the franchise.	California, Illinois, Iowa
10.	Imminent danger to public health or safety.	California, Nebraska, Iowa
11.	Failure to act in good faith and in a commercially reasonable manner.	Arkansas
12.	Impairment by the franchisee of the franchisor's trademark or trade name.	Arkansas
13.	Written agreement to terminate.	California, Iowa

14. The franchisee's failure to comply   California
    with any law applicable to the op-
    eration of the franchise.

15. Governmental seizure of the fran-   California, Iowa
    chised business or foreclosure by a
    creditor.

Procedural Requirements for Termination and Nonrenewal

Arkansas

The franchisor may not terminate or fail to renew without giving the franchisee ninety days' notice. In the case of termination, the franchisor must give the franchisee thirty days in which to cure.

Notice and cure are not required for termination due to:

(1) voluntary abandonment,
(2) criminal conviction,
(3) any act by the franchisee that substantially impairs the franchisor's trademark or trade name,
(4) institution of insolvency or bankruptcy proceedings by or against a franchisee or an assignment for the benefit of creditors,
(5) loss of either party's rights to occupy the premises, or
(6) failure to pay sums due to the franchisor within ten days after receipt of notice.

A ten-day cure period is required for termination or failure to renew due to:

(1) repeated deficiencies, within a twelve-month period, giving rise to good cause based on noncompliance with the franchisor's requirements, or
(2) failure by the franchisee to act in good faith and in a commercially reasonable manner.

California

Termination: The franchisor must give notice "and a reasonable opportunity, which in no event need be more than 30 days, to cure." The notice period is not specified.

Nonrenewal: The franchisor must give the franchisee at least 180 days' notice of its intention not to renew.

Connecticut

The franchisor may not terminate or fail to renew without giving the franchisee sixty days' notice.

Six months' notice is required if the franchisor elects not to renew because the franchisor intends to sell or lease the premises on which the franchise is located, or to convert the premises to another use, or the lease to the franchisor is about to expire.

Thirty days' notice is required in the case of termination or failure to renew due to voluntary abandonment by the franchisee.

Immediate notice is permitted if the cause for termination or nonrenewal is the conviction of the franchisee of a criminal offense directly related to the franchise business.

No opportunity to cure is required.

Delaware

Ninety days' notice is required both for termination and nonrenewal. No opportunity to cure is required.

District of Columbia

The franchisor may not terminate or fail to renew without giving the franchisee sixty days' notice. The franchisee must be afforded sixty days to cure before any termination or failure to renew.

Notice may be given fifteen business days in advance when the grounds are voluntary abandonment.

Immediate notice is permitted in the case of criminal conviction.

Written notice must be given to the Advisory Neighborhood Commission and ward councilmember sixty days before closing.

Hawaii

Termination requires written notice and an opportunity to cure "within a reasonable period of time."

There is no notice requirement for nonrenewal.

Illinois

Termination requires notice "and a reasonable opportunity to cure such default, which in no event need be more than 30 days."

Six months' notice is required for nonrenewal.

Indiana

"Unless otherwise provided in the agreement," termination and nonrenewal both require ninety days' notice.

No opportunity to cure is required.

Iowa

The franchisor may not terminate without giving written notice, stating the reasons for termination, and a reasonable period of time to cure the default, which in no event shall be less than thirty days or more than ninety days.

The franchisor may terminate upon notice, without an opportunity to cure, if:

(1) the franchisee is declared bankrupt or there is a judicial determination of insolvency,

(2) the franchisee voluntarily abandons the franchise,

(3) the franchisor and franchisee agree in writing to terminate,

(4) the franchisee knowingly makes a material misrepresentation or omission relating to acquisition or ownership of the franchise,

(5) the franchisee repeatedly fails to comply with the same material provision of a franchise agreement,

(6) the franchised business is seized by a government authority,

(7) the franchisee is convicted of a felony that materially and adversely affects the operation of the franchise, or

(8) the franchisee operates the business in a manner that imminently endangers public health and safety.

Michigan

Termination requires notice "and a reasonable opportunity, which in no event need be more than 30 days, to cure such failure."

There are no procedural requirements with respect to nonrenewal.

Minnesota

Termination requires ninety days' notice and failure to cure within sixty days of receipt of the notice.

Notice is effective immediately in the following cases:

(1) voluntary abandonment by the franchisee,

(2) conviction of the franchisee of an offense directly related to the franchise business, or

(3) failure to cure a default that materially impairs the goodwill associated with the franchisor's mark or name after being given notice and twenty-four hours to cure.

Nonrenewal requires 180 days' notice.

Mississippi

Termination and nonrenewal require ninety days' notice; but ninety days' notice is not required in the following cases:

(1) criminal misconduct,

(2) fraud,

(3) abandonment,

(4) bankruptcy or insolvency of the franchisee, or

(5) giving a no account or insufficient funds check.

No opportunity to cure is required.

Missouri

Termination and nonrenewal require ninety days' notice; but ninety days' notice is not required in the following cases:

(1) criminal misconduct,
(2) fraud,
(3) abandonment,
(4) bankruptcy or insolvency of the franchisee, or
(5) giving a no account or insufficient funds check.

No opportunity to cure is required.

Nebraska

Termination and nonrenewal require sixty days' notice, or fifteen days' notice in the case of voluntary abandonment. Immediate notice is permitted in the following cases:

(1) conviction of the franchisee of an offense directly related to the franchise business,
(2) insolvency or the institution of bankruptcy or receivership proceedings,
(3) default in payment or failure to account for proceeds of a sale of goods by the franchisee,
(4) falsification of records or reports,
(5) existence of imminent danger to public health or safety, or
(6) loss of the right to occupy the premises.

No opportunity to cure is required.

New Jersey

Termination and nonrenewal require notice at least sixty days in advance. Fifteen days' notice is permitted in the case of voluntary abandonment.

Immediate notice is permitted where the grounds are conviction of the franchisee of an offense directly related to the franchise business.

No opportunity to cure is required.

Virginia

There is no statutory notice or cure requirement.

Washington

The franchisor may terminate only after giving the franchisee notice and a reasonable opportunity, which in no event need be more than thirty days, to cure, or if the default cannot reasonably be cured within thirty days, and the franchisee has failed to initiate within thirty days substantial and continuing action to cure the default.

No notice or cure are required in the following circumstances:

    (1) after three willful and material breaches of the same term of the franchise agreement within a twelve-month period, of which the franchisee has been given notice and an opportunity to cure,

    (2) if the franchisee is adjudicated bankrupt or insolvent,

    (3) assignment for the benefit of creditors,

    (4) voluntary abandonment, or

    (5) conviction of violating a law relating to the franchise business.

Nonrenewal requires one year's notice.

Wisconsin

Termination and nonrenewal require ninety days' notice and must give the dealer sixty days in which to cure.

No notice is required if termination or nonrenewal is for insolvency, an assignment for the benefit of creditors, or bankruptcy.

If the reason is nonpayment or sums due, a ten-day cure requirement is required.

Examples of Other Unlawful Practices

Unlawful Practice	States
1. Restricting the right of free association among franchisees for any lawful purpose.	Arkansas, California, Hawaii, Illinois, Iowa, Michigan, Minnesota, Nebraska, New Jersey, Washington
2. Discriminating between franchisees in the charges for royalties, goods, services, equipment, rentals, advertising services, or in any other business dealing, unless such discrimination is based on reasonable distinctions and is not arbitrary.	Hawaii, Illinois, Indiana, Minnesota, Washington
3. Imposing unreasonable standards of performance on a franchisee.	Hawaii, Minnesota, Nebraska, New Jersey, Washington
4. Requiring or prohibiting any change in management of any franchisee except for reasonable cause.	Arkansas, Minnesota, Nebraska, New Jersey
5. Obtaining money, goods, services, or any other benefit from any other person with whom the franchisee does business on account of such business except under certain conditions (e.g., disclosure).	Hawaii, Indiana, Washington
6. Requiring a franchisee to purchase goods or services from the franchisor or from designated sources of supply unless such purchase is reasonably necessary for a lawful purpose justified on business grounds.	Hawaii, Indiana, Iowa, Washington
7. Establishing a similar business or granting a franchise for the establishment of a similar business at a location within the franchisee's exclusive territory, if any.	Hawaii, Indiana, Minnesota, Washington
8. Requiring that arbitration or litigation be conducted outside the state.	Michigan, Washington
9. Enforcing any unreasonable covenant not to compete after the franchise relationship ceases to exist.	Indiana, Minnesota

10.	Providing for a term of less than three years and for successive terms of not less than three years thereafter unless cancelled, terminated, or not renewed pursuant to this section.	Connecticut
11.	Allowing substantial modification of the franchise agreement by the franchisor without the consent in writing of the franchisee.	Indiana
12.	Limiting litigation brought for breach of the agreement in any manner whatsoever.	Indiana
13.	Requiring the franchisee to participate in any advertising or promotional campaign at an expense that is indeterminate, determined by a third party, or determined by a formula, unless the franchise agreement specifies the maximum amount that the franchisee may be required to pay.	Indiana
14.	Selling, renting, or offering to sell to a franchisee any product or service for more than a fair and reasonable price.	Washington
15.	Requiring a transfer fee in excess of an amount necessary to compensate the franchisor for expenses incurred as a result of transfer.	Washington
16.	Substantially changing the competitive circumstances of a dealership agreement without good cause.	Wisconsin

About the Editors

RUPERT M. BARKOFF is a member of the law firm of Kilpatrick Stockton LLP of Atlanta, Georgia, and specializes in the practice of franchise law. A native of New Orleans, Louisiana, he received his B.A. degree from the University of Michigan in 1970, graduating with high distinction. He received his J.D. degree, graduating *magna cum laude* in 1973, from the University of Michigan Law School where he was a member of the Order of the Coif and articles editor of the *Michigan Law Review.*

Mr. Barkoff served as chair of the ABA Forum on Franchising from 1989 to 1992, and as its immediate past chair from 1992 to 1995. He first joined the Forum's Governing Committee in 1986 and before that served as an associate editor of the Forum's *Franchise Law Journal.* He is the co-editor of the ABA *Franchise Law Bibliography* (1st ed.). He has been an active member of the Franchising Committee of the ABA Section of Antitrust Law since 1981. Mr. Barkoff was also chair of the Franchising Subcommittee of the ABA Business Section's Small Business Committee and acted as liaison between the ABA and the Drafting Committee of the National Conference of Commissioners on Uniform State Laws' Franchise and Business Opportunities Act project. He served as chair of the ABA Standing Committee on Forums from 1992 to 1996 and presently serves as a member of the Industry Advisory Committee to the North American Securities Administrators Association's Franchise and Business Opportunities Committee. He has written over thirty articles on franchise law.

In addition to franchise law, Mr. Barkoff's areas of practice include corporate, securities, unsecured financing, distribution matters, and general business counseling.

ANDREW C. SELDEN is a shareholder in Briggs and Morgan, P.A., Minneapolis, Minnesota. He served as chair of the ABA Forum on Franchising from 1985 to 1989, as a member of its Governing Committee from 1983 to 1989, and as its immediate past chair from 1989 to 1992. Mr. Selden's practice is concentrated in the area of advising franchisors and various franchisee associations and purchasing cooperatives. He also advises manufacturers on antitrust, trademark, and product distribution and dealership matters.

Mr. Selden was the reporter of the Uniform Franchise and Business Opportunities Act promulgated by the National Conference of Commissioners on Uniform State Laws. He is a member, and was chair (1983–87), of the Industry Advisory Committee to the Franchise Regulation Committee of the North American Securities Administrators Association. He has published several articles on franchising in the *Franchise Law Journal, Business Lawyer, Franchise Legal Digest,* and other publications and has spoken at numerous programs on franchising and antitrust issues sponsored by the Forum on Franchising, the International Franchise Association, the Practising Law Institute, and the ABA Sections of Antitrust Law and Intellectual Property Law. He is a member of the Legal/Legislative Committee of the International Franchise Association.

Mr. Selden is chair of the Board of Directors of the Better Business Bureau of Minnesota. He is a past chair of the Hennepin County Bar Association Business Law and Franchising Committee. Mr. Selden is also president of the Minnesota Association of Railroad Passengers.

About the Contributors

JUDITH M. BAILEY is a partner in the law firm of Quarles & Brady, which has offices in Wisconsin, Arizona, and Florida. She has specialized in licensing and intellectual property matters throughout her professional career. She also serves as counsel to the Arizona Licensor/Franchisor Association, the first state franchisor trade association. Ms. Bailey served for three years on the Governor's Regulatory Review Council of Arizona and has been appointed to the Franchise Advisory Committee of the Securities Division of the Arizona Corporation Commission. She has also been an adjunct professor of law at Arizona State University. She is a past member of the Governing Committee of the ABA Forum on Franchising, has been a panelist at many of the Forum's annual programs, and chaired the Forum's 1982 Annual Program. Ms. Bailey received her J.D. degree (magna cum laude) in 1975 from Arizona State University College of Law, where she was articles editor of the *Arizona State Law Journal* and was selected by the faculty as the "Outstanding Graduate" of her class.

ANDREW A. CAFFEY practices law in Bethesda, Maryland, in the boutique law firm he founded in August 1993. He specializes in franchise, trademark, business opportunity, and distribution law. Mr. Caffey received his law degree from the University of Maryland School of Law in 1977 and his B.A. degree, cum laude, from Amherst College. He is a member of the bars of Maryland, New York, and the District of Columbia. Mr. Caffey served as a member of the Governing Committee of the ABA Forum on Franchising and was program chair of the Forum's 1992 Annual Program. He is former general counsel of the International Franchise Association (1983–85). Mr. Caffey is presently a member of the International Franchise Association's Legal/Legislative Committee.

M. CHRISTINE CARTY is a member of the Litigation Department of the New York City law firm of Schnader, Harrison, Segal & Lewis. She has litigated numerous dealer and distribution cases. Her experience in this area includes the full range of pretrial, trial, and alternative dispute resolution procedures. Her practice also includes labor litigation and counseling, especially employment discrimination, and trademark and other commercial litigation. Ms. Carty is a contributor to and associate editor of *Covenants against Competition in Franchise Agreements,* published in 1992 by the ABA Forum on Franchising. She is also a member of the Forum.

MICHAEL M. EATON is a partner in Arent, Fox, Kintner, Plotkin & Kahn, a Washington, D.C., law firm that also has offices in New York City and in Budapest, Hungary. He is a graduate of the University of Chicago Law School and the University of Virginia. Mr. Eaton writes and speaks on franchising, antitrust, and litigation topics and has spoken at programs of the International Franchise Association, the ABA Forum on Franchising, the ABA Section of Antitrust Law, the University of Missouri/Kansas City Bar Association, and the Bureau of National Affairs. He is a co-editor of the *Franchise Law Bibliography* (1st ed.). Mr. Eaton is a member of the bars of the District of Columbia, Florida, and Virginia.

WILLIAM A. FINKELSTEIN is vice president and intellectual property counsel of PepsiCo, Inc., in Purchase, New York, whose divisions and subsidiaries include Pepsi-Cola, Frito-Lay, Pizza Hut, Taco Bell, Kentucky Fried Chicken, and their respective worldwide businesses. He was president of the International (formerly United States) Trademark Association (INTA) from 1985 to 1986 and has been on the INTA Board of Directors since 1980. He served for six years as a Governing Committee member of the ABA Forum on Franchising and has been active on numerous ABA committees within the Intellectual Property Law Section. A frequent lecturer on trademark and franchise law matters, Mr. Finkelstein completed his undergraduate work at the University of Virginia and obtained a J.D. from Boston University School of Law and an L.L.M. in trade regulation from New York University School of Law.

MARK B. FORSETH is an associate in the Washington, D.C., office of the Dallas-based law firm of Jenkens & Gilchrest. He was formerly the senior franchise examiner of the Maryland Attorney General's Office, Division of Securities, from 1985 to 1990. Before joining the Maryland Attorney General's Office, Mr. Forseth was employed by the Department of Commerce, International Trade Administration. Mr. Forseth currently works in the Franchise and Distribution Law Practice Group at Jenkens & Gilchrest. Mr. Forseth is a member of the Advisory Committee to the North American Securities Administrators' Association's Franchise and Business Opportunity Committee, the Legal/Legislative Committee of the International Franchise Association, and the ABA Forum on Franchising. His publications include "The ADR Alternatives: Survey of Providers of Alternative Dispute Resolution Services" in *Franchise Law Journal* and "Fiduciary Duty between Franchisor-Franchisee? Texas Supreme Court Says No" in *Franchise Legal Digest,* as well as other articles for trade publications.

LAURENCE R. HEFTER specializes in intellectual property law. He has served as a professional lecturer in trademark law at the National Law Center, George Washington University, and was a member of the Board of Directors of the American Intellectual Property Law Association (formerly AIPLA) and the International (formerly United States) Trademark Association. He has also served as a member of the Governing Committee of the ABA Forum on Franchising and as chair of the Trademark Committee and Unfair Competition Committee of the ABA Intellectual Property Law Section. Mr. Hefter is on the Trademark Mediation Panel of the International Trademark Association/CPR and was a member of the Trademark Review Commission that drafted the Trademark Law Revision Act of 1988. He obtained a B.M.E. and M.S.M.E. from Rensselaer Polytechnic Institution and a J.D. with honors from the National Law Center of George Washington University, where he was an associate editor of the *George Washington Law Review* and a member of the Order of the Coif.

STUART HERSHMAN is a partner with the law firm of Rudnick & Wolfe in Chicago, Illinois, and has focused his practice in the franchising, antitrust, trademark, and general trade regulation areas for twelve years. Mr. Hershman received his B.A. degree in history, with high distinction, from the University of Michigan in 1981 and his J.D. degree, cum laude, from the University of Michigan in 1984. He has authored and co-authored, or contributed to, numerous articles and seminar materials on various franchising, antitrust, and bankruptcy topics including "Information and Switching Costs in the Franchise Context: Does *Kodak* Affect

Franchisors Complying with the New Uniform Franchise Offering Circular Guidelines?" and "Federal Antitrust and Trade Regulation Law: Problems and Concerns in Franchising." Mr. Hershman is a member of the Chicago Bar Association's Antitrust Committee, the ABA Forum on Franchising, the Franchising Committee of the ABA Section of Antitrust Law, and the Robinson-Patman Act Committee of the ABA Section of Antitrust Law. He has also served as a vice chair of the ABA Section of Antitrust Law Franchising Committee's Task Force on Legislation and Regulation.

ROBERT T. JOSEPH is a partner in the Chicago, Illinois, offices of Sonnenschein Nath & Rosenthal, where he specializes in commercial litigation, with emphases in antitrust, trade regulation, and franchising. A magna cum laude graduate of Xavier University, he received his B.A. in 1968. He earned his J.D. degree, cum laude, in 1971 from the University of Michigan Law School, where he was a member of the *Michigan Law Review.* Mr. Joseph was a staff attorney at the Federal Trade Commission's Bureau of Competition from 1971 until 1976. From 1973 to 1974, he also served as assistant to the director. He joined the Sonnenschein firm in 1976. He is currently a member of the Council of the ABA Section of Antitrust Law. He previously served as chair and vice chair of that Section's Franchising Committee and also as chair and vice chair of its Publications Committee. He was chair of the ABA Task Force on the National Conference of Commissioners on Uniform State Law's Uniform Franchising and Business Opportunity Act.

ALAN H. MACLIN is a shareholder in the St. Paul, Minnesota, law firm of Briggs and Morgan, P.A. His commercial litigation practice includes antitrust, trade regulation, franchise, and consumer class actions, as well as government investigations. Before joining Briggs and Morgan, Mr. Maclin served as special attorney general for Minnesota, where he headed the Antitrust and Commerce Divisions. He received his law degree from the University of Chicago in 1974 and his undergraduate degree, magna cum laude, from Vanderbilt University. He has served as a member of the Civil Litigation and Antitrust Sections of the Minnesota State Bar Association, the Ethics and Judiciary Committees of the Ramsey County Bar Association, the ABA Section of Antitrust Law, and the ABA Forum on Franchising.

THOMAS M. PITEGOFF is a founding partner in the law firm of Halket & Pitegoff, L.L.P., in Larchmont, New York. His practice covers a broad range of corporate and commercial matters, including technology and trade regulation. Mr. Pitegoff is on the Franchise Mediation Panel of the CPR Institute for Dispute Resolution. He has served as a member of the Governing Committee of the ABA Forum on Franchising. He is also chair of the Intellectual Property Law Subcommittee of the ABA Business Law Section's International Business Law Committee. He was formerly chair of the Franchising Subcommittee of the ABA Business Section's Small Business Committee and an associate editor of the *Franchise Law Journal.* Mr. Pitegoff's publications include: "Choice of Law in Franchise Relationships: Staying within Bounds," (*Franchise Law Journal*); "Product Supply in International Franchise Agreements," (*World Franchise & Business Report*); "Ways to Avoid Being a Franchise," (*Franchise Law Journal*); "Franchise Relationship

Laws: A Minefield for Franchisors," (*The Business Lawyer*); and "Choice of Law in Franchise Agreements," (*Franchise Law Journal*).

LEWIS G. RUDNICK is a partner in Rudnick & Wolfe and heads the firm's franchising and distribution law department. Mr. Rudnick is a graduate of the University of Illinois, Columbia University Graduate School of Business, and Northwestern University School of Law. He has practiced law in the fields of franchising and distribution law since 1964. Mr. Rudnick is counsel to the International Franchise Association and a member of the Association's Legislative Action Group and was the principal author of the Code of Principles and Standards of Conduct recently adopted by the association. A member of the Governing Committee of the ABA Forum on Franchising from its establishment in 1977 until 1984, Mr. Rudnick served as chair of the Forum from 1981 to 1983. Mr. Rudnick has been a member of the Illinois Franchise Advisory Board since 1974 and has served on the Advisory Committee to the Franchising Regulation Committee of the North American Securities Administrators Association. Mr. Rudnick is an editor of the *Journal of International Franchising and Distribution Law* and of the *Franchise Legal Digest.*

ROCHELLE BUCHSBAUM SPANDORF is a shareholder in Shapiro, Rosenfeld & Close, P.C., of Los Angeles, California. Her practice concentrates in the areas of franchising, licensing, and distribution law, both domestic and international. Ms. Spandorf is currently the chair of the ABA Forum on Franchising, the nation's leading franchise law association with over 2,400 members. She served as a member of the Forum's Governing Committee from 1992 through 1995 and as program chair of the Forum's 1994 Annual Program. She is a former topic and articles editor and associate editor of the *Franchise Law Journal* and has written extensively for the *Journal.* She also is past chair of the Franchise Law Committee of the California State Bar Business Law Section. Ms. Spandorf is a member of the Board of Editors of *Leader's Franchising Business & Law Alert.* She has also developed and taught franchise courses for the University of California at Santa Barbara and California State University.

DENNIS E. WIECZOREK is a partner with the law firm of Rudnick & Wolfe, with offices in Chicago, Tampa, and Washington, D.C. He is practice group leader of his firm's Franchise and Intellectual Property Team. He has concentrated in U.S. and international franchising, licensing, antitrust, and distribution law matters for over nineteen years. He holds a law degree from Duke University and a bachelor's degree, magna cum laude, from Washington University. He is a co-author of *Franchising: A Planning and Sales Compliance Guide,* published by Commerce Clearing House. He has written extensively for franchise and other legal and business publications, including the *Franchise Law Journal* and the *Franchise Legal Digest,* and has contributed materials to various programs of the Illinois Institute for Continuing Legal Education. In 1990, he was appointed a member of the Advisory Committee to the North American Securities Administrators Association Franchise and Business Opportunities Committee. In 1993, he was appointed chair of the Advisory Committee. He is a member of the ABA Section of Antitrust Law, Section of Business Law, and Forum on Franchising and also the IFA Legal/Legislative Committee.